Derby County
*Champions of England
1971-72 & 1974-75*

DESERT ISLAND FOOTBALL HISTORIES

Club Histories

	ISBN
Aberdeen: A Centenary History 1903-2003	1-874287-57-0
Aberdeen: Champions of Scotland 1954-55	1-874287-65-1
Aberdeen: The European Era – A Complete Record	1-874287-11-2
Bristol City: The Modern Era – A Complete Record	1-874287-28-7
Bristol City: The Early Years 1894-1915	1-874287-74-0
Cambridge United: The League Era – A Complete Record	1-905328-06-0
Cambridge United: 101 Golden Greats	1-874287-58-9
The Story of the Celtic 1888-1938	1-874287-15-5
Chelsea: Champions of England 1954-55	1-874287-94-5
Colchester United: Graham to Whitton – A Complete Record	1-874287-27-9
Coventry City: The Elite Era – A Complete Record	1-874287-83-X
Coventry City: An Illustrated History	1-874287-59-7
Derby County: Champions of England 1971-72 & 1974-75	1-874287-98-8
Dundee: Champions of Scotland 1961-62	1-874287-86-4
Dundee United: Champions of Scotland 1982-83	1-874287-99-6
History of the Everton Football Club 1878-1928	1-874287-14-7
Halifax Town: From Ball to Lillis – A Complete Record	1-874287-26-0
Hereford United: The League Era – A Complete Record	1-874287-18-X
Huddersfield Town: Champions of England 1923-1926	1-874287-88-0
Ipswich Town: The Modern Era – A Complete Record	1-874287-43-0
Ipswich Town: Champions of England 1961-62	1-874287-63-5
Kilmarnock: Champions of Scotland 1964-65	1-874287-87-2
Luton Town: The Modern Era – A Complete Record	1-874287-90-2
Luton Town: An Illustrated History	1-874287-79-1
Manchester United's Golden Age 1903-1914: Dick Duckworth	1-874287-92-9
The Matt Busby Chronicles: Manchester United 1946-69	1-874287-96-1
Motherwell: Champions of Scotland 1931-32	1-874287-73-2
Norwich City: The Modern Era – A Complete Record	1-874287-67-8
Peterborough United: The Modern Era – A Complete Record	1-874287-33-3
Peterborough United: Who's Who?	1-874287-48-1
Plymouth Argyle: The Modern Era – A Complete Record	1-874287-54-6
Plymouth Argyle: 101 Golden Greats	1-874287-64-3
Plymouth Argyle: Snakes & Ladders – Promotions and Relegations	1-874287-82-1
Portsmouth: From Tindall to Ball – A Complete Record	1-874287-25-2
Portsmouth: Champions of England – 1948-49 & 1949-50	1-874287-50-3
The Story of the Rangers 1873-1923	1-874287-95-3
The Romance of the Wednesday 1867-1926	1-874287-17-1
Stoke City: The Modern Era – A Complete Record	1-874287-76-7
Stoke City: 101 Golden Greats	1-874287-55-4
Potters at War: Stoke City 1939-47	1-874287-78-3
Tottenham Hotspur: Champions of England 1950-51 & 1960-61	1-874287-93-7
West Ham: From Greenwood to Redknapp	1-874287-19-8
West Ham: The Elite Era – A Complete Record	1-874287-31-7
Wimbledon: From Southern League to Premiership	1-874287-09-0
Wimbledon: From Wembley to Selhurst	1-874287-20-1
Wimbledon: The Premiership Years	1-874287-40-6
Wrexham: The European Era – A Complete Record	1-874287-52-X

World Cup Histories

England's Quest for the World Cup – A Complete Record	1-874287-61-9
Scotland: The Quest for the World Cup – A Complete Record	1-897850-50-6
Ireland: The Quest for the World Cup – A Complete Record	1-897850-80-8

Miscellaneous

Red Dragons in Europe – A Complete Record	1-874287-01-5
The Book of Football: A History to 1905-06	1-905328-00-1
Football's War & Peace: The Tumultuous Season of 1946-47	1-874287-70-8

DERBY COUNTY

*Champions of England
1971-72 & 1974-75*

Series Editor: Clive Leatherdale

Edward Giles

DESERT ISLAND BOOKS

First published in 2005
by
DESERT ISLAND BOOKS LIMITED
7 Clarence Road, Southend on Sea, Essex SS1 1AN
United Kingdom
www.desertislandbooks.com

© 2005 Edward Giles

The right of Edward Giles to be identified as author of this work has been asserted under The Copyright Designs and Patents Act 1988

British Library Cataloguing-in-Publication Data
A catalogue record for this book is available from the British Library

ISBN 1-874287-98-8

All rights reserved. No part of this book may be reproduced or utilised in any form or by any means, electronic or mechanical, including photocopying, recording or by any information storage and retrieval system, without prior permission in writing from the Publisher

Printed in Great Britain
by
Biddles Ltd

The photographs in this book were kindly provided by the *Derby Evening Telegraph*, County Press (Wigan), Anton Rippon and Neville Pyne

Contents

	Page
Author's Note	6
Foreword by Roy McFarland	7
1. From Hartlepool to Derby via Scotch Corner	8
2. Boro unrest amid Clough's Glut of Goals	19
3. Rams' Rebuilding off to a False Start	29
4. Perseverance pays off with Mackay coup	45
5. Promotion! and memorable League Cup nights	55
6. Spurred to Success, but barred from Europe	69
7. What they did not want was Watney win	80
8. Champions in Season of Three Trophies	93
9. Twist in the Tale of Two Moores	107
10. Contract distractions after record transfer	116
11. Epic FA Cup replay and European semi-final	127
12. Warnings, Discord and Temptations	164
13. Resignations spark Players' Rebellion	174
14. End of Protest after Boardroom Siege	186
15. Two Riochs and three van Goghs	197
16. Francis Lee gives lift to another title	208
17. A Cup Clash of 18 Penalties	222
18. Real Dazzlers reach European Pinnacle	234
19. Dave Mackay's Biggest Disappointment	247
20. The Vote of Confidence that never came	260
21. Hapless short reign of 'an Apprentice'	273
22. No Taylor-made answer as problems mount	285
23. The Break-Up of a Big Friendship	300
Guide to Seasonal Summaries	307
Seasonal Summaries	308
Subscribers	320

Author's Note

When my third book about Derby County was published I said it would be the last, so some explanation is called for with this production of a fourth. It was suggested to me by Clive Leatherdale, of Desert Island Books, as an addition to his excellent series on occasional English and Scottish national club champions. With his indulgence, I have gone outside the usual format in covering the period from 1967, when Brian Clough became the Rams' manager, to 1984, when his former partner Peter Taylor's return from brief retirement to take up that post ended as the club headed back to the Third Division. So this is a story not only of glory but also of gloom – a repeat, in nine years, of the descent, with two relegations, that befell Derby County within seven years of their winning of the FA Cup in 1946.

There are three titles in the telling, though the first one was of the then Second Division – a stepping stone to the major triumphs that were first interrupted by a players' rebellion, then dramatically undone as a financial crisis drove the club to the very brink of extinction. Two managers, Brian Clough and Dave Mackay, piloted Derby to the pinnacle; six others were pulled into the decline that gathered momentum after a Cup and League double had been in sight.

I attended a number of the Rams' games during the seasons under review, but am indebted to the *Derby Evening Telegraph*'s reports by George Edwards and Gerald Mortimer. Without them I could not have recalled so much detail, or compiled the statistics of the League championships of 1971-72 and 1974-75 that Rob Hadgraft has so skilfully assembled at the end of the book. Gerald has also readily responded to my requests for clarification of a number of important points.

Thanks, too, for the help given by Neil Hallam and Anton Rippon, to Roy McFarland, who was the Rams' captain, then assistant manager and manager, for providing the Foreword, and to Ken Smales, former secretary of Nottingham Forest, for checking the chapter recalling the Rams' abortive attempt to sign Ian Storey-Moore.

Sticklers for accuracy will note that my figures for appearances and goals differ from those usually given in regard to certain Derby players. This is because I have taken into account the three games the club played in winning the Watney Cup in 1970.

Edward Giles
July 2005

Dedication:
This book is for Ben, Charlotte, Lucy and Sam

Foreword

When I was dragged from my bed in Liverpool in the middle of the night to sign for Derby County at the start of the 1967-68 season, I knew very little about the man who had made himself at home downstairs with my Mum and Dad and who refused to leave without my somewhat reluctant signature on the transfer forms. I was vaguely aware that he had been a goalscoring hero in the North-East, but the achievements which were to create one of soccer's great legends were still to come.

Now, getting on for forty years later, Brian Clough is famous and hugely respected wherever football is played and the incredible things he and his partner Peter Taylor achieved with Derby County and Nottingham Forest have become part of the game's folklore. Brian is firmly established among this country's sporting giants and the fact that he achieved success at the very highest level with two clubs outside the big city elite convinces many people that he deserves to be rated English soccer's best manager of all time. I am certainly not going to argue with that judgment.

He and Peter introduced a personal style of management which shocked some and aggrieved a few, but produced teams totally committed to playing intelligent, creative football based on possession and high standards of discipline. They knew exactly what they wanted and they could be ruthless in ensuring that their players did things their way, but those who claim that Brian ruled by fear miss the point. Yes, he could make grown men tremble when he felt they had let him or themselves down but knocking people back was a very small part of his managerial method. Building them up and making them 'feel a million dollars' was a far more important aspect and made players desperate to win his approval. Laughter was never far away. He enjoyed debunking pomp and pretence and was a merciless critic of unearned privilege, but he was not the anarchist that some people saw him as. In management terms he was a revolutionary and a genius, and his death at the tragically early age of 69 has deprived the game of a great source of wisdom and original thinking.

For the fans of both Derby and Forest there is the recollection of golden eras to make them grateful that he dared to be different and their pride will be stirred again by the painstaking research which Eddie Giles has put into this detailed and comprehensive account of the events which went into the making of the Clough legend.

For many fans, almost every page will rekindle a treasured memory and for those of us who had the good fortune to play under Brian, the feelings of gratitude can never fade.

Roy McFarland

From Hartlepool to Derby via Scotch Corner

Derby County, original members of the Football League in 1888, had to wait 84 years before winning the title of its top division for the first time. They then became champions twice in four seasons, yet on both occasions soon parted company with the manager who had guided them there.

Brian Clough departed with his deputy, Peter Taylor, in the seismic sequel to months of friction with chairman Sam Longson and his board that threatened to spark a players' mutiny; Dave Mackay was sacked with his assistant Des Anderson after seeking the board's vote of confidence.

Until their League title triumphs of 1972 and 1975, Derby's lone major honour was the belated FA Cup final victory of 1946, gained with a team inspired by the celebrated inside-forward partnership of Raich Carter and Peter Doherty. Before that, the tale of the curse supposedly laid by disgruntled gipsies who had been turfed off what became the club's Baseball Ground home was magnified in the eyes of the superstitious, as the game's biggest prizes remained tantalisingly just out of reach.

In the FA Cup, the Rams were seven times semi-finalists in nine seasons around the turn into the twentieth century. They were beaten on each of the three occasions they got through to the final, before at last landing the trophy – in 1903 by the record margin of 6-0, against Bury. They failed again at the penultimate fence in 1909. Defeat fourteen years after that cost them the chance of being in the first Wembley final, and they have been losing semi-finalists three more times since then.

In the League, they were thrice First Division runners-up before finally claiming the title, third in three seasons, and four times fourth. In the last pre-War season of 1938-39 they really did seem set for the championship at long last when they topped the table for fifteen weeks up to early February, only to tail away to a final sixth place. Ten years on, they made their best-ever start to a season by going through their first sixteen matches undefeated, but then suffered such a slump that a late revival was not sufficient to catch Portsmouth, champions for the first time in their Jubilee year (and again the following season).

On the downside of Derby County's existence in the League before they eventually joined the elite, they had four spells in the Second Division. Worse still, within nine years of their FA Cup win they began a couple of seasons in the wilderness of the Third Division's Northern Section.

For those who believe in such things, the crossing of a gipsy's palm with silver broke the Cup hoodoo, but life in the League after the escape from its lower reaches was largely confined to the bottom half of Division Two until the cyclone called Clough swept in from the North-Eastern outpost of West Hartlepool. The brazen young man whose playing career had been cruelly cut short by a torn cruciate ligament in his right knee, after scoring 204 goals in 222 games for his home club Middlesbrough and 63 in 74 for Sunderland, arrived at the Baseball Ground on the strong recommendation of Len Shackleton, the self-styled Clown Prince of Soccer who had himself been forced out by injury while playing for Sunderland.

It was fortunate for Derby that Shackleton, scorer of six goals on his debut for Newcastle after being barracked out of Bradford, bore them no ill-will for having ruined his debut for Sunderland with a four-goal broadside from that club's former captain, Horatio Stratton Carter.

With Hartlepools United, Clough, at thirty, became the youngest manager then in the League, after a change of Sunderland manager had cost him his job in charge of the youth team at Roker. The newcomer, Ian McColl, the former Rangers and Scotland wing-half who had been managing his national team, wanted his own men around him. The manager who left, the former Middlesbrough and England full-back George Hardwick, was the man who set Clough on the path to management by encouraging him to take the FA coaching course from which he emerged as one of the youngest in the game to earn a full badge. 'I got a coaching badge through the FA in seven weeks,' Clough recalled, 'first the preliminary badge, then the full one.'

Clough had no hesitation in accepting the offer he received from Hartlepools' chairman, Ernie Ord, a millionaire tailor who had made a fortune during the War. It came straight after an appropriate scoring farewell in his testimonial match at a packed Roker Park, but, as with Longson at Derby, it was a relationship that deteriorated. He might have taken some warning from the fact that the man he succeeded, Geoff Twentyman, the former Carlisle and Liverpool defender, had lasted only four months in the job. There was also the disturbing fact that Hartlepools had regularly been compelled to seek re-election to the Football League.

Neither Clough nor Peter Taylor, who had rejoined him from Burton Albion after they had first struck up a friendship while clubmates at Middlesbrough, felt appreciated at Victoria Park, where they kept an improving team in a respectable Fourth Division position despite money being so short in that austere sphere that buckets were needed to catch the rain water which dripped through holes in the roof. Clough constantly went round the colliery clubs touting for donations, and at one point, when Hartlepools were in acute financial straits, he offered to work without pay to help them out – a gesture that prompted contributions from businesses in the town.

For someone as independent as Clough, the diminutive Ord's attempts to interfere in the running of the club became a constant irritation. The situation worsened when Ord tried to get rid of Taylor, arguing that there was no need for the two of them. That having failed, he announced that the board had decided to dismiss them both, but they simply refused to go. In the end, it was the chairman, not the manager and his assistant, who toppled, though he remained the biggest shareholder and eight years later was reappointed in averting a cash crisis that threatened the club's existence. By then Clough, whom he regarded as 'a decent fellow, but one with whom I did not see eye to eye', had become widely acknowledged elsewhere as one of football's greatest managers.

Ord did not end his original spell as chairman without trying a parting shot. When a sufficient number of the other directors came round to the view that he should go, he threatened to put the club out of business by trying to reclaim in one lump sum the £7,000 he was owed from a long-standing loan, but he eventually agreed to be repaid in instalments.

The successor in 1967 as chairman, John Curry, was, in complete contrast, an ideal man to work with, but the damage had been done. The urge to move to a bigger club was most keenly felt by Taylor, who persuaded Clough to lend a receptive ear to the approach Derby made on deciding not to renew the contract of the gentlemanly Tim Ward. Even so, quite apart from the fact that Clough was not all that sold on the idea at the outset, negotiations almost broke down after Len Shackleton, at that time a football journalist who was in close touch with Taylor, had arranged for Clough to meet Sam Longson and three other members of the Derby board, Sydney Bradley, Harry Payne and Bob Kirkland, at a hotel at Scotch Corner on the A1 (Bob Kirkland was the brother of Jack and uncle of John, who both followed him onto the Derby County board). Curry recalled:

'Brian rang me one day and told me that Derby had approached him. They had not contacted me, and I was upset. When Brian told them he had put me, his chairman, in the picture, they apparently replied that they would have preferred him to have kept quiet. He told them that if the negotiating couldn't be done in an above-board manner there was no point in discussing the job further. When, however, he did agree to go to Derby, I did my utmost to persuade Peter to stay and be manager at Hartlepool, but he went with Brian, and that turned out to be the right decision.'

It was ironic that Taylor was the one who was really eager to get to Derby, for Longson and his fellow directors did not at first appreciate that he was part of the package. Clough was the prime target, though Longson's companions were rather reluctant passengers in his Rolls-Royce on the journey from Derby because they felt that Clough should have been travelling to see them, rather than the other way round.

As a Nottingham man (born on 2 July 1928), Taylor was more aware than Clough of Derby's tradition as a football town, and of the potential there was to build a successful team there with an increased following. He, even more than the Derby County contingent, had to do a lot of hard talking to get his partner to leave his native North-East. They had undoubtedly done much to revive Hartlepools' fortunes, but Peter Taylor's claim that 'we gave them a promotion team' was robustly refuted by the man who succeeded them, Angus McLean, a Welshman (born at Queensferry) of Scottish parents who had been a doughty full-back with Wolves. Indeed, McLean remembered Clough's description to him of the players he was handing over as: 'They're a boat-load of rubbish. They are willing to run for you, and that's about it.' As McLean also saw it:

'I had my own ideas of how to run the team. I changed it and rearranged it and when, after a sticky start to the season, we gained promotion, half the side were my own signings. Much the same team went down the following year, but I have heard no claims about that!'

Brian Clough was born on 21 March 1935, the sixth of nine children. There were six brothers, Joe, Des, Bill, Brian, Gerald and Barry, and three sisters, Doreen, Deanna and Elizabeth. Betty, as Elizabeth was known, died of septicaemia as the age of four, before Brian was born. The family was brought up on the Grove Hill council estate in Middlesbrough. Brian was so reluctant to move from that part of the country that he agreed to go only after his family and Taylor's had spent the weekend weighing up all the pros and cons at a Scarborough hotel.

Clough's appointment at Derby broke with the Rams' tradition of mainly having one of their former players as manager, yet it also re-established a connection in that post with the North-East. After Jimmy Methven, who would surely have played for Scotland but for the strong bias against choosing Anglo-Scots in his day, had ended his dozen seasons as their manager in 1922, the job was held first by Cecil Potter, like Clough recruited from Hartlepools United, next by George Jobey, a Geordie who was an FA Cup finalist with Newcastle United, and then by Newcastle-born Ted Magner, before three other ex-Derby players, Stuart McMillan, Jack Barker and Harry Storer, preceded Tim Ward.

Potter piloted the Rams to the FA Cup semi-finals, and twice to the brink of promotion from the Second Division – they failed by only 0.015 of a goal on the first occasion – before Jobey, Derby's most successful manager in the years BC (Before Clough), got them back into the top flight in 1925-26, the first of his fourteen League seasons at the County's helm.

Following a varied playing career in which he had the distinction of scoring Arsenal's first goal at Highbury, Jobey made an unhappy start as a manager with a Wolves team that dropped out of the Second Division, but he quickly guided them back before unexpectedly going into the hotel business for the year out of soccer from which Derby County recalled him. His stay with the Rams ended on another sad note as, with five directors, he was suspended from all football in 1941 by an FA-League Commission which found that illegal bonuses and inducements had been paid to players since he had joined the club. The ban on Jobey was lifted four years later, but it was some time after that before he secured his only other managerial appointment, a short-lived one at Mansfield that led to his dismissal for alleged 'neglect of duty'. It was a wholly inappropriate conclusion to the career of one of the game's most respected managers, a disciplinarian after Clough's own heart.

The gap left by Jobey at Derby was not filled until 1944, when Ted Magner, who had played against the Rams for Gainsborough Trinity and Everton before going into Scottish football and breaking St Mirren's individual scoring record with five goals against Queen's Park, swiftly made his mark by linking Carter and Doherty in a team that carried off the League North title and Midland Cup in one season. There was quite a surprise, therefore, when he suddenly returned to coaching abroad, in Denmark, while the FA Cup run to the first final at Wembley after the Second World War was into only its fourth round.

Stuart McMillan, whose father also played for Derby County, made only one first-team appearance for the Rams in a playing career he shared with six other clubs, but his managerial reign included the Cup win at Wembley and two signings, respective replacements for Doherty and Carter, that broke the transfer record – £15,500 for Scottish international Billy Steel from Morton, £24,500 for Johnny Morris, who was capped by England while with the Rams, from Manchester United. How paltry those deals, so breathtaking at the time, appear in comparison with the millions splashed out these days.

Jack Barker, a centre-half who would have played more than eleven times for England if the national selectors had not so often preferred pivots who were less robust and attack-minded, served Derby resolutely as a player throughout the 1930s, becoming one of their most commanding captains, but as a manager he was a huge disappointment. After forestalling a sacking by resigning in the turbulent wake of relegation to the Northern Section of the Third Division, he talked in the big-money terms of the day in telling Gerald Mortimer, who reported on Derby's matches for many years: 'It was a rotten experience. I wouldn't be a manager again for £10,000 a week. The trouble is that the people you are working for know nothing about the game.'

Similar sentiments were expressed by Brian Howard Clough when he also vacated the manager's chair at the Baseball Ground. 'There's a seven-man board at Derby,' he said in firing off one of his parting salvoes, 'and I wouldn't give tuppence for five of them.' The Infamous (in his eyes) Five were the inevitable Sam Longson, Bill Rudd, a quietly-spoken solicitor with offices in Derbyshire, Sydney Bradley, a former chairman who had gents' tailors shops in the Derby area, Bob Innes, a golf-playing Derby estate agent, and Jack Kirkland, a businessman, one of the club's major shareholders, who was the newest member of the board.

The two exceptions were Mike Keeling, the youthful (compared with the rest) manager of a transport company, who resigned when Clough and Taylor left, and Sir Robertson King, who, said Clough, 'had sympathy for us.'

Harry Storer, who had made a big impression on Taylor when having him as one of his goalkeepers while manager of Coventry City, also exerted an important influence on Clough's abrasive management style in meetings with him, but came to regret that he did not sign him as a player for Derby when he had the chance. Taylor tipped him off about the young centre-forward who had then not yet established himself in Middlesbrough's League side, but Storer decided he could not afford even the nominal fee that would have been needed.

Even so, Storer completed his third promotion success as a manager (the others with Coventry and Birmingham) in getting Derby out of the Third Division at the second attempt in 1957. It was also his second promotion with the Rams, having helped them back to the First Division as a player under Jobey's direction, but he was unable to engineer another one before retiring at the end of the 1961-62 season with Derby no more than just a very ordinary team only six places off the foot of Division Two. Despite that subdued ending, Storer could rightly look back with pride on a sporting career in which he fully lived up to the family traditions set by his father, also Harry, who kept goal for Woolwich Arsenal and Liverpool, and his uncle William, one of four Derbyshire and England cricketers who played for Derby County. Harry Storer, whose father also played a few games for Derbyshire, crowned his own career with the county, stretching across sixteen years up to 1936, by helping them, as an opening batsman, to win the Championship for what was then for the second time, but now is only the first. Until 1963 Derbyshire were also listed in Wisden as the champions of 1874, but that is among the seasons no longer officially recognised. In 1874 the placings were decided by 'least matches lost'. Derbyshire, though unbeaten, fulfilled only four fixtures.

The forthright, outspoken Storer, though widely respected for his deep knowledge of the game, was a very daunting character for the often caustic tone of his comments – as memorably aired in public as a member of the panel on a sports programme the BBC used to broadcast in the

Midlands – and his withering criticism of those who displeased him. One day I was among those below stairs at the Baseball Ground when he pointed in turn at each of the portraits of Derby County's international players that then lined the walls and dismissed a good many of them as having been nothing special. I felt somewhat aggrieved because those so dispassionately discounted included my step-father George Richards, who during most of the years in the twentieth century leading up to the 1914-18 war exceeded 300 appearances for the Rams despite several absences through injury, but I wisely refrained from saying so. In any case, Storer himself was among the pictured capped men he professed not to rate at the highest level.

Brian Clough was even more dismissive of those portraits. Not long after he had breezed into the Baseball Ground they were all taken down. He was aiming for a bright new future, not looking back over past glories. Swiftly though he supplied some new heroes and achievements for the club's fans to enthuse over, it was too much to expect a ready compliance with his urging that they should stop dwelling on the great days of Carter and Doherty, let alone those far-off ones of Steve Bloomer, the free scorer who Sir Frederick Wall, then FA secretary, said was 'the greatest of the old-timers'.

Although born on Merseyside, at West Derby while his father was with Liverpool, Harry Storer staunchly regarded himself as a Derbyshire man. He was only four years old when he moved with his parents on their return to live in their home county. After starting his soccer career with Ripley Town, he had a spell as a Notts County amateur before entering League football with Grimsby Town, the club from which he was transferred to Derby County for £4,500 in 1921. Over the next eight years before his departure to Burnley he totted up 274 appearances for the Rams, and 27 of his 63 goals came in the 1923-24 season for which he was switched into the forward line. Twice he scored four times in a match, including the club's record 8-0 away win against Bristol City.

In taking over from Storer as Derby's manager, Tim Ward embarked upon five years of struggle on a tight budget that he looked back upon as the unhappiest of his career. Like Storer, Ward was a former Derby and England wing-half, as one of the midfield links between defence and attack was then known, but unlike him he was a stylish, cultured player as opposed to one noted for the wholehearted, combative methods Storer employed, and for which that embattled old warhorse looked in the men he managed. Clough said that one of the most telling pieces of managerial advice Storer gave him was to 'count the number of hearts' when leaving for an away game. Harry had no time for those who lacked courage, both moral and physical.

Ward was certainly never found wanting in that regard, combining class with determination. A £200 bargain signing by George Jobey from Cheltenham, he established himself in Derby's League side before the War, but had the misfortune to miss the chance of a Cup winner's medal because he was not demobilised from the Army until shortly before the final in which the Rams defeated Charlton Athletic after extra-time. Ward, who later that year was the subject of a £10,000 bid by Arsenal, considered himself lucky to have survived the War, rather than unlucky not to play at Wembley.

He had good reason, however, to regard himself unlucky as an international player. Dropped after his debut display for England in a comfortable defeat of Belgium had encouraged one critic to say that he was 'here to stay', he was once more left out despite again giving a good account of himself in another win, against Wales, after a reshuffle through injury to Arsenal's Laurie Scott had caused him to play all but the first 25 minutes of the match in the unaccustomed position of full-back. After that he had to be content for representative recognition with an FA tour of Canada.

Ward became Derby's fourth captain after the 1939-45 war, following Jack Nicholas, Raich Carter and Jack Howe, before leaving for Barnsley in a rushed transfer deal that was completed only five minutes before 1951's March midnight deadline. With the experience gained from 260 League and Cup games with the Rams, he was regarded as just the man to fill the vacancy caused by Irish international Danny Blanchflower's move to Aston Villa, but he played in only about two dozen more before first becoming player-coach with Barnsley's Yorkshire League team and then hanging up his boots to go into management with the Oakwell club.

At first, he seemed set to take that turn in his career with Exeter City, who wanted him as player-manager to replace Norman Kirkman, a former Rochdale, Chesterfield, Leicester and Southampton full-back who had left to manage Bradford. Ward travelled to Devon to discuss their offer when Barnsley decided to invite applications from outside following the death of their manager, Angus Seed, and his appointment at Exeter was actually announced almost four weeks before he took over as Barnsley's manager on the last day of March in 1953.

The snag for Exeter was that the Barnsley board decided not to release Ward after all, and they finally chose him for their own manager's chair from a short-list of four that had been whittled down from more than fifty. The three to whom Tim was preferred were Harry Catterick, the Crewe player-manager who went on to guide Everton, the club for which he had played, to two League championships and two FA Cup finals (once as winners), Gordon Pallister, a former Barnsley full-back, and Alf Young, a pre-war centre-half with Huddersfield and England.

Joe Richards, Barnsley's venerable chairman, thanked Exeter by telegram for agreeing to keep Ward in limbo until he and his fellow directors had reached a decision. In view of the high opinion he had formed of Ward's ability and character while with him on the Canadian tour as one of the FA officials, it was to be wondered why this future League president, later knighted, did not favour him as a manager as readily as he had strongly influenced his signing as a player.

So Tim Ward, at 34, became, by a rather roundabout route, the youngest manager then in the League. With Barnsley already five points adrift at the foot of the Second Division, he was powerless to prevent their relegation in the remaining seven games, but they went back up in his second full season in charge after narrowly missing promotion the year before as runners-up to Port Vale. As they climbed out of the Third Division North, so Derby County tumbled into it with their second demotion in three seasons.

Although Barnsley soon slipped out of the Second Division again, Ward went on to pull off another promotion with Grimsby Town immediately before rejoining Derby in the summer of 1962. After flirting with a return to Division Three in his first season back with his old club he got them into more respectable final positions, with a highest of eighth, before they again went near the drop in what was to be his last campaign with the County.

He made a rod for his own back by achieving several successful signings at modest fees – notably Alan Durban from Cardiff City, Bobby Ferguson and Gordon Hughes from Newcastle United, Billy Hodgson from Leicester City, and, in particular, Eddie Thomas from Swansea Town. Derby's directors expected him to keep picking up such bargains, and it came as a real shock to the system when, in the September of 1966, they reluctantly allowed him to splash out around £40,000, a tidy sum for those days, on a forward he had been after for some six months – the 1965-66 season's top marksman in the League with 44 goals in the Fourth Division, plus another in the FA Cup.

That was the deal which brought to Derby one of the club's most prolific scorers and most popular players, a deal for which Brian Clough and Peter Taylor were truly thankful when they inherited him. The 21-year-old snapped up so perceptively from under the nose of Leeds United was Kevin Hector, 'Zak the King' as Rams fans were to hail him, scorer of 113 goals in 176 League games for Bradford (the Park Avenue one), with whom he made his first-team debut at the age of sixteen, and 203 more in a record 592 competitive appearances for Derby County. Only the renowned Steve Bloomer, with 332, has scored more goals for the Rams.

Hector was one of the five players Tim Ward left behind him who featured prominently during the purple patch that brought Derby the championships of the Second and First Divisions under the direction of Clough and Taylor, and the First Division title again under Mackay and Anderson. The others were Durban, a forward turned midfielder who for a time was the Rams' most-capped player with 27 call-ups for Wales, Colin Boulton, a goalkeeper snapped up after being dropped from his police cadet course for playing too much soccer and cricket, and two defenders who were local finds – Ron Webster, from Belper, and Peter Daniel, from Ripley. (Boulton, incidentally, had a cricket trial with Gloucestershire, but decided to concentrate on his goalkeeping. He was a prominent member of Derby County's cricket team, and on one occasion, at Derby in 1973, he fielded as a substitute for Derbyshire against Kent – during an opening stand of 256 for the visitors by Brian Luckhurst (215) and Graham Johnson (130).)

It was just a coincidence that Boulton, like Ward, was born at Cheltenham and went to the school in that Gloucestershire town which Tim had attended. Boulton was recommended by a young player on the club's staff who happened to overhear Ward tell Sammy Crooks, then the chief scout, that they could do with a youngster to take over when the time came for former England goalkeeper Reg Matthews (a Storer signing) to be replaced. 'I thought it was a chance worth taking,' said Ward, 'so I told him to bring the lad along for us to have a look at him.'

That look did not have to be very long for the manager to decide that the eighteen-year-old Boulton was just what was needed, but the patience of the young man with the West Country burr was sorely tried as he had a long wait in the reserve side before establishing himself in the first team. Despite deputising promisingly for Matthews in the last six games of the 1964-65 season, he had such limited opportunities over the next two that he hankered after a move several times, and he might well have been lost to the Rams if there had then been a loan system to give another club's manager the chance to see for himself that he was worth offering a contract. It was Derby's good fortune that he stayed and made good with them. From originally also having no place in Brian Clough's first-team plans, he progressed to alone playing in all 84 games of the Rams' two First Division championship seasons and went on to make more appearances, 344, than any other goalkeeper in the club's history.

Ron Webster played his first League matches as a wing-half towards the end of Harry Storer's last season as manager, and was kept there for much of Tim Ward's reign, but he flourished as a full-back when Brian Clough was in control. He held the club's appearances record with 538 (five of them as substitute) until overtaken by Kevin Hector, and altogether served under eight managers in his 22 years at the Baseball Ground, latterly as youth coach. Peter Daniel hardly had a look-in when Clough chose the teams, yet, after rejecting the chance to join Luton Town, he did Dave

Mackay proud for most of the run to the title in 1974-75 as centre-half replacement while Roy McFarland, one of the Clough-Taylor era's first and most important signings for the Rams, was out of action with a severe Achilles tendon injury suffered while playing for England.

Just over a year after leaving Derby County, Tim Ward secured his last managerial post with Carlisle United, but resigned when they made a poor start to his second season with them. He then scouted for Nottingham Forest and took a job outside football as a representative for a concrete-making firm near Burton-upon-Trent. For all the tribulations of his second stint at the Baseball Ground as manager, he still had a soft spot for the Rams, and, well into the veteran stage, maintained a close connection with some of his former County colleagues by playing alongside them in the ex-Derby All-Stars team. He was also the first chairman of the Derby County Former Players' Association for a little more than a year before his death at Barton-under-Needwood early in 1993 at the age of 75.

Boro unrest amid Clough's Glut of Goals

Peter Taylor took only two days to recognise Brian Clough's footballing talent after joining him at Middlesbrough from Coventry City in the summer of 1955. He admitted that his touting in the Ayresome Park dressing room of Clough's claims to a first-team place 'made more enemies than friends', but he saw it as the reason why they were brought together. 'If that situation hadn't arisen,' he said, 'I'm sure we would have gone our different ways in football. It was the start of our friendship.'

Taylor first became fully aware of Clough's potential as a player during a pre-season friendly match. He recalled:

'Brian came on in the second half. I hadn't seen anything like him. I said so to the rest of the lads, but I was shouted down. I didn't know him at all then. He was only the fourth choice centre-forward, but the only person who agreed with my judgment of him was Brian Clough. He thought I was a great judge.'

The expounding of Clough's cause by Taylor was spread through the coaching staff of Harold Shepherdson, a former Middlesbrough centre-half who was for many years also England's trainer, Mickey Fenton, a free-scoring centre-forward with the club who had played for England, and Jimmy Gordon, the ex-Newcastle and Boro wing-half who was later trainer with Clough and Taylor at both Derby County and Nottingham Forest.

Neither did Taylor's championing escape manager Bob Dennison, a Cumbrian who had played for Newcastle, Nottingham Forest and Fulham before the 1939-45 War, originally as an inside-forward, but had caught most attention as the Northampton Town centre-half given the daunting task of marking Tommy Lawton when England's attacking spearhead made his much-publicised Third Division debut after his startling £20,000 transfer from Chelsea to Notts County in 1947. Lawton scored County's first goal in their 2-1 win at Northampton on 15 November 1947, but Dennison ('I did not lose any sleep') came out of their duel with credit.

Taylor asked Dennison, who was a good friend of his, to put Clough in the League side even though the nineteen-year-old centre-forward who had caught his eye was then well down the pecking order behind Charlie Wayman, Ken McPherson and Doug Cooper, but it was not until a year later, on 17 September 1955, that Clough was given his first senior chance in a home match with Barnsley. McPherson, a £15,000 signing from Notts County who had displaced the veteran Wayman, was himself dropped to make room for Taylor's protégé.

Only bad luck prevented Clough from making it a scoring League debut. He cracked the ball into the Barnsley net just as the referee whistled to award Boro a free-kick because Joe Scott had been fouled in supplying the pass. The goal that rescued a point was netted six minutes from time by Arthur Fitzsimons, who had also gone through the frustrating experience of being kept waiting an undue length of time for his first opportunity in Middlesbrough's Second Division side. Indeed, along with fellow forward Peter Desmond, he was first capped by the Republic of Ireland well before playing in the Football League. They were both chosen for a World Cup qualifying game against Finland in Dublin in 1949, four months after moving together to Ayresome Park from Shelbourne – and Fitzsimons had a further wait of eight months for his first League game with Boro after that.

Desmond, who had the contrasting experience of playing for the Teessiders' second team against Eppleton Colliery Welfare at Hetton-le-Hole the weekend after facing Finland in the return World Cup qualifier in Helsinki, made only two appearances in the club's first team before drifting into the Third North with Southport, but there were to be 230 more for Fitzsimons after his delayed League debut at West Bromwich. Fitzsimons, who also played for Lincoln and Mansfield, had a habit of waltzing past two or three defenders in the penalty area only to shoot wide, and it was said that after one such sortie the exasperated Clough told him: 'You make the bloody goals. I'll do the scoring.'

And do the scoring the cocky Clough emphatically did. In continuing to find the net with the ease he had shown with local clubs South Bank, Billingham Synthonia and Broughton Rangers before giving up his clerical job with ICI and turning professional with Boro, he rattled up, in 218 games, the quickest 200 goals in first-class football – but not the fastest 100. It took Clough 109 matches to reach his first century, whereas Jimmy Cookson, who played for Chesterfield and West Bromwich Albion, got into three figures in his 89th game, in December 1927.

Yet Boro had what George Camsell, the most prolific of Clough's predecessors at the head of the club's attack, called 'an awful job to persuade him to sign'. This was how Camsell recalled the scouting mission on which he was sent to watch a minor game at Guisborough:

'There was this kid of about 16 playing for Broughton Rangers against much older men. He didn't give a damn. He wanted the ball all the time. He was well balanced, had two good feet, was courageous in the air, but more than that he was greedy for goals. All great centre-forwards must have that, otherwise they get snuffed out. The first difficulty was to get him to Ayresome Park to meet our manager, Walter Rowley. When we did get him there he actually told Rowley he didn't particularly enjoy football. I couldn't believe my ears. Fortunately, we were able to talk him round and he signed for us. He was the best player I ever found.'

The first of the many goals Clough was to score in League football came in his fourth game – one of four in a narrow home win over Leicester City. With Wayman, Cooper and a new rival, Alan Peacock, then gaining preference at various stages, he had only limited further chances before ousting Cooper after the first match of the next, 1956-57, season.

From then until his transfer to Sunderland nearly five years later, he was an automatic choice. Bob Dennison came to consider him 'the greatest goal-scorer I ever saw – and I saw a great many of them, from the days of Dixie Dean'. McPherson moved to Coventry City, Wayman, a free scorer with Newcastle, Southampton and Preston before helping Middlesbrough to avert relegation in the first of his two seasons with them, joined Darlington, Cooper faded out of the picture, and Peacock formed a formidable twin strike force with Clough from inside-left after Fitzsimons fell out of favour.

Peacock twice scored four goals in a match. When he first did so, in 1959, Boro equalled their record 7-1 away win at the ground where Clough, who, remarkably, did not score that day, was first to become the most talkative, and most talked-about, manager in the game – the Baseball Ground in Derby. Peacock's other four-goal feat came in a 5-1 home win over Rotherham in 1961, his first game at centre-forward after Clough's departure to Sunderland.

In successive seasons with Middlesbrough, Clough scored 40 goals in 44 games, 42 in 42, 43 in 43, 40 in 42 and 36 in 42. Admittedly, all those goals, except half-a-dozen in Cup competitions, were amassed in the Second Division, but the mind boggles at the thought of how many millions would have to be splashed out these days for a forward capable of such consistent scoring.

Against Brighton on the opening day of the 1958-59 season, Clough equalled Boro's individual scoring record for one match, hitherto shared by Andy Wilson and George Camsell, by contributing five goals to a 9-0 victory, the club's biggest in the League. He had previously scored five for an FA XI at Old Trafford in a 6-3 defeat of an Army side for which Bill Curry, the Newcastle (and later Derby) centre-forward who was one of his chief rivals for an England Under-23 place, netted twice. Clough scored three of his five that night in five minutes early in the second half.

For Middlesbrough, Clough five times scored four in a game (once on his 24th birthday), and one of his eleven 'ordinary' hat-tricks for the club came in the rarity of a 6-6 draw at Charlton, where Dennis Edwards countered with three goals for the home side and Johnny Summers, twice a five-goal man for the Athletic on other occasions, grabbed the final equaliser in the last minute. Tragically, Summers, whose first nap hand transformed a 1-5 deficit into a 7-6 win against Huddersfield, was stricken with cancer the summer after the high-scoring draw with Boro, and died in 1962, aged 34.

Effectively though Peacock combined with Clough on the field, they did not get on well off it – and therein lay an example of the undercurrent of unrest that Boro's outspoken centre-forward stirred up behind the scenes. With promotion to the First Division remaining elusive, team spirit suffered as Clough complained he was 'sick and tired' of scoring goals at one end only to see his team's defenders letting in plenty at the other. Matters came to a head in November 1959, shortly after he had applied unsuccessfully for a transfer and been appointed captain.

Nine players signed a petition asking manager Dennison to take the captaincy away from Clough. Several of them made it clear they thought it should be given to Brian Phillips, the centre-half signed from Altrincham six years earlier whom Clough regarded as the ring-leader. Only a few weeks later, however, Phillips himself asked for a transfer in anticipation of the arrival from Stoke City of Ken Thomson, the man who was to replace him, and, in any case, he dropped out of the side through injury before the big former Aberdeen player's transfer went through.

On his return to fitness early the following year, Phillips renewed the request which, along with those of Clough and right-winger Billy Day, had been turned down, and this time it led to his transfer to Mansfield. The discord he was leaving behind was made abundantly clear when he said:

'I did not wish to waste valuable time regaining the first-team place I lost through injury, and not loss of form. But the underlying reason for my renewed transfer request was that I haven't been happy at Ayresome Park for some time because of the dressing-room bickerings. The outcome of the recent dressing-room controversy over the round-robin about the club captaincy was far from satisfactory. I was one of the players who signed the document which asked for the captaincy to be changed. Things have not improved at all since that fuss.'

When the rumpus was at its height Cliff Mitchell said in his report in the *Evening Gazette* of Middlesbrough's home match with Bristol Rovers that when Clough led his team onto the field 'there were loud cheers, with the odd boo from one or two spectators', and that when he went up to the centre spot for the toss-up 'there was loud applause'. Furthermore, the central figure in the Boro storm completed his hat-trick shortly after the interval 'to deafening cheers from the crowd and to handshakes all round from his team-mates'.

Clough's request for a transfer had been refused only a few days earlier at a board meeting which lasted 2½ hours. His claim that some members of the team wanted to drive him from the club was discounted by a spokesman for the players who said that they realised his value to the side, but added: 'He always seemed to think he was a little more important than the rest of us, and most of us resented it.'

Hard as the club tried to smooth things over, the dispute was too fundamental and personal to go away, and although Clough stayed for another season after at first refusing to re-sign for it, the break came with his move to Sunderland in July 1961. Unwelcome as it was for fans who deplored the loss of such a human goal machine, his exit was eased for Middlesbrough by the competent manner in which Peacock switched position to fill the gap he had left. Peacock did so well, in fact, that he was chosen to play for England against Austria at Wembley the following April, but his cap debut was delayed because just a few days before that match he fractured a cheekbone in only the second minute of the game in which Clough first returned to Ayresome Park. Sunderland won that day by the only goal, and there are no prizes for naming the scorer.

Peacock, later of Leeds, played six times for England and was in the squad for the World Cup finals in Chile, whereas Clough had to make do with just a couple of full caps to add to his one appearance for England 'B' (in which he scored twice in a 4-1 defeat of the Scots) and three (two more goals) with the Under-23s. Clough would have played a fourth time at England Under-23 level but for an Asian flu epidemic that caused a number of League games to be called off. Peter Taylor was among the victims as Ayresome Park was particularly affected.

Clough would have been an automatic England choice if the majority of the public had had their way – just as he would have been the popular appointment as England manager when, nearly twenty years on, a successor was being sought after Don Revie had suddenly been lured away by a lucrative tax-free contract to coach in the United Arab Emirates.

England were seeking a new centre-forward for the approaching 1958 World Cup finals in Sweden when Clough boarded the plane for Belgrade as a member of a senior England squad for the first time in May 1958. Tommy Taylor had been among those killed only a few months earlier in the Manchester United plane disaster at icy, snow-covered Munich airport on the way home from a European Cup-tie in the Yugoslav capital, and Bolton's Nat Lofthouse was nearing the end of his career. But the manner in which Clough was treated on that short tour left him, with good reason, feeling hard done by. Walter Winterbottom, the England manager, and the national selectors were not convinced that he was the man for the job because he was with a Second Division club, and he was therefore left out of the match with Yugoslavia in favour of the less mobile Derek Kevan, a big and willing worker who, as mainly an inside-left, did not even play regularly at the head of the attack for his club, West Bromwich Albion.

After England had been thrashed 0-5, trainer Harold Shepherdson told Clough he was 'an absolute cert' for the next game in Moscow. And so he should have been. But no. Clough overheard skipper Billy Wright whisper to Kevan that he was in the side again, and when this was confirmed by Winterbottom the Boro sharpshooter felt cheated – that he had been invited to join the England party under sufferance, just to keep the critics quiet.

It is interesting to note what Tom Finney, the gifted and versatile Preston forward, had to say on this subject in his book *Finney on Football*: 'Walter Winterbottom must have been wondering just how to solve his forward problems, because during one training session he came over to me and casually discussed possible inside-forward combinations to face Russia. This informal chat apparently made big news for the English football writers, and at least one newspaper suggested that the international team had been selected – or partly selected – by Tom Finney and Billy Wright. I certainly picked no team, but I did pass an opinion. After the match in Belgrade Derek Kevan had been given his customary grilling from the press, and it was assumed that Middlesbrough's Brian Clough would be our centre-forward in Moscow. Unfortunately, I had seen very little of Clough, and was in no position to comment on his ability as an international centre-forward.'

On returning home after the 1-1 draw with the USSR in which Kevan scored, Clough had his hopes of being in the final selection for Sweden turned into seeming reality when he was measured for a World Cup blazer, but after a hard morning's training during the final get-together at Roehampton, where he played in only the first half, though proficiently enough, of a full-scale practice match, he and Jimmy Langley, the Fulham left-back, were called aside by Winterbottom and quietly given the bad news that they were being omitted. It took another five-goal onslaught by Clough, for the Football League in their 5-0 win against the Irish League in Belfast on his wife's birthday, to give the selectors the final nudge and make him one of the five newcomers they introduced for England's game against Wales in Cardiff on 17 October 1959. The others were full-back Tony Allen, of Stoke City, the Birmingham centre-half Trevor Smith, and wingers John Connelly (Burnley) and Clough's clubmate Eddie Holliday.

England did not win, and Clough did not score. The ploy of putting him between Jimmy Greaves, Chelsea's own scoring sensation, and Bobby Charlton, maturing survivor of the Munich tragedy, simply did not work. There had been a warning of this during the team's preparations in the week before the match, when those three had not combined well in England's 1-3 defeat by a mixed Arsenal side at Highbury. At Ninian Park, a first-half goal by Greaves was cancelled out in the last minute by the Welsh 'wonder boy' Graham Moore, an eighteen-year-old former pit worker who was then the third youngest to be capped in the home international championship. Lack of support from his inside men left Clough thoroughly frustrated, although Donald Saunders stated in *The Daily Telegraph* that 'despite his limited opportunities he looked more like an England leader than any of the several who had held the job in the preceding 18 months'.

The absence of a scheming type of player such as Johnny Haynes, who was impressively back in the Fulham side but not considered for England because he had only just recovered from a knee operation, again counted against Clough when he kept his place in an unchanged team to face Sweden, the World Cup runners-up, at Wembley the same month. Again he was not among the scorers, but he provided the pass from which Connelly, later of Manchester United, neatly side-footed England into an early lead, and he went close to putting them further ahead near the interval. The Swedes then hit back with three goals in two dozen second-half minutes, and a late reply by Charlton was all England could muster as they slipped to their first failure at home against a team from abroad since the 3-6 humiliation by Hungary in 1953 had ended their immunity from defeat by Continental visitors.

That was the end of Brian Clough's international career, deepening the hurt for a goal-hungry young man who was already narked about not being chosen for the Royal Air Force side during National Service. And his feeling of unfairness in being dropped, along with Greaves and Charlton, for England's next game against Northern Ireland at Wembley was made all the more acute because Haynes was recalled to give support for his successor, a former Scotland Boys player, the son of an English sailor but with a Scottish mother, who had a broad Scottish accent because he had left his Liverpool birthplace for Motherwell at an early age. This was Hibernian's Joe Baker, later of Arsenal, Forest and Sunderland after a spell in Italy, and then of Hibs again, who became the first to win a full cap for England while with a club north of the border.

Baker scored the first of the goals that gained a very fortunate 2-1 win over the Irish. Jimmy McIlroy, of Burnley, lost the chance to equalise by repeating his penalty miss of the previous month, against Scotland, and the decider was not snatched until the last seconds of injury-time only two minutes after Luton's lively winger Billy Bingham, formerly of Sunderland and later of Everton, had brought the scores level. The grabber of that dramatic late winner, from Baker's low centre, was Raymond Parry, a skilful inside-forward, making his England debut, who had been whisked away off Derby County's doorstep by Bolton Wanderers. Parry, previously a team-mate of Haynes with England Boys, was the youngest to play in the First Division, three months from his sixteenth birthday, when he turned out at Wolverhampton in 1951 – a distinction taken from him when Derek Forster kept goal for Sunderland against Leicester City at the tender age of fifteen years 184 days in 1964.

Derby County did acquire two of the other Derby-born Parry brothers, Glyn and Jack, but another one, Cyril, slipped off to Notts County. Glyn never progressed beyond the reserve team, whereas Jack played in more than 500 first-team games for his only League club, turning out in all five forward positions of the then accepted formation, and also at wing-half. For League appearances alone, discounting those as a substitute, he even outdid Kevin Hector with 482 to 478, despite not always being available while on National Service in the Sherwood Foresters. One of the Rams' most loyal players in a twenty-year stay that ended with his free transfer to Boston United only the month before the coming of Clough, Jack Parry was also a worthy addition to the list of those who have scored a century of goals for the County.

His best season as a scorer, with 27 goals, was that of 1955-56 in which Derby might have made an immediate escape from the Third Division's Northern Section if he had not been injured in a crucial promotion clash with Grimsby Town and missed the remaining eleven matches. The Rams lost to the Mariners, and finished runners-up to them, five points behind, in failing to score in three of their last half-dozen games, losing two of these.

Jack Parry might, like brother Ray, have won his way into the England team if he had been with a more fashionable, or more successful, club than Derby County were during the years he was at his peak. But at least he did something Brian Clough could not do by playing in senior Services soccer, gaining valuable experience in Army sides that included the redoubtable Welshman John Charles and two of the men who kept Clough out of the England line-up – Tommy Taylor and Bobby Smith, top scorer for Tottenham Hotspur's League champions and FA Cup winners of 1960-61.

Besides Smith, Clough was down the England queue during his short stay with Sunderland behind Ray Pointer (Burnley), Ray Crawford (Ipswich Town), Gerry Hitchens, who had left Aston Villa for Inter Milan, Middlesbrough's Alan Peacock and Ray Charnley (Blackpool). And up-and-coming challengers, latest leaders of the Under-23 forward line, included Ted Farmer (Wolves), 'Budgie' Byrne, whose £65,000 transfer from Crystal Palace to West Ham broke the record for a deal between British clubs, and Derek Stokes (Huddersfield Town).

With such an array of talent ranged against him, it was perhaps not surprising that Sunderland's sparky newcomer was unable to compel an international recall before injury put him right out of the running for club as well as country – not even when he repaid the then Roker Park club for their £45,000 outlay by ending his first season with them, 1961-62, with 34 goals in 43 games. Of those goals, 29 came in the Second Division, relegation to which three years earlier had deprived Sunderland of their proud unique record of holding unbroken First Division membership since their admission to the League in 1890. The local football paper had literally turned blue in mourning, and did not get back into the pink until promotion was achieved.

For Sunderland in 1961-62, Clough added to his already impressive array of hat-tricks at the expense of Bury, Plymouth, Swansea and Huddersfield in the Second Division, and against Walsall in the League Cup. In the following season he had 28 more goals to his name, further hat-tricks against Southampton and Grimsby among them, when, on a Boxing Day afternoon of biting wind and sleet on Wearside, his barnstorming progress was brought to a shuddering halt.

With Sunderland pressing for an opening goal to bolster their hopes of a quick return to the top flight (they had to wait a further season for that), Clough tore in across the heavy, muddy surface, head down with eyes only for the through pass he was chasing. That made him wide open to a hefty collision with the outcoming Bury goalkeeper Chris Harker, whose shoulder crashed into Clough's right knee as he flung himself down in an attempt to intercept. Momentarily dazed, Clough instinctively tried to get to the ball as it ran loose, but he was unable to regain his feet and had to be carried off to hospital, where he underwent an operation on the medial ligament as well as the torn cruciate one. For three months he had a plaster on his right leg from ankle to groin, with the damaged knee in a bent position.

The all-out dash for goal that ended so traumatically for Clough was typical of his simple and direct methods which not a few people considered counted against him. His repeated exclusion by England was just one cause of the nationwide controversy that was to be a constant companion throughout his career as both player and manager. Some said he was overlooked for caps because he was too big for his boots, a dressing-room lawyer. Others viewed his style of play as a drawback at a time when the all-purpose player, the non-stop runner with a high work-rate, was coming strongly into fashion. Clough saw no sense in blunting his scoring power with a lot of ineffective running about the pitch.

Sunderland were back in the First Division by the time Clough attempted a comeback. He scored on his return against Leeds United on the September day in 1964 that sadly coincided with the death of his wife's mother while she was staying at their house, but he managed only two more matches before having to accept that his knee could no longer stand up to the strains of League football.

The refreshing ideas on coaching with which he first invigorated Sunderland's youngsters gelled perfectly with the talent spotting of Peter Taylor, who accepted his invitation to rejoin him at Hartlepools despite having to take a drop in wages from £34 a week to £24 on leaving Burton Albion. Taylor, a Nottingham Forest amateur during the Second World War before being signed by Coventry City, took over in Burton's goal after ending his Football League playing career of more than 200 games with just one appearance in Port Vale's Third Division side, and it was only through a chance meeting that he became the Albion's manager.

He had been a player with the Staffordshire club for just a few months when the holder of that post, Bill Townsend, a former Derby County goalkeeper, was given six weeks' notice. Before that period expired, the team travelled for a game at Hastings, and next morning Taylor came across Townsend and the Albion chairman on leaving the hotel for a walk along the pier. A talk between the three of them over coffee at a nearby café resulted in the chairman inviting Taylor to apply for the manager's job in a phone call to his home the following evening. He did so, and was appointed. Putting into practice the pattern that was to serve him so well – observe, expose, replace – he had practically a brand new team by the start of the next season. Burton promptly won the Southern League Cup, and a year later, in 1965, they were at the top of the league when the call from Clough came.

The blend that broke Hartlepools' habit of having to seek re-election transformed Derby County into the top team in the country, yet for this ambitious pair life at the Baseball Ground was at first found to be anything but rosy.

Rams' Rebuilding off to a False Start

The managerial whirlwind which, after a frustrating first season, blew away the Baseball Ground cobwebs of stagnation with the appointment of Brian Clough and Peter Taylor in the summer of 1967 also swiftly swept out the last of the players who had shared their cricket and soccer between Derbyshire and Derby County since the Rams' formation as an offshoot of the county cricket club way back in 1884.

Foremost among the new management team's requirements was the acquisition of a new centre-forward. On their arrival, they were dismayed to find that the occupier of that position for most of the past three seasons had been a player they considered to be little more than a part-timer because he played cricket for Derbyshire and had a clause in his contract allowing him a holiday at the end of the cricket season. Derby County, opined Clough, were being run 'like an amateur club'.

This criticism was no reflection on the ability of the man in question, Ian Buxton, but there was no argument about it. Even after scoring, and giving a good account of himself, in the only League game he was allowed under the new regime, he had to go. Clough and Taylor blithely ignored the fact that injury had also been a reason for his missing just a few matches over those three seasons in altogether making just over 150 first-team appearances and scoring getting on for fifty goals.

Buxton, born within the county, at Cromford, and a product of Wirksworth Grammar School, was an unused substitute for three successive games immediately after that lone League opportunity before playing what was to be his last senior game for the Rams, out of position at wing-half, in a League Cup-tie against, of all clubs, Hartlepools United (who would change their name to Hartlepool in 1968, then Hartlepool United in 1977). Within a fortnight, priced at about £10,000, he was on his way out to Luton Town, with whom he promptly won a Fourth Division title medal. From Luton, where his team-mates included Bruce Rioch, who was to be a Division One champion with Derby County under Dave Mackay's management, he joined Port Vale after a short stay with Notts County and also helped them to climb out of the League's basement. He continued playing for Derbyshire until 1973, captaining the county for three of the fifteen seasons he spent with them as an accomplished all-rounder.

Although, with the seasons increasingly overlapping, and the demands of combining the two sports at the first-class level becoming too taxing, Derby County have not fielded a Derbyshire cricketer since Buxton,

Derbyshire have called upon a League footballer and the Rams have had the services of a county cricketer. Chris Marples was a goalkeeper with Chesterfield when he temporarily ousted Bernie Maher as wicketkeeping successor to Test player Bob Taylor in the mid-1980s, and Alan Ramage, a centre-half for whom Derby paid Middlesbrough £150,000 in 1980, was a fine fast-bowling prospect with Yorkshire until his dual career was blighted by a knee injury.

Since then, Derbyshire's only top-soccer connection has been in name only – during the years when their team contained a Finney and a Mortensen. Roger John Finney was a right-hand batsman and left-arm bowler from Darley Dale, Ole Henrek Mortensen a fast bowler who gave up his job in a tax office and became the first Dane to make good in English county cricket.

The centre-forward signed to succeed Ian Buxton in the Derby County side was John O'Hare, one of the youngsters with whom Brian Clough had worked at Sunderland. Clough was well aware of this sturdy Scot's ability – O'Hare had, indeed, been one of his favourites up there – but Peter Taylor was even more determined to have him on Derby's books. At £21,000, O'Hare proved to be one of their outstanding bargains, though not always appreciated by the more critical of the County's often hard-to-please supporters. He was never able to shake off all his detractors, but he gradually won many of them round – just as he himself came to amend the unfavourable first impressions he formed of Derby ('dreary') and its football stadium ('dilapidated') as he pondered somewhat gloomily on what he had come to while he was initially based at the Midland hotel that was more like headquarters for the Rams' players in those days. Others also had it as a home before obtaining houses of their own, and the first-team squad spent Friday nights there before home games.

In common with many others who had no previous connection with the Derby area before joining the Rams, O'Hare was to find it sufficiently to his liking to settle there after finishing with football. And although the Baseball Ground certainly was not noted for its attractiveness, he was also to appreciate that there was nowhere quite like it for its atmosphere when a packed crowd, encroaching so close to the pitch, was in full cry on a big-match occasion.

One of the worst examples of the unfair treatment meted out at times to O'Hare occurred at a home match with Liverpool early in the season following Derby's first winning of the League championship. It provoked Clough into such fierce condemnation of the fans responsible that Sam Longson felt compelled to disassociate himself and his board from what he had said. At one stage when O'Hare was injured, somebody shouted: 'Goood! Now he'll have to go off.' He quickly recovered, however, and although he continued frequently to run into difficulties and lose the ball in one of his less convincing performances, he typically never gave up trying and in the last few minutes provided the perfect answer to his critics by scoring the winning goal.

Clough not only spoke out about the barracking of O'Hare but also complained that 'the crowd only started chanting when we were a goal in front near the end'. He added: 'I wanted to hear them when we were a goal down. Champions should have the blind support of their fans.'

O'Hare was born on 24 September 1946 at Renton near Dumbarton, home of the first Scottish League champions (jointly with Rangers after an indecisive play-off) way back in 1891. His value to Derby was well appreciated by discerning supporters, and above all by team-mates who knew that 'Solly', as they called him, was an ideal target man for their passes.

Pace was not prominent among this modest Scot's assets. Nor was he a battering-ram out-and-out goal-getter on the lean lines of Jack Bowers, for two successive seasons the First Division's leading scorer while with the Rams in the 1930s. Clough and Taylor wanted O'Hare for his strong points, which enabled him to slot admirably into their team pattern. Broad shouldered – so much so that it seemed he was padded like an American footballer – and a strong resister of tackles, he was a difficult man to play against because he shielded the ball in receiving it with his back to a defender and was adept at bringing it under control. His colleagues in defence and midfield were grateful that he consistently made himself available to receive their passes, and that when he got the ball he was not liable, even when below form, to let it promptly return in their direction. Brian Clough, whom he also followed to Leeds and Nottingham Forest, said he had 'a heart as big as a bucket'.

Sir Alf Ramsey, when England's manager, was heard to express regret that O'Hare was not an Englishman after seeing him give one of his finest displays, despite defeat, in an FA Cup-tie at Leeds early in his Derby career. He gave Jack Charlton, one of England's World Cup winners of 1966, a right runaround that afternoon towards the end of January in 1968. In the *Derby Evening Telegraph*, George Edwards reported:

'He gave Charlton the complete works, beating him on both sides and rendering the ultimate humiliation of pushing the ball through the England man's legs and leaving him sitting on his pants. It was said afterwards that Charlton was not happy about a neck injury, but it looked more a case of injured pride when he went off 11 minutes from the end, to be replaced by Madeley. Charlton was given "the bird" for much of the match, and Madeley was welcomed with a terrific cheer.'

Impressed as Sir Alf was, it took Scotland's selectors almost two years after that to award O'Hare the first of his three Under-23 caps, by which time he had helped Derby to promotion and proved himself in the First Division, but they then chose him thirteen more times in full internationals. Only twice in his dozen starts at the senior level (on the other occasion he went on as a substitute) were Scotland beaten.

Two of the Scots' four goals O'Hare obtained on his Under-23 debut against France at a sparsely populated Hampden Park on a dismal Wednesday evening in December 1969 ensured his retention for the next month's match with Wales at Aberdeen, in which he also scored to earn a draw. He was kept quiet, however, in defeat at Sunderland soon afterwards by an England Under-23 defence that included one player who was among his colleagues with Derby County, two others who were later to join him at the Baseball Ground, and a fourth, Peter Shilton, who was to keep goal for the Rams after he had left the club. The three with whom he played for Derby were Roy McFarland, the centre-half who followed him as the club's second signing by Clough and Taylor, Colin Todd, captain of the England Under-23 side at what was then his home ground, and David Nish, at that stage one of Shilton's team-mates at Leicester. Todd became one of the most gifted defenders Derby County have ever possessed, but on the day he opposed O'Hare he had the misfortune to put the ball into his own net for Scotland's only goal.

There was also just the one goal for Scotland, but the winner each time, in games O'Hare played for the senior side against Northern Ireland (on his full international debut in Belfast in 1970), Denmark and Belgium – and he was the scorer of all three. He also netted in victories over Portugal and Peru, but the unselfishness of his play was reflected in the fact that he was a steady, rather than a ready, scorer, averaging just under a goal every four matches with 82 in his 311 first-team appearances for Derby County.

The first of those goals for the Rams, with a well-placed right-foot shot in the 48th minute of his debut, completed their scoring in a 3-2 home win against Charlton Athletic in their opening match of the 1967-68 season. It was the only real opportunity he had that afternoon as Derby embarked upon a campaign in which, after a misleadingly promising start, they again went uncomfortably close to relegation instead of making the anticipated thrust for promotion under the new management.

Prospects looked bright when they won seven of their first nine League games, especially when four of those victories came in succession, culminating in a 5-1 eclipse of Cardiff City at Ninian Park, where Hector did the hat-trick, and a 4-1 home success against Rotherham United that included two more goals for 'King' Kevin, but after that the rot set in. Only two more wins were gained in fifteen Second Division matches up to the turn of the year, as against eight defeats, and in the remaining eighteen League fixtures after that losses outnumbered successes by nine to four. It would have been a dismal season indeed but for the League Cup run to the last four that is still the furthest the club have gone in that competition.

The transformation of League fortunes that was so rapidly to follow looked a long way off as the Rams faded to a final eighteenth place in the Second Division – one lower than where Tim Ward had left them. With only one win in the final eight games, fears of the drop persisted uncomfortably late.

The week after their narrow defeat of Charlton on the first day, Derby disappointed in failing to find any response to a headed goal by Crystal Palace's Bob Woodruff at Selhurst Park, but on the following Monday evening they opened their away account in impressive style as Roy McFarland made a remarkably mature Second Division debut for a nineteen-year-old in a 3-1 victory at Rotherham.

The match with Palace marked the 113th and last appearance in Derby's first team of Eddie Thomas, who took over for the second half when wing-half Phil Waller dropped out with an ankle injury. Before that last week of August was out so was Thomas. For a fee £1,000 less than the £6,000 Tim Ward had paid Swansea for him, he preceded Ian Buxton in becoming the first departure of the Clough era with his transfer to Third Division Orient.

A Lancastrian, born at Newton-le-Willows, Thomas played in the First Division with Everton and Blackburn before joining Swansea in the Second, and he turned up at Derby with a century of goals already under his belt. For the Rams he scored only one short of fifty more after getting off to a flying start by netting in each of his first six games, forming a productive inside-forward partnership with Alan Durban that touched its peak during the 1964-65 season in which they both scored two dozen times. In a short stay with Orient, Thomas took his career goals tally to just beyond 150 in little more than 300 games before going on loan to Nuneaton and then returning to Derbyshire with Heanor Town.

Popular and unassuming, Eddie was one of the former Derby players I had the pleasure of meeting at matches at Pride Park, to which the Rams moved from the Baseball Ground in 1997, until he was taken seriously ill shortly before his death towards the end of 2003, at the age of seventy. We were all guests of Lionel Pickering, then the club's chairman, who has been a friend of mine since we worked together in the sports department of the *Derby Evening Telegraph* way back in the 1950s.

Phil Waller was another who did not long survive the Clough-Taylor clear-out, but, although rarely called upon to add to the hundred League games he had played while Ward was the manager, he stayed on long enough to feature prominently in the side that reached the League Cup semi-finals. A product of the Rams' junior teams during Harry Storer's time, the Leeds-born Waller moved to Mansfield Town for £6,000 on the eve of 1968's March transfer deadline, the month after Derby's hopes of taking part in another Wembley final had been dashed.

Four years later, Waller had a spell as Ilkeston Town's player-manager before signing for Boston United, who were twice Northern Premier League champions while he was with them, and in whose team he reappeared at the Baseball Ground in a third-round FA Cup-tie in 1974.

That return visit so nearly resulted in a repeat, if on a less grand scale, of one of the biggest bombshells in the whole of Cup history that Boston had exploded at the same venue almost twenty years before. With a team including six former Derby County players, the Lincolnshire club had gained a staggering 6-1 victory in the second round against the very same Rams who had themselves hit Darlington for six in the League the previous Saturday. The skeleton so nearly rattled in the County's Cup cupboard when Boston, with Waller, were drawn to play at Derby again – this time against recent First Division champions, by then managed by Dave Mackay, instead of humble members of the Third North.

The game remained goalless only after a future caretaker coach of the England team, the Lincolnshire club's player-manager Howard Wilkinson, had put over a perfect cross that led to the ball, from Alan Tewley's header, spinning off one Derby upright and trickling tantalisingly right across the goalmouth, inches from the line, with no Boston player able to apply the finishing touch before it was scrambled behind for a corner. In the replay the Rams exactly reversed that shocking 1-6 scoreline as another of the Clough-Taylor bargains, Archie Gemmill, strayed from his industrious midfield role to score the only hat-trick of his career with the aid of a penalty.

From Boston, Waller went via Matlock Town to Burton Albion, where he returned for just over a season as manager after service with Belper Town, as player-coach, and Kimberley Town.

Roy McFarland's wearing of Derby County's black and white was pre-destined from the time Brian Clough and Peter Taylor were together at Hartlepools United. While there, they saw two players in opposing Fourth Division teams they particularly coveted and bore in mind for when they were in a position to afford such luxuries. One, Kevin Hector, was already at the Baseball Ground when they arrived. The other, McFarland, became an immediate objective. Born at Liverpool on 5 April 1948, he was even younger than O'Hare, and a still more exciting prospect. Taylor waxed most enthusiastically about him, saying:

'I became obsessed with him after he'd played for Tranmere Rovers against us at Hartlepool. He was then under 18, and looked younger. I couldn't believe my eyes. Twelve months later we were appointed at Derby, and I missed our opening League match to watch Mac again. Soon afterwards we signed him for £24,000 under the noses of Everton and Liverpool. He ranks as my No 1 discovery.'

It was not, however, a straightforward signing. Far from it. Taylor may have been the motivating force behind it, but it took the tenacity Clough was to display in pulling off other big deals to complete it. And even then McFarland was to admit that he woke up in the morning wondering what on earth he had done, beset by regrets that he had committed himself to a lowly Second Division club, as Derby then were, instead of awaiting the call from thriving Liverpool for which he had been hoping. That afternoon, standing on the Kop at Anfield, he felt that he had just made the biggest mistake of his life as he watched the team he would have preferred to join score six goals against Newcastle without reply.

Amazed because neither of Merseyside's two big clubs had yet moved in for such a highly promising teenager, Clough and Taylor were so anxious not to miss signing him that they knocked on his front door at such a late hour the previous night that his father had to get him out of bed. At first the reluctant and half-awake McFarland said he would let them have a decision on their offer after he had enjoyed a good night's sleep, but when Clough made it clear he was not leaving without getting his name on the transfer form this young Englishman with the Scottish-sounding name felt unable to sustain his resistance with the clock having ticked past midnight, and, rather bemusedly, he gave in – if only to have some peace and quiet, and get back to bed. His father, an admirer of Clough the player, was also an important influence, observing that if he was wanted that badly he really ought to sign.

The doubts that assailed him when he awoke again in the clear light of day took a little time to be dispelled as Derby struggled for much of his first season with them, but subsequent events proved that he had made the best decision of his career. The doubts Derby's directors felt about forking out so much money, for those days, on such a young and inexperienced player also quickly faded away. McFarland, fresh from helping Tranmere out of the Fourth Division, was a success from the start, regularly earning rave reviews even when he lacked support as others in the Derby defence were too often found wanting before Clough and Taylor remodelled it to their satisfaction. Skilful on the ground and strong in the air (as befitted someone who had competed in the national schools' trampoline championship), he could well have made a name for himself as a forward if he had not been a defender. As it was, he ended only just short of a half-century of goals for Derby County.

Only occasionally did McFarland falter during that difficult first season with the Rams. His lack of experience showed when Ray Crawford, one of the men who had kept Clough out of the England team, gave him a hard time in a 0-4 defeat by an Ipswich side bound for the Second Division championship. He also failed to master the lively John O'Rourke, an England Under-23 cap who did the hat-trick against him at Derby shortly before leaving Middlesbrough, for whom he had been top scorer in their rise from the Third Division the previous season, to give Ipswich's push to promotion a final boost that included another goal at the Baseball Ground as the Suffolk club completed the double over the Rams.

Otherwise, McFarland was almost invariably impeccable, dominating even during an April snowstorm in Birmingham, and as the team at last settled into a formidable force the following season he rapidly developed towards becoming the best central defender in the country – and one of the most stylish since the Second World War. After playing five times in the England Under-23 side, he eventually overtook Durban as Derby's most-capped player, reaching a total of 28 senior international appearances which, but for the serious injury he suffered in making his 24th, plus other absences while under treatment, he might well have increased beyond the reach of the three players who have since surpassed it while with the club. Peter Shilton took part in 34 of his record number of 125 games for England during his Baseball Ground days, Mart Poom made 37 appearances in Estonia's goal, and Deon Burton played 42 times for Jamaica before rejoining Portsmouth.

Bob Saxton, the resolute, wholehearted Yorkshireman from whom McFarland took over in the Derby team, continued as captain at wing-half until shortly before his £12,000 transfer to Plymouth Argyle early in February 1968, though he was required again at centre-half in the League Cup, for which McFarland was ineligible that season because he had played for Tranmere in the opening round. Saxton, a product of Denaby United, the club a few miles from Rotherham in South Yorkshire that had provided the Rams with Jack Barker, was the first-choice defensive pivot for much of Tim Ward's last two seasons with Derby, but it was as a substitute that he gained a special place in the club's records. On 21 August 1965, the first day on which substitutes were allowed in the Football League, he became the first one to be used by the Rams when he went on in place of the injured full-back Geoff Barrowcliffe after only a quarter of an hour's play in a 0-3 home defeat by Southampton.

Saxton's last game for Derby was the first leg of the League Cup semi-final they undeservedly lost to Leeds – only ten days before their FA Cup defeat by the same club – through a penalty he conceded by handling the ball in the scramble that ensued from a corner. He went west only a few days before the second leg, in which Phil Waller filled the gap he had left and Leeds progressed by a 4-2 aggregate to a narrow victory over Arsenal in the final. It was no consolation for the County that Hector, who was born at Leeds, scored the best goal of that return match at Elland Road, where the home side, then one of the strongest in the country, were unquestionably good value for their victory. The margin by which they gained it would have been a little more in keeping with the balance of play if Eire international Johnny Giles had not hit a post with another penalty kick.

Subsequent moves took Saxton to Exeter, where he was player-manager when they won promotion from the Fourth Division with an overdraft limit of £25,000, back to Plymouth as manager, and then to other managerial posts at Blackburn and York. He was also caretaker manager at Newcastle – between the departure of Jim Smith, who a few years afterwards guided Derby County into the Premiership, and the appointment of the Argentinian Ossie Ardiles – and later was with Manchester City as chief scout, then Sunderland as assistant manager.

Other players who did not last out the first season of the Clough era at Derby were Billy Hodgson, who cost Rotherham £7,000 but soon left them for Lincoln; Derek Draper, who followed a short stay at Bradford with more than 300 League games for Chester, whom he helped out of the Fourth Division; Gordon Hughes, a £6,000 signing by Lincoln who was later with Boston; and a couple of young wingers, Nigel Cleevely and Ron Metcalf, who both went to Burton Albion.

Glaswegian Hodgson, almost thirty when Tim Ward signed him, gave his best years to Sheffield United, but he was a regular choice for two seasons at the Baseball Ground and enjoyed one of his most memorable afternoons in scoring a hat-trick against Clough's old club Middlesbrough.

Hughes, short, stocky and speedy, added just over 200 League and Cup matches for the Rams to the near-150 he had played for Newcastle before losing his place on the right wing after the Leeds leg of the League Cup semi-final. It was testimony to the consistency and unsparing effort of this no-frills player that until then, amid frequent changes in other positions, he had not missed any of the 35 fixtures Derby had fulfilled since Clough's appointment.

Draper, a former Welsh Under-23 international from Swansea, Cleevely, who hailed from Ward's home town of Cheltenham, and Metcalf, a North-Easterner from Marsden Colliery's junior team, had made fewer than thirty first-team appearances between them. Metcalf's only League game was the last one of the 1966-67 season, for which the side was selected by the directors after Ward had left.

Those outgoings, added to the transfers of Buxton, Thomas and Waller, brought more than £40,000 into the County's coffers, whereas expenditure on players during that first season with Clough and Taylor in charge approached £100,000. The costliest player of that period was Alan Hinton, a left-winger who had drifted into such a lean spell with Nottingham Forest that the committeemen of those East Midlands neighbours (Forest were run by committee until becoming a limited company in 1982) positively rubbed their hands with glee on offloading him to Derby for £30,000 in the month following the signing of O'Hare and McFarland. One of them even suggested that the Rams would be asking for their money back.

Never one to cope well with tough tackling, Hinton had been nicknamed Gladys and taunted from the terraces by fans who asked what he had done with his handbag. Hinton also at first found it difficult to please at the Baseball Ground, but the last laugh was on Forest, whom he had joined from Wolverhampton Wanderers in exchange for another winger, the Channel Islander 'Flip' Le Flem, after winning the first of his three full England caps against France at Hillsborough in 1962 – just three days before his twentieth birthday, and after only 27 League appearances.

Hinton also played in the England Youth and Under-23 teams. His other two full caps were gained while with Nottingham Forest against Belgium and Wales, both at Wembley, in 1964. He scored one of the goals in the 2-2 draw with Belgium. England also drew, 1-1, when he made his debut against France, and they defeated Wales 2-1 with a couple of goals from Frank Wignall, who began his League career with Everton and, like Hinton, played for Forest and Wolves before joining the County.

Hinton was out of the Derby team for a time when troubled by a leg injury, but he became an integral member of it after crowning an excellent display with two goals on his recall early in 1968 for a match at Plymouth that Derby battled back to win 4-3 after being 1-3 down half-an-hour from the finish. Having wiped out the lead that relegation-bound Argyle had been given in only 38 seconds by John Mitten – son of the former Manchester United winger – Hinton started the late recovery by halving the deficit on the hour.

Those goals were the first two of the 84 Hinton was to score in 319 matches for Derby County, most of them with shots of the explosive power he packed into both boots, the left one especially. Though unable to get back into the England team, he massively influenced the Rams' march to the championships of the Second and First Divisions in the space of four seasons, and when the League title was won again under Dave Mackay's guidance he provided new impetus at a critical time on being restored to the side for most of the run-in. Hinton readily conceded that with Forest his game had gone stale, draining his confidence. He added:

'Clough put that right. At the team talks he'd make me feel ten feet tall. He would tell the other lads: "Give it to Alan. He'll show you how it's done.

He'll make a goal for you." Maybe it was only psychology, but it worked. Clough and Taylor saved my career. They gave me eight of the best years of my life. I'm sure it was Taylor who saw something in me that Derby needed when they signed me.'

The secret of Hinton's success was that Derby's managerial pair ignored his understandable distaste for the rough stuff, of which some opponents were only too ready to try to take advantage, and gave full rein to his strengths. And those strengths were considerable. Having modelled himself on Jimmy Mullen, the Wolves and England winger noted for his skill in crossing the ball, he was unmatched in his time for the accuracy of his centres, from any position and with either foot. With the placing of his corner-kicks also exceptional, many were the goals he made. On top of that, especially from free-kicks, there was his shooting, so often spectacular and invariably, for goalkeepers, frighteningly fierce. That made him an obvious, though surprisingly not immediate, choice as penalty-taker, and there were eight successful spot-kicks among the fifteen goals that made him Derby's top scorer when they were League champions for the first time in 1971-72.

Not that Hinton was all perfection from the spot. I was among the incredulous onlookers when he failed with two penalties in one home match with Sheffield United, the club against which he had converted a couple in the corresponding fixture of the first title-winning season the year before. The man responsible for the 'minor miracle', as Gerald Mortimer described it in the Derby evening paper, was goalkeeper Tom McAlister, who saved on both occasions – although on the first one the ball was immediately returned into the goalmouth for O'Hare to score what proved to be the deciding goal.

Only a few months later, on an April evening in 1973, I was again at the Baseball Ground (perhaps I should have stayed away!) when Hinton recorded the most memorable, and costly, of his rare penalty lapses. We shall be coming to that match more fully in due course. Suffice to say for now that he struck the ball wide as Derby were striving to wipe out a controversial 1-3 deficit from the first leg of a European Cup semi-final against Juventus. With the game remaining goalless, out they went on aggregate, and the Italian champions got through to the final in Belgrade, where they were beaten by an only goal as Ajax, of Amsterdam, won the trophy for the third consecutive year.

Hinton took over Derby's penalty-taking only after Kevin Hector, the fans' big favourite, had missed from the spot in successive games with Bristol City and Carlisle United. Hector was called upon to take two penalties against City, and he might also have failed with the first one if Mike Gibson, a Derby-born goalkeeper from Gresley Rovers, had stayed where he was instead of diving hopefully to his right.

The Rams' key player that day was Richie Barker, whose two goals in a 3-1 win increased his tally to a dozen in twenty matches since his £2,000 bargain signing from Burton Albion – in his second spell with whom he had played in the Southern League under Peter Taylor's management after assisting Loughborough United and Matlock Town. Those goals also had him spoken of as 'the new Jack Stamps', if a rather flattering reference to the extra-time hero of the 1946 FA Cup final triumph who gave the Rams sterling service during three decades.

Barker, who gave up his job as a draughtsman to join Derby, varied from looking very ordinary to being surprisingly effective for someone who had entered the Football League at the advanced age of almost 28. Although he could not be regarded as a long-term investment for the higher echelons of the game at which Clough and Taylor were aiming, he rendered his home-town club commendable service before leaving for Notts County midway through the Second Division promotion season. The move brought Derby a profit of several thousand pounds on what they paid for him.

A broken leg while with Peterborough United ended Barker's playing career after he had helped Notts to the 1970-71 Fourth Division title. Instead of sticking to his original intention of returning to his old job outside football, he entered management as assistant to Alan Durban, who had by then become player-manager of Shrewsbury Town – the club whose first manager in the Football League had been Sammy Crooks, the former Derby and England winger whose return to the Rams as chief scout had ended abruptly with the advent of Clough and Taylor. Durban and Barker started Shrewsbury on their climb from the Fourth Division to the Second that was completed under the player-management of Graham Turner.

Barker briefly succeeded Durban as Shrewsbury manager when his former Derby team-mate left to manage Stoke, and, after being assistant manager with Wolves, he also replaced him at the Potteries club on the Welshman's departure to Sunderland. While at Molineux, Barker was in charge of the Wolverhampton team for a match with Derby in the absence of manager John Barnwell, who was recovering in hospital from serious injuries sustained in a car crash. The Rams were well beaten on that occasion, by 0-4, and only just avoided the relegation that befell them a year later.

Sacked at Stoke amid discord behind the scenes and a poor start to the 1983-84 season, Barker had a similarly unhappy experience on rejoining Notts County as manager, ending with their descent to the Third Division, and he coached in Greece and Egypt before finding his next post in England at Luton, as head coach. He stayed at Kenilworth Road for just a few months, however, then taking the gamble of going from one First

Division club that was heading for Wembley to another for which relegation was looming.

In leaving Luton early in 1989, not long before they lost to a Nottingham Forest side managed by Brian Clough in the final of the Littlewoods Cup (as the League's knock-out trophy was then known), Barker joined Sheffield Wednesday as assistant to Ron Atkinson even though he was warned he might be out of work if they were unable to avoid the drop. But they survived, and although they did go down the following season they climbed straight back up, winning the Rumbelows Cup (the League's competition under its new guise with another change of sponsor) on the way. It was not until the summer of 1996, when his contract, by then as Director of Football, was not renewed, that Barker left Hillsborough – and he could have been manager there before that.

The experience he had gained both in England and abroad prompted Wednesday to ask him if he fancied taking over when Atkinson moved to Aston Villa, but at that time he preferred to remain an assistant. He modestly explained:

'I felt they needed another high-profile manager, and I knew I wasn't that person. I was ready to fill in if required, and said I'd be happy to work with a new man. I was delighted they chose Trevor [Francis, the former England forward who became Britain's first £1 million footballer when Brian Clough signed him from Birmingham City for Nottingham Forest in 1979], and my role suits me. I could be a No 1, but I think I'm a better No 2 because it's where I do my best work. I provide the opposite view. I've never been a "yes" man, and I know it doesn't help a manager to agree with all he says. As you get older [he was then in his fifties] and gain experience you can stand back and take a broader view you don't see when you're younger.'

After parting company with Sheffield Wednesday, Barker became West Bromwich Albion's chief scout, and he was caretaker manager at the Hawthorns between the departure as manager of Ray Harford (later also briefly coach at Derby) and appointment of Denis Smith. After that, Barker had just under a year as assistant manager at Halifax.

On the last day of September in 1967, between the signings of Hinton and Barker, Brian Clough and Peter Taylor made one of their rare unsuccessful ventures into the transfer market for Derby in paying about £6,000 to Shrewsbury Town for Pat Wright, a full-back who had started out with Birmingham City. Wright was given only nine games at right-back before losing his place after a 2-4 home defeat by Middlesbrough, but, with constant changes being made in the attempt to find the right blend, he had three partners on the opposite flank during that short run – John Richardson, Peter Daniel and Mick Hopkinson.

Of those three, Daniel, known as 'Ticker' to his team-mates, was the only one to survive the Clough-Taylor era. Unspectacular but dependable, he was taken on by Tim Ward as an apprentice in 1963 after playing in a Sunday morning trial game, and it was not until early in 1979 that he finally left the club. He moved only a short distance, first to Burton Albion, then Belper Town, not long after having gone to the other extreme in Canada on loan to Vancouver Whitecaps. Despite being a reserve – though a very valued one – for all but three seasons during his many years with the Rams, he totted up almost 250 League and Cup appearances, including substitutions.

Richardson, who was born just outside Derbyshire, over the border with Notts at Worksop, and Hopkinson, who came from within the county at Ambergate, were both gradually phased out after having played more than a hundred first-team games for Derby. Hopkinson was the first of them to go, transferred to Mansfield Town in the 1968 close season for £5,500. Richardson, the first product of the Rams' apprentice professional scheme, stayed for three years after that, but with only limited opportunities in the senior side, before joining Notts County for a fee of about £10,000. He was then still only 26, but he had the misfortune to break a leg soon afterwards and left for King's Lynn after turning out only twice in the Magpies' League side, both times as a substitute.

Hopkinson, a versatile signing for Derby from the local West End Boys' Club, graduated through the juniors to the first team, at wing-half, in Harry Storer's last season as manager. 'Hoppy,' whose wholehearted efforts made him a popular figure with fans, did not get many goals, but is best remembered by those who saw it for the cannonball shot with which he scored in the defeat of promotion-bound Liverpool in 1961. From Mansfield he moved on a free transfer to Port Vale in the summer of 1970, a week before the Town's manager, Tom Eggleston, a former Derby wing-half, left to coach in Greece. After that, Hopkinson went out of the Football League with, in turn, Boston United, Belper Town, whom he managed, and Burton Albion, where he was coach and assistant manager.

Pat Wright, having been displaced at Derby when Brian Clough first switched Ron Webster back from wing-half, added only four first-team appearances to his original nine, one of them as a substitute, but the best part of two more seasons went by before, in March 1970, he went on loan to Southend United. The manager newly appointed there was Arthur Rowley, holder of the Football League scoring record with 434 goals, who had been player-manager at Shrewsbury during Wright's stay at Gay Meadow. Wright signed for Rotherham United after the cancellation of his contract with Derby the following August. He later coached at Portsmouth and in Zambia, Saudi Arabia and the United Arab Emirates.

The match with Middlesbrough in which Wright ended his short sequence as Derby's right-back also marked the debut for the club of Arthur Stewart, a Northern Ireland international wing-half from Glentoran who was pitched straight into the team even though he did not sign the transfer forms until less than three hours before the kick-off after a tiring overnight journey from Ulster. Under those difficult circumstances he did well enough in defeat to raise hopes of justifying the £12,000 fee, and soon afterwards was promoted to captain. As Derby's fortunes declined, however, so did his own. He won four of his seven caps while with the Rams, but too often in the Second Division his lack of pace was exploited, and it was only on the few occasions he was used as a sweeper that he looked really comfortable. Soon he was on his way back to Ireland, rejoining his first club, Ballymena, with whom he became player-manager. From there he also rejoined Glentoran, as manager, before coaching on the other side of the Atlantic in New Jersey.

Derby County's other newcomers in the first Clough-Taylor season were Jim Walker and John Robson. The slimly-built Walker, signed from Northwich Victoria after arriving on trial towards the end of 1967, showed flashes of pace and trickery in holding a first-team place up to Christmas in the Second Division championship season, and although he was then restricted to only occasional first-team outings, mainly as a substitute, and was loaned out to Hartlepool, he captained the Reserves to the Central League title in the 1971-72 season that also ended with the Rams' senior side as First Division champions.

When Walker left Derby in September 1974, it was to rejoin Peter Taylor, then newly installed as Brighton's manager, in company with Tony Mason, a young reserve player, in a deal worth some £20,000. After that he was with Peterborough and Chester before coaching in the Middle East and then turning to physiotherapy with Blackburn Rovers and Aston Villa. For unearthing a find from the obscurity of junior football, Derby really came up with the goods in signing Robson. Or, to be exact, Peter Taylor did. Although he rated McFarland his top discovery, the reputation Taylor had for spotting talent was rarely – if ever for someone so unknown – more justified than when he recognised the potential of the seventeen-year-old he saw playing for Birtley Youth Club on one of his return trips to the North-East. It has to be said, though, that the first thing about Robson that caught Taylor's attention was his neat, short-cut hair, a rarity in those days of extravagant styles.

Promptly signed, after Taylor had laid a smokescreen for any other interested parties by making a point of complaining to the scout who had tipped him off about having his time wasted, Robson made a most promising League debut at wing-half against Ipswich Town despite its coinciding with one of the nine home defeats Derby suffered that season. After also doing well in a couple of drawn games, he was the Rams' outstanding player, besides scoring their only goal, when Blackpool became the third successive winning visitors on the final day.

Fortunately, Robson's confidence was not undermined by being introduced into a team whose inconsistency and defensive weaknesses combined to plummet them into the Second Division's depths after deceptively rising as high as fourth in the early weeks. On being converted into a full-back, he formed an efficient partnership with Ron Webster over the following four seasons that contributed considerably to the club's rise to the top of the English game.

No defence in Division Two conceded more goals than the 78 put into Derby's net in 1967-68. Even Fourth Division Darlington scored four at the Baseball Ground in a League Cup-tie the Rams were lucky to win, as the last of the five with which they responded was an own-goal. How different it was all so swiftly to become under the expert influence of the footballing legend Clough called 'the most effective signing of my entire managerial career'. Few Derby followers, surely, will not know who that was before going on to read about him in the next chapter.

THE COMPASSIONATE SIDE OF BRIAN CLOUGH

Brian Clough was first on the telephone with offers of help when Mick Hopkinson, a player he had sold to Mansfield for a nominal fee, broke a leg while playing for Boston United. He not only arranged for Hopkinson to enter hospital as a private patient, and to receive later treatment at a rehabilitation centre, but also for his leg to be reset by a leading surgeon, with Derby County footing the bill.

'What more can you say about a man like Mr Clough?' said Hopkinson. 'He told me that if Roy McFarland had suffered the same injury he would get no better treatment than me. All that for an unknown player. He's magnificent.'

Perseverance pays off with Mackay coup

Of all the many incoming transfers Brian Clough negotiated during his often stormy, always eventful, managerial career, one stands out for the sheer audacity of its conception and his completion of it after the odds had been heavily stacked against him. What he himself called his most effective signing brought to the Baseball Ground David Craig Mackay, 22 times a Scottish international (he deserved a lot more), a League champion and Cup winner with Hearts, and strong man king-pin in Tottenham Hotspur's League and Cup double team of 1960-61.

Hearts were also runners-up for the Scottish League title, and once third, during his four full seasons with them, and they again finished second a few weeks after he had left. He was therefore a key member of their team throughout one of the most successful periods in their history – an achievement he was to repeat with both Tottenham and Derby County.

Born in Edinburgh on 14 November 1934, the well-built, barrel-chested Mackay, who was also capped as a schoolboy, joined Hearts from Newtongrange Star, a Midlothian junior side, in the spring of 1952, around the time of his call-up for National Service in the Royal Engineers, and he made the first of his 135 appearances in their Scottish League side in the 1953-54 season. He was the driving force behind their winning of the Scottish League Cup in 1954, their first victory in a Scottish Cup final for fifty years in 1956, their League championship triumph of 1958 (by the biggest margin, thirteen points, for nearly thirty years), and another Scottish League Cup success a few months before his sudden and unexpected move to Tottenham on the eve of the transfer deadline on 16 March 1959.

Until then, Spurs had seemed set on signing Mel Charles (younger brother of John, who comes into these Derby memories later), the Welsh international who soon afterwards left Swansea for North London's other big club, Arsenal. The fee Tottenham paid for Mackay was a British record for a wing-half, just exceeding the £30,000 they had shelled out to sign Northern Ireland's Danny Blanchflower from Aston Villa nearly five years before.

When Mackay arrived, Blanchflower had only recently been reinstated as captain after having been dropped, so it was under the Irishman's leadership that the sturdy Scot, who was made skipper of Hearts at 22 and of Scotland the month before his 24th birthday, added to his string of honours with the Football League and FA Cup double in 1961, and the FA Cup again in 1962, before captaining Spurs to another Cup win at Wembley in 1967, three years after Blanchflower's retirement. He also had the distinction of playing for the Football League as well as the Scottish League, once turning out against his compatriots.

Mackay had no hesitation, nor later any regrets, about joining Tottenham, yet he had been hopeful of entering English football with Manchester United, whose manager, Matt Busby, was then also Scotland's team manager. After signing for the London club, he said:

'When Matt Busby started grooming me for the Scotland captaincy job I pictured myself in the Manchester United strip, but Matt never made the approach to Hearts. Although I play at right-half for Scotland, Mr Nicholson, Spurs' manager, has given me the concession of allowing me to play at left-half, my favourite position, behind the most fabulous outside-left in Britain, Cliff Jones.'

That arrangement also suited Nicholson because it enabled Blanchflower to continue on the opposite flank, putting an end to speculation that he was to be replaced by Mackay. After completing the deal, Tottenham's manager stayed on in Scotland that evening to watch a Scottish FA trial match in which his new capture, from left-half, scored a couple of typically hard-hit goals for a Scotland XI against a Scottish League representative side. What was not so typical was the start Mackay made to his captaincy of Scotland against Wales in Cardiff the previous October. He led his country to victory right enough, in only his third international match after graduating from the Under-23 team, but he failed to score from a penalty in the first minute.

The qualities Mackay had shown as a captain from an early age were what Brian Clough and Peter Taylor were looking for, besides his exceptional strength as a defender, when they decided that, at 33, he would be just the man to put the right sort of experience into a Derby line-up they were rebuilding with an emphasis on youth. In the eyes of many, Mackay was the best captain Derby County ever had. You only had to look at him on the field to know that he was the player in charge. Combining inspiration with reassurance, he led by example and would be as ready to give a congratulatory pat on the back for something well done as to shake a fist in admonishment for an avoidable error – accompanied by an urging-on to do better.

There is one vivid memory, graphically preserved for posterity on camera, of the time when, in a face-to-face confrontation with a fellow Scottish international, that fist was clenched as it pulled upwards in a vice-like grip on the front of Billy Bremner's shirt after the Leeds captain had incurred Mackay's displeasure during a match at White Hart Lane. It was an unsavoury image that was to haunt Mackay, one that he said made him look like 'Desperate Dan on steroids', and he was asked to sign the picture of it many more times than any other from his entire career.

As his prison warder namesake in the television comedy *Porridge* claimed to be, Mackay was firm, but fair, and he expected others to be the same. He was quite prepared to receive strong tackles as well as dish them out, but woe betide anybody who transgressed against him or his teammates. The Mackay tackle was one to be feared. The late Bryon Butler, a respected commentator on the game in both print and on the radio, wrote that 'it could have earned him a good living felling trees, demolishing walls or breaking up tanks'. Someone else likened it to a clap of thunder.

Twice, however, Mackay's combative style rebounded on him as he suffered serious injury, and he needed all of his fighting spirit to make the comebacks without which he would never have been seen at Derby. It was bad enough that he should have the misfortune to miss the European Cup-Winners' Cup final victory against Atletico Madrid at Rotterdam in 1963 because of pulled stomach muscles. A still bigger blow was awaiting him when Spurs went to Old Trafford later in the year aiming to complete the first stage of their defence of that trophy after gaining an advantage of two goals (one of them scored by Mackay) at home to Manchester United. In the eighth minute of the return game he broke his left leg, and ten-man Tottenham, beaten 1-4, went out 3-4 on aggregate. Nine months later, just as he was beginning to look forward to his return to the first team, he broke the same leg again in a try-out with the Reserves in a Football Combination match against Shrewsbury Town. In his autobiography *The Real Mackay*, he said that in the shirt-grabbing incident he was momentarily furious after being kicked by Bremner because 'he could easily have broken my leg for a third time'.

After being kept out of the whole of the 1964-65 League season, Mackay came back with such undiminished power that in the next one he was only one game short of making, for the first time, the then maximum 42 First Division appearances. It was a cherished objective he was eventually to realise in the last of his three seasons with Derby County.

It spoke volumes for his playing ability that he stood out as much amid Spurs' established stars as he did among the Rams' aspiring ones. The Tottenham of his time were a major force in English football, a collection of talent assembled at a cost of well over half a million pounds — nothing extraordinary these days, but awesome enough then to attract the tag of 'Bank of England team'.

When the warrior-like figure of Mackay was added to that select gathering, it already included Maurice Norman and Bobby Smith, who both played for England, and Welsh caps Terry Medwin and Cliff Jones, in addition to Blanchflower. Quickly in Mackay's wake came two other capped

Scots who also made big contributions to the team that did the double – goalkeeper Bill Brown and John White, a silkily skilful inside-forward whose career was tragically cut short in his mid-twenties when he was fatally struck by lightning while sheltering on a golf course in a thunderstorm.

Later, between the first Football League and FA Cup double of the twentieth century and Mackay's departure, came Jimmy Greaves, the free-scoring most expensive of the lot at just under £100,000 (Spurs wanted to spare him that millstone), Pat Jennings, Alan Mullery, Alan Gilzean and Terry Venables. Internationals all. Greaves paid Mackay the finest of compliments when he said:

'He was the greatest professional I played with. If he was ever missing from the Tottenham side every one of us had to work twice as hard to make up for it.'

When word at last got around at the end of the 1967-68 season that Mackay, after more than 300 games and just over fifty goals, was on his way out of White Hart Lane, released on completion of his contract, Brian Clough at first resisted Peter Taylor's insistence that he should try to sign him for Derby, regarding it as a forlorn hope, but he was finally persuaded to drive down to North London to test his luck.

Admitting to feeling 'nervous as hell' when he arrived there, Clough promptly came up against a couple of rebuffs that would have deterred lesser mortals. First Bill Nicholson, and then Mackay himself, told him that next day the man he coveted was off to Scotland to rejoin Hearts as assistant manager.

Clough, persevering despite being kept waiting about for some time, still refused to take 'No' for an answer even when Mackay insisted that he would not sign for Derby during a chat they eventually had in the players' lounge. 'I wouldn't come to you for ten thousand quid,' he said. When Clough asked him what he would come for, he replied that he would consider fifteen thousand. This is how, in the autobiography he wrote with John Sadler, Clough recalled what happened next:

'Maybe these were the negotiations in which I learned my trade. Don't let the player have the last say if you can avoid it. Or maybe it was just the old Yorkshire trait of giving away as little as possible, because if a few thousand quid had been the difference between landing Mackay or losing him I wouldn't have resisted for too long. "I can't get fifteen thousand," I said. "Well, if you can't get it you might as well get off and thanks very much," he said, making as if to get up. "But I can get fourteen thousand," I returned, and he said: "Done!", just like that.'

The £14,000 was a signing-on fee, to be spread over a three-year contract on top of Mackay's wages. To say that for Derby it was money well spent would be an outsize understatement. For Mackay it was, as he said later, 'a marvellous sensation' to be part of the Rams' revival, and he was to look back with a warm feeling of pleasure on his years as their captain. He also recalled:

'When I think back, I marvel at the way I made up my mind. Brian Clough told me he had a good side with a lot of young players. I'd never seen them play, so I took his word for it. And he was right.'

To begin with, however, Mackay was to have qualms about climbing aboard the Clough bandwagon similar to those that had at first troubled O'Hare and McFarland – especially after being on the losing side against St Johnstone in a pre-season friendly match in Perth. And Dave Mackay had a fierce aversion to losing. He was as fired up for five-a-side games in training as he was for the serious stuff out in the middle. 'I have always been terrified of losing,' he once said, 'and I think this has rubbed off on other people.'

That sobering defeat back on his home Scottish soil – which was akin to the disturbing eye-opener Clough and Taylor had themselves experienced on having the first sight of their new charges on a close-season tour of Germany – was not the only shock in store for Mackay. Another one was sprung on him when he was told he would no longer be an attacking wing-half. He was required to play as a sweeper – and, despite all his protestations that he was not up to that job, a sweeper he became. A sweeper of such authority that this formidable man who was four months older than his manager gained a new lease of footballing life and, with his unflurried expertise, made better players of those around him. It was under the Mackay influence that Roy McFarland, building on natural ability, blossomed into Britain's best central defender.

The signing of Dave Mackay was the second step taken during the 1968 close season to correct the defensive flaws that had undermined the initial phase under new management. The first one brought a change of goalkeeper, but still left Colin Boulton fretting in the Reserves. Reg Matthews, to whom Peter Taylor had lost his place with Coventry City almost thirteen years before, gave way to Les Green, who had been signed by Taylor for Burton Albion and had been taken by him from there to Hartlepools United.

Matthews, a rugby player at school, took part in the soccer match in which he was spotted by a Coventry scout only because the chosen goalkeeper failed to turn up. Signed during Harry Storer's second spell as Coventry's manager, he showed extremely promising form in his home club's nursery team, who were beaten just once in four years, before being called up for National Service, and it was only a week after his return from Germany, on being demobilised, that he made his debut in the Southern Section of the Third Division in the spring of 1953, at the age of nineteen.

His first game for the reserves three days earlier had been his first for a Coventry team in two seasons.

From entering League football in front of fewer than 10,000 people at Southend United, where Coventry were beaten by an only goal, Matthews progressed in just over three years to playing his first game for England in a 1-1 draw with Scotland before a crowd of 132,817 at Hampden Park. He was the first Coventry player to become a full England international, and the second goalkeeper from the Third Division to play for England. Millwall's Fred Fox was the first, with just one cap in 1925.

Matthews didn't, however, immediately establish himself in Coventry's first team. Peter Taylor was recalled a few matches into the 1953-54 season, and it was not until just over a year later that Matthews displaced him for good. Taylor, who had originally been kept waiting for several years to take over from the long-serving Alf Wood, had to bide his time again at Middlesbrough before succeeding Rolando Ugolini, a naturalised Briton who was born in Italy. Matthews had also moved on by the time Wood kept goal for Coventry for the last time, briefly recalled in an emergency towards the end of 1958 after Jim Sanders, an FA Cup winner with West Bromwich Albion, had broken a leg. Then older, at 43, than he admitted to being, Wood had rejoined Coventry from Northampton as assistant trainer.

Matthews made his England Under-23 debut after only thirty Division Three games, and he also played for England 'B' and the Football League before being capped five times while with Coventry. England were unbeaten in those five matches, yet this natural goalkeeper, courageous and agile, with acute positional sense and lightning reflexes, was never called upon by his country again during his four seasons as a first choice in the First Division after Chelsea, then recent League champions managed by Ted Drake, the former Arsenal and England centre-forward, had made him the costliest goalkeeper in the game, at £20,000, in December 1956.

That was a move he came to regret, saying that he did not think he should have left Coventry ('where my heart lay'), but his League career was revived at Derby for the best part of seven seasons after he had been ousted by Peter Bonetti at Stamford Bridge. As Bonetti — nicknamed 'The Cat' for his athleticism but, like Matthews, soon discarded by England — went on to break the Chelsea appearances record, so Matthews did for a goalkeeper with the Rams. To his 116 first-team games for Coventry and his 148 for Chelsea, he added 246 for Derby (the same number Wood had made for Coventry) before falling victim to the Clough-Taylor purge. It was a splendid return on the £6,300 his old Coventry boss Harry Storer paid to bring him to the Baseball Ground. Before Matthews, the highest number of games played by a goalkeeper for Derby was 240 by Ben Olney, a Londoner raised in Birmingham who had been in George Jobey's Second

Division promotion team during the 1920s. Colin Boulton is the only County keeper to have exceeded the Matthews total.

Derby fans thrilled to the sight of Matthews' daring dives at the feet of rampaging forwards, and to the numerous other spectacular saves he made in playing a crucial part in the preservation of the club's precarious hold on Second Division status. When the dynamic new managerial pairing came in, however, he was in his 34th year and past his best. During that first season after Tim Ward's departure his displays, like those of some of the other defenders, seriously lacked consistency.

Magnificent saves in League Cup victories against Birmingham and Lincoln, penalty saves in successive home games with Cardiff and Queen's Park Rangers, and a string of great saves that helped to gain a point at Millwall were offset by uncertainty in defeat by Crystal Palace at Selhurst Park, costly errors in defeats at Blackburn and Villa Park, and bad positioning that led to a winning visit by Ipswich. The crunch came when he showed a complete loss of confidence in a mid-March match at Huddersfield, where what George Edwards described in his report as 'a very poor Town team' won comfortably at home for the first time since Boxing Day.

Mind you, Matthews was far from alone in being at fault. Brian Clough was so incensed by a generally appalling performance, from which only McFarland emerged with any real credit, that he panned them good and proper:

'I told them that I'd taken responsibility for them right through the season, but not this time. They were absolutely disgraceful, and I went into the dressing room and told them so. I was ashamed of them. They let me down and they let the club down. Some of them have had enough "last chances" to find their form.'

For the next game, at home to Bolton Wanderers, nine positional changes were made, McFarland alone staying put at centre-half, but Matthews was the only player to be dropped. Colin Boulton was brought back in, making several outstanding saves in a 2-1 win, and he would no doubt have stayed in for the rest of the season but for being injured in the draw Derby salvaged at Carlisle with a last-minute goal by Alan Durban after one of Kevin Hector's penalty misses.

So Matthews was restored for the last five matches of the 1967-68 season, none of which Derby won, and his continued fall from grace made it inevitable that he would be on his way. Even at his best he was a victim of nervous tension before the kick-off, the subject of some amusement among team-mates who regularly saw the cigarette smoke rising from the cubicle in the dressing room where he took refuge just before going onto the field, but until those nerves got the better of him towards the end of his Derby days he was an entertaining and high-class performer, remembered with genuine regard.

From Derby he went to Rugby Town as player-manager, but that was not a role suited to his highly-strung nature and he left there after only one season. When he died in October 2001, aged 67, the obituary by Gerald Mortimer, former Sports Editor of the *Derby Evening Telegraph*, summed him up well in these words:

'Matthews was often heroic – and had to be. He was sharp and agile, but the quality that stood out was his courage. He was in the "so brave as to be daft school" of keepers, and if the ball was around his area he meant to have it. It mattered not who was in the way, and defenders found there were sharp edges in Matthews' physique. They suffered along with the forwards. The Baseball Ground crowds loved his agility.'

The choice of successor to Matthews in Derby's goal was a curious one, and not only because Boulton was kept in the background to make room for him. Clough and Taylor had seen fit to let Leslie Green leave Hartlepools United for Rochdale, but it was to him that they turned, securing his transfer from that Lancashire club at a fee of £7,000. There was also the disturbing fact that Green was small for a goalkeeper, at 5ft 9in, but he had long arms, unusually big hands ('as big as shovels' said Clough), and was a good organiser of his goalmouth. His manager at Derby also rated him better than even the peerless Peter Shilton in one respect – punching the ball clear.

Those attributes made Green another inspired signing. For two seasons he was an ever-present, and he altogether made 133 consecutive appearances before it all came to an abrupt end after his lack of height had been shown up in a pulsating 4-4 draw with Manchester United at the snow-covered Baseball Ground on Boxing Day 1970. Boulton then at last had the chance of a sustained run in the first team that he literally took with both hands, and Green never again played in the Football League he had first entered with four games for Hull City between spells at Atherstone Town, his home club, and Nuneaton Borough before first joining Peter Taylor at Burton. Off he went to join Durban City in South Africa, where a broken leg finished his playing career.

After Green and Mackay, the next important newcomer to Derby's ranks, near the end of August in 1968, was the 'Mighty Midget' Willie Carlin, a 5ft 4in bundle of midfield energy and enterprise who was imported from Sheffield United at a cost of £60,000 that made him the Rams' most expensive player until the then record £110,000 for a defender was paid to Nottingham Forest for Welsh international Terry Hennessey some eighteen months later. Clough and Taylor had tried to bring Carlin into their fold a year earlier, but had been forced to back off when Carlisle

United, who transferred him to Sheffield United for £40,000 soon afterwards, reported them to the Football League for an alleged illegal approach.

To Liverpudlian Carlin's intense dismay, it was because he was so small that Liverpool discarded him after he had played just one League game for them, in a Second Division home draw with Brighton in October 1959, shortly before Bill Shankly stormed in to transform the Anfield club's fortunes. For £1,500 he drifted off to Halifax Town, with whom his career was in danger of foundering before he was transferred to Carlisle for £10,000 in time to play a leading part in their Third Division promotion of 1964-65.

With Sheffield United he had the contrasting experience of dropping out of the First Division, though that did give him an early opportunity to remind Clough and Taylor of what they were missing (not that they really needed it) when he guided the Blades to a defeat of Derby County at Bramall Lane. The first of the two goals to which the Rams had no reply was hit home from the penalty spot by Colin Addison, later one of the managers who were unable to arrest the decline into which Derby plunged after peaking under the stewardship of Clough and Mackay. The second scorer was none other than Carlin, who strayed from his creative role to smash a left-foot shot into a top corner of Green's goal after jinking away from two tackles.

Six days later Carlin signed on the dotted line at the Baseball Ground. His arrival was hailed as 'the last piece of the jigsaw' in the construction of the team that soared out of the Second Division. It did indeed herald the start of the zoom to the League heights, but there was still one more key ingredient to be added to the potent mixture before the long-awaited return to the top flight was achieved. We shall be coming to that in the next chapter.

In the meantime, a young forward was released who was to attract a price tag of more than £200,000 and play for England. The then raw nineteen-year-old Phil Boyer was allowed to leave for £3,000 simply because no room could be found for him amid the wealth of talent that was being brought in. Clough told him: 'You're not going to make the first team for a long time, and I've had an offer from York.' So off Nottingham-born Boyer went into the Fourth Division, 'in the hope that I would get a few goals and be noticed.'

And get noticed he did – especially by John Bond. From York he was signed by the former West Ham full-back, who was then managing Bournemouth, for £20,000, then followed him to Norwich for £145,000, was sold by him to Southampton for £125,000 (only because Norwich ran into financial difficulties), and rejoined him at Manchester City for

£225,000. After all that, it was scarcely surprising that Boyer said he had learned everything he knew about football from Bond. He admitted he had played 'off the cuff' before the flamboyant much-travelled manager who signed him three times in almost a dozen years 'taught me technique and encouraged me to express myself as a player'.

Boyer arrived at Maine Road with his quest for goals having brought him just over 150 in a little more than 500 games, and earned him the Golden Shoe for outscoring every other First Division forward with 23 for Southampton in the 1979-80 season, but he was playing only his tenth match for Manchester City when he suffered the injury that was to cut short his career. In a fourth-round FA Cup-tie with one of his former clubs, Norwich City, in January 1981, a tackle ripped the ligaments and muscles at the back of his left knee so badly that the surgeon who carried out the operation gave him no more than a 50-50 chance of playing again. Ironically, the defender who made that fateful tackle was Bond's son Kevin, who later that year joined Manchester City after a spell in American football and was among Boyer's team-mates when the Derby cast-off made a short-lived comeback.

After being loaned out to the Hong Kong club Bulova, Boyer made only a few further appearances for City before being forced into retirement early in 1983 as his clubmates slithered towards relegation from the First Division.

He never considered himself international class – 'just a good club player' – but while with Norwich he was mystified when Don Revie, then England's manager, failed to call upon him again after he had made what he thought was a reasonably sound, if goalless, debut in a victory over Wales at Wrexham.

As will be recalled, one of the forwards who kept him out of the Derby County team, Kevin Hector, was unfairly to be given even shorter shrift by an England manager.

Promotion! and memorable League Cup nights

After their first five games of the 1968-69 season Derby County, David Mackay and all, were still without a win, down in the Second Division depths with only three points. It was just the sort of dismal start to fuel the fires of criticism stoked up by Fred Walters, the anti-Clough director who had been heard complaining loud and long in the Baseball Ground corridors as the club's home reverses had mounted the previous season.

Yet how different it all was as the Rams entered the New Year. By then they were three points clear at the top of the table, having lost only twice more in nineteen matches. And there were only two further League defeats to come, for an economical total of five, as they swept to the title seven points ahead of runners-up Crystal Palace. Of their last fifteen games they won thirteen, the last nine of them in a row.

In those days, when two points, not three as nowadays, were awarded for a win, clubs came out of Division Two by bigger margins, but none with such a final flourish. Not even Middlesbrough when they romped away with the 1973-74 title by a record fifteen points. They had two defeats and a draw in their last nine games. Not even West Ham when they pulled thirteen points clear in 1980-81. They drew three of their last nine. Nor Everton and Tottenham in their respective promotion seasons of 1930-31 (by seven points) and 1949-50 (by nine) which they both directly followed with the First Division championship. Everton lost five times, Spurs four, on the run-in. In 1893-94, unbeaten Liverpool ended eight points in front, but they fulfilled only 28 fixtures and drew two of the final nine.

Derby County altogether won 26 of their Second Division matches in 1968-69, breaking the club's record for a League programme of 42 fixtures. That was two fewer than they gained when runners-up in the Third Division North in 1955-56, and equalled the number obtained as champions of that section the next season, but on both those occasions they played 46 games. Jobey's promotion winners of 1925-26, who were not champions but runners-up, set the previous best total of 25 wins from 42. The 63 points achieved by Clough's men were also the most the club had attained up to that time over 42 games, matching the tally of each of the two Division Three seasons, though more have been gathered since the increase to three points for a win. Discounting the 33 wins of the 1944-45 wartime season, the club record was raised to 84 in 1985-86, when the Rams rose from the Third Division (46 games) in third place, and equalled the following season when they were champions of the Second (42).

Another significant Derby County statistic of 1968-69 was that the number of goals conceded, 32, was the second lowest for one season in the club's history, demonstrating the extent to which the defence, hitherto so suspect, had been tightened. Four fewer were let in during the 1911-12 escape from Division Two.

Those supporters who saw the Rams start the second season under Clough and Taylor by drawing 1-1 at Blackburn had reason to return home satisfied that newcomer Les Green was not too small to be a top-class goalkeeper. His saves included three that were right out of the ordinary, and he even got his finger tips to the ball the only time he was beaten – by a well-struck, but controversial, penalty-kick as early as the second minute after the taker, Dubliner Eamon Rogers, a Republic of Ireland international, had fallen over what appeared to be a fair tackle by Stewart. The equaliser five minutes later was brilliantly headed from a Hinton corner by McFarland.

The Rams' up-and-coming centre-half, watched by England manager Sir Alf Ramsey, was the man of the home match with Blackpool a week later, when another player named Green, the Seasiders' brilliant young Scottish forward Tony, punished an inaccurate clearance by Richardson with a fierce shot that entered his namesake's net off the angle of post and crossbar after O'Hare had opened the scoring. Derby could have gone two goals ahead but for being denied what they felt was a clear case of handball in the penalty area, and they were thwarted of victory when Hector had a shot kicked off the goal-line in the last minute.

After those two draws came two defeats. Between the setback at Sheffield which Willie Carlin masterminded for the Blades and Carlin's debut for Derby the following midweek, a Saturday visit to Huddersfield brought a repeat of the adverse 0-2 Bramall Lane scoreline as Jimmy Nicholson, a former Busby Babe, showed the midfield mastery the Rams were still seeking. There was little wrong with Derby's defence, which already had Webster and Robson settled at full-back in front of Green, with Mackay sweeping up and McFarland dominant in the middle, but the attack lacked support and sharpness. Both Huddersfield goals resulted from Green's inability to cling onto crosses, though each time he had the excuse of being impeded.

Derby's new goalkeeper next had an off-putting start to the Wednesday evening home game against Hull City in which Carlin first played for the County, having his name taken before the kick-off for contravening a new ruling by marking the pitch with the heel of his boot to help him get his bearings. With wee Willie augmenting the midfield, brought in at right-half to the exclusion of Stewart, home hopes of a first League victory at the fifth attempt were high, but a third draw was the best Derby could manage. Hector timed his leap perfectly to head them into a 34th-minute lead, yet

Hull hit back so smartly that the visitors would have been ahead at the interval but for Barker's swift reply to their second goal late in the first half.

That was the end of the scoring, Derby eliminating the defensive errors that had enabled Hull to score twice in four minutes, and Carlin, though troubled by a heavy cold, gave an encouraging indication of the good things to come by warming up from a quiet start to enjoy a splendid second half. Three days later, the tonic the doctor gave this busy little grafter was also just the booster Derby needed. Galvanised by Carlin, they at last gained their first League win of the season, sending Oxford home thankful not to be beaten by more than 2-0. Both goals, scored by O'Hare and McFarland, were set up by Carlin, who was moved into the inside-right position he was to occupy for the rest of his Derby days, with Durban recalled at right-half. The first-choice line-up that was to romp away to the title was almost complete, just a couple of adjustments remaining.

One of those alterations took Hinton back to the left wing from his one-match switch to the right. The other was the final key ingredient in the Second Division promotion team referred to in the previous chapter – the introduction of a youngster whose £7,500 signing from Hartlepools attracted little attention compared with the other deals with which Clough and Taylor brought the Rams back into the national limelight. This was John McGovern, a deceptively frail-looking midfielder who went on to captain two European Cup-winning teams in successive seasons on following Clough, along with John O'Hare, to glory with Nottingham Forest after all three had made an ill-fated move to Leeds.

McGovern first met Clough while a sixteen-year-old pupil at a rugby-playing grammar school who indulged on Sundays in the soccer he preferred. As he recalled it, he said 'Hello', and Clough replied: 'Get your bloody hair cut.' No wonder the boy admitted he was 'scared to death', but he agreed to be taken on by Hartlepools' new manager even though both his widowed mother and his headmaster were keen for him to stay on at school – Mrs McGovern because she wanted him to have a good education and then fulfil his declared ambition to be a sports master, the headmaster so that he could study for his 'A' levels and go on to university. Clough had to do a lot of his persuasive talking to change their minds and complete what he looked back upon as 'one of the most significant signings of that era'. McGovern's grandmother, who thought what 'a nice kind man' Mr Clough was on meeting him during his frequent visits to the family's home, also had quite a bit to do with it.

Still only sixteen when drafted into Hartlepools' League side, McGovern was able to continue his studies when Clough compromised by allowing him to attend a college of further education two mornings and two evenings a week. They developed something of a father-son relationship (McGovern's father, a former paratrooper, had been killed in a road accident), but even some ten years later, after they had been together at four clubs, McGovern was to say that 'I am nobody special to him', adding:

'I am no closer to him now than when I first met him, and that is the way it should be. It is a good relationship. He is a man who has very few rules and everybody had to stick by them. On any matter his word is final, so you know exactly where you stand. All he asks is that a man plays to his strengths and works on his weaknesses. Watching him on telly some people may think he's putting it on a bit, but he isn't. As long as I've known him he's said what he thinks. The fact that I've been with him over the years won't make any difference in his handling of players. There are no favourites, and certainly no favours for old times' sake.'

Clough also had to contend with some opposition when he took McGovern to Derby. A director complained that the newcomer was splather-footed (a northern expression) and a waste of money. How wrong he was proved to be! Though slimly-built and with what Clough conceded was 'a funny waddle', McGovern gave full value to each of his clubs – with the cruel exception of Leeds, where he was pilloried so mercilessly that his manager felt 'desperately sorry' for him – and collected a host of honours unrivalled by many of the biggest names in the whole history of the game. He also had the distinction of being the youngest of the players (Willie Carlin was among the others) to appear in all four divisions of the Football League, as it was then constituted. Earlier, from the time when the Third Division was divided into North and South sections, another who was with Derby, the Ilkeston miner Ray Straw, became the first to play in all six divisions after the change to one Third and the addition of a Fourth.

The subdued manner of McGovern's arrival at the Baseball Ground in mid-September was accentuated by the fact that it was not until early November that he made the first of his 190 appearances in Derby's League side. By then, things were really buzzing in the County camp. The Rams were a dozen games into a Second Division sequence of 22 in which their only defeat was inflicted, and by an only goal at that, in the return meeting with Hull, and they had pulled off a couple of giant-killing acts in another League Cup run that had come to a most unfortunate end just a few days earlier.

That run began comparatively uneventfully in pouring rain on a Wednesday evening in August with a 3-0 home victory over a Fourth Division side, their Derbyshire neighbours from Chesterfield, gained with the team that had opened the season at Blackburn the previous Saturday (Green; Richardson, Robson; Stewart, McFarland, Mackay; Walker, Barker, O'Hare, Hector, Hinton, to list it in the 1-2-3-5 formation of the time). Durban was again an unrequired substitute. Hector and Hinton scored either side of an own-goal debited to the Saltergate club's goalkeeper, Alan Humphreys, who lost balance as the ball, passed low inside by Barker instead of coming over as an orthodox centre, cannoned off him into the net.

In the next round, Third Division Stockport County were outclassed at the Baseball Ground on the Wednesday following the defeat of Oxford that got the Rams going in the League. For the first time since they had scraped through against Darlington in the previous season's competition, Derby scored five goals, but on this occasion they conceded not four, but just the one – and that was not let in until three minutes from the final whistle. Alan Hinton hit home a couple of first-half penalties and whipped in two more goals as Stockport wilted in face of persistent attacks. Kevin Hector, back in form after a lean spell, was Derby's final scorer.

That took the Rams to the first of the ties in which they made the country fully aware of their rising power by overcoming strong First Division opposition. With the exception of Hector keeping the No 10 shirt and Jim Walker still wearing the one at No 7, which McGovern was soon to inherit, the team had otherwise been completely rebuilt by that stage. Apart from Hector, only Webster and Durban remained from the Derby side Clough had first fielded in a competitive game, and they had been moved to new positions – Webster from right-half to right-back, Durban from inside-forward to right-half.

Drawn away to Chelsea, who had ended sixth in the League's top section that year and were to finish fifth in the next, the new Derby County forced a well-deserved replay by more than just holding their own in a scoreless draw. And that brought them to one of the truly memorable Baseball Ground nights, one that many of those who had the good fortune to be there still rate as the most memorable of them all – and that is including the other epic wins that were to come against the might of Benfica and Real Madrid in European competitions.

A delighted Brian Clough hailed it as 'easily the best performance since I came to Derby'. Len Shipman, president of the Football League, said it was 'a wonderful match', adding: 'It reminded me of the Derby of 20 years ago.' In the *Derby Evening Telegraph*, George Edwards wrote:

'And not just the younger Rams fans are getting excited now. Men who have been watching Derby County for 30 years and more were hailing this display as one of the best they could remember.'

Wednesday, 2 October 1968 was the date; Derby 3, Chelsea 1 the score. Even when the Rams were a goal down from the 26th minute to the 77th they were in full cry, with the old stadium reverberating to the thunderous urging-on from the crowd of almost 35,000. What an intimidating place it could be for visiting teams in such a deafening atmosphere – something that Dave Mackay said had particularly impressed him ('playing in front of crowds like that, I never noticed that I'd dropped down a division when I left Spurs.') It certainly was intimidating for Chelsea, who, as the game built up to its tremendous climax, finally crumbled under the sustained assault that conjured up three goals in the last thirteen minutes.

The goal that gave the London club the lead was a breakaway one, but brilliantly taken by the tall, blond Alan Birchenall, a former Nottingham Boys forward for whom Chelsea had paid Sheffield United £100,000, a sum they were to recoup when he left them for Crystal Palace. Receiving a pass by Peter Houseman, who nearly a decade later met his death in a car crash that also killed his wife, Birchenall gave Green no chance with a blistering shot into the corner of the net from some thirty yards. Who better to score the dramatic equaliser than Dave Mackay? Carlin, a constant tormentor, suddenly back-heeled the ball as he tore through the middle, and the skipper, following up, emulated Birchenall by hammering in a shot from a similar distance. Bonetti was completely deceived as the ball dipped late in its flight.

Chelsea's goalkeeper, but for whose excellence Derby would already have scored several times, was beaten again six minutes later, when Durban headed the Rams in front from a cross by Walker, who only moments before had made a last-ditch saving tackle as Ian Hutchinson, a Derbyshire-born former Burton Albion player, had been shaping to shoot from an unmarked position only a few yards out. Then, with three minutes to go, Robson, again a big success, put over the centre from which Hector completed the scoring.

One of the Chelsea players was to join Derby, and another one almost did. David Webb, a promotion winner with Southampton in 1966 and scorer of Chelsea's winning goal in the 1970 FA Cup final, was a popular, if short-term, signing during the turbulent management of Tommy Docherty that accelerated Derby's decline after the heady days under the control of Clough and Mackay. Peter Osgood decided against teaming up with the Rams after Chelsea had accepted an offer for him while Mackay was manager, and he moved to Southampton instead.

The draw for the fourth round of the 1968-69 League Cup gave Derby an even more formidable task than Chelsea had presented in taking on Everton at Goodison Park. The Merseysiders were going strongly for the First Division title, having been unbeaten in fourteen matches, and although they were pushed into a final third place that season behind Leeds and Liverpool, they had assembled, under the direction of their former centre-forward Harry Catterick, a classy side whose installation as champions was delayed for only another year. It included Gordon West, Catterick's first signing for the club, whose transfer from Blackpool had cost a record

£27,000 for a goalkeeper, the much-envied half-back line of Howard Kendall, Brian Labone and Colin Harvey, Alan Ball, who helped England to win the World Cup in 1966, and Joe Royle, a centre-forward whose progress had been rapid since making his First Division debut, also in 1966, as Everton's youngest newcomer at sixteen.

In that distinguished company Derby County produced another superb performance which, again with a goalless draw, provided a further foretaste of the Division One opposition that promotion was so soon to bring to the Baseball Ground on a regular basis. Everton gave them a torrid time in the first twenty minutes, during which Green made two great saves, the magnificent Mackay blocked a fierce drive with that mighty chest of his, and Carlin, the best midfielder on view, cleared another shot off the line, but after that the longer the game went on the better they became.

Every man in the Derby team was right on top of his form. Up front, Hector was in his element – especially after the interval, when he ran rings round Roger Kenyon, a second-half substitute for the injured Jimmy Husband. Derby fans, estimated to number nearly 10,000 in the near-45,000 crowd, roared unsuccessfully for what appeared to be a clear-cut penalty for a foul on Hector by Kenyon, and Everton ended relieved to have a second chance after West had needed to be at his best to keep out powerful efforts from O'Hare and Hector.

The replay was not the Derby-dominated bonanza of the Chelsea clash, and the Rams had to endure a tense finish as Everton battled away in search of an equaliser, but the win gained with a splendidly-taken goal on the half-hour was well deserved. Hector, who at this stage of the season was at his peak, had his back to goal when the ball, centred by Walker under pressure, reached him, but he smartly brought it under control, turned swiftly, and struck a powerful shot that glanced off Labone on its way into the net.

The end came with Carlin, this time the man not only of the midfield but also of the match, engaged in one of his time-wasting jaunts out towards a corner flag. Harvey brought him down in a desperate attempt to wrest possession, and from the free-kick Carlin was still dribbling with the ball in that corner of the field when the whistle went to the accompaniment of a last rousing roar from home fans in another crowd of more than 34,000. The only disappointment from a Derby viewpoint was that some of those so-called supporters had seen fit to jeer John O'Hare, who came off battered and bruised from his duels with the uncompromising Labone. Theirs was certainly not a verdict shared by officials of other clubs who were onlookers that night. They were full of praise for the plucky centre-forward who had once more played a valuable, if not blatantly obvious, role in another victory there was special reason to relish.

To get through to the semi-finals, Derby were faced with overcoming what appeared to be a less taxing obstacle after Swindon Town, of the Third Division, had won the right to meet them by seeing off First Division Coventry City with a convincing 3-0 win in their fourth-round replay – particularly as this time the Rams were drawn at home. On closer examination, however, it was not as straightforward as that. And when the midweek Baseball Ground confrontation resulted in the Rams' third score-less draw of the competition the odds swung, albeit narrowly, in favour of these 'minnows' from Wiltshire.

This was because Swindon, going smoothly for the promotion they were to gain with Watford, were undefeated at their County Ground for more than twenty matches – a home record then third only in Britain that season behind those of Chelsea and St Mirren. Moreover, they held an ace in Don Rogers, a tricky free scorer who was one of the finest wingers in the country.

Goalless though the first meeting was, it was far from bereft of thrills. Both sides had hair-raising escapes in front of Derby's biggest home crowd of the season, boosted to just over 35,000 by about 7,500 Swindon followers. The Rams, who were without Hinton due to a knee injury that had caused his early exit from the previous Saturday's narrow home win over Birmingham City, went closest to breaking the deadlock when substitute Owen Dawson headed out from off the line following the second of two corners during a hectic goalmouth scramble. But the best chance of the game was missed, ironically, by Rogers, who temporarily tarnished his goal-getting reputation by lifting the ball over the bar from an excellent position after cutting through the middle and tempting Green into advancing to meet him.

The balance tilted still more in favour of Swindon for the replay when Derby were deprived of not only Hinton but also O'Hare, who was confined to bed with a feverish cold. Critics of the centre-forward were confounded as the attack misfired without him. His deputy Barry Butlin, called upon four days before his nineteenth birthday, could not be faulted for lack of effort, but, with only three first-team games behind him, one of them as a substitute, he had a dearth of experience and was out of his depth.

Butlin, who came from Rosliston, a village in South Derbyshire not far from Burton-upon-Trent, benefited soon afterwards from an extended loan spell with Notts County, but he made only nine senior appearances for Derby before, in November 1972, Luton Town considered him worth £50,000 of their money. That was the biggest fee the Rams had received for a player up to that time, and he lived up to it by heading the Hatters' scoring list, with seventeen goals, when they regained First Division status in 1974. Down they went again straightaway, but without Butlin. After scoring three of Luton's first four goals back among the elite, he cost Nottingham Forest £120,000, then the most money they had paid for a player, and 88 games and twenty goals later, interspersed with loans to Brighton and Reading, he wound up his League career with the Uniteds of Peterborough and Sheffield. He later became secretary of the Derby County Former Players' Association.

As I was then working in Bristol, I motored over to Swindon for the Town's fifth-round replay with Derby, and was therefore among the mortified County fans who saw them lose their opportunity to reach the League Cup's last four for the second successive season. I have to admit that I made the journey hoping for the best but fearing the worst – and the worst, from a Derby point of view, happened in the 28th minute.

It was then that Swindon scored the only goal of the game, and what a flukey one it was. There appeared to be no threat to Green's goal when Rogers hoisted the ball back into the penalty area after the goalkeeper had punched it out, but it struck Robson on the shoulder, looped slowly into the air, and dropped just beneath the crossbar as McFarland failed in a desperate attempt to hook it clear.

Until then the Rams had been showing signs of settling down despite the absence of O'Hare's craft in the centre of their forward line and the pinpoint accuracy of Hinton's centres. Afterwards, they were thrown out of their stride for a while, and when their more controlled football enabled them again to step up the tempo of their attacks that man Dawson, who this time was on the field from the start, repeated his off-the-line rescue act at the expense of Hector. The only other close approach to another goal was made a dozen minutes from time by Rogers, from whose free-kick, swerved round the defensive wall, the ball was deflected onto a post by the fully stretched Green and rebounded into the goalkeeper's arms.

So Swindon progressed to a semi-final that they extended from the stipulated two legs to three by beating Burnley 2-1 at Turf Moor but losing to them at home by the same score. Helped by an own-goal, they won the decider 3-2 at West Bromwich Albion's ground, then caused one of Wembley's biggest upsets with a 3-1 win after extra-time against Arsenal, who the year before had been runners-up to Leeds for the trophy that the Town's captain, Stan Harland, received from Princess Margaret. Rogers scored twice in the extra period, but the man who made it all possible with a string of amazing saves was Peter Downsborough, who at school had played fly-half at rugby and centre-forward at soccer before turning to goalkeeping in an emergency.

The only changes Swindon made for the final compared with the side that defeated Derby were at full-back. John Trollope, whose son Paul later played for the Rams during Jim Smith's time as the club's manager, returned to partner Rod Thomas, destined to be a Mackay signing for the County, who switched from the left flank to the right. John Trollope holds Swindon's record for League appearances with 770; Welshman Thomas remains their most-capped player with thirty out of his total of fifty.

From their reverse at Swindon, Derby County kept firmly on course for promotion in the League with a narrow, but worthy, home victory over Charlton Athletic in which John McGovern made a quiet first-team debut and John O'Hare a triumphant return. It left them second in the table, a point behind pace-setting Crystal Palace with a game in hand, yet the moaners still made their presence felt as the standard of play, already harmed by the visitors' over-emphasis on physical strength in defence, fell away after Hector's neat right-foot shot had gained a winning 2-1 lead in the 65th minute.

George Edwards said he sometimes thought those critics hoped the opposition would score, so that they could have the opportunity to jeer. He also observed that it was no wonder a few members of the Rams' team preferred to play away from home. What a sad commentary on the attitude of some alleged fans towards a team clearly on the up. Peter Taylor had already put the position in its true perspective, since the arrival of Carlin, by urging people to 'put your money on us because we are going up'.

Against Charlton, the stoic O'Hare for a change did not have to bear the brunt of the barbs aimed by impatient frequenters of the Baseball Ground. Indeed, he gave them not the slightest encouragement to barrack him in showing the form without which both points might well have gone south. Uncomplainingly taking most of the hard knocks, he held and shielded the ball in his best manner, headed the goal that gave Derby a briefly-held lead in the first half, then created the opening for their second, scored by Hector, by sending Charlton's defenders the wrong way with a deft header direct from a long clearance by Green, the Rams' other outstanding player.

Three weeks later, after dropping one point at Cardiff and another in a 3-3 home draw with Carlisle on a day when the notorious Baseball Ground pitch was covered in mud and standing water in a downpour, Derby took over at the top of the table by deposing Crystal Palace at an almost as muddy Selhurst Park. To concede three goals to Carlisle (after leading 2-0 early on) was untypical, even allowing for the difficult conditions, of a defence which stayed intact in two dozen games that season. But that defence was back to its best in restricting London's high-flyers to one goal in reply to the two the County snatched in as many minutes around the hour. Carlin and McFarland were the scorers for the new leaders, the centre-half giving his usual polished performance despite feeling a bit under the weather.

Not until the return game with Charlton in mid-January did Derby lose in the League for the first time since the setback at Hull in October, though they went perilously close to it at home to Norwich the week after their Palace visit. They were one down from midway through the first half, and the match was well into injury-time when McFarland was on the mark once more to grab a point, throwing himself at the ball to head in a curling cross from Mackay.

After the next game, at Preston, was also drawn, only two points covered the top seven teams, and the Rams again had to dig deep to win a fast and bruising encounter with Middlesbrough on Boxing Day, when the first of six League crowds in excess of 30,000 at the Baseball Ground that season saw John Hickton knock them out of their stride with two goals in quick succession after going off to change his boots. The first of those goals, wiping out a lead gained with another of the nine that made McFarland Derby's third highest scorer of the campaign behind Hector and O'Hare, came from a penalty awarded against Mackay for handling a bad bounce in the fortieth minute, and it was from another spot-kick, conceded when a Boro defender handled in trying to cope with the County captain, that Hinton made it 2-2 with twenty minutes to go. Five minutes later, Hinton scored again, heading the ball just inside a post for the winner that McFarland had to make a goal-line clearance to preserve.

Defeat at Burnley at the first FA Cup hurdle left Derby free to concentrate on promotion, and after they had missed their chances in the failure at Charlton their only other reverse on their path to it was the ending by Palace in March, by a lone breakaway goal and in the absence of the injured Carlin, of their unbeaten run of 22 home League and Cup matches.

The Cup exit to a First Division side at Turf Moor was a most undeserved outcome for a team deprived by injury of Mackay (it was only the second of Derby's 51 matches he missed that season) and reduced to ten men by the debatable sending-off near the interval of Robson, the player who moved forward to deputise most capably for him. Robson claimed he was trying to kick the ball, not the player, as Ralph Coates, a coming England international, strove to keep possession as he lay on the ground, but referee Kevin Howley ruled otherwise.

Acrobatic goalkeeping by Harry Thomson, though he knew nothing about two Hinton thunderbolts that hit him, limited the Rams to a late reply by Durban to Burnley's three goals. Brian Clough applauded his players off the pitch and said afterwards: 'It's a new experience for us to play well and lose. We murdered them at football and lost 3-1.' Bob Lord, Burnley's outspoken chairman, admitted his side 'had all the breaks', adding: 'I can't think of many sides that could have bothered us with ten men like Derby did.'

For John McGovern, as he saw it himself, this Cup-tie was the match in which it all began to come right for him. After a couple of muted Second Division games as an orthodox outside-right, he had found playing in midfield for the Reserves much more to his liking, and he was such a success when recalled in that role at Burnley that from then on it was only rarely that he was not a first choice until he followed Clough to Leeds in the autumn of 1974.

It was around the time of the Turf Moor tie that another young player, Jeff Bourne, was added to the reserve forward strength. Signed from Linton United, a club near Swadlincote in South Derbyshire, he had to wait until Dave Mackay became manager to have an extended run in the first team, but in the meantime his goals made a major contribution to the Central League championship win of 1971-72.

Soon after Bourne's arrival, a signing of more immediate impact was made to provide some experienced forward cover for the run-in towards the Division Two title. For an outlay of around £20,000, the powerfully-built 29-year-old Frank Wignall was brought in from Wolverhampton Wanderers, and, although unable to establish himself at Derby (almost a third of his 59 appearances were as a substitute), he did just what was asked of him before leaving for Mansfield Town, the last of his five League clubs, nearly three years later. After Mansfield, he played for King's Lynn and Burton Albion, was national coach in Qatar for five years, then managed Shepshed Charterhouse.

He led Shepshed, a Leicestershire club, to eleven trophies during the 1981-82 season, including league and cup doubles for both the first team (Midland League) and Reserves (Derbyshire Premier League), and in the following one he guided them to the first round proper of the FA Cup for the first time in their history and to the quarter-finals of the FA Vase. In the spring of 1983, however, he reluctantly resigned because he wanted to devote more time to his businesses in Nottingham and Lancashire.

Wignall's best playing days were with Nottingham Forest, who signed him from Everton. While with them, he played twice for England, scoring both goals in a 2-1 win on his debut against Wales at Wembley in 1965, and after recovering from a broken leg he was in the Forest team that in 1966-67 finished runners-up to Manchester United in the First Division and reached the last four of the FA Cup.

It was as a substitute, because of injuries to first Carlin and then McGovern, that Wignall scored two of the four goals with which he helped Derby to clinch promotion. He opened his account for the club by rounding off a 4-2 home win over Blackburn, whose right-half, George Sharples, suffered a double fracture of the right leg in falling awkwardly, then five weeks later, on the second day of April, scored the crucial only goal at relegation-bound Fulham. That was the Rams' fourth successive clean sheet, and in six games, five of them away, they had dropped only one point, at Carlisle, since the home defeat by Crystal Palace.

On the following Saturday, the return to the First Division, sixteen years after they had left it, was assured by a resounding 5-1 beating of Bolton at the Baseball Ground in which Wignall was again a scorer. The champagne flowed after Roy McFarland, yet again dominant in defence, had fittingly applied the finishing touch on his 21st birthday, after other goals from O'Hare, Hector and Carlin, with a fierce right-foot drive just inside a post. Peter Taylor missed the celebrations because he was away watching a player, and within half-an-hour of the end of the game Brian Clough, who was said to have lost a stone and a half in weight since the season began, was back at work meeting the parents of two teenage trialists.

That was also the day on which Sheffield Wednesday, for whom relegation from the First Division was only a season away, were considering approaching Clough with a view to his taking over as their manager from Jack Marshall, a former Burnley full-back who had guested for Derby County during the War. But within 24 hours of the Rams' promotion being assured any remote chance of such a move had evaporated with the decision at a Baseball Ground board meeting to award their bright young manager a 'handsome bonus'. At the same time, Peter Taylor was granted an overdue contract and the go-ahead was given for the construction of a new grandstand.

Sydney Bradley, who had taken over as chairman from Sam Longson under a new arrangement whereby the holder of that office changed every two years, said that Clough had 'built an ocean-going liner out of a shipwreck'. He added:

'Brian Clough is the sort of man to succeed in any business. He deserves his bonus, and I've also told him that if he needs money for team building we'll do all we can to find it. I would be glad to have his drive in my own business, and I know what this season has taken out of him mentally and physically. I like the man – he's had to fight his way up.'

After seeing off Bolton on the back of a geeing-up during the interval by the manager, who accused them of letting him down in the first half, Derby had to battle to beat their next visitors, Sheffield United, in front of 34,976, their biggest home League gate of the season. It was not until five minutes from the end that Durban scored the only goal from an opening created by McFarland as the centre-half again found the chance to advance into the attack.

The next game, at Millwall, was the one in which the Rams made sure of the title. They won it by the same slender margin, Carlin scoring in the 22nd minute with a header also set up by McFarland, but in a far more convincing manner. In the first half, particularly, Green had so little to do that he spent much of his time peering through the clouds of dust swirling in the strong wind as his team-mates, clad in Millwall's second strip of red shirts and black shorts – borrowed because an all-white outfit they had intended to wear was being used by the home side – concentrated play at the other end. Though easing off after going ahead, Derby were never in real danger of losing the initiative, not even when Millwall moved the lofty Barry Kitchener into their forward line and resorted to long punts upfield with the wind behind them after the interval.

Four days later, on 16 April 1969, an emphatic 4-1 win at Norwich established a Derby record of eight victories in a row, five of them away. Since the defeat at Hull on 9 October they had lost only one of fourteen League matches on their travels, drawing three and winning ten. In the same period they had won eleven home games, drawn two and lost just the one. It was championship form with a vengeance. Carlin again literally used his head to score two of the goals against Norwich – not bad going for a little 'un – and he went close to his first hat-trick. O'Hare and Wignall, who also hit the bar after an eight-man move, were the other scorers before Ken Foggo's late reply from a penalty, awarded when Webster handled as he was flattened, was Norwich's first direct attempt at goal.

So the scene was perfectly set for a fitting farewell to the Second Division. To Bristol City fell the unenviable role of being the whipping boys as Derby steamrollered them at the Baseball Ground with a first-half hat-trick by Durban, one of the most explosive of Hinton's bombshells, and a powerful late header by Hector. Even then, five goals without reply were something of a let-off. McFarland hit the bar with a header and a left-foot volley, then had a strong right-foot shot deflected wide. And Hinton registered one of his rare penalty misses, his spot-kick bouncing to safety off goalkeeper Barry Watling.

To cap this triumphant season, the Football Writers' Association voted 34-year-old Dave Mackay joint Footballer of the Year with 32-year-old Tony Book, captain of First Division Manchester City's FA Cup winners. It is still the only time two players have dead-heated for the award. Admitting that this honour came as 'a real shock', Derby's skipper said:

'I'd long since stopped dreaming of titles like that, even before I bowed out at Tottenham. I thought I might have had a chance during the Spurs' glory years when we were winning everything in sight, but the nearest I got was in 1963 when Stanley Matthews beat me by just one vote. I've had many thrills in my career, but this is as great as any of them. I've played more matches this season than in any of my years with Spurs.'

Spurred to Success, but barred from Europe

It did not take Derby County long to make the rest of the First Division sit up and take notice when they re-entered it for the 1969-70 season. Cynics who had suggested they would find the going hard with their small squad were silenced as they soared to the top of the table and crowned their startling start by thrashing Dave Mackay's old club Tottenham 5-0 in front of the Baseball Ground's record crowd of 41,826.

At that stage, with eighteen points from eleven games, the Rams were the only unbeaten team in the division and had conceded a mere four goals. Of course, it could not last, and it did not. But although they lost eleven of their next nineteen League matches, they then perked up again to go undefeated through the last dozen and finish in a respectable fourth place that would have qualified them for Europe if accountants making a routine check had not found discrepancies in the club's finances.

The raising of the record home attendance from the 38,063 who had watched an FA Cup-tie with Northampton Town almost twenty years before was made possible by the increased accommodation provided by the erection of a £150,000 cantilever stand along the popular side of the ground where there had been standing room only. Before the new stand was built, a small section of the terracing alongside the pitch opposite the main stand, which housed the office and dressing rooms, was divided off by railings and incurred a slightly bigger charge of admission than the rest. The cheaper part remained known as the popular side to fans who dubbed the costlier section the unpopular side.

The new Ley Stand (later Co-op and later still Toyota) was given its name in appreciation of the Ley's Malleable Castings firm whose factory bordered that part of the Baseball Ground, and from whose chimneys drifted the acrid fumes which gave such a distinctive flavour to the famous atmosphere. Ley's made additional land available for its construction, agreeing to have the boundary moved back all of eighteen inches – but only after Brian Clough and gone round to talk the managing director into it with the promise of a few season tickets to go with the Ley name on the new stand.

Theoretically, the capacity was boosted to 42,000, though, from my own experience, a good many had a far from clear view of the action once the size of the crowd rose to around the 35,000 mark. I well remember when I took my fourteen-year-old son Chris to see the first match of the 1971-72 season that ended with the Rams League champions for the first time.

We arrived early to make sure of a good vantage point for him on the terracing in front of the Normanton Stand at one end of the ground, but had to withdraw to give him more air when he complained at half-time of feeling unwell in the crush. After he had recovered it was impossible to get back to where we had been, so, as he became more and more frustrated at hearing all the cheers and groans without being able to see what was happening – and I, though over six feet tall, could view precious little of it – we cut our losses and left. To make up for his disappointment, we called in at the club's souvenir shop, which was then near the town centre in Osmaston Road, and besides buying some memento we were gratified to learn there that Derby, two down to Manchester United when we departed, had hit back to salvage a point.

The contractors had their work cut out to have the new stand in use for the return of First Division football to the Baseball Ground on 9 August 1969, and they only just managed it. The goalless game with Burnley that resulted would have been quite a let-down for County fans but for Les Green making them grateful for the point by saving an 81st-minute penalty taken by Frank Casper after McFarland had clearly handled. Green dived correctly to his left and the ball flew off his body to safety. 'I've seen Casper take penalties on television,' said the Rams goalkeeper, 'so I knew which way to go.'

That opening month of the season ended with a win at West Bromwich which left the Rams with the best defensive record in the First Division and brought Brian Clough one of his many Manager of the Month awards. A spokesman for Bell's, the sponsors, stated:

'His Derby County team is probably the first side since Ipswich under Alf Ramsey to make such an immediate impact on the First Division. Mr Clough has succeeded in restoring genuine enthusiasm to one of the great traditional strongholds of football – and in re-establishing the soccer prestige of Derby County and the Midlands.'

I travelled up from Bristol with my son to see that match. We were sitting in the stand right behind the flight of the ball as Dave Mackay deceived the Albion defenders, and both of us too, by blasting the ball just under the bar from a free-kick the hovering Hinton was expected to take. It was a lead Derby never looked like losing, and one Hector increased in the last few minutes. A week later, I missed the treat of watching Everton's champions-to-be outplayed, fortunate to lose by only the odd goal of three. Instead, I opted that day to go to Lord's, hoping to see Derbyshire defeat Yorkshire in the Gillette Cup final. It was a forlorn hope, but the news from the Baseball Ground did much to make up for that.

Another week on, Liverpool lost their unbeaten record at Old Trafford and Derby displaced them from the top of the table by becoming the first visitors to win at Newcastle for almost a year despite having Hinton little more than a passenger with a thigh injury, Green needing Mackay to take goal-kicks because of tendon trouble in his right foot, and McFarland bothered by a groin strain. Handicapped though the centre-half was, however, he was still able to nip in for the diving header with which he scored the only goal – and to run about sixty yards to deliver the left-foot shot that very nearly produced another, the ball flashing out of play off an upright.

Derby followed that defeat of the holders of the Fairs Cup (forerunner of the UEFA Cup) with the demolition of Tottenham which had Bill Nicholson hailing them as 'a very, very wonderful team'. The Spurs manager added this accolade:

'They humiliated us. They are very talented and they don't just run, they know where to run and when. Their midfield players were great. Carlin was brilliant, and that lad McGovern was tackling somebody in his own penalty area one moment, then having a shot at the other end. The centre-forward? You can watch Spurs play for the next five years and you won't see Mike England be made to struggle like that again. Dave Mackay? If I wanted all this to happen for anybody it would be him. Six Dave Mackays and you wouldn't need anybody else. He's an inspiration to everybody and a credit to the game. One of the all-time greats.'

The delighted Mackay said it was 'the best we have played since I came here'. He was happy for both himself and the team – 'not because it was Spurs we beat, but because you can't be anything but happy when you are in a team which plays like that.' Brian Clough said he thought that 'even the real idiots who don't understand football twigged John O'Hare this afternoon'. He described Mike England, a seasoned Welsh international, as 'a centre-half stumbling about like a blind man'.

Spurs came with the best away record in the First Division, having won on successive visits to Burnley, Crystal Palace, West Ham and Arsenal since losing at Leeds on the first day of the season. And they might well have got back into the game to extend it if Les Green had not made a truly remarkable save from their ace marksman, Jimmy Greaves. A goal seemed certain when the England forward volleyed viciously from only fifteen yards, but Derby's goalkeeper leaped to his left and caught the ball in both hands. It would still have been an exceptional save if he had just managed to tip it away to safety. Greaves acknowledged it as 'a brilliant effort'. Mackay's adjective was 'fabulous'.

So Spurs were as good as finished off by the three-goal onslaught that hit them in the eight minutes from the fifteenth to the 23rd. Durban began it by pouncing on a misplaced pass by the bemused England, Hector hammered in a spectacular shot from O'Hare's through pass, and little Carlin outsmarted six-footers England and Peter Collins to head home a Hinton corner kick. Other well-taken goals by O'Hare, after some nifty footwork by Carlin, and Durban, from Hector's centre, completed the rout in the second half, and there was no hint of even a consolation response by the ten men to whom Tottenham were reduced, after having already used their substitute, when John Pratt limped off twenty minutes from time.

The Rams' undefeated start to the season stretched to thirteen games with the inclusion of League Cup victories at Hartlepool (their second meeting in this competition in three seasons) and at home to Hull before it came to an unexpected end against relegation-bound Sheffield Wednesday. Hartlepool were back to the bad times away from which Clough and Taylor had pointed them, heading for the first of two consecutive applications for re-election to the League after having speedily returned to the Fourth Division, but Derby needed a late penalty to make sure of again beating them – on a pitch that was in an even worse condition than the much-maligned one at the Baseball Ground could ever be. Second Division Hull, though handicapped by an early injury to the free-scoring Ken Wagstaff, who had been a Raich Carter discovery for Mansfield, also proved testing opponents, ahead until the last twenty minutes and with hopes of a replay until the final four, during which they conceded two more goals.

Defeat at Hillsborough three days after being given that scare by the Humbersiders was all the harder to bear because Derby had more of the play than they had enjoyed against Tottenham, yet failed to break down a packed defence which conceded a succession of free-kicks. Danny Williams, the Owls' manager who had piloted Swindon to promotion and their League Cup final success against Arsenal, admitted he was 'a very lucky man'. The winning goal, prodded in by big Alan Warboys seven minutes before half-time, resulted from a mix-up between Webster and McFarland, who limped almost throughout with his continued groin problem. Just over four years later Warboys was to help deal Brian Clough and Peter Taylor the most devastating blow of their managerial careers. More about that in its proper turn.

The brightest spot for Derby during the mid-season dip in form which set in after their first setback was a crushing of Liverpool that could have been as big as that against Spurs if 'iron man' Tommy Smith had not been overlooked on the goal-line when the whistle went for offside as O'Hare back-heeled the ball into the net. Hector was at his best with two of the four goals that did count against a square defence that misguidedly persisted in trying to operate an offside trap. Unfortunately for the Rams, however, there were too many other occasions around that time when they did not live up to the unstinting praise heaped upon them by Bill Shankly, the dynamic manager who had transformed the Anfield club into a feared First

Division force. The disturbing number of matches in which they failed to score included exits from the League Cup and FA Cup (in a fifth round they reached for the first time for twenty years) before they finished with an unbeaten flourish of a dozen games.

While goals were in short supply there was much astonishment when Clough and Taylor put priority on tightening up the defence. Their argument was that when things were going wrong in both departments the rearguard had to come first. It therefore also soon became common knowledge that their target was Terry Hennessey, and the Welsh international duly made the short trip across from Nottingham on 7 February 1970. The six-figure transfer fee, paid in instalments, temporarily made him the costliest defender in English football.

Then seven months from his 28th birthday, Hennessey was younger than his premature baldness made him look. Born at Llay, near Wrexham, he joined Birmingham City as an amateur in 1957 after catching their attention with Wales Boys. He turned professional on his seventeenth birthday, 1 September 1959, and just over a year afterwards played in the two-leg final of the Fairs Cup against Roma, who won in Italy after a draw at St Andrew's. He was still only eighteen when he made his League debut in a home win against Manchester City in March 1961. Two seasons later he was voted Midlands Footballer of the Year after figuring prominently in the team that defeated Aston Villa over the two-legged League Cup final.

After several close brushes with relegation, however, Birmingham dropped into the Second Division in 1965, and towards the end of that year Hennessey moved back into the top section with Nottingham Forest at a fee of £70,000. To the 202 League and Cup games he had played for the Blues he added 183 for the Reds, captaining Forest to second place behind Manchester United in the final First Division table, and to the semi-finals of the FA Cup, in the 1966-67 season. As he was such a powerful personality and performer, it came as quite a surprise when manager Matt Gillies, who had himself been a strong central defender (with Bolton and Leicester), agreed to release him – and to deadly rivals Derby County at that. Added to the success Alan Hinton was making of his departure to the Baseball Ground by the same route, there were to be repercussions from the Hennessey transfer to the Rams' detriment when they tried to pluck other plums off the Forest tree.

There was a Carlin-like air of *déjà-vu* about Hennessey's debut for Derby. As with the pint-sized Scouser, it came in a midweek home match straight after two defeats in which the Rams had failed to score, and it produced the same result: a 2-2 draw that his new club salvaged after falling behind. What was more, the Welshman made it in the same position as Carlin temporarily had done, as wearer of the No 4 shirt then known as the right-half. Durban moved forward from there to displace McGovern temporarily at No 7 in those more straightforward pre-squad days when players were numbered, excluding the goalkeeper, from 2 to 11. 'We have not bought Hennessey as a direct replacement for anybody,' said Clough. 'His signing gives us a reasonable first-team squad of about 13 players, and it will be good to have a bit of a choice after operating for so long with a skeleton first-team staff.'

The opponents in Hennessey's first game for the Rams were Chelsea, who looked comfortably cast as party poopers when they were two goals up only twelve minutes from time – and there could have been more. One of the immensely long throw-ins for which Ian Hutchinson was so noted (on another occasion the distance was measured at 112 feet) caused the frantic scramble from which Osgood struck the first blow just before the interval, and there had still not been a serious threat to the visitors' goal when a Hudson volley made the score more in keeping with what had gone before. Within a minute, however, Durban halved the deficit with a firm header after a scorching drive by Mackay had been turned against the crossbar by Bonetti, and two minutes after that Hennessey fittingly made the equaliser, a Hector header, by charging across the goalmouth to deceive the defence with a back-header from one of the corners forced in quick succession as Derby belatedly piled on the pressure.

That was the start of the unbeaten sequence with which the County ended their first season back in the First Division since 1952-53. Hennessey took on the guise of a lucky talisman as victories in each of the remaining five home games were interspersed with the transformation of a dismal away record. From gleaning only three points out of twenty on their travels since winning at Newcastle, the rejuvenated Rams dropped just three, in drawn matches, of the last twelve when visiting. That revival included a sequence of three away wins, beginning with the emphatic completion of the double over Liverpool in their Anfield stronghold.

Beginning that game in midfield but then taking Mackay's place in the back four when the skipper reverted to sweeper in a preconceived tactical plan, Hennessey augmented his impeccable display by joining in the attack to head his first goal for Derby from Hinton's chipped free-kick in the fourteenth minute. And before O'Hare rounded off a brilliant Webster-Hector move to increase that lead an hour later it was Hennessey who protected it by hooking the ball off the goalline when Liverpool were allowed their one clear scoring chance. The win, and so deserved, made my long trip up from Bristol, where I was then with the *Evening Post*, well worth while.

After also enjoying a winning return to Forest's City Ground, the lanky Hennessey gave further evidence of his adaptability by ending the season as a capable replacement in the absence through injury of first Mackay, then McFarland. Moreover, he was again a scorer in the final home game, against Wolves. All therefore seemed set for him to continue another prosperous phase of his career when he reported back after the summer break, but how abruptly that bright outlook was to change. While with Derby he was to win the last eight of the 39 Welsh full caps he added to the six he had gained at Under-23 level, yet he was limited to 82 first-team appearances for the Rams, three of them as a substitute, because of injuries to his knees and an Achilles tendon.

The trouble began in a practice game against Port Vale in the warm-up to the 1970-71 season. Brian Clough said he considered Hennessey 'so vital to our plans that we want the injury cleared up straightaway', but fluid and swelling on the right knee led to the first of two cartilage operations. He was able to play in no more than a dozen League matches that season, and only eighteen, including one as a substitute, in the championship-winning side of 1971-72. He managed almost thirty, but with several interruptions, the season after that, before leaving to manage the Staffordshire club Tamworth in April 1974, though he did have the satisfaction of being in the team that defeated mighty Benfica in the European Cup.

Hennessey was also in Midlands non-League football with Kimberley Town and Shepshed Charterhouse, and he coached in the United States and Canada before emigrating to Australia. He looked back upon his time at Derby with some bitterness. In 1977, when he was a packaging company's sales director, he was quoted as saying:

'I've got no reason to like Clough. He bought me and he finished me. If I'd been treated differently I'd still be playing today. Maybe not in the First Division because I'm 35, but at least playing. My problems started when I was injured in a pre-season game. If you were injured Clough didn't want to know you, although he was still sympathetic. That's the impression I got. Sometimes I could hardly walk on the field, but what really hurt was that there were people at the club who didn't believe I was injured. They thought I was swinging the lead. But I had to have two cartilage operations on that knee. I was never fully fit for the rest of my career. Despite everything I have to respect Clough. Whatever I think of him, and whatever anyone says about him, he's always got the perfect answer – he gets results.'

Hennessey's first stint in America was as assistant coach with Tulsa Roughnecks. He returned to that post after his spell back in England at Shepshed, then became the Roughnecks chief coach and led them to victory in the North American Soccer League Bowl final in Vancouver in 1983. One of the two goals with which they defeated Toronto Blizzard was scored by a player who had incurred suspension after passing the penalty points mark, but was cleared to play by the NASL president, Howard Samuels. This was Ron Futcher, whose twin brother Paul's clubs included Derby County.

The victory over Wolves with which Derby completed their home programme on 4 April 1970 assured them, in theory, of a place the following season in European competition, in the Fairs Cup. All the hard work that had been put in to bring that about was undone, however, by what two accountants revealed in one of the sudden spot checks to which clubs were subject under Football League regulations. They found that money had been paid out without being recorded in the books, including a sizeable amount to Mackay for articles that had appeared under his name in match programmes. Neither had the sales of season tickets and the payment of petty cash been properly documented.

On the day, the Wednesday after the defeat of Wolves, when the findings of a joint FA and Football League Commission were announced, Derby's officials had to endure an extra eight hours of suspense because the special delivery letter containing the verdict and sentence, posted by the FA in London at midday the previous day, was mislaid en route and did not arrive until the afternoon. They then learned that the club had been fined £10,000 and banned from playing in Europe during the season for which they had qualified. A full list of the charges was as follows:

THE EIGHT CHARGES AGAINST DERBY COUNTY – April 1970

1 – That FA Rule 44 (A) had been contravened with regard to discrepancies in club finance.
2 – That FA Rules 25 (A), 26 (B) and 27 (A) had been contravened.
3 – That there had been a breach of FA Rule 27 (A) and League Regulation 40 (A) regarding a variation of payments made during the playing season without the consent of the Management Committee.
4 – That there had been a breach of FA Rule 27 (A) and the League Regulation 42 as no new contract in respect of player F Wignall had been lodged with the FA and the League. These breaches also applied to J Richardson and L Green.
5 – That on November 7, 1968 the club had asked the League to confirm that it would be in order for Dave Mackay to be paid a fee for providing articles in the first-team programme at about £20 per article. On November 11 the League secretary had replied: 'I doubt whether the Committee will approve . . . and in the meantime I would ask you not to include any such articles in your programme.'
On November 26, following the Management Committee meeting held on November 14, the club had been informed that the Committee

refused to give their consent. The payment of £2,000 on November 14, although made to D Mackay Limited, for programme articles had been a breach of League Regulation 42.

6 – That there had been a breach of FA Rule 25 (A) as junior players who had taken part in trial matches were amateurs.

7 – That there had been a breach of League Regulation 47 in respect of lodging allowances for apprentices.

8 – That there had been a breach of League Regulation 47 and FA Rule 27 (A) as the amount had not been entered in Mackay's contract.

Sydney Bradley, the Derby County chairman, made the following statement after the joint FA and Football League Commission had announced their findings – a fine of £10,000 and expulsion from European competition in the next season:

'The club obviously accept the findings of the Commission. They are pleased that the Commission appreciate that the process of rearranging the club's administration had commenced prior to the inquiry. Every effort will be made to complete the process and ensure there is no further cause for complaint. The club are very disappointed that European football will not be possible this year, but we assure the supporters that every effort will be made to maintain the high standard achieved.'

Sir Robertson King, the Derby County president, said the charges covered a period of 'dramatic success' for the club. This and the growing volume of work were contributory reasons for the charges.

Brian Clough was joined in blaming the directors by Alderman Tom Taylor, the Mayor of Derby, who called it 'a terrible injustice' and said that 'the players will be penalised for something which is the responsibility of the board'. Sam Longson, however, maintained that the manager had to take his share of the responsibility because, without a strong secretary to restrain him, he had taken decisions without regard to the rules. It was an annoying and frustrating outcome to a first season back in Division One that had begun and ended on a high note in other respects, with the team recovering splendidly from the mid-season slip-ups and home League gates only once falling below 30,000 – and then, on the opening day, by fewer than 550. Six times, including an FA Cup-tie, the Baseball Ground attendance exceeded 40,000.

In the administrative shake-up that followed, Bob Innes, Bill Rudd and Mike Keeling were appointed to the board, and soon afterwards Bob Kirkland, who was very anti-Clough, Harry Payne and vice-chairman Ken Turner were dropped from it. During my time at Derby I met both Payne, a former Derbyshire Amateurs footballer who had been a director since the 1950s, and Turner, who ran a firm of industrial cleaners at Borrowash. I found both of them most amenable, though Ken Turner, who was also a member of the Derbyshire CCC committee, had reason to regard me with less approval. While bowling against him in a cricket match I struck him on the forehead, fortunately with no dire results, when the ball suddenly flew up to the great surprise of both of us.

The coup that unloaded those three directors also restored Sam Longson to the chairman's seat he had surrendered to Sydney Bradley because the board had voted to have a new man in that position every two years. On having that rotation rapidly rescinded, Sam Longson OBE remained as chairman until George Hardy eased him out, sidelined into the post of president in succession to Sir Robertson King KBE, in February 1977. Full of upheaval and controversy though Sam's seasons as chairman were, they also included some of the most prosperous in the Rams' history, a far cry from the parlous state they were in, newly relegated to the Third Division for the first time, when this wealthy representative from the north of Derbyshire, at Chapel-en-le-Frith, entered the board in 1955. The time he was able to devote to the club he had supported as a season-ticket holder since the 1930s was made possible by his sale of the road haulage company whose lorries bearing his name were a familiar sight as they trundled about the North-West.

After all the flaws unearthed in the keeping of Derby County's books in 1970, Alan Collard, an old friend of mine who was a prominent figure on the local cricket scene (he captained Derbyshire's second team for a time) was brought in temporarily to fill the gap left by the resignation owing to pressure of work of Malcolm Bramley, who, at 22, had been the youngest club secretary in the League. The appointment of another full-time secretary clearly became an urgent necessity, but the first rifts in the relationship between the reinstated chairman and his manager developed from the fact that the appointment was made after Brian Clough had conducted the interview along with vice-chairman Bradley instead of with an 'extremely annoyed' Sam Longson, who was away on holiday.

The choice fell on Stuart Webb, a smart-looking young man who was to have a profound influence on the club's future. Webb came from Preston North End, where he was assistant secretary, on the recommendation of Jimmy Gordon, who had been brought in as Derby's trainer in place of Jack Burkitt, skipper of the Nottingham Forest teams that won promotion to the First Division and the FA Cup in the 1950s.

Burkitt, who held the record for the number of Nottingham Forest appearances before Bob McKinlay, Terry Hennessey's predecessor as the club's captain, boosted it from 503 to 685, made a typically conscientious contribution to Derby County's progress after joining the staff in the 1967 close season, but his health had already suffered during a difficult time as

Notts County's manager, leading to his resignation at Meadow Lane after being given a month's leave because of nervous strain brought on by overwork.

Webb had an uneasy relationship with Clough and Taylor, resulting from his increasing influence on the Rams' affairs that included the organisation of their travel arrangements through the agency he formed, but years later Derby had the best of reasons to be thankful to him when he played a key role in saving them from bankruptcy. His interrupted connection with the club included spells as vice-chairman, managing director, chief executive and briefly chairman. Michael Dunford, in those early days a young assistant secretary but destined to end his long service at the Baseball Ground as secretary/general manager, and then become Everton's chief executive, often had to bear the backlash of the fragile alliance between Clough and the new secretary. Webb was horrified to find the books in such 'utter disarray' when he first had the chance to examine them after agreeing to leave Deepdale.

Gordon, too, was no yes-man. Indeed, he had made no secret of his dislike for both Clough and Taylor while on the Boro's coaching staff during their playing days there, and he was therefore taken aback when he was invited to rejoin them while a trainer with Blackburn Rovers. Because Derby's resources were then thin, they were not in a position to pursue their interest when they made their first approach soon after taking over at the Baseball Ground, and they again found him unwilling to make the move when they repeated their offer on reaching the First Division. Clough promptly turned up on Gordon's doorstep in Lancashire, asking what Blackburn paid him. On being told, he said he would double it, and that was enough to land the man he saw as a 'fair-minded old pro I could trust with my life'.

For all his misgivings, Gordon, veteran of almost 400 games with Newcastle and Middlesbrough before becoming a trainer, had reason to look back on his decision to accept the offer as the best he ever made, taking him to a close association with most of soccer's big prizes. It culminated shortly before his retirement in 1980 with the honour of leading out Nottingham Forest at Wembley for a League Cup final while Clough and Taylor made their way round the track to their touchline seats.

WHAT THEY DID NOT WANT WAS WATNEY WIN

With the benefit of hindsight, the Watney Cup win with which Derby County prefaced the 1970-71 season was, as Brian Clough put it, 'the worst possible thing that could have happened.' It bred a misguided feeling of well-being among both players and supporters that was shown to be seriously misplaced as the club slipped as low as nineteenth in the First Division table before another late improvement lifted them to the respectability of a final ninth place just inside the top half.

At one point, after only one win had been gained in ten League games, Clough sought to put some new life back into his jaded stars by packing them off to Majorca for five days of straight talking and self-examination. 'The players have been told a few home truths,' he said, 'and everybody has had to sit back and take stock.'

Later in the season, he was stung into condemnation of complainers in the crowd, telling them that 'if they don't like what we are doing they can stay away'. He was particularly angered when Les Green and John McGovern were barracked during Ron Webster's testimonial match with Coventry City – a game which he said 'did not matter tuppence in terms of points or trophy'. He went further:

'Neither I nor my players have to stand for louts. Generally our fans are superb, among the best in the world, but if a few louts want to get at anyone for our comparative lack of success this season they should blame me. I won't tolerate those who come along just for a 90-minute knock at some of my players. They are so wrong that I would stake my job against the players they are getting at being released.'

The Watney Cup, a new, but short-lived, competition for the previous season's two highest-scoring teams in each of the four divisions of the Football League that had not won promotion, was a consolation prize for the Rams because it was also not open to clubs with the European involvement they had forfeited through their financial irregularities. Introduced with the intention of encouraging attacking play, it experimented unsuccessfully with the offside law, though not in the inaugural season in which Derby County won it. A similar plan, restricting offside to the eighteen yards at each end of the pitch with the penalty-area markings extended to both touchlines, was also quickly abandoned in Scotland.

Derby went into the Watney Cup still smarting from losing the European place they had earned, but with a side buoyant from the successes of their first season back among the country's top 22 clubs, and with some stability – if, as it transpired, only temporary – established behind the scenes by the changes in the boardroom. Most important of all, unsettling talk of Brian Clough being lured away to Birmingham City had died out, though that was but the first of several temptations he had to better himself elsewhere before the split-up that threw the club into turmoil.

From the playing aspect, the only drawback as Derby embarked upon the new season was the unfitness of Terry Hennessey, but the team's performances during the Watney Cup games he missed were so impressive, with Durban back at wing-half and first Wignall, then McGovern, at No 7, that the main problem then appeared to be the question of where to fit him in when he was available again. At least, those displays were impressive after the recovery from conceding three goals to Fulham in seven sizzling minutes at sun-baked Craven Cottage in the first round.

All seemed well with the experiment of a 4-2-4 formation when O'Hare opened the scoring in the second minute and Wignall had the ball in the net again in the sixth, only for Bob Matthewson, a referee rarity of having been a professional footballer (with Bolton Wanderers), to rule against Hector for pushing. The inadvisability of putting only two men in midfield was then shown to throw too great a burden on the back four as the Third Division side stormed into a 3-1 lead with just under a quarter of an hour gone.

To a quick equaliser by Steve Earle two goals were added almost as swiftly by Vic Halom, a sturdy Derbyshire-born striker whom Bobby Robson, while briefly Fulham's manager, had narrowly beaten Brian Clough to sign from Leyton Orient nearly two years earlier. Halom, who hailed from Swadlincote, helped the Cottagers to promotion before leaving for Luton, then gained an FA Cup winner's medal with Sunderland besides assisting the Wearsiders back to the First Division. Derby County were given three other good reasons to regret not landing him when he did the hat-trick against them for Sunderland in a League Cup second replay shortly after Dave Mackay had taken over as the Rams' manager. Burton Albion were among the clubs Halom later managed.

Although Hector reduced the deficit with a long shot goalkeeper Malcolm Webster misjudged, Fulham for the rest of the first half scarcely felt the absence of their long-time star man Johnny Haynes, who preferred to play golf and was soon off to finish his footballing in South Africa, but everything changed when Derby reverted to 4-3-3 with the introduction of McGovern for Hinton about twenty minutes from the end of the ninety. Within five minutes Durban brought the scores level to force the extra-time in which he crowned the comeback with the best goal of the game's eight, a blistering first-time shot into the far corner of the net, shortly after Hector had regained the lead.

Just one goal, finely struck by McGovern on the half-hour, accounted at the Baseball Ground for Derby's next opponents, Sheffield United, who had demolished Aldershot, one of Division Four's representatives, with six. The Blades, who went on to win promotion as Second Division runners-up to Leicester, had a strong team that included, in addition to future Rams manager Colin Addison, Alan Hodgkinson, a former England goalkeeper, Welsh caps David Powell and Gil Reece, internationals-to-be in Tony Currie (England) and skipper Eddie Colquhoun (Scotland), and one of the game's most dangerous raiding wingers, Alan Woodward.

So to the final, for which Derby again had home advantage in meeting the challenge of Manchester United, who had followed a narrow and unimpressive win at Reading with a Boothferry Park semi-final that Second Division Hull City, first-round conquerors of Peterborough United from Division Four, had lost only on a penalty shoot-out after extra-time. Hull, under new player-manager Terry Neill, the Northern Ireland half-back who had been the youngest captain in Arsenal's history and was later to manage the Highbury club as well as their North London rivals Tottenham, gave a real fright to a United team attempting to regroup under the ill-fated coaching control of Wilf McGuinness, whose promising playing career at Old Trafford had been ended by injury at the age of 22.

That, however, was a minor embarrassment compared with the 4-1 drubbing Derby gave Manchester's creaking stars. Whereas McGuinness had looked to the final of Britain's first sponsored tournament as an ideal stepping stone to First Division prosperity, it led within five months to his demotion back to trainer-coach of United's reserve team, as the legendary Sir Matt Busby took charge once more until the appointment as manager of Frank O'Farrell, another who failed to fill the great man's shoes. The sequel was to be deflating for Derby County too, but on that day, 8 August 1970, they basked in the warm glow of a job magnificently done. In the *Guardian* Paul Wilcox observed that 'Derby would still have missed a few had it been 8-1'.

From the twentieth minute in which man-of-the-match McFarland opened the scoring with an opportunist shot, the Rams were what the onlooking Hennessey said was 'different class' to labouring United, who, in a reversal of the home team's tactics, had switched back to a 4-2-4 formation instead of persevering with the 4-3-3 line-up that had won them points, but few friends, the previous season. Further goals flowed from Hinton, with an astute back-heel after 23 minutes, a Durban header (35) and, seventeen minutes from time, Mackay's fierce repetition, but slightly more accurate, of the free-kick with which he had struck an upright while the scoresheet had still been blank. The lone reply, by George Best in the 32nd minute, was scant consolation.

Sir Stanley Rous, the former FA secretary who was then President of FIFA, called Mackay 'the old warrior' as he handed the trophy to Derby's inspiring captain.

Regrettably, there was one big blemish on Derby's big day. Football hooligans from Manchester provoked havoc in the streets around the Baseball Ground before the match. The main bar at the Baseball Hotel had to be closed because of what licensee Ronald Sutton called 'indescribable' damage, a milk float was overturned in Bloomfield Street, and running fights broke out all over the area. One of the glasses that were thrown in the hotel, breaking mirrors, after a fan had been ejected struck a barman on the head, causing him to require medical attention, and the floor was covered in beer and broken glass.

Police had to use emergency measures to bring the situation under control, but there was a steady flow of more disturbances on the popular side during the game after Derby had gone into the lead. Coins were among the objects thrown, and according to the front-page report in the *Derby Evening Telegraph*, 'a stinging liquid resembling ammonia was squirted as the crowd struggled on the centre of the terraces.' Four adults and nine juveniles were arrested before half-time; others were later taken to the special police room at the ground, charged with a variety of offences.

Brian Clough was also displeased by the behaviour of young fans inside the ground. He complained: 'If it means hemming in the young fans the way they do in South America, then that is what we will have to do. It was heartbreaking the way hundreds of kids ignored repeated warnings to keep off the pitch. Their stupidity could cost Derby points later in the year. Anyone paying schoolchildren's admission could be put in a very tight pen, and if that didn't work the reduced price would be scrapped altogether.'

In common with other grounds in the country, fences did have to be installed at the Baseball Ground to prevent pitch invasions, but all were removed in accordance with the Taylor Report after the crowd tragedy at the abandoned FA Cup semi-final between Liverpool and Nottingham Forest at Sheffield Wednesday's ground in 1989.

As if all those deplorable scenes at the Watney Cup final were not enough to anger the Derby manager, he took his team to London the following weekend, for their opening League match with Chelsea, still irked by the refusal of many sceptics to recognise either the talent of his team or the merit of their success in a competition those same critics had belittled. He welcomed the challenge that the Rams had to prove themselves all over again, but added:

'It's about time people realised just how good a side we are. I could give you now the five teams who will be disputing the title this season, and Derby will be one of them. I will go further and say that I want Derby to be on top of the table by the time we meet Leeds in October, and I believe we can be. It's absolute rubbish for anyone to decry our performances over the last couple of seasons. After we had won the Second Division title our critics were saying we wouldn't last the pace in the First Division. We answered that by finishing fourth, but still there were those who claimed it was something of a fluke. The same people were saying Dave Mackay was finished. Diamonds don't lose their shine, do they?'

For once, however, Clough was way out with his forecast. By the time Leeds United visited the Baseball Ground it was they, not the down-table Rams, who were on top of the heap. And the Elland Road club achieved their 2-0 win without three of their first-choice players – full-back Paul Reaney, who had not fully recovered from the broken leg suffered at West Ham towards the end of the previous season which kept him out of England's World Cup squad for Mexico, Johnny Giles, the Republic of Ireland midfield general, and Eddie Gray, the bemusing Scottish international winger whose career was continually threatened by injuries.

Leeds, indeed, were Derby's bogy team while Brian Clough was with them (and afterwards too. The Rams' 2-0 home victory on 27 January 2005 was their first against Leeds for eighteen years, since 2 May 1987). County won only two of the fourteen matches between the clubs during Clough's tenure – and one of them, by 4-1 in their penultimate home fixture of 1969-70, was gained over a side that did not contain even one regular member, a diminution that cost Leeds a £5,000 fine as well as the two points. In the midst of a busy Easter programme that for Leeds included the first leg of a European Cup semi-final against Glasgow Celtic two days later, with an FA Cup final in the offing, Don Revie greatly annoyed an Easter Monday crowd of 41,011 at the Baseball Ground by delaying the news that he would be fielding a second-string side until after they had all been locked in about half-an-hour before the kick-off. Some cynics were heard to suggest that the gates had been closed to prevent disgruntled fans getting out when this Leeds line-up was announced: Harvey; Davey, Peterson; Lumsden, Kennedy, Yorath; Galvin, Bates, Belfitt, Hibbitt, Johanneson. The team that faced Celtic at Elland Road on the Wednesday was: Sprake; Reaney, Cooper; Bremner, Charlton, Madeley; Lorimer, Clarke, Jones, Giles, Gray (E). It was on the following day that Reaney broke a leg, so for the return match at Celtic Park Hunter returned in place of Madeley, who was switched to right-back.

The version of the Revie Plan perpetrated at Derby (the more acceptable one helped Manchester City to win the FA Cup while he was a player) rebounded on the Leeds manager as the Scottish champions scored the only goal of the first leg and went on to progress by a 3-1 aggregate to a final in which they only narrowly failed to win the trophy for the second time. In 1967, Celtic had become the first British winners by defeating Inter-Milan 2-1 in Lisbon. This time they lost by the same score to the Dutch champions Feyenoord in Milan, but only after extra-time.

For Leeds in 1970 there was also the disappointment of losing to Chelsea in a replay of the FA Cup final at Old Trafford, where future Derby player David Webb scored the winning goal in extra-time, and of finishing second to Arsenal in the First Division. During ten successive seasons after returning to the top section in 1964, Leeds were twice winners, five times runners-up, once third and twice fourth in the League, once winners, three times losing finalists, and twice beaten semi-finalists in the FA Cup, and once holders of the League Cup. It was a remarkable record, if frequently falling just short of the honours, that Brian Clough strove to emulate. He told Mervyn Thomas, a *Daily Mail* reporter on the West Country beat whom I got to know while working in Bristol:

'We want to be like Leeds. They have the strongest squad either side of the Channel. Don Revie has set a standard to which we all aspire. Everybody is aiming for their kind of reserve strength and consistency, and I hope people will soon be saying the same things about Derby.'

The Rams' manager was later to have some less complimentary views to express about Leeds United, views that were held against him when he sank to the lowest point of his career during his short and stormy stay with the Yorkshire club, but first he gave vent to some of his harshest words for his own players after the heaviest of the defeats handed out to them by Leeds. Humiliation was the only word for it as the County tarnished their champion crown by capitulating to a truly United side that crushed them 5-0 at Elland Road, easing up, in the autumn of 1972.

Derby's sad sequence of results against Leeds in Clough's time stretched from their expulsion from the FA Cup's third round and a League Cup semi-final in the first few weeks of 1968 to another FA Cup failure, at home in the quarter-final, in March 1973. The only genuine victory for the Rams over Leeds between those dates was gained on what turned out to be the run-in to the League title on the first day of April in 1972, when they themselves would not have been flattered with five goals. As it was, they had to make do with two, one of them an own-goal by Norman Hunter after John O'Hare had opened the scoring. Twice Paul Reaney cleared off the Leeds line. Both squads were just one man below full strength on that April Fools' Day. Derby lacked Alan Hinton; Leeds were without Mick Jones.

The defeat by Leeds in October 1970 that completed the contradiction of the table-top prophecy Clough had made after the lifting of the Watney Cup left the Rams with only four victories (three of them misleadingly in succession straight after starting with a defeat at Chelsea) in their first fourteen League games of the season. By that time, one new player had come in and one who had contributed greatly to the climb under Clough had gone out. The newcomer was Archie Gemmill; the man who left, reluctantly, was Willie Carlin.

Gemmill, another dynamic little 'un, all of 5ft 5in, had not long turned twenty when he entered English football in May 1967 (at about the same time that Brian Clough and Peter Taylor took over at Derby) by joining Preston from St Mirren, the club in his home town of Paisley with which he had become the first substitute to be used in a cup-tie in Scotland. He went on to play 93 League games for North End, scoring thirteen goals from midfield, and to captain the Scotland Under-23 team, before Clough nipped in to beat Everton for his signature. The £66,000 fee gave the Deepdale club a nice little profit on the £13,000 they had paid for him. Their manager, Alan Ball Senior, father of the England player, was forced into the sale by financial difficulties. 'I wish,' he said, 'I had £100 for every game Gemmill will play for Scotland while with Derby.' On that reckoning he would have picked up £2,200 – and this indefatigable human dynamo made 21 more appearances for his country after moving to Nottingham Forest and Birmingham City.

The deal, which increased Derby's spending to around £350,000 in three years, provided a classic case of Clough's persistence in pursuing a player he felt he must have. Refusing to be put off by his quarry's insistence on sleeping on his offer, he decided that he would sleep on it himself – also at the Gemmill home, without waiting for an invitation. Mrs Gemmill, who was pregnant with the son, Scot, who was to play for Clough at Nottingham Forest, was not all that welcoming at first, but Derby's volatile young manager could turn on the charm when he wanted, and he felt that she looked upon him more favourably after he had helped with the washing up the next morning. A hearty breakfast put them all in a good mood and Gemmill duly signed. 'This is a marvellous surprise for me,' he said, 'after being relegated with Preston to the Third Division last season.'

Starting with a trademark display of determination and perpetual motion at West Bromwich, where two more defensive slip-ups led to another defeat, Gemmill made his first four appearances for Derby alongside Carlin, the player he had been bought to replace. Two of those games were lost, the two others drawn, and after the last of them, another defeat by Chelsea in the return fixture at the Baseball Ground, Carlin, a special favourite of the fans, was transferred to Leicester City for a fee of £38,000 – the biggest paid for a Derby player in twenty years, since Billy Steel's £23,000 move to Dundee. In saying that he and Peter Taylor were 'genuinely sorry' to see Carlin go, Brian Clough admitted it was not an easy decision to make in paying this tribute:

'Willie was indispensable for two seasons. He was, and always will be, the complete professional. He gave us what we lacked. He grafted for us and gave us strength, skill and character in midfield, but we needed the money. We knew that Willie's style of play, a non-stop runner, would catch up with him some time, but he is the ideal man to help Leicester out of the Second Division.'

Although Carlin's thirtieth birthday was less than a fortnight away, he still had two more promotions ahead of him to add to those he had gained with Carlisle United and Derby – first with Leicester, then Notts County. Cardiff City were his last League club, after which he took over a newsagent business and later lived for a time in Majorca. In recent years he has been back with Derby County as one of the hosts at Pride Park's hospitality boxes.

Derby's next important team change after Gemmill's inclusion at Carlin's expense resulted from the Boxing Day extravaganza they had to come from behind to draw with Manchester United after being two up at half-time. That was one of the first games on which I reported for *The Daily Telegraph*, and as I drove down in icy weather from Manchester I had the alarming experience of fearing I would be unable to get to the Baseball Ground in time when I encountered several other cars that were stranded on a snow-covered hill just outside Ashbourne. More by luck than good judgment, I was able to slither my way around the obstructions, to be rewarded with the treat of a real Christmas cracker that provided high entertainment for a crowd of more than 34,000, but defensive nightmares for the management of both clubs.

It was not a spectacle the purists could appreciate, though the treacherous surface, turning from snow-covered to mud, made many of the mistakes excusable. Unfortunately for Les Green, however, mistakes he made were avoidable and costly – costly both for his team and himself personally. From being not far short of international class, he had for several weeks been on the wane, his form affected by the distraction of gambling debts and other problems in his private life. Now came his comeuppance. As Peter Taylor saw it, he played 'a stinker in the second half', and was never to keep goal for Derby County's first team again.

The lead the Rams gained through Mackay and Wignall was frittered away as United hit them with three goals in five second-half minutes. Green's lack of height was shown up when he was caught out of position as Denis Law headed the ball over him from a corner, and his fumble then let in George Best for a simple tap-in, but the crestfallen goalkeeper was let down by a lack of cover as the unmarked Law beat him with another header. The balance of play swiftly tipped back in Derby's favour as a penetrating dribble by Gemmill gave Hector the opening to equalise and the little

Scot put the County ahead again with a shot that went in off a post – only for Green to cancel out a superb reflex save from Best by failing to gather the corner-kick from which the leaping Brian Kidd completed the scoring.

For Derby's next match, a third-round FA Cup-tie at Chester on an icy January day darkened by the disaster at Ibrox, where 66 people were trampled to death after tumbling down a stairway on leaving a Rangers-Celtic game, Colin Boulton at long last ended his wait for a first-team recall. And for all but three (two of them through suspension; the other when rested before a European Cup trip) of the Rams' following 243 fixtures, he kept his place before being temporarily dislodged by Graham Moseley, a six-footer from the Urmston district of Manchester who cost the Rams £20,000 as a seventeen-year-old in September 1971, within a few hours of turning full-time professional with Blackburn Rovers and just two weeks after being spotted by Peter Taylor in a reserve game. Ken Furphy, the Lancashire club's manager, not keen to sell but needing the money for rebuilding, had to make a hurried car journey to Moseley's home to get him to sign full-time terms before the deal could go through.

Boulton, who was to make nearly fifty more appearances after winning back his place from Moseley, might have established himself in the side earlier but for not always being on the same wavelength as Brian Clough, and for attracting criticism because of an often lackadaisical attitude to training that made him not over-keen to bother saving shots directed at him in practice matches. This almost brought him to blows with Roy McFarland, as the centre-half recalled in a contribution he made to the brochure that was brought out for Boulton when the goalkeeper was awarded a testimonial after ten years' service. McFarland wrote:

'To me, he was idling in training, not putting his lot in and not trying to better himself. I thought he had a chip on his shoulder, and I told him so. That led to some violent arguments, and more than once Col and I nearly went outside the dressing room to fight. I'm glad it didn't happen, because I punch so strongly I might have robbed Derby County of a fine goalkeeper! That is what Bernie, as we call him, has become [after "Bernie, the bolt!" the catchphrase of Bob Monkhouse's TV game show The Golden Shot]. He has never let us down and I would rate him certainly among the top half-dozen in the country. His handling is great and he has improved enormously in the way he deals with crosses, something which I know bothered him in his early days in the side.'

Boulton was a reformed character in training after getting the big chance that came his way not only belatedly but also ironically because he owed it not so much to his own efforts as to the loss of form of Les Green, like whom he was small for a goalkeeper. Boulton, also belatedly, set about working assiduously at his game, to the extent that he eventually met all the major requirements set by Derbyshire-born Bob Wilson, a highly respected goalkeeping coach after ending his playing career between the posts for Arsenal and Scotland. Wilson listed them as the six Cs: Competitiveness, Concentration, Confidence, Courage, Consistency, Composure. And consistency was Boulton's speciality.

Of Brian Clough, Boulton was to admit that 'affection for him didn't come into it', but he came to recognise that 'he had this knack of making us play to the limits of our ability'. When Clough left, Dave Mackay had his difficulties, to put it mildly, with Boulton before they were resolved. More about that in its turn.

Another alteration to Derby's regular line-up was made within days of the ending of the club's interest in that season's knock-out competitions. The Rams lived dangerously before being beaten by an only goal in both of them. In the League Cup, they struggled at home against Halifax, then had to come from two down to overcome Millwall before losing away to Coventry City, who in a League match at the Baseball Ground had been stung into also recovering from a two-goal deficit by the disparaging pen pictures of their players in the match programme. In the FA Cup, the win at Chester was followed by an even narrower one at home to Wolves, O'Hare snatching victory in the last minute, before an exit at Everton as David Johnson, later of Ipswich, Liverpool and England, added to his debut goal in the League, at Burnley, with another in his first FA Cup-tie.

The new addition to Derby's playing strength in the wake of that Goodison defeat was the considerable one of Colin Todd, the 22-year-old Sunderland and England Under-23 captain. His signing for £175,000 came not long after Brian Clough had indicated that such an expense could no longer be afforded, and at a time when a crisis at the Rolls-Royce works in the town had Derbyshire folk queuing up to get their money out of the local building society. It was then the biggest fee to change hands for one player in Britain. Martin Peters, one of England's World Cup heroes, had left West Ham for Tottenham Hotspur in a £200,000 transfer almost a year earlier, but that sum had included £45,000 for Jimmy Greaves in part exchange.

Clough was in no doubt that he was bringing in another winner, having had this king of defenders under his wing while coaching the youngsters at Sunderland, but, as had been the case with Stuart Webb, he gave Sam Longson reason to fret by doing the deal while the chairman was again on holiday. The old man could scarcely fail soon to appreciate what an excellent bit of business it was, but the first he heard of it was in the telegram Clough sent to him. Not good for a harmonious relationship, another early source of the barbs that swelled a festering sore for Longson as directors of other clubs, also concerned about the gathering momentum of Clough's controversial pronouncements, eventually began to ask him who exactly was running the Rams.

Todd first turned out for Derby in a 2-0 home win against Arsenal, a rare check in the Gunners' progress to the League title they clinched for a then record eighth time just a few days before also winning the FA Cup. He was seen as the long-term replacement for Mackay, but Durban was the man who initially had to make room for him – unfortunate because the manager admitted to wishing that the Welshman, scorer of his 100th goal for the club earlier in the season, 'had got a couple of goals last week to force me to keep him in the side because he has qualities that other players do not possess.' The newcomer was to strike up as formidable a partnership for England as he did for Derby in playing alongside McFarland, newly an international on being called up for a Nations Cup match in Malta after Everton's Brian Labone had dropped out with a badly gashed leg that also caused him to miss the Cup clash with the Rams.

Derby's next home match after Arsenal's visit was marred by serious injuries to three Manchester City players. Mike Summerbee broke a leg for the third time in twelve months, Alan Oakes suffered a knee injury that required a cartilage operation, and skipper Tony Book badly dislocated a shoulder in only the second minute. Neither Summerbee, who played on for fifteen minutes, nor Dave Mackay, the other player involved, realised at first how bad his injury was. Derby's captain said afterwards:

'It was one of those terribly unfortunate accidents that happen at times. It wasn't so much a tackle as a collision. As I was about to play the ball, Mike nipped in between it and me and I caught him. I didn't even feel sorry at the time because it was the sort of collision you get so often in a game.'

City, already without goalkeeper Joe Corrigan and Book's usual full-back partner Glyn Pardoe, who had also broken a leg, were reduced to ten men when Oakes went off, young Mike Brennan, the only substitute then allowed, having been sent on for his first taste of League football after the loss of Book. In those circumstances, they were grateful to glean a point from a scoreless draw – especially as referee Ron Challis disallowed a goal for pushing when O'Hare forced the ball through a crowded goalmouth past eighteen-year-old Ron Healey, the deputy goalkeeper, in the fourth minute of injury-time.

With City facing a two-goal deficit from the first leg of their European Cup-winners' Cup quarter-final against Gornik Zabrze, the Polish club they had beaten in the previous year's final, manager Joe Mercer was both alarmed and annoyed to see his forces so depleted, but he made it clear that his criticisms were not aimed at Derby County when he said: 'This wasn't a rough game, but when Mike Summerbee's leg was broken it was the sad old story of a tackle from behind. I'm not complaining about Derby. I just want the tackle from behind cut out of our game. It is dangerous. It can be deadly. Time after time I have implored referees to put a stop to this kind of tackling, no matter whether it is from our own players or from opponents. It is the cause of most of the serious injuries in the game.' Prophetic words! The League imposed a disciplinary crackdown for the next season.

Below strength though they were, the Manchester club themselves scored twice without reply when they met Gornik at Maine Road, then won the replay in Copenhagen, but they were beaten in both legs of their semi-final against Chelsea, who succeeded them as holders by defeating Real Madrid in Athens.

The month after City's injury-hit visit to the Baseball Ground, Ron Webster had to drop out of Derby's team after taking an ankle knock in his 300th League game, narrowly lost at Tottenham, but Todd smoothly moved back to deputise for him, allowing the return of Durban, as the Rams went unbeaten through the remaining half-dozen games. That run of four wins and two scoreless draws began most impressively at Old Trafford, where Manchester United had not been beaten for four months. I was among the admiring onlookers as John O'Hare gave one of his greatest displays, to which Richard Bott paid this tribute in the *Sunday Express*:

'There was scope at Old Trafford yesterday for the preparation of an illustrated manual on centre-forward play, with Derby's John O'Hare the subject of the still camera. By freezing the action you could have caught him displaying every facet of his trade, including the scoring – with head and foot – of two majestic goals. O'Hare left us all asking, incredulously, why Scotland have dropped him from their international squad.'

Everton, Burnley and West Bromwich were the other teams convincingly defeated on that impressive run-in, and Dave Mackay was given a rousing, emotional send-off against Albion by a crowd that would otherwise have been nowhere near topping 33,000 for an end-of-season game that had no bearing on the final positions. News that he was leaving for Swindon Town, after talk of Hull City's player-manager, Terry Neill, showing some interest, had been given a fortnight earlier by Sam Longson shortly before the kick-off in the Everton match. The transfer was delayed to enable Mackay to realise his ambition of getting through a season without missing a match, and also because Brian Clough had still seen him as an important player while Todd was settling in.

Mackay, who, like the club, had a one-year option to extend his three-year contract, said he was not really sorry to be going. He explained: 'I think the time is just right, just as it was when I left Tottenham. I have enjoyed every minute of it at Derby, but I think the move is best for both of us. I shall have a rest, go to a health farm to get some weight off, and then try to lead Swindon to the Second Division championship.'

In his three seasons with the Rams, this redoubtable Scot was out of the team only six times, making 148 League and Cup appearances and scoring eight goals. Right to the end of his farewell game he was still urging his men on, even though victory had well before then been assured by goals from Durban and Hinton against a club that in recent weeks had beaten Leeds and drawn with Arsenal. At the final whistle off he sprinted with a last wave to fans saddened by his departure but grateful for having had their team so inspired by his leadership. How even more momentous were to be the events that brought him back.

Champions in Season of Three Trophies

For neutral observers, apart from those indifferent to it, there were two ways of looking at Derby County's first winning of the Football League's top title in 1972.

They could either welcome it, as many of them did, because the addition of a new name to the roll of honour breathed fresh life into a competition which, in an inescapable consequence of the lifting of the maximum wage, has since become a Premiership monopolised by a small group of the wealthiest clubs. Or, as the other faction more vociferously did, they could see it as a victory 'by default' because it was assured by the shortcomings of their closest rivals while the manager was on holiday with his family in the Scilly Isles and his players were sunning themselves with his assistant in Majorca.

Incredibly, events off the field might well have left Derby with no championship to celebrate in any case. Almost a dozen games from the finishing post there was a real danger of Brian Clough and Peter Taylor being tempted away, with a resulting threat of disruption similar to the one that caused a dip in form when they did finally depart. There had already been one big scare of losing them since the approach from Birmingham City had been warded off by the boardroom changes and Sam Longson's reinstatement as chairman. Clough admitted they had gone very close to accepting an offer to manage the Greek national team – so close that he had had three talks with that country's Minister for Sport, and had also consulted George Brown, a former Foreign Secretary. 'If it hadn't been for my politics,' he said, 'we might well have done so,' but Taylor had a more straightforward reason for staying put at that stage: 'Derby County were just beginning to tick.'

Clough went into more detail: 'They would have given us the earth if we could have got Greece's team up to the standard where it could qualify for the 1974 World Cup. Peter and I were both to receive a £5,000 signing-on fee for the 3½-year contract. Then we were to get £15,000 a year each at an Income Tax rate of ten per cent. If we succeeded in getting Greece into the last 16 of the World Cup we could have named our own bonuses. I doubt if there's ever been a contract like it in the history of football. I was tempted. I met George Brown at the Mackworth Hotel. He was utterly fair about it and didn't attempt to dissuade me. He even gave me the phone number of the British Ambassador to Greece so that I could find out more about the conditions we would have to work in. But then I came to my senses. With my mouth and my political views I would have been in jail inside a week.' (The Labour Party twice tried to persuade Clough, a lifelong left-wing socialist, to be a parliamentary candidate. He was not tempted when asked to contest the Richmond seat in Surrey, but thought seriously about the second approach concerning Moss Side in Manchester before also rejecting it. Instead, he campaigned effectively for Phillip Whitehead, MP for Derby North, 1970-83.)

Clough's name was also linked with the Manchester United vacancy Frank O'Farrell filled, but that was a certain non-starter because he would not have been interested in it while Sir Matt Busby was still there. 'That was Frank's big mistake,' he said. 'Jock Stein got as far as the chairman's house, but wouldn't take it in the end. Matt has a great record. I take nothing away from him, but I wouldn't have gone within 100 miles of that job while he was still at Old Trafford.'

No, the offer that so nearly took Clough and Taylor away from Derby County while they were in the running for the 1971-72 championship was made by Coventry City, who were seeking a successor to the sacked Noel Cantwell. Derrick Robins, their chairman, first talked to them at the Midland Hotel in Derby after obtaining Sam Longson's permission. A week later, they were in another hotel, in London, the morning after Alan Hinton had given the Rams both points at Tottenham with a late penalty, his tenth of the season, when Robins rang to say he had his Rolls-Royce waiting outside to take them to Coventry.

But he was one match too late. Clough had recently admitted in public his disappointment at the level of support for Derby, and had even stated with some bitterness that the club were not big enough to become champions. He had also fancied the possibility of more scope at Highfield Road, where, in his words, 'we could have made three times the money we were getting at Derby.' The Coventry offer was said to be worth £40,000 a year for the pair, £25,000 of it to Clough.

When Robins made his second call, however, the win at White Hart Lane had swung the odds against him, although a countering increase in salaries at Derby no doubt also had something to do with it. By then, Clough felt that the Rams did have a chance of taking the title, close behind the two clubs above them, Manchester City and Leeds United, with eleven games to go. He therefore said that he and Taylor now had to stay where they were to try to see the challenge through, but maybe they could all talk about it again afterwards. Within 24 hours Robins withdrew his offer.

Instead, who should he turn to but Clough's old boss at Boro, Bob Dennison, who had joined Coventry as chief scout after he had followed what was held in court to be unfair dismissal from Ayresome Park (he was awarded £3,200 damages) with a quick Southern League promotion in charge at Hereford.

Derby County's start to the 1971-72 season was not wholly convincing for potential champions, with four draws in the first six matches, and three more in the next half-dozen, but it was not until they then visited leaders Manchester United in mid-October that they lost the last unbeaten record in the First Division – and that was by just one goal, scored by George Best early in the second half, although Brian Kidd and Alan Gowling hit the crossbar with headers. There had, however, been one defeat shortly before that – one of those Leeds inflicted in the League Cup, after a scoreless draw at the Baseball Ground. Leeds, who earlier in the year had won the Fairs Cup for the second time, were knocked out by West Ham in the next round after extra-time in a replay, but went on to win the FA Cup before being denied the double in finishing runners-up to Derby in the League.

During the first few weeks of the season, the Rams made up for their early League Cup exit by embarking upon a run in the Texaco Cup tournament, played throughout over two legs, that was to take them to the trophy they added to those for the championships of Division One and the Reserves' Central League. Qualification for the Texaco Cup was by invitation to clubs from England, Scotland, Northern Ireland and the Republic of Ireland who were not in European competitions. Though without Gemmill and McFarland, Derby began with a 6-2 home win against one of the Scottish representatives, Dundee United, and advanced clearly on aggregate despite fielding only five first-team regulars for a second leg they lost 2-3 after increasing their advantage with two goals inside the opening twenty minutes.

Among the reserves who played at Tannadice that evening was Tony Bailey, a young wing-half who had been signed from Burton Albion on the day of Terry Hennessey's arrival from Forest. Bailey was to play twice more in the Texaco Cup – once as a substitute when Hennessey had to be carried off in the first leg of the next round against Stoke with a recurrence of his knee trouble – but he had only one chance in the League, as deputy for Todd in one of the defeats at Leeds, before going to Oldham on loan early in 1974. Oldham signed him soon afterwards, but before the end of that year parted with him to Bury. His stay with the Gigg Lane club lasted until late 1980, when, after taking his total of League appearances beyond 150, he went into the Northern Premier League with Mossley.

Stoke were overcome only narrowly in the Texaco Cup's second round, by 4-3 on aggregate. At the Baseball Ground they trailed to two goals by O'Hare and one by Hector after fifty minutes, but recovered to score twice – first through John Mahoney just before Hennessey's 65th-minute exit on the broad back of Jimmy Gordon, then, three minutes from the end, with a header by Denis Smith from a corner. The Potters' centre-half was left unmarked to deliver that late blow only in the sense that nobody was keeping a close watch on him, for in those days he was the most marked man in football. In sixteen seasons with Stoke he broke a leg five times, his nose four times, an arm twice and had five knee operations. His other breakages included those of his collarbone and fingers, and his body was, as he said himself, 'a patchwork of scars.' Not for nothing was he known as the 'Iron Man'.

Smith scored again in the second leg at the Victoria Ground, this time with a speculative long-range drive, but too late to do more than just equalise a freakish goal by Wignall, from whose shot, partially blocked as full-back Mike Pejic challenged him, the ball looped into the air and flew into the net over the head of the outcoming Gordon Banks.

The first of those two matches with Stoke, played on the evening of Wednesday, 20 October 1971, has a special place in Derby County annals because Steve Powell, at sixteen years and thirty days, became the youngest ever to play in the club's first team. And an astonishingly assured job he made of it, the portent of a commendable career with just the one League club in which he followed his father, Tommy, who was also sixteen when he made his debut for the Rams on the third Christmas Day of the 1939-45 war, to more than 400 games in the County's colours. Between them they played 826 times for the Rams, but hopes of service to the club stretching to the third generation of this Derby family were dashed when Steve's son Stevie was released without getting into the senior eleven.

The most youthful Derby debutants before Steve Powell were Fred Flanders, who played against Birmingham in 1910 at the age of sixteen years and 287 days, and Roy Patrick, introduced at Sunderland in 1952 at sixteen years and 277 days. Powell remained the youngest of all until Boxing Day 2002, when Lee Holmes was sent on as a substitute in a home match with Grimsby Town when fifteen years and 268 days old.

While a pupil at Derby's Bemrose School, which his father had also attended, Steve Powell captained Derby Boys at fourteen, and at the same age gained a place in the Derbyshire Boys side, also as skipper. In the following season he played nine times for England Boys, whom he captained for the first time in the March before his debut for Derby when they drew with Northern Ireland Boys at Wembley. Two years later, with almost thirty League and Cup games behind him, he led England to victory in the international youth tournament in Florence, where they won the trophy for the third successive season by beating East Germany 3-2 in excessive heat with a 'sudden death' goal scored three minutes from the end of extra-time by one of their substitutes, Steve Phillips, a Londoner who was then with Birmingham City and later Northampton Town.

Tony Waiters, the former Blackpool and England goalkeeper who was the manager of that England Youth team, said of Powell: 'He has natural qualities of leadership. Although he is one of the youngest in the squad of 16, he is by far the most experienced. He has had responsibility thrust on him at an early age, but he has responded to it well and is sensible enough to do well at any level.'

Like his father, however, Steve was to get to the fringe of the senior England team, but never into it. The problem in that respect was that the best things came first; later he was caught up in a declining Derby team. And despite making so many appearances in his fourteen seasons with the Rams, a distinct asset in midfield or defence, injuries also had a lot to do with his failing to progress beyond one Under-23 cap gained against Scotland at Aberdeen the week before Christmas in 1974. Back and pelvic troubles, a broken jaw and damaged knee ligaments were the more serious of the misfortunes that blighted his career.

The England Youth team which Powell led to victory also included Alan Lewis, an Oxford lad who, at full-back, first entered Derby County's senior side with Powell in the first leg of that Texaco Cup-tie with Stoke City. Unlike Powell, he played only twice in the Rams' League side, in the 1972-73 season, but, after short spells with Peterborough United, Sheffield Wednesday (both on loan) and Brighton, he was a regular member of the Reading team that would win the Fourth Division championship in 1978-79.

After accounting for Stoke City, Derby County had two more tough tussles with Newcastle United. In the first of them, on a treacherous frozen pitch at the Baseball Ground, they were thankful for O'Hare's skilful control when the centre-forward kept his balance to retrieve a pass from Gemmill that was going behind him and neatly tucked the ball into the corner of Irish international Willie McFaul's net. Newcastle had reason to be well satisfied with only a one-goal deficit, especially as for the last half-hour they were under the handicap of losing their play-maker Tony Green with a stomach upset, and they seemed the better bet for the final when, against a team lacking the injured Gemmill, McFarland and Robson, they led 2-0 after 78 minutes' play back at St James' Park.

Both clubs then resorted to a substitute, and Derby's, Walker for Hinton, brought the aggregate scores level within five minutes, courtesy of some good work by Durban. That forced extra-time, in which McGovern, direct from a corner, and Todd, joining in the attack from his emergency role of full-back, scored the goals that took the Rams to a final against Airdrieonians, conquerors of Manchester City, Huddersfield Town and, in their semi-final, a Ballymena team containing Arthur Stewart. Malcolm ('Super Mac') Macdonald scored Newcastle's first goal and had another shot cleared off the line by Webster just before the extra period, but Bailey, despite having to tread carefully after being booked in the opening minute, otherwise did well against this bow-legged goal-getter who is one of the few to have scored five goals in one match for England (if against Cyprus, not one of the strongest teams in international football).

There was a gap of three months, from 26 January to 26 April, between the two legs of the Texaco Cup final because the return match at the Baseball Ground had to be postponed from its original date due to bad weather. Another young player was brought into the Derby team in each of those games. One, Tony Parry, was to have only six opportunities in the First Division side, two of them as a substitute, before going on loan to Mansfield, but the other, 6ft 3in-tall Roger Davies, totted up more than 150 League and Cup games, including substitutions, in two spells with the Rams. Davies twice hit the headlines with outstanding scoring feats, but more about them in their right sequence.

In the absence of McGovern (and also McFarland, O'Hare and Hector), 26-year-old Parry took the step up to the first leg of the final of what could loosely be called an international competition at Broomfield Park, Airdrie, within a week of being signed for £3,000 from Hartlepool, where he had previously played for Clough and Taylor after starting out with his home club Burton Albion. He later returned to the Burton area in having two spells with Gresley Rovers, whom he captained.

Parry's tackling and running on a heavy surface nobly plugged one of the gaps in a below-strength side against the robust tactics employed by the Scottish club, who put up far stronger resistance than was to be expected from a team at the foot of their First Division. Captained for the first time by Colin Todd, who was shaded out of being the game's best player by the busy Gemmill, the Rams were both relieved and satisfied to come away with a scoreless draw. Four members of their patched-up formation, Butlin, Daniel, Hennessey and Walker, were playing their first match for more than three weeks.

With the second leg of the final coming at a crucial time – between the last two games of the League season and just two days after the Reserves had celebrated their Central League title success – the team that defeated Airdrieonians 2-1 at the Baseball Ground to clinch the trophy also contained five players who were not regular choices. Mind you, as far as fixture congestion was concerned Derby County were not as hard hit as Arsenal and Leeds, for, regardless of strident protests, those rivals to the Rams for the First Division title were both ordered by the Football League to play important First Division games on the Mondays preceding and following their meeting in the FA Cup final. No wonder Don Revie declared himself 'speechless'. And no wonder there were those snide remarks about the championship going to Derby 'by default', though Brian Clough still had good reason to consider them 'an insult'.

Gemmill and O'Hare were out of the return game because they were at Hampden Park playing for Scotland against Peru (O'Hare scored one of their goals in a 2-0 win), and but for injuries Todd and McFarland would have been with the England squad for the following Saturday's game in which West Germany won 3-1 at Wembley. Fortunately for the Rams, all four were available for the vital closing League fixtures. Indeed, excluding the Texaco Cup, Gemmill, Todd and O'Hare each missed only two matches all season, and McFarland just four. Only sixteen players were called up for the whole First Division campaign, and three of them, Bailey, Powell and Walker, mustered only half-a-dozen appearances between them. The fact that a settled side could be fielded so often had a big bearing on the final outcome. Hector, like Boulton, played in all 42 matches; Robson took part in 41.

Derby were deserving winners of the Texaco Cup on their form overall, but, as in the first leg, they had to survive quite a battering at the Baseball Ground, especially up to half-time – so much so that another of my old friends, Derek Hodgson, observed in his *Daily Telegraph* report that 'the Texaco Cup seems to be meeting a long-felt need in Anglo-Scottish relations as a kind of minor substitute for the Border Wars'.

Hodgson also looked knowingly into the future in saying that 'Davies, like most men of his size, will be either a sensation or a laughing stock'. Jolly Roger, who in recent seasons has been back at Pride Park commenting on matches for closed-circuit television, is remembered by many supporters as much for his astounding miss at Chelsea, seen by the millions on the *Match of the Day* programme that evening, as for his major scoring feats. Sent clear by McGovern two minutes from time with the score 1-1, he ran almost the length of the home half and was confronted with an unguarded net after rounding the goalkeeper, but the ball trickled wide off his shin for a goal-kick. In referring to a recent visit by a curvaceous film star, George Edwards said 'it rivalled Raquel Welch as the Miss of the season at Stamford Bridge'. Davies later explained: 'Few people realised I stumbled and the ball bobbled at the same time. It wasn't quite as bad as it looked.'

Given his first senior game before a crowd of more than 25,000 in the second leg of the Texaco final the month after being snapped up from Southern League Worcester City for £12,000, then a record for a player from outside the Football League, Davies marked the occasion with a magnificent header of power and accuracy from Butlin's cross in the 51st minute. That increased a lead gained five minutes before half-time when Hinton blasted a typical penalty just below the bar after Hector had fallen under a challenge by goalkeeper McKenzie, and Hector hit a post before

Whiteford replied in the 78th minute. Even with only one goal separating the teams Derby's superiority was never in doubt, a late flurry of seven corners in five minutes almost making the score more in keeping with the balance of play.

Davies had also scored on his debut for the Rams in a reserve match with West Bromwich Albion at the Baseball Ground, getting the only goal a minute from the end, but it was as a Preston player, while on loan, that he first turned out in the Football League – against Queen's Park Rangers and Burnley, without scoring, in the Second Division early in the 1972-73 season. His first League match for Derby was lost 0-4 to Manchester City at Maine Road several weeks later. He was promptly dropped, and after giving another poor display back in the Reserves he was horrified to find his name was not there when he sought it on the team sheet for the next Central League game. From the despondency he felt in thinking he had been relegated to the third team, he was transformed to the delight of suddenly realising that he should have looked at the first-team list. He was back in the First Division side for a home match with Arsenal.

For Davies that, on 25 November 1972, was the turning point. The Gunners, then managed by Bertie Mee, a pre-war Derby County reserve, were stung into a close examination of their deficiencies after being thrashed 5-0, and Davies, who scored the final goal, broke O'Hare's hold on the No 9 shirt. It remained Arsenal's heaviest defeat of that season until they lost 1-6 on the final day at third-placed Leeds to finish runners-up to Liverpool, three points behind.

In 1971-72, Arsenal came fifth, six points behind Derby's champions, but they ended the Rams' interest in the FA Cup, if only at the third attempt, in the fifth round. After scoring eight goals without reply in dismissing Shrewsbury Town and Notts County from the competition, Clough's men drew with Arsenal at both the Baseball Ground and Highbury, but lost by an only goal in the second replay at Filbert Street.

Derby ended the old year with another chastening visit to Leeds that stung Clough into saying his team were 'not big enough and strong enough to dish it out when it needs to be dished out', but they began the new one, if somewhat tentatively, by keeping in touch with the First Division leaders, the two Manchester clubs and Leeds, with their first defeat of Chelsea since returning to the top sphere. The victory at Southampton and Cup win over Third Division Shrewsbury that followed encouraged belief in Peter Taylor's forecast that Kevin Hector's goals could lift the Rams to the top of the table as the 'King' struck a rich vein of his best form.

The year before, Hector, with John Robson, had gained a place in the Football League team against the Irish League at Norwich, scoring one of their five goals, only because of the withdrawal of other players through injury. This time, with McFarland (Todd came on as substitute), he helped the League to another victory, against the League of Ireland in Dublin. His resurgence was attributed by Brian Clough to tougher refereeing that lessened the battering he took from defenders by giving him more room in which to operate ('the difference has been tremendous,' said the manager), but the predicted England cap was still further away than it should have been – and then ridiculously limited to just a couple of short substitute appearances, one of them of less than two minutes in which he very nearly grabbed the goal that would have earned a place in the World Cup finals. Again, that is something we shall be coming to in more detail later. Clough partly blamed himself for the delay in Hector's international breakthrough. He explained: 'After four seasons we have now admitted that we have been asking Hector to play an unnatural role. It has finally dawned on us that he is not physically equipped to play as an orthodox striker, and we have given him the freedom to move deep and take on defences at speed. Now he has hit peak form.'

Hector scored both the goals that ousted Shrewsbury, and was again on the mark, but outscored by Durban's hat-trick, in the 6-0 eclipse of Notts County, whose defence fell four times in eighteen minutes (Derby banned TV cameras from the tie because the fee of £87.50 was considered too small). It was the first time the Rams had scored so many goals in a Cup-tie since crushing Luton (four for Stamps) and Brighton (three for Carter) on the way to Wembley in 1946. Hector did not score in any of the three fifth-round meetings with Arsenal, but he sent over the perfectly-flighted centre from which Durban forced the first replay inside the last two minutes. That wiped out the lead which future Derby player Charlie George, also the scorer of both Arsenal goals in their home League defeat of the Rams a fortnight earlier, had regained in the eightieth minute after having his first beating of Boulton, five minutes from half-time, nullified by a Hinton penalty awarded when O'Hare was tripped in the area one minute after the interval.

Those home ties with Notts County and Arsenal both attracted a crowd of almost 40,000, and the attendance of more than 63,000 for the replay at Highbury on the following Tuesday was exceptional because it was played in the afternoon, owing to a power crisis that prevented the use of floodlights. So many were crammed in that fifty of them were injured when a crush barrier collapsed. Touts had a field day, collecting £20 for tickets priced at £1. One of Derby's best performances of the season was rewarded with a goalless draw after extra-time. O'Hare might have earned another penalty under a dubious challenge by George Armstrong, but much of the play was in midfield as defences dominated. The partnership between McFarland and Todd was seen at its most impenetrable.

The goal by which the Rams, despite playing the more attractive football, lost the second replay at Leicester would not have materialised but for a blunder. The game was less than five minutes old when McGovern intercepted Arsenal's attempt to break out down their left flank after withstanding fierce opening pressure. I can see him now in my mind's eye as I sat high in the stand behind the Gunners' goal. The obvious next move was a pass forward to the waiting Hinton, but instead the young midfielder elected to try to send the ball back to Boulton. To the anguish of all with Derby County's best interests at heart, it glanced off Todd to the feet of Ray Kennedy, who advanced a few yards in the clear before neatly placing a left-foot shot past the goalkeeper. After that there was the all-too-familiar sight of Arsenal shutting up shop, under the expert organisation of skipper Frank McLintock, for yet another of their 'lucky' 1-0 victories.

Arsenal next disposed of Orient, though again by only one goal, and then were taken to another replay before accounting for Stoke City, but in the Centenary final they succumbed to a lone score by 'Sniffer' Allan Clarke as Leeds United won the trophy for the first time. For Stoke there was the consolation of picking up the League Cup, their first major prize in 109 years of competitive football; for McLintock the disappointment of being on the losing side at Wembley for the sixth time (in two FA Cup finals with Leicester and one with Arsenal, two League Cup finals with Arsenal, and one of his nine appearances for Scotland). McLintock was also a runner-up for the League title with Arsenal in 1972-73, and again with Queen's Park Rangers in 1975-76, but he led the Highbury club to the League and Cup double in 1970-71, when he was Footballer of the Year, and was also in their team when they won the Fairs Cup.

For Derby County, not to coin a phrase, expulsion from the Cup was a blessing in disguise. Aside from the second leg of the Texaco Cup final, in which they did not field a full-strength team anyway, it allowed them to devote their attention to the League, where they won seven of their remaining eleven games, drawing two and losing two. Kevin Hector did not exactly bear out the suggestion that his goals would clinch the title, for he finished third in the club's First Division scoring list with a dozen – behind Hinton (eight penalties in his fifteen) and O'Hare (thirteen) – but the four he contributed during those closing weeks included a winner against Ipswich that kept them in second place behind Manchester City.

One of the defeats on the run-in was the anti-climax of an Easter Monday failure at home to Newcastle just two days after the solitary success that a Derby team managed by Brian Clough gained against the strongest side, with the one exception of the injured Mick Jones, Leeds could field. The other reverse came in the Rams' penultimate match at Maine Road, where Manchester City lost their chance of the championship despite winning 2-0. In completing their programme with 57 points, City knew they were bound to be overtaken, at least on goal-average (goal-difference had yet to become the deciding factor), as a result of Derby's concluding home match with Liverpool on the evening of the Monday's May Day – quite apart from the fact that the Anfield club and Leeds both had two games in hand. In the event, City had to be satisfied with a final fourth place, leaving Malcolm Allison open to criticism for upsetting the balance of the team with the late £200,000 signing of the gifted, but mercurial and individualistic, Rodney Marsh from Queen's Park Rangers.

With Arsenal having dropped out of the title race, undermined by consecutive defeats at the hands of Manchester City, Newcastle and Leeds, Liverpool arrived at the Baseball Ground linked with Leeds as Derby's only remaining challengers. They also turned up with the intimidating record of not having conceded a goal in each of their last six away games – more than 600 minutes of defensive solidarity on their travels since Ally Brown had scored Leicester's winner against them not long before continuing his goal-packed career with West Bromwich Albion.

Just one goal also did the trick for the Rams against the Merseysiders, John McGovern breaking the deadlock with a fine shot midway through the second half. Liverpool, according to manager Shankly, should have had a penalty for a foul on Kevin Keegan – the player a part-time scout named George Pycroft claimed Derby missed by not acting on his tip while the future twice European Footballer of the Year was in the Fourth Division with Scunthorpe United – but the formidable visitors were allowed few chances by a defence in which Steve Powell gave a display far in advance of his tender years as deputy for the injured Webster. In his third appearance in the League side, following the last 22 minutes of a home win over Arsenal and all ninety in the defeat of Forest at Nottingham back in October, this £8-a-week apprentice produced such an assured performance that Shankly, a man whose opinions merited the highest respect, was unstinting in his praise. The cheeky confidence Powell radiated peaked in the memorable moments when he flicked the ball over the head of Emlyn Hughes, then ran round the England player to collect it and coolly pass to a team-mate.

'Why am I considering a 16-year-old for such a vital match?' countered Clough in response to those who questioned the wisdom of it before the match. 'Because he's good enough. That's all you have to worry about. I wouldn't care if he was 14, providing I thought he was ready. I shall have no qualms about putting him in. He's a regular right-back in the Reserves, and he's been playing some superb stuff.'

Derby's victory took them back to the top of the table with 58 points – one ahead of Leeds as well as Manchester City, with Liverpool a further point away. While the Rams were outsmarting Liverpool, Leeds moved into second place on goal-average by beating Chelsea at Elland Road in the first of their three games (one of them the Cup final) in eight days. The Yorkshire club, who had begun the season under the handicap of having to play their first four home games on neutral grounds because of crowd trouble at Elland Road, were then 7-2 favourites for the title, with Derby at 9-2 and Liverpool 8-1. In the *Daily Express*, Alan Thompson said that Liverpool's chances hung on 'a thread so gossamer thin that only the blindly faithful can believe it is still there', and Derby had 'even less hope of finishing champions'. And so it seemed to the great majority, yet how wrong we were all proved to be. This was the situation after the May Day games:

	P	W	D	L	F	A	Pts
DERBY	42	24	10	8	69	33	58
Leeds	41	24	9	8	72	29	57
Manchester C	42	23	11	8	77	45	57
Liverpool	41	24	8	9	64	30	56

Those figures meant that on the following Monday, two days after playing at Wembley, Leeds needed only one point from their away match with Wolves to make sure of becoming champions because of their superior goal-average, and that Liverpool required Leeds to lose that evening while they themselves collected both points from Arsenal at Highbury in order to overtake Derby on goal-average. The ideal scenario for Liverpool was for Arsenal to beat Leeds in the Cup final, thus making deflated United more vulnerable at Molineux, besides wrecking their bid for the double, and for the Highbury club's resulting victory celebrations to leave them less efficient on the League's last day.

Meanwhile, Clough and his men were not staying to await the outcome. The manager went off to the Scilly Isles for a holiday with his family and Peter Taylor took the players away for a ten-day break in Majorca. Clough left saying he was 'over the moon, delighted with the victory [over Liverpool] and the whole season', but not expecting to see his team carry off the title for the first time in the club's history.

That possibility seemed even more remote when Leeds, though newly deprived by a broken leg of their regular left-back, Terry Cooper, landed the first half of the double with their win at Wembley, but the elation of that long-awaited triumph was diluted by the loss also of Mick Jones for their vital match at Molineux – plus the fact that the centre-forward's strike partner Allan Clarke and midfield general Johnny Giles were able to play there only after having pain-killing injections for groin strains. Jones, who had become Leeds' first £100,000 player when sold by Sheffield United, dislocated an elbow in the last minute of the Cup final and was led up to the Royal Box with his arm in a sling to receive his medal from the Queen.

Manager Don Revie said that Clarke and Giles had 'soldiered on bravely and unselfishly for many weeks' with injuries for which the only genuine cure was rest. It was therefore no surprise when, after Leeds had been controversially beaten 1-2 by Wolves, Clarke withdrew from the England squad for the return European Championship clash with West Germany in Berlin, where Alf Ramsey was criticised for selecting a defensive 4-4-2 formation as his team failed, in a 0-0 draw, to wipe out a 1-3 deficit incurred at Wembley.

The defeat that condemned Leeds to being League runners-up for the third successive year, and meant that the double had narrowly eluded them for the third time in seven years, was especially galling for them to bear because they claimed they should have had two penalties for handling offences by full-back Bernard Shaw in the 23rd and 51st minutes. Donald Saunders reported in the *Daily Telegraph* that on the first occasion 'Shaw quite clearly beat the ball down with both hands', and although referee John Gow was unsighted it was amazing that the nearest linesman did not spot the infringement. Manager Don Revie also thought his team ought to have been awarded another penalty 'when Clarke was flattened in the box'. As it was, a late shot by skipper Billy Bremner was the only reply they could muster to goals by Frank Munro and Derek Dougan – largely due to an inspired display by Phil Parkes, at 6ft 2in one of the tallest goalkeepers ever to play for Wolves.

The other result essential to Derby's retention of top place came when Roger Kirkpatrick's ruling-out of an 88th-minute 'goal' by Liverpool's John Toshack ensured a scoreless draw at Highbury. Bill Shankly, not unexpectedly, did not agree with that decision, but it was generally accepted that the Welsh international was clearly offside when he touched in a pass from Emlyn Hughes. For the watching Sam Longson it was the end of 'a terrible week in which I've died a thousand deaths'.

The holidaying Brian Clough, who had told his chairman he was convinced the title would go to Liverpool, was kept in touch with what was happening in the closing stages by telephone, and, with Leeds so distressingly thwarted, he was hardly overstating it when he said: 'It is incredible. I do not believe in miracles, but one has occurred tonight. I heard they played 4½ minutes of injury time at Molineux. It seemed like 4½ years to me. There is nothing I can say to sum up how I feel, although I suppose we could have won the Cup as well. For a team and a town like Derby to win this title is a credit to all concerned.'

John O'Hare's wife Valerie professed not to be surprised by the outcome. 'Alan Hinton and a few of the other lads laughed at me,' she said, 'when I told them I had dreamed we would lose to Manchester City, beat Liverpool, and still win the title.'

Leeds had responded superbly to their early-season exile by dropping only two points from their remaining seventeen home games, and would surely have emerged champions with better away form. Disappointed as he was, Revie said that 'all of us at Leeds are pleased that Derby have won the title. They are a very fine side, and I had the foresight to tip them at the start of the season.' Shankly also paid tribute to the Rams, conceding that 'the best team we have played this season has won the League'.

For Brian Clough, the reward was revealed the following November when Derby County's balance sheet for the year ending 31 July showed that one member of the club's staff, presumably the manager, earned between £20,000 and £22,500 in the championship season. Another earned more than £15,000 and five others upwards of £10,000.

With only £23,000 spent on transfers during that period, the club made a profit of more than £27,000, boosted to more than £87,000 by a donation from Derby County Promotions. This compared with a loss of £624 the previous year. How glowing those accounts look when set against the desperate financial situations into which the Rams have since floundered.

Twist in the Tale of Two Moores

Brian Clough twice wanted Moore, but, like little Oliver Twist, he had to stay wanting.

Ian Storey-Moore – to give him his full name, though he was generally known simply as Ian Moore – cost Derby County £5,000 for a breach of the Football League's regulations instead of the £225,000 for which Clough claimed he had signed him from Nottingham Forest early in March, 1972. Robert Frederick Moore, captain of England's 1966 World Cup winners, was not averse to the idea of joining the Rams when Clough 'tapped' him in the summer of 1973, but Ron Greenwood, his manager at West Ham, definitely was.

Ipswich-born Ian Moore had an impressive strike rate for a player who was primarily a wing forward, but illness, injury and Alf Ramsey's reluctance to have wingers in his England teams combined to curb his international appearances. He was carried off injured from his second and last Under-23 game, then broke a leg in a League match with Leicester, damaged leg ligaments in a scoring comeback at Coventry, and had to pull out of England's squad for the 1970 World Cup finals in Mexico with more ligament trouble after winning what was to be his only full cap, against Holland at Wembley.

That game with the Dutch was goalless, yet Moore might have had a hat-trick. He had two shots cleared off the line, and when he did get the ball in the net a team-mate was ruled offside. With Forest, for all his fitness problems, he was top scorer in all but one (when he was second) of his six seasons as a first-team regular after having been turned down by Blackpool for being considered too small. And in the season he left the City Ground his thirteen goals remained almost double the number obtained by Forest's next highest scorer. He altogether totalled 118 in just over 270 first-team games for the club, and that was good enough to offset any worries about his susceptibility to injury among the managers who were hot on his trail once word got around that he was unsettled.

Moore signed a new four-year contract with Forest at the start of the 1971-72 season, but sought to escape from it in the January when the crisis of a relegation battle in which they were immersed was intensified by an immediate FA Cup exit at Millwall. 'Everything is dead for me now,' he said. 'In three years' time I'll be 30, and past the point where clubs would be willing to pay a big fee for me.' Forest at first insisted that he must stay to help them try to preserve their First Division status, and Cliff Lloyd, secretary of the Professional Footballers' Association, had repeatedly said that his members were expected to honour their contracts. Nevertheless, Moore was so desperate to get away that within a few weeks Forest were compelled to accept they could no longer hang on to him, and manager Matt Gillies was authorised to invite offers. Manchester City were willing to pay about £120,000, plus one of their reserve players, or even two, when they made an inquiry, but their interest cooled as the fee required rose to the region of £200,000 after Forest had got nowhere with trying to arrange a part-exchange deal. Malcolm Allison, the Maine Road club's manager, considered it too high for a 27-year-old.

That left Wolves and Everton at the head of the queue. Wolves' manager, the former England wing-half Bill McGarry, a long-time admirer of Moore, was first in with his bid, only to find it insufficient. Everton, who had recently received a record £220,000 from Arsenal for Alan Ball, were in urgent need of a new big name to stimulate both their team and supporters after a Cup defeat by Tottenham had left them with the only aim that season of seeing how far they could finish off the foot of the First Division. At that point, however, Manchester United entered the reckoning. Until then the Old Trafford club had gone so far as to express disinterest, and their sudden emergence from their smokescreen was quite a surprise considering that they had just spent £125,000 on Martin Buchan, the young Aberdeen captain, and could not field Moore in that season's FA Cup, the only competition in which they then still had a chance of some silverware (they later lost to Stoke in a replayed quarter-final) after a run of poor results in the League and defeat in the League Cup.

Everton, given first refusal, were not prepared to indulge in an auction after having their bid of £170,000 rejected. United's manager, Frank O'Farrell, also publicly ruled himself out of the race, describing the price demanded by Forest as 'unrealistic,' yet within 24 hours he slipped quietly away from Manchester instead of travelling with his team for their next day's match at Tottenham and entered into secret talks with Matt Gillies and the player at the Edwalton Hotel in West Bridgford.

Moore was upset because it was from the radio that he first heard he was being put up for sale. 'It's amazing that I had to hear of it this way,' he said, 'after ten years' loyal service to the club. Even in the next 48 hours nobody from the club phoned to tell me personally.' He had not discussed his future with Gillies for six weeks until he received a phone call to tell him that the hush-hush rendezvous had been arranged with O'Farrell. He likened it to a 'James Bond existence' on being told to switch to a green Aston Martin car to shake off any pursuers after driving into Nottingham in his own car. The cloak and dagger aspect of it all was heightened when he learned that the venue for the meeting had already been changed twice.

Forest saw the need for such subterfuge because by then the plot had also thickened with the intervention of Derby County, even though Brian Clough had been suggesting he could no longer afford to compete for top-price players unless the fans turned up in greater numbers. Forest were soon to make it abundantly clear that the Rams were the last club they wanted Moore to join, not that this was much of a revelation. The fact that Henry Newton had moved to Everton instead of Derby had already made their attitude clear enough. After having seen Hinton, Hennessey and Wignall (via Wolves) find their way to the Baseball Ground, they were dead against another of their stars reaching the same destination – and taking with him a good chunk of the support that floated in the short distance between the two clubs. That was accentuated in Moore's case because Forest were then sliding towards the Second Division whereas Derby were heading for the top of the First.

Earlier in the day – Friday, 3 March 1972 – of Moore's clandestine get-together with Manchester United's manager, Brian Clough rang Matt Gillies to put in a firm bid for the winger, but was informed that Forest first preferred Frank O'Farrell to see the player at a place they were not willing to divulge. They were obviously hoping to reach some agreement with United before Derby could make a direct approach.

Moore was joined by Gillies and Ken Smales, the Forest secretary, soon after arriving at the Edwalton Hotel. O'Farrell turned up a few minutes later, and had a private talk of some twenty minutes with the player. The transfer fee he was willing to pay was acceptable to Forest, but Moore asked for more time to consider the personal terms after having learned that Derby had also made a bid. Naturally enough, he wanted to hear what they had got to say too. He therefore phoned Clough to tell him where he was, and that he would like to have discussions there with him. When O'Farrell heard of this he left in a huff to continue his journey to London, angered by the new development, but under the impression that his negotiations were interrupted, not abandoned. On his arrival in the capital he was briefly to fear he had been beaten to the deal before being reassured that he was still the frontrunner.

Significantly, Gillies and Smales had also departed by the time, about half-an-hour later, that Clough and Peter Taylor arrived at the hotel in a white Mercedes to find Moore on his own. Clough was at his persuasive best. It did not take him long to impress Moore with talk of Derby's tremendous potential and the exceptional quality of the players with whom he would be teaming up. There was an even more compelling reason why what the Rams' manager had to say was more attractive than O'Farrell's overtures. In addition to matching United's offer to Forest, he topped the terms the Old Trafford club had promised the player.

So, after careful consideration, Moore rang Gillies, who was back at Forest's ground, to ask him to inform O'Farrell that he had decided to choose Derby. 'I fully expected to sign for Manchester United early in the evening,' he said, 'but then Derby stepped in and Brian Clough's offer was too good to turn down.' He signed transfer forms which Clough took to Nottingham to have them counter-signed by Forest's secretary, while Moore went with Taylor to the Midland Hotel in Derby, where the Rams' players were staying before the next day's home match with Wolves. That was where everything started to go wrong as far as Derby County were concerned. Smales's signature was not forthcoming – nor would it be, by order of the Forest's committee.

In their approach to Moore the Rams had done everything by the book, but they had now made their first mistake by as good as kidnapping him while he was still not their legally signed player. They made another, and an even more serious one, by introducing him on the pitch as their new signing before the game against Wolves that he watched from the directors' box. Clough went further, saying that Moore would make his debut for Derby in the second leg of their Texaco Cup final against Airdrieonians on the following Wednesday night (though he would not have played on that occasion in any case because the match had to be postponed when two days' heavy rain left the notorious Baseball Ground pitch deep in mud). Smales was to denounce it all as a gimmick, 'a bit naughty to parade a player knowing that the transfer would not go through.' It also grossly misled the fans who besieged the club's offices to cause a run on tickets for the Scottish club's visit. Neither was Alan Hardaker, secretary of the Football League, best pleased. 'We will say when Moore makes his debut for his new club,' he growled.

Stuart Webb, who had put his required signature to the transfer forms in his capacity as the County's secretary and kept the League informed of what was going on, was quoted as saying: 'We have been in touch with our chairman, Mr Sam Longson, who has been in London at the League Cup final. He has discussed the matter of Ian Moore's transfer with the chairman of Nottingham Forest, Mr Jack Levey, and they have come to an agreement over the payment of the fee. It does seem that things are now to be settled, and Mr Levey assures us that it will all be finally resolved on Monday when the Forest committee meet.'

And so it was, but entirely to Derby County's discomfiture. Far from forcing Forest's hand, the bold but misguided bluff served only to strengthen it – in favour of Manchester United. Levey promptly made it clear that his talks with the worried Longson had not resolved the situation, and that he had also spoken to the United chairman, Louis Edwards, before reporting back to his eight colleagues on the committee that then ran the club in those days before it became a limited company. In the meantime, O'Farrell had been told by Tony Wood, the Forest vice-chairman, that Derby had not completed the deal, and Ken Smales had emphasised that there was 'no point in Derby contacting us, or sending transfer forms, because we are not prepared to sign them'.

At their emergency meeting on the Monday, which Gillies and Smales also attended, the Forest committee gave O'Farrell the go-ahead to carry on with the negotiations Clough had so sensationally disrupted. Derby had by then made their third mistake of keeping Moore with them in training when Gillies had demanded his return to the City Ground, but a phone call from his wife Carol summoned him back to their home in the Nottinghamshire village of Bingham. Shortly afterwards, the United manager turned up on their doorstep accompanied by Sir Matt Busby, the club's former manager who was then one of their directors. They confirmed to Moore that Forest would give their approval if he signed for United, so, after talks lasting two hours, the deal was done, the forms correctly signed by Moore, Smales and United's secretary, Les Olive. The fee of £225,000 included the ten per cent levy – half of which went to the League and the remainder to Moore, since he had not specifically asked for a move.

The part played by Carol Moore, a demonstrator with a cosmetics firm, produced headlines such as: HOW I MADE IAN SIGN FOR UNITED and MOORE CHANGES HIS MIND ON HIS WIFE'S ORDERS.

Disappointed when he acted without consulting her in deciding on Derby, she undoubtedly had much to do with his altered outlook, and he afterwards conceded that 'I have a lot to thank my wife for; she has given me a lot of advice at the right time'. There was, however, an over-riding influence on his thinking. During the weekend he had come to realise that Forest would not contemplate his move to Derby, and in an interview with Frank Butler in the *News of the World* he admitted:

'With only 48 hours remaining to the transfer deadline I panicked at the thought of facing the next season in the Second Division. I could protest until I was blue in the face, but unless Forest released me I was stuck, and Brian Clough was as dumbfounded as myself by Forest's attitude. Then along came Sir Matt Busby with Frank O'Farrell to my house to assure me that Forest would give their immediate permission if I signed for Manchester United. Just think of it. Sir Matt Busby in my own front room persuading me to play for United. I felt I had no option. The Derby deal was doomed anyway.'

Moore maintained that he had really wanted to join the Rams, but from telling the Baseball Ground crowd that he was 'looking forward to playing for Derby County for many years to come', he unexpectedly, but diplomatically, revealed after going to Old Trafford that 'at the bottom of my heart I have always wanted to join United – my dream has come true'. At least he had the grace to confess that 'it might seem strange to say this'.

The difficult situation in which he had found himself should have spared him the rough reception he was given when he returned to Derby for the first time as a United player the following Boxing Day. He had expected some abuse, but not to the extent of the storm of anger that greeted him. He said 'it was as if Judas had taken to the field'. Tommy Docherty, who only four days before had left the Scotland's team manager's job to follow O'Farrell as the Manchester club's manager, told Moore to 'go out there and prove that Brian Clough was right to try to sign you', and this strong, direct winger did just that after being stung into some of his best form by the boos, shaken fists and clearly heard four-letter words directed at him practically every time he touched the ball. He looked back upon it as the worst treatment he had ever heard handed out to any player. United lost, but their only goal was scored by Moore, who could not resist giving his tormentors what he called 'a footballer's Churchillian gesture' as the ball hit the net.

Forest's fans also expressed themselves most forcibly over the Moore transfer. Mounted police dispersed an angry crowd after a home defeat by Ipswich in the club's first match after his departure, and cushions were thrown at members of the committee as they left the stand. Nor were tempers eased as none of the money received from Manchester United was used in an attempt to strengthen an ailing team before the transfer deadline, leading to relegation after fifteen unbroken seasons back in the First Division.

There was an unhappy sequel all round. Gillies, in the wake of relegation, resigned from his post even more quickly than O'Farrell was sacked from his; Clough, whose telegram of protest to the League was of no avail, not only missed a player he badly wanted but also gave Longson something more to complain about by jumping in for him without prior consultation while the chairman was again out of town; Derby County fell foul of the Football League; and Manchester United and Moore fared badly out of the deal because he played only 43 games for them, scoring a dozen goals, before injury forced him out of top-class football.

Fearing that their reputation for fair dealing might be impugned, Forest asked for an investigation into the Moore transfer squabble. It resulted in this announcement by the League on the first day of August 1972:

'The committee considered the evidence, verbal and written, from Nottingham Forest, Derby, Moore and Mr Hardaker. It transpires that although the player had signed a transfer form for Derby it was never signed by Forest. The player could not remember signing a contract for Derby, and it was admitted that Mr Hardaker had told the Derby secretary that until the transfer form was completed by Nottingham Forest the player was not registered by Derby. The committee was satisfied that by taking the player to Derby and announcing publicly that he was their player whilst he was still registered with Nottingham, Derby had committed a breach of League regulation 52 (A). It was felt that this was a very serious offence which strikes at the foundations of the Football League regulations about the registration and transfer of players. Because a club is responsible for the actions of its officials a fine of £5,000 was imposed.'

This latest punishment for the Rams was accompanied by a warning about the manner in which they carried out any future transfers. The letter conveying it reached the Baseball Ground while most of the club's players and officials were away on a tour of the Netherlands and West Germany. Brian Clough and the assistant secretary, John Howarth, had stayed behind, but both refused to comment.

Injury ended Moore's career at the top level after he had played in just two League matches during the 1973-74 season in which Manchester United dropped out of the First Division. He was therefore denied the chance to share in their immediate return, so had the sad experience of bowing out with a relegated club after a change of mind had cost him the opportunity to win a championship medal and take part in a run to the semi-finals of the European Cup.

In 1975 he made a comeback in the Southern League with a Burton Albion team that reached the last four of the FA Challenge Trophy before losing over two legs to Matlock Town, who convincingly defeated Scarborough at Wembley. For a while he entertained hopes of getting back into the Football League ('my ankle has stood the test and I've retained my speed'), but those dreams were dispelled by a League official who said it was virtually impossible for a player in Moore's position to be registered in the League again. A club might have been prepared to refund the £20,000 compensation he had received from Manchester United, but not the £200,000 insurance awarded to the Old Trafford club.

Moore also played for, and managed, Shepshed Charterhouse, besides having a few games for Chicago Sting in the North American League, and also touring in South Africa, before becoming a turf accountant and contributing to radio programmes in the Nottingham area. He also turned full circle by rejoining Nottingham Forest as chief scout.

Brian Clough's attempt to sign the other Moore came when the West Ham and England captain was nearing the end of an illustrious international career in which he became only the third player, after Billy Wright and Bobby Charlton, to reach a century of appearances for England. His total of 108 has since been exceeded only by Peter Shilton.

In his autobiography, Ron Greenwood recalled that Clough walked into his office and said that he wanted to sign Bobby Moore and Trevor Brooking. This was how the ensuing conversation went according to the then West Ham manager:

'You can't be serious,' I replied. 'Every man's got his price,' he insisted. I told him there was no point going on because neither was for sale. 'Well, if I can't have Moore can I have Brooking? And if I can't have Brooking can I have Moore?' Clough continued. 'They're not available, Brian,' I said, 'but I'll pass your offer on to my board.'

There were no raised eyebrows when the offer for Moore was speedily refused by West Ham's directors, and no business was again done by Derby a few months later when a showdown between Moore and his manager did appear likely to lead to a transfer. The Rams, indeed, were reported to be favourites to sign him at that time, but Clough, after having visualised Moore as another Mackay, was no longer quite so enthusiastic about it. He said he could understand the frustration of a player who, at 32, had probably only a couple of seasons left and wanted a change because West Ham had made a poor start to the new season ('any player worth his salt would want to get out of a side like that'), but he added that if Moore went on the list it would be a question of making some reassessment to see if he could be fitted into Derby's formation.

But Moore did not go on the list. He had not asked for a transfer, and when West Ham announced that he would be staying they also suggested that newspaper speculation had manoeuvred the player, manager and club into a difficult situation. No blame was attached to Moore, but he did not last out that 1973-74 season with West Ham. He lost his first-team place after his 642nd senior game for the club, a drawn home FA Cup-tie with Third Division Hereford (who won the replay), and last played for them in the obscurity of a reserve match with Plymouth.

In the last few hours before the deadline for unrestricted transfers in March 1974, off Bobby Moore OBE went to Fulham, at a fee of £25,000, for a reunion with a former England colleague, Alan Mullery MBE, and a final appearance at the Wembley stadium where he had been the first captain to lift a trophy in three consecutive years (the FA Cup in 1964, when he was Footballer of the Year; the European Cup-Winners' Cup in 1965; the World Cup in 1966). In 1975 he was back there with Fulham for another FA Cup final – against (who else?) West Ham, winners with a couple of goals from Alan Taylor, a new arrival from Rochdale who had also scored twice at the quarter-final and semi-final stages.

Moore had almost 800 League and Cup appearances behind him when he retired on the completion of his contract at the end of the 1976-77 season in which he helped Fulham to stave off relegation from the Second

Division. He then turned out for San Antonio and Seattle in North America before returning the England to find, amazingly, that there were no ready openings for his potential for coaching. He applied unsuccessfully for several jobs – including, after being persuaded by friends, the England managership vacated by Don Revie – before having a spell as player-coach with Herning, a Third Division club in Denmark.

In addition to several business ventures, he next took part-time footballing posts with Oxford City of the Isthmian League, the fourth team of Crystal Palace, and in Hong Kong. After that came what he correctly predicted 'could be my last chance to break back into the game' with his appointment as chief executive of Southend United, the club in his home county of Essex he also served as manager and director up to 1986, when he left to become Sports Editor of *Sunday Sport* and match analyser for Capital Gold Radio. He also worked on sports promotion projects in the United States.

On 14 February 1993, he revealed for the first time his fight against cancer, and ten days later he died at the early age of 51. Conscientious as ever, he had taken up his commentary position for the London radio station at England's World Cup qualifier against San Marino at Wembley only a week earlier, and, although his gaunt appearance showed how ill he was, it was only because he felt he would be mobbed by well-wishers that he abandoned plans to attend the top-of-the-table match between West Ham and Newcastle on the Sunday before his death.

Contract Distractions After Record Transfer

Twelve days into the 1972-73 season, Brian Clough bounced back from his failure to sign Ian Storey-Moore by forking out £250,000, a British record fee for a defender, to bring in the cultured David Nish from Leicester City. The basic figure was £225,000, plus the League levy and player's share.

Long and loud were the howls of incredulity that so much should be spent for a full-back, especially for one who was not yet a full international. There had been a similar outcry when £170,000 had been lashed out on Colin Todd, but his value had considerably increased since then, and the same would soon apply to this latest newcomer as he smoothly made it clear that Derby's manager had picked up yet another bargain.

After all, forecasts of doom for those who made expensive (for the time) forays into the transfer market had been bandied about ever since a forlorn attempt had been made to limit the size of fees to what were considered the astronomical heights of £350 early in the twentieth century. And even before the floodgates were opened by the abandonment of the maximum wage in 1961 money had continued to flow through the game's coffers after the Rams had twice raised the record in the 1940s – to £15,500 for Billy Steel, then to £24,500 for Johnny Morris. What those decriers of days long gone would think of the current deals done in millions does not bear thinking about.

One thing, though, is certain – unless, perhaps, a Russian benefactor suddenly appears on the horizon. Derby County will never again be setting new transfer targets. And, in view of the obscene heights to which fees and salaries have soared, a good thing too.

Back in 1972, however, the Rams were the champions, and nothing less was expected of them than to add a player of Nish's quality to the awesome array of talent with which Brian Clough and Peter Taylor had put the buzz back into the Baseball Ground. Here was one of soccer's rarities – a defender with polish and style, fit to rank high on the list of Derby County full-backs that included other such cool and dependable players as Jimmy Methven, Charlie Morris, Tommy Cooper, Jack Howe and Bert Mozley, to name but a few.

Only a few weeks before signing Nish, Brian Clough described as 'absolute rubbish' talk of a rift with Sam Longson, yet, incredible as it may seem considering how much of Derby's cash was involved, he upset his chairman yet again by going behind his back to negotiate the deal. Longson bemoaned the fact that 'the close consultation that had existed in the early years has disappeared completely', but he still had so much respect for the manager that he was 'prepared to swallow as best I could the irritations that were cropping up'.

Len Shipman, the Leicester chairman who, as president of the Football League, had presented the Rams with the First Division trophy, was also put out by Clough's tactics. He had to ask him to wait outside after this brash young man had burst into the City's boardroom during a meeting saying that he had come to buy their full-back.

The row with Longson which Clough denied was said to have resulted from the manager's withdrawal from the club's Continental tour. The reason he stayed behind, said Clough, was that he wanted to be available for any signings. He believed in pre-season tours, and he had arranged this one. 'I didn't want to miss it, but I make the signings and pick the team here, and if there's work to be done this is the place I should be.' Clough was also miffed because he could not take his sons Simon and Nigel on tour.

On the eve of the 1972-73 season, Clough forecast that seven clubs had about an equal chance of winning the title, but in his opinion Derby, defending it, were the only ones yet to reach their peak. A cloud was cast over the Rams, however, when they were ordered by the FA to post warning notices for three weeks because of crowd disturbances at the end of the previous season, and this deepened as they lost half of their first sixteen League games. During a slump on their First Division travels they were kept afloat, if in the lower half of the table, by six consecutive wins at home, though all by only a one-goal margin.

It was around this time that Clough said 'nobody will get me out of Derby's front door now unless they shoot me', yet with the season almost three months old he had still not signed the new contract offered to him. Differences had arisen over clauses that would have prevented him saying and writing what he liked, and fresh doubts about his future at Derby had developed from the linking of his name with Aston Villa, where a battle was going on for boardroom power. There were even suggestions of something that was to become a reality a year later – the return in his place of Dave Mackay, who was then player-manager at Swindon.

The team's lack of consistency during this period was due in no small measure to the fact that Clough and Taylor were distracted from their running of it by the protracted negotiations for their new contracts. Clough, hitherto a constant exhorter of his men on the training ground, was no longer to be seen regularly supervising their preparations. There was perhaps some excuse for a 0-4 defeat by Manchester City at Maine Road because Gemmill, Hector and O'Hare were rested with European action in Portugal a few days later in mind, but a 0-3 beating by Manchester United and a 0-5 thrashing by their jinx side at Leeds were especially hard to take.

In the *Derby Evening Telegraph*, Gerald Mortimer put everything sharply in perspective when, in the aftermath of what he called 'the shambles at Old Trafford', he wrote:

'I went to see Mr Clough and Mr Taylor three times last week. On each occasion it was almost impossible to turn the conversation to that of football. They were preoccupied with their position within the club. Two-thirds of the way through last season the situation was similar. At that time the *Telegraph* appealed to the board and management to concentrate on football, and the club, astonished that anybody should have the temerity to criticise them, lashed out clumsily. We were "rocking the boat". I have news for Derby County. The average fan knows now that the boat is lying very low in the water, weighed down by jealousy and the sort of pettiness which is old hat at prep school. It is time Brian Clough and Peter Taylor closed their minds to this sort of thing instead of joining battle. It is time Mr Clough concentrated on being manager and Mr Longson let him get on with it. The players, without any doubt, are being affected by the off-the-field disputes.'

While this crisis behind the Baseball Ground scenes was going on, another disturbing influence arose. An article in the *Sunday People* alleged that several Wolverhampton players were offered bribes to 'throw' the championship decider against Leeds at the end of the previous season. Percy Woodward, the Leeds chairman at the time, said his club had nothing to do with any attempts to 'buy' the game, and manager Don Revie stated that there was no need to speak to his players on the matter because they had nothing to hide. Nevertheless, an investigation was ordered when Bernard Shaw, the Wolves right-back, revealed that an approach had been made to him to 'sell the match', but he had spurned it. In view of the seriousness of the allegations, the Football Association sent all the statements they and the *Sunday People* had obtained to the Director of Public Prosecutions. All this was bound to arouse much concern at Derby because it threatened to detract from the merit of the Rams' title win, but after weeks of uncertainty nothing was found to justify proceeding.

That was also the case when new allegations of 'fixing' in that match were made in a *Daily Mirror* article some five years later. It was claimed that a former Wolves and Leeds player had acted as middle-man in an unsuccessful attempt to guarantee Leeds at least the point they had needed, but Alan Hardaker, the League secretary, said the only thing new to him was the name of the supposed go-between, which was not divulged publicly. Don Revie, who by then had left Leeds and was working in Dubai, and Billy Bremner, the Leeds captain, were also accused in the *Mirror* and *Sunday People* of trying to affect the results of other matches, but, although the names of several witnesses were published, both men vigorously denied all the allegations and an FA inquiry again led to no further action being taken.

Terms for Brian Clough's new contract were eventually settled two months after his bold venture back into the transfer market for David Nish, following a further delay due to Sam Longson's absence on holiday. Billy Wright, the former Wolves and England captain, arranged, as head of sport in commercial television, for Clough and Peter Taylor to sign their new five-year contracts in the middle of the Baseball Ground pitch during ITV's lunchtime soccer progamme *On the Ball* on the last Saturday of October, but the plan was in danger of misfiring because some 200 Sheffield United fans who had gathered early for that afternoon's match would not keep quiet.

As Wright said, however, 'it was the personality of Brian that saved the show.' Clough told the television engineers: 'I didn't think this lot would be in already. I'd better go and see what I can do.' So he vaulted over the barriers, stood among the rowdy visitors, and asked them for silence. The response was immediate and complete. A hush settled over the ground as the contracts were signed and Clough was interviewed. Then he stood up, thanked the Sheffield supporters, and was given a cheer to rival any that his players earned in going on to gain a 2-1 victory, despite the usually reliable Alan Hinton's two failures from the penalty spot to which reference was made in an earlier chapter. It could therefore be said that the man who had refused to sign his Derby contract until the removal of a clause curbing his comments on football, in the press and on television, scored another triumph by 'gagging' other people, although his expression of those often inflammatory views was ultimately to be a crucial factor in preventing him from seeing out that contract.

There was one topic, though, on which Brian Clough spoke out with particular justification. Guest speaker at a sportswriters' lunch, he roundly condemned the two-year international ban that had been placed on Colin Todd for pulling out of the England Under-23 squad's tour of East Germany, Poland and the Soviet Union in June, 1972. With his customary bluntness, he declared:

'Toddy has been banned because he isn't a cheat. He told me he did not want to play for the Under-23s well before the squad was due to leave. He told Sir Alf Ramsey personally four times, and sent a letter explaining why. If he had come to me and asked for a medical certificate I could have got on the phone to the club doctor and got him one in 15 seconds. Damaged ankle ligaments! He didn't do that because he is honest. And there are enough cheats in this game without me turning Toddy into one.'

Todd, whose full debut for England at Wembley the previous month had unfortunately coincided with their first defeat by Northern Ireland for nearly fifteen years, asked to be left out of the tour because he was tired after a strenuous domestic season. Alan Hudson, the Chelsea midfielder whose other clubs included Arsenal and Stoke, also declined to go, citing domestic reasons (he finished decorating his new house), and a two-year ban was imposed on him too. Denis Follows, the FA secretary, said there was no question of an appeal 'because the players have not been charged, as they might have been – they have just been told they are not wanted by England for two years'. The ban was confirmed the following April, but lifted at the beginning of July, by which time Todd had written to apologise and Derby County had asked for his case to be reconsidered. Follows said the International Committee felt that the lesson had been learned generally. Of the 36 players chosen for England teams that summer only one had not accepted – and he had mumps.

Todd heard that he was no longer banned while on holiday in Malta with his wife Jennifer, their two-year-old son Colin junior, and Roy McFarland and his fiancée, Linda. He and Hudson were therefore available for the Wembley matches with Austria, Poland (a vital World Cup qualifier) and Italy that autumn, yet neither played in any of them. Todd, though in squads in the meantime, had to wait for his recall until the following April, against Portugal in Lisbon. Without the ban, he might well have become the player most often chosen for England while with Derby – surpassing McFarland, whose chance of retaining that record was so undermined by injuries, and Peter Shilton, the current holder of it – instead of being limited to 27 appearances in full internationals, all with the Rams, after fourteen with the Under-23s. As for Hudson, well, just a couple of senior caps (in successive games against West Germany and Cyprus at Wembley in 1975) to go with his ten at Under-23 level were a most undeserved reward for a player of such undoubted skill.

Todd's punishment, however, did not leave McFarland without a Derby County companion when Sir Alf Ramsey named a squad of 22 for a friendly match with Yugoslavia at Wembley on 11 October 1972. The inclusion of David Nish brought back memories of the swift advance to the national ranks that Jack Lee had made after leaving Leicester for the Rams 22 years before, but whereas Lee had played (his only cap despite scoring in a 4-1 win in Belfast), Nish had to wait until the following May before getting into the England team – also against Northern Ireland, at Goodison Park – despite again being in the squad in the interim.

Even then, he would not have had that chance but for the postponement until two days before the game with the Irish of the first leg of Liverpool's UEFA Cup final against Borussia Moenchengladbach. He was called back from Derby County's holiday break in Majorca to take over from Emlyn Hughes, the Anfield club's captain, and made his England debut along with John Richards, the Wolves striker who later had a spell with Derby County on loan. Richards was another late addition to the squad in the absence of Leeds United's Allan Clarke through injury. England won (by 2-1) – and so did Liverpool, by 3-0 in the home leg and 3-2 on aggregate.

When Nish was first the member of an England squad, for the visit of the Yugoslavs in the autumn of 1972, McFarland also did not get to play. He became the tenth withdrawal from the original selection when he injured a leg in a League Cup replay Derby lost at Chelsea two days before the international match. Nish was unlucky not to be among the four newcomers in the side that drew 1-1 with a goal from Joe Royle.

That was just one of the occasions when injury denied McFarland international honours and thus prevented him from becoming the Derby player to make the most appearances for England. Alf Ramsey complained about so frequently finding him unavailable, and McFarland felt no less frustrated in saying that 'things were against me' before he eventually won his first full cap on what was termed a 'gravel strip' in Malta. In the *Daily Mail* he told Brian James: 'The Under-23 squad is supposed to be the way up, isn't it? But for every game I actually played for Young England [five] I missed at least one more. Little things just kept cropping up – silly little injuries that got better a day or so after it was too late.'

One of the four newcomers (the others were Mick Mills of Ipswich, Frank Lampard of West Ham, and Southampton's Mick Channon) for the match with Yugoslavia that Nish and McFarland missed was the Derby centre-half's replacement, Jeff Blockley, who was then newly transferred from Coventry to Arsenal for £200,000, but later with Leicester when he was signed on loan for Derby by Tommy Docherty. That was early in 1978, when McFarland, then in his thirtieth year, was so plagued by injuries that Docherty first sought Gordon McQueen in what would have been a record £450,000 deal from Leeds, but the Scottish international, who had made his League debut against Derby nearly five years previously, moved instead for £495,000 to Manchester United, the 'bigger club' he said he wanted. Because of icy weather, Blockley was unable to play for the Rams until near the end of his month's loan, in a fifth-round home FA Cup defeat by West Bromwich Albion, and the option they had of completing his transfer for £50,000 was not taken up.

McFarland, Todd and Nish finally came together for England in the first match played with Joe Mercer as caretaker manager after the dismissal of Ramsey in May, 1974. Sir Alf could have stayed until his contract expired at the start of the next month, but he refused to do so and was away on holiday when Mercer's short, but more lighthearted, tenure began with a 2-0 victory over Wales in Cardiff. Four days later, the Derby trio played in the same England team for the last time, for that was the match with Northern Ireland – won by a goal from Keith Weller, one of Nish's former Leicester clubmates – in which McFarland suffered the serious Achilles tendon injury that was to keep him out of League action until the last four games of Derby's second Division One championship season of 1974-75.

That match with the Irish was played at Wembley, where in 1969 Nish had been the youngest captain in an FA Cup final at the age of 21 years 212 days. Another cool and assured display by this accomplished defender, who while still at school had been good enough to be a Leicester substitute, indicated that he was settling in for a long international career, but it was all over after just one more game.

Defeat at Hampden Park, compelling England to share the home championship with Scotland instead of claiming it outright, was not the reason for his exclusion after he had added only a fifth full appearance to those he had made in youth and Under-23 teams. Late in that month of May he was rushed to hospital in Derby after collapsing so suddenly that Mercer did not have time to send for a replacement before the England party flew out from London for their summer tour of East Germany, Bulgaria and Yugoslavia. Nish's wife Carole feared he was dying. 'David seemed all right until the afternoon,' she said. 'Then he very suddenly became ill, violently sick, and started bleeding from the mouth.'

An immediate operation had to be performed for a perforated ulcer. Nish made a full recovery and was fit again for the start of the following season, but there were no more cap calls for him even though he played a prominent part in the winning of Derby's second League title in 1974-75. Quite apart from his intervening illness, however, such a rapid rise to a championship medal scarcely seemed on the cards in the early stages of his County career.

The doubts about the value of the Rams' claim to the First Division title in 1972 that arose from the claims of malpractice elsewhere caused the circumstances in which Nish was drafted into their defence to be most distracting, aggravated for him personally by the fact that for a few matches he was pulled out of it to play in midfield – a role he had filled before developing into one of the finest left-backs in the country. There was also the unsettling fact that during the 1972-73 season the Rams fielded no fewer than eleven full-back combinations – one of them a teenage partnership between Steve Powell and Alan Lewis immediately before Nish's arrival. Nish himself had four partners, and it was greatly to his credit that, after understandably showing some initial uncertainty as the whole side struggled, he took it all in his elegant stride to maintain a consistently high level of performance that did much to help stabilise a defence which as late as March had let in more goals than every other team in the First Division except Manchester United's. If that makes strange reading in these days of the United's prosperity, it was also most contradictory for a back four as distinguished as Derby's then was. And it would have been even worse but for the heroics of Colin Boulton, who had ample opportunity to demonstrate that he was at the top of his form.

Nish reverted to his usual full-back position in mid-November when John Robson dropped out of the side after disappointing in a home draw with Crystal Palace, who were relegated that season along with West Bromwich Albion. A month later – just before Christmas, by which time Nish had become eligible for the European Cup – Robson was sold to Aston Villa for £90,000, then a record incoming fee for Derby. It was a handsome profit on a player, still only 22, who had come a long way in the eight years since he had started out as an outside-right with the Birtley Youth Club near his home industrial town of Consett. For four seasons Robson had been a Rams regular, missing no matches as, at eighteen, the youngest member of the 1968-69 Second Division title side, and only one with the First Division champions of 1971-72 when Steve Powell, who played just twice, was alone younger.

Having entered a Villa team that also included Bruce Rioch, who was soon to move in the opposite direction, Robson lost his place for a while to John Gidman, a key figure in the club's FA Youth Cup triumph of 1972 after being discarded by Bill Shankly at Liverpool, but he was recalled in midfield by Ron Saunders, successor to Vic Crowe as manager, before being restored to full-back when Gidman suffered a serious eye injury as a firework exploded in his face on Bonfire Night in 1974. During that season Robson was only once out of the team as Villa, runners-up to Manchester United, coupled promotion back to the First Division with a run to victory over Norwich City in the League Cup final at Wembley. Two years later, at left-back in partnership with Gidman, he helped Villa to win the League Cup again, though it was only after extra-time in a second replay that they accounted for Everton in the final.

A then record fee of £650,000 changed hands when Gidman moved to Everton, but it was again against the Goodison club, after being Ron Atkinson's first signing for Manchester United, that he collected an FA Cup winner's medal in 1985. His transfer to United involved the part exchange of Mickey Thomas, a much-travelled Welsh international who had a spell on loan to Derby County towards the end of the 1985-86 season in which, from Division Three, they gained the first of two successive promotions under the management of Arthur Cox.

To his 214 senior appearances for Derby, John Robson added 174 for Villa before being forced into premature retirement by multiple sclerosis after the 1977-78 season in which he played the last three of his 315 League games. It was a devastatingly early end to a fine career that brought him three more medals with Villa to add to those he had gained with Derby, plus seven matches with the England Under-23s and one in the Football League representative side. An International XI provided the opposition for a testimonial game Villa arranged for him in October, 1978. He was only 53 when he died in May 2004. It was especially sad that, at such a relatively young age, he was the first of Derby's First Division champions to pass on.

Following Robson's move from the Baseball Ground, David Nish linked up at full-back with Ron Webster, who had only just been restored to the team, after being prematurely omitted since the third match of the season, for the visit of Crystal Palace that coincided with Robson's final first-team appearance. That was Webster's 173rd game in tandem with Robson, and he then formed a similarly fruitful partnership with Nish that endured for another century of matches, tapering off after Dave Mackay had made Rod Thomas, a Wales regular, his first signing for the Rams on taking over as manager from Brian Clough.

The drawn home match with Palace came straight after the trouncing by Manchester City at Maine Road and was the beginning of a mini-revival of ten points out of the next twelve in which the highlight was the 5-0 defeat of high-flying Arsenal at the Baseball Ground – Derby's biggest win in the League since they had seen off Spurs in their first season back in Division One. Alan Hinton was the man mainly behind that shooting down of the Gunners, scoring one of the goals with a drive of trademark force and making three of the others. It made for a most miserable return to League action, after seven months out following a cartilage operation, for Chesterfield-born Bob Wilson, a former England Boys goalkeeper who had won a couple of full Scotland caps through a parental qualification. The 'inquest' that manager Bertie Mee conducted had the desired effect as his team lost only three of their remaining 22 League matches (one of them at home to Derby), though Liverpool denied them a ninth First Division title for which they had to wait sixteen more years in those pre-Premiership days.

In six weeks Derby rose from sixteenth to sixth, but promptly slipped back to mid-table, undermined by the delicate skills of the veteran George Eastham in a 0-4 defeat at Stoke as Hinton registered another of his rare penalty misses. The last faint hopes of retaining the League title then disappeared in a beating at Birmingham, where Tony Parry made his first Division One appearance, and John Sims his first full one, in a side deprived of Hennessey, Hinton, O'Hare, Powell and Todd. Sims, a twenty-year-old forward from Belper who was leading scorer for the Reserves, had been sent on as a substitute in a drawn home game with Newcastle a few weeks earlier, but he was to be given only one further first-team chance, as Stoke completed the double, before going out on loan to Luton, Oxford and Colchester.

In December 1975, Sims was the first signing for Notts County by Ronnie Fenton, a former West Bromwich, Birmingham and Brentford forward who had joined the Meadow Lane club as coach to the youth team and earned his promotion to manager after helping Jimmy Sirrel, later Derby's chief scout, to raise them from the Fourth Division to the Second. Fenton, who engaged future Derby manager Colin Addison as coach, lost his job two years later when Notts were at the foot of the table, but crossed the Trent to work with Brian Clough at Nottingham Forest after Peter Taylor had gone into what turned out to be a premature retirement.

Sims, first sought by Notts County nearly two years before, during the first of Sirrel's three stints as their manager, thought he had missed the transfer he said would have suited him down to the ground ('I wouldn't even have had to move from Ripley') when Kevin Randall, a former Chesterfield forward, left Meadow Lane for Mansfield. Within a fortnight, that disappointment was dispelled by Notts' choice of himself to replace Randall, so he joined a club then near the top of Division Two when he would have been content with one at the bottom of Division Three.

After three years with Notts County, during which he made 74 first-team appearances and scored seventeen goals, Sims played for all three Devonian clubs, Exeter, Plymouth (both under the management of Bobby Saxton) and Torquay. He had two spells at Exeter and Torquay, but enjoyed most success with Argyle, scoring 48 times in 182 games. His return to Torquay began as player-coach, then ended as manager – a post in which he lasted for only 33 days. After that he stayed in the West Country, playing for Saltash United and Waldon Athletic (where he was also manager) before becoming a licensee in Torquay.

Sims, who had gained a Central League championship medal in 1972, was one of four reserves Derby County fielded in the return game with Stoke, and Parry became the fifth when he went on as substitute for Walker about twenty minutes from time. That depletion of the team, and the defeat which went with it, provoked Bert Head, manager of Crystal Palace, to call it 'a farce'. He had a vested interest. Stoke, like his own club, were candidates for relegation. Head, whose team did drop (with West Brom) gave vent to his feelings by adding: 'Our boys are wild about it. There is no action I can take. It is a ridiculous situation. When the European Cup gets more important than the Football League it's time to pack up.'

Brian Clough, beset by injuries, strongly refuted Head's complaint, pointing out that Derby, although then still with the chance of qualifying as European Cup holders, needed to finish among the leading places in the First Division to make sure of again entering European competition the following season. After controversially losing to Juventus in their champions' semi-final (more about that in the next chapter), they at first thought they had still got through to Europe when the three successive home victories with which they completed their League programme secured a final seventh position – but no. Yet again Leeds United thwarted them, if unintentionally. The Yorkshire club's failure to win either the FA Cup or the European Cup-Winners' Cup, after getting into the final of both, meant that they were reduced to filling the last UEFA Cup place left to English representatives which otherwise would have been Derby's.

Epic FA Cup replay and European semi-final

Derby County's campaign on three Cup fronts in season 1972-73 began before a crowd of fewer than 16,000 at Swindon on the first Tuesday of September and ended the following April with a two-leg semi-final that attracted a combined crowd in excess of 100,000.

The second-round League Cup-tie in Wiltshire brought revenge of a kind for the Rams' quarter-final defeat there four years earlier, but it was a scrappy affair, decided unimpressively by a reversal of the 0-1 scoreline. Both clubs fielded four players who took part in the 1968 encounter – Peter Downsborough, Rod Thomas, Joe Butler and Don Rogers for Swindon; Roy McFarland, John O'Hare, Kevin Hector and Alan Durban (who replaced Archie Gemmill during the second half) for Derby.

A fifth member of the County's team on that former occasion was also present – Dave Mackay, the Swindon manager whose forceful words at half-time spurred his men to give their off-colour visitors some uncomfortable second-half moments after having fallen behind to the goal that went in off Terry Hennessey's bald pate from an Alan Hinton corner around the half-hour. Colin Boulton had to be at his brilliant best to avert another humbling exit from the County Ground, saving with particular expertise at the expense of David Moss and Ray Treacy as the Rams clung on to their slender lead.

Treacy, Mackay's first signing for Swindon at £40,000 from Charlton Athletic, was such a handful for McFarland that the Derby captain was fortunate not to be sent off. Frustrated by the centre-forward's shielding of the ball, McFarland was booked the second time he brought him down, then was reprieved when he did it a third time even though a free-kick was awarded. That rare loss of composure spread an unsettling effect throughout the side. Even Colin Todd, though sharing the defensive honours with Boulton, was not immune from indiscretion – fortunate that the referee did not spot his tugging of Rogers' shirt to prevent a late breakthrough by the tricky winger.

Derby's next engagement in a knock-out competition brought FK Zeljeznicar to the Baseball Ground from Sarajevo for the first leg of a European Cup-tie. Shaking off worrying League form that had gleaned only six points out of sixteen and just cost a third successive away defeat, they overcame a nervous start to gain a two-goal advantage with a magnificent all-round performance. McFarland and Todd were their usual efficient selves in a defence in which Daniel deputised ably for the ineligible

Nish alongside Powell, but the player who stood out above them all was Hennessey, who during those early months of the season was enjoying the most prosperous phase of his injury-hit career with the club. Midfield, indeed, was where Derby's main strength lay that night, Gemmill and McGovern also excelling.

Hennessey, ever eager to attack, had a shot cleared off the line before the scoring was opened by McFarland while strong appeals were being made for a penalty. Spreco appeared to handle the ball as it was on its way across the line from the centre-half's header, but the referee, Anton Buchell from Switzerland, sensibly awarded a goal instead of pointing to the spot. In the second half the lead was several times almost built up beyond the shot by Gemmill, with his improving right foot from Hector's centre, that entered the net off the goalkeeper. Hennessey, on three more occasions, Hector and Gemmill all went close.

The return game in Yugoslavia, as it then was, a fortnight later produced a closer result, 2-1, but it was as good as over after the opening quarter of an hour. By then Hinton and O'Hare had silenced the hooters and sirens in the crowd of about 60,000 (more than double the disappointing gate for the first leg) by leaving the home team in need of five goals to progress. The Zeljeznicar players resorted to some very dubious tactics, with much blatant tripping, in their desperate attempts to make some inroads into their deficit, but the Austrian referee was reluctant to produce even a yellow card until two minutes from time, when he sent off Jankovic for kicking at Todd from behind. The home team were fortunate to finish with as many as ten men.

Boulton did not have a shot to save until the game was nearly half-an-hour old, so dominant were Derby as they played the ball about accurately despite the bumpy surface. Hinton struck the first blow in the ninth minute from McGovern's pass after the fleet-footed Hector had broken away down the left, and six minutes later McGovern was again the provider for O'Hare's quickly-taken scoring shot. Spreco replied on the hour, at the second attempt after eluding Daniel. Too little, too late.

Those who looked askance at Clough for his often vitriolic comments would surely have amended their opinion of him if they had been there when he insisted that his players should meet the tiny band of supporters who had travelled to the game. 'These people have come 2,000 miles to see you,' he said. 'Go and shake their hands and thank them.'

Victory earned a mouth-watering tie with Benfica, the Portuguese champions managed by Jimmy Hagan, the skilful former Sheffield United and England forward whose transfer from Derby in the late 1930s was arguably the biggest of the few mistakes George Jobey made as the Rams' manager. First though, there was a third-round League Cup date at the

Baseball Ground with Chelsea, winners of the first League match to be played there that season. The London club were without four of their experienced players (Baldwin, Dempsey, Hudson and Hutchinson), and employed the versatile Webb as a striker, but again Derby failed to beat them. They did the next best thing by drawing, no goals being scored, but on the run of play they should have won comfortably.

An unusual note was struck when two referees shared the four bookings of an often unattractive game. Tommy Dawes took the names of McFarland (his fourth booking of the season) and Chelsea's Droy and Houseman before having to leave the field suffering from double vision. Linesman D L Stanton replaced him after 34 minutes and early in the second half added Ron 'Chopper' Harris to the list.

In those days when there was no long wait for replays unless bad weather intervened, it was on the following Monday, only five days later – and in the turbulence of the Rams' 0-5 League thrashing at Leeds on the Saturday – that the teams met again at Stamford Bridge for the right to visit Fourth Division Bury in the fourth round. With only one change from the original tie, Powell displacing Durban, and also just one from the debacle at Elland Road, McGovern resuming to the exclusion of Daniel, Derby were transformed from dross to brilliance, dictating much of the play and twice scoring in splendid style. Yet defeat was once more their lot. Chelsea – even more makeshift, with Droy and Garland added to the absentees – countered with three goals and were the width of an upright from another.

The match could hardly have begun more dishearteningly for Derby. Only five minutes were on the clock when McGovern played his own personal replay of the blunder that had enabled Arsenal to knock the Rams out of the FA Cup the previous March. The back-pass he again intended for his goalkeeper went straight to Steve Kember, for whom scoring was simplicity itself. Hinton's equaliser soon afterwards was a contrasting classic. Making one of his frequent forays into the attack, McFarland slipped the ball across the face of the goal, and the left-winger closed in to meet it with one of his specials, bending it just inside a post.

Three minutes later, and with only a quarter of an hour gone, Webb put Chelsea back in front when a left-wing corner-kick was headed to him from the near post by Osgood, who but for Boulton would have scored earlier than the 53rd minute in which he increased the lead with a superb effort from Houseman's accurate cross. Another thirteen minutes went by, discounting the time taken up while Gemmill and O'Hare received treatment after a hefty collision, before McGovern narrowed the gap with a firm header from a Hinton centre, and, although Kember almost widened it again when he hit a post, it was only on a linesman's intervention that Hector was denied the second equaliser.

So Chelsea went to Gigg Lane, where they won with a goal by Chris Garland, the £100,000 England Under-23 forward who found his way back to Bristol City after costing Leicester nearly another six-figure fee, and they progressed to the last four before going out to Norwich, runners-up to Tottenham for the trophy.

It was after another disconcerting defeat in the League, at Ipswich, that Derby County returned to the cup trail towards the end of October with a win that ranks high among their most glorious achievements. Critics became the County's spur as they prepared for the first leg, at home, of their second-round European Cup-tie against the renowned Benfica. Peter Taylor, who was in charge while Brian Clough was away making on-the-spot plans for the return leg in Lisbon, pinned abusive letters and dismissive headlines on their dressing-room notice-board and told the Derby players: 'Read them, get mad about them – and then go out and prove them all wrong.'

The poison-pen letters ridiculed the team's chances of getting further along the European road. The newspaper headlines included YOU'RE FOR IT, DERBY, and EASY PREY FOR EAGLES. Taylor commented:

'I usually tear up anonymous letters, but these could do us a great favour. One of them says we will lose by a cricket score and all of them, along with many recent headlines, reckon we will be easy meat for Benfica. But I am using all this stuff to help us make those responsible look silly. When the players see those letters and headlines as they walk in and out of the dressing room during the next few days it will put them in exactly the right frame of mind for the game. There's nothing like a sense of grievance to make proud men respond by producing the goods, and I believe Derby are entitled to feel that anyone writing us off is being unjust.'

On past form Benfica were indeed a formidable proposition. They were firmly established as a national institution, winners up to that point of the Portuguese League title nineteen times and their country's cup competition on eighteen occasions. In 1950 they had also won the Latin Cup, forerunner of the European Cup, under the management of Ted Smith, a former Millwall player who later coached the Portugal team, and they had broken Real Madrid's grip on the European Cup by carrying off that trophy in 1961 and 1962. They had also since been runners-up for it three times, most recently to Manchester United in 1968.

But by the time, the year after being losing semi-finalists, they met Derby County in their 66th European champions tie (as against the Rams' third), they, like their star player Eusebio, were no longer such a fearsome force. Indeed, when Brian Clough saw them play while he was over there they were so out of touch that he dared not give Taylor his true impression on his return for fear that word would get back to his players and put them in danger of becoming complacent. Instead, he made no reference to what he saw as Benfica's shortcomings but took the precaution of having the Baseball Ground pitch well watered. Sir Stanley Rous, the venerable FIFA president, expressed surprise that it had rained so heavily in the night as he sat in the directors' box to watch the match.

The doubters and detractors were quite correct to suggest that it would be a one-sided affair. Far from dispatching Derby out of sight, Benfica were never in the hunt from the seventh minute, in which the Rams scored the first of the three goals they put past keeper Jose Henriques inside the first forty minutes. In the *Daily Mirror*, Frank McGhee said that 'Benfica, used to a more leisurely pace, must have felt at times that they were at war against the Chinese army as the Derby hordes kept pouring forward.'

The first goal came after Gemmill, playing one of his most influential games, forced a corner on the left. Hector pushed a short kick to Hinton, whose cross was headed firmly down over the line by McFarland. Another corner led to the lead being increased in the 27th minute. This time Hinton took the kick, from which McFarland back-headed the ball for Hector to volley it home off the far post with Henriques hopelessly out of position. There was no easing-up of the pressure, and in the 39th minute Hector won the ball in the air after Daniel had hit it upfield, giving McGovern the chance to strike a smartly-taken shot into the far corner. It was heady stuff, fittingly reflected in Donald Saunders' *Daily Telegraph* report when he declared: 'I have not seen Derby play with the verve and assurance they displayed in that one-sided first half for many a day.'

After all that, the second half was bound to be something of an anticlimax because there were no further goals, but the Rams mostly remained right on top and twice went close to extending their advantage before Boulton safeguarded it with a couple of excellent saves as Benfica desperately tried to grab a crucial away goal during the last five minutes. More than an hour went by before Eusebio threatened real danger, and even then his close-range shot skidded several yards wide.

Boulton was the hero of the second leg in Lisbon's huge Estadio Da Luz (Stadium of Light). Largely due to his brilliance, nonsense was made of the defensive flaws Derby had been displaying in the First Division as the red-shirted Portuguese champions, urged on by their shrieking fans, who vastly outnumbered Derby's contingent in the crowd of 75,000, launched themselves into wave after wave of relentless attacks.

The pressure was at its fiercest in the opening half-hour, during which Boulton blunted it with three exceptional saves from the revitalised Eusebio. He hurtled off his line to the rescue when a rare lapse let the danger-man through for the first time. Within minutes he repeated the feat with another brave dive at Eusebio's flying feet, then was again equal to the emergency when the same player showed an electrifying burst of speed in pursuit of a penetrating through ball. Even when Baptista fastened onto a rebound Boulton claimed possession at the second attempt.

Jimmy Hagan introduced Artur Jordao, Portugal's top scorer for the past two seasons, shortly after half-time, but to no avail, and he virtually conceded defeat when, to the accompaniment a chorus of disapproving whistles, he replaced Baptista with a defender, Rodrigues, in the 65th minute. Eusebio, the Mozambican 'Black Pearl' from Lourenco Marques formally known as Eusebio Da Silva Ferreira, held his head in his hands in obvious dismay as he watched his strike partner leave the field.

As the minutes ticked away Benfica gradually lost the momentum with which they had sought to wipe out their arrears amid an early spate of corner-kicks. They lost heart against a sterling defence in which the celebrated McFarland-Todd link-up exerted an increasingly tight hold and Ron Webster settled into his old dependable self on his recall for his European debut in his first senior match for nearly three months. To prevent a club with such an exalted reputation from scoring over the two legs was an exceptional achievement, especially as Derby's team included three players, O'Hare, Hector and, most notably, Hinton, who had gone into the match from the treatment table.

To Benfica's discredit, they employed some very dubious methods as their hopes dwindled. Jeff Farmer told his *Daily Mail* readers that they 'used every trick they could recall from their long history in European combat, and some of their tactics shamed their legendary name'. Hinton, who operated in a withdrawn position because of his lack of full fitness, was blatantly punched on the head by full-back Da Silva, McFarland was surprisingly able to carry on after being viciously fouled, and Hector would almost certainly have given Derby victory on the night as well as overall if he had not been, as Gerald Mortimer put it, 'almost sawn in half' when a deplorable assault by the goalkeeper deprived him of a straightforward scoring chance. The free-kick awarded on the fringe of the penalty area was hammered wide by Hinton.

Defeat put Hagan's future with Benfica in doubt, but he stayed for almost another year, leaving only a few months after they had completed their third hat-trick of Portuguese League titles in eleven years. The cause of the split was therefore not poor results, but an argument over the selection of players for Eusebio's testimonial match. After coaching in Kuwait, Hagan ended his managerial career back in Portugal with first Sporting Lisbon, then Porto (where those who followed him included that man of many clubs, Tommy Docherty).

Eusebio, European Footballer of the Year in 1965, played in North America after leaving Benfica in 1974 with 316 goals in 294 league games, and 38 in 46 internationals, behind him. Three years later he returned to Benfica as coach. In 1992 a statue of him was unveiled at the entrance to the Estadio da Luz, and a film of his life was released entitled *Sua Majestade o Rei* (His Majesty the King).

With the European Cup put on hold until the competition was resumed the following March, Derby County's next Cup date in the 1972-73 season was in the FA Cup. The draw for the third round pitted them against Peterborough United at the lowly Fourth Division club's London Road ground. A crowd of more than 20,000 saw them wriggle through by just one goal, luckily credited ten minutes before half-time to Roger Davies as the ball nestled in the net off his right leg after two shots had been blocked on the line. Brian Clough, whose views on centre-forwards carried particular weight, rated Davies the most exciting discovery since John Richards, of Wolves, and considered that he was fast approaching Peter Osgood's skill, but in this match the young man had a lean time, unsettled by swift and sharp tackling.

Alan Hinton was again out with his troublesome groin strain when Derby met Tottenham Hotspur in the next round – but once more Davies scored the goal that kept the Rams in the competition, earning a White Hart Lane replay in which he hit the headlines on the night he came right into the full glare of national publicity. At the Baseball Ground, however, he was three times in danger of being substituted before he toe-ended the 85th-minute equaliser, eight minutes after Martin Chivers had given the visitors the lead. Brian Clough said afterwards:

'The lad did not have a good game for us, did not do as well as he had been doing. I kept going to take him off, and each time I decided to stick with the players we believed in. In the end Roger toed one in, and he swears it wasn't a fluke because he meant it. I believe him because he's too young to lie.'

So remorselessly did Derby attack in the second half of a nerve-tingling tie, drawing most inspiration from Hector and McGovern in a display of all-round quality, that it came as a real stunner when Spurs suddenly went ahead at such a late stage. The excellence in Tottenham's goal of Pat Jennings, who that season polled more than twice as many votes as runner-up Paul Madeley in being elected Footballer of the Year by the Football Writers' Association, threatened to have provided a solid foundation for the London club's advance into the fifth round when Hennessey, who otherwise had another marvellous match, miskicked in attempting to clear a free-kick from Cyril Knowles. The Welshman made a valiant effort to retrieve his error when the ball bounced out off Boulton, but Jimmy Pearce, who only a minute earlier had gone on as substitute for Alan Gilzean, nipped in to serve up a sitter for Chivers. To make it all the more galling for Derby, and the magnificent McFarland in particular, it was the only sniff of a chance the centre-forward was allowed all afternoon – and he would still have been denied it if referee Ken Burns had not decided that Martin Peters was not interfering with play in an offside position.

The goal that wiped out Tottenham's lead also resulted from a free-kick, with a decided tinge of luck. Todd miscued his shot after Hector had played a short pass to him, but the ball went straight to Davies, who swivelled smartly to poke it home. Derby's lanky No 9 ('My height has made me a bit lazy, so I'm trying to speed up a fraction') thus atoned for frittering away a good opportunity in the first half, when he had lost the ball to Jennings instead of passing to either of two better-placed colleagues. Hennessey almost shared that making-up for an earlier lapse, going close to a last-gasp winner.

As at Derby, so at Tottenham. Spurs, though again having the worst of the exchanges, seemed set for victory in the replay when they led 3-1 with only twelve minutes left of the normal ninety, but Davies was again their undoing. This time he did even better. He not only brought the scores level, but also completed a hat-trick in the extra period to give the Rams a long overdue lead which Hector increased for a pulsating 5-3 triumph. It was one of the truly great FA Cup fight-backs, memories of which were so recently stirred at the same ground when Manchester City transformed a three-goal half-time deficit into a remarkable 4-3 win despite having one of their players sent off.

It was right against the run of play for Derby to have been two down at the interval, and then to concede a third goal, to a dubious penalty converted by Mike England, after Hector had halved the deficit by hooking a 68th-minute shot just beneath the bar. Tottenham scored their three goals with only four attempts. The one that failed was foiled by Boulton, with a daring save at the feet of Chivers two minutes into the second half.

As in the first meeting, Chivers, England's centre-forward, was second best to McFarland, England's centre-half, but he underlined the threat that brought him 25 goals that season by slickly opening the scoring in the twentieth minute. Knowles broke down Spurs' left flank and Chivers timed his run perfectly to finish firmly at close range from the full-back's low diagonal centre. Derby retaliated with a left-foot drive by McGovern from Hector's back-heel that went only inches wide, a low shot by Davies which Jennings tipped behind for a corner, an effort by Hector that hit the bar, and a shot by Gemmill which Gilzean knew little about when it hit him as he stood near the goal-line. Then, to rub it in, Tottenham broke away again and increased their lead in the last minute of the first half. Gilzean, the oldest player afield, headed against the bar following a throw-in by Chivers, but nodded in the rebound.

The penalty with which Spurs appeared to have put themselves out of reach against all the odds was doubly contentious from the Derby viewpoint. First, referee Don Biddle, a fingerprint expert with Bristol Police, gave a free-kick for hands against Webster after the full-back had fallen on the ball when pushed in the back by Ralph Coates. Then the driven-in ball struck O'Hare and the spot-kick was awarded.

Far from being down and out, however, Derby County were just about to begin one of the most sensational comebacks in FA Cup history. Better balanced with Durban on for Hennessey from the start of the second half, they hit back within two minutes of the penalty, Davies punishing some uncertainty in the Spurs' defence by beating Jennings with a strong shot through a crowded goalmouth. Six minutes later, he brought the scores level with the goal of the game. O'Hare skilfully brought the ball under control near the by-line and pulled back a knee-high centre which Davies volleyed powerfully into the roof of the net from a position well short of the near post. In afterwards paying tribute to 'the tremendous football Derby played throughout the match', Bill Nicholson, Tottenham's manager, singled out that equalising goal for special praise.

The Rams were complete masters of the extra thirty minutes which Hector almost made unnecessary with a shot that hit Jennings, but it was not until the second minute of the second additional period that they at last went in front. Hector's corner-kick landed the ball just beyond the far upright, and as the goalkeeper hesitated Davies rose to head past static, demoralised defenders. 'It's just great to score my first hat-trick for the club,' he said later. 'But for a long time it seemed as if it would not be my night. Mike England is one of the best centre-halves I've played against, but suddenly everything changed and the ball just went in.'

Six more minutes went by before the seal was set on Derby's night as Hector chased a long clearance that caught tiring Tottenham square, and he placed the ball beyond Jennings as the goalkeeper came out. After that, dismayed home fans began to drift away from White Hart Lane's biggest crowd of the season, 52,736, but there was still time for the rampant visitors to go close to widening their winning margin in three further attacks. Spurs, holders of the UEFA Cup and finalists for the League Cup (they defeated Norwich City at Wembley the following month) were outclassed.

Davies was brought down to earth next day. Brian Clough fined him £20 for allowing his photograph to be taken for a newspaper. 'Davies has a weakness,' said the manager. 'He thinks everything in the garden is lovely. He thinks all those in football are nice, friendly people. He will soon find the truth.'

In the next round, at home to Queen's Park Rangers, Derby served up a devastating display of attacking football, going 4-0 up after just over half-an-hour's play. Davies was again on target, with a header from the sixth corner they forced inside the first ten minutes, but this time Hector was the hat-trick hero. Gordon Jago, the London club's manager, spoke of the onslaught with considerable feeling: 'We were lucky it was not six or more by half-time. They came at us with the sort of football we have never met before. We came up to play the best team in the country. I'm happy that we came out and showed some character in the second half.'

QPR hit back with two goals after the interval as Derby, deprived of an accurate flow of centres when Hinton limped out of the action, went off the boil in failing to add to their first-half flurry. It was greatly to the visitors' credit that they made a game of it after heading for humiliation, but not entirely unexpected because their team included players of such outstanding ability as skipper Terry Venables, Dave Thomas, Gerry Francis and Stan Bowles, internationals all. And that was the season in which they regained First Division status.

The draw gave the Rams another home tie in the quarter-finals, but it also paired them with Leeds United. Sure enough, their bogy team were the winners, and although it was by only one goal – Peter Lorimer scored in the thirtieth minute when referee Harry New decided that Allan Clarke, though offside, was not interfering with play – there could be no reasonable complaints. Norman Hunter and Paul Madeley scarcely put a foot wrong at the heart of a superbly-organised defence. As for skill, well, on the day Derby had to give second best. Hinton, whose replacement, Powell, was himself supplanted by Durban in the second half, was again badly missed, and Gemmill had probably his most ineffective game for the County.

On the Wednesday after that failure to qualify for the FA Cup's last four, Derby returned to the European Cup with the task of overturning a one-goal deficit from the first leg in Czechoslovakia of a third-round clash with Spartak Trnava. They welcomed back Hinton for the second leg, but he was still troubled by his groin injury and, with Nish also not fully fit, Spartak reaped the greater benefit from the return to their team after suspension of Ladislav Kuna, a player of world class.

The one goal conceded in Trnava, spectacularly scored by Horvath, would have been two if Boulton had not left his line to smother a shot from Masma in the last five minutes. Both those Czech players had to be substituted at the Baseball Ground – Masma with an ankle injury as early as the seventh minute, Horvath with a thigh strain in the 58th – but their withdrawal was determinedly shrugged off as the Rams, winners by 2-1 on aggregate, were made to battle right to the end.

With Derby's quest for a quick equaliser repulsed, there was much anxiety in the home camp before Hector brought the overall scores level in the second half from McGovern's low centre after Gemmill had done the spadework. Hector also obtained the vital second goal, with a coolly controlled volley as friend and foe around him froze in expectation of a penalty for a foul on Davies after one of Hinton's teasing crosses, but the inability to add to that lead kept Spartak hopes alive in the knowledge that if they had scored they would have gone through on the away goal. It took a series of wild, undignified clearances to keep them out in a hectic final quarter of an hour, and although Boulton did not have a serious save to make he was fortunate not to give away a penalty with one over-robust challenge.

Of all the goals he scored for Derby County, Hector rated those two against Spartak Trnava as his most memorable. The winner was the one to which he gave pride of place. In *The Ram*, a newspaper the club used to bring out instead of the normal programme, this was how he modestly looked back on it: 'It was a volley from outside the box and, to be honest, it could have gone anywhere.'

At the first attempt, Derby County were into the semi-finals with a distinct chance of becoming the second English club, after Manchester United, to lift the European Cup. Brian Clough regarded it as 'a magnificent piece of luck' when the postponement of a League match with Wolves allowed his players an unexpected rest before the next big hurdle had to be faced, but the prospect of further progress receded in front of 72,000 at the Communale Stadium in Turin on the evening of Wednesday, 11 April 1973.

Watched by hundreds of their fans for whom a special smallpox vaccination unit had been set up at East Midlands airport, they gave a spirited, disciplined performance that was not quite good enough to prevent Juventus, the Italian champions, emerging from an exciting first leg 3-1 ahead. Not until as late as the 83rd minute, however, was the gap widened to two goals by Jose Altafini, the Brazilian-born veteran who had been known as Mazzola, because of his resemblance to the Italian star of the late 1940s, while with the Palmeiras club of Sao Paulo.

Altafini also scored the opening goal in the 28th minute, but within two minutes Hector collected a return pass from O'Hare, who gave one of his finest displays for Derby back at centre-forward in the absence of Davies with a groin strain, and eluded two defenders before expertly planting the ball past the great Dino Zoff. It was no mean feat to beat a goalkeeper of that calibre, one who the following year set a world record by going through a dozen international matches without conceding a goal. Hector's goal was also the first to be scored for an English club in a European Cup-tie in Italy, and it kept Derby level until the 66th minute in which Causio made up for missing a good first-half opening by restoring the home club's lead.

The provider of the pass from which that goal was scored, only four minutes after going on as a substitute, was Helmut Haller, who had been in West Germany's team against England in the 1966 World Cup final. And thereby hangs a tale that made the next day's headlines, best told by the man who was at the centre of it – Peter Taylor. The Rams' assistant manager said that he might have been put in prison over a half-time incident but for the intervention of John Charles, the Welshman dubbed Il Buono Gigante (the gentle giant) by the Italian crowds who idolised him while he was a player with Juventus after leaving Leeds, who had accompanied the Derby party to Turin as an adviser. This is what Taylor had to say:

'I noticed that Helmut Haller was talking to Gunther Schulenburg, the referee, who is also a West German, as we were walking back to the dressing rooms. I thought this was very odd, so I walked behind them and said: 'Carry on, gentlemen, I am listening.' Immediately I was elbowed in the ribs and kicked and pushed. By the time I left the pitch I was being shouted at by a Juventus official, who then called in the police. The police demanded my passport and later started to question me. I thought I would miss the second half and possibly end up in jail because everybody was in such a frenzy. But John Charles remained very calm and told me not to let them keep my passport. Eventually, a senior Juventus official came along and at his request the police left me alone. Everyone seemed to think I had struck Haller, which is not true. I was just disturbed to see him talking to the referee and later learned that he had also been seen in the referee's room before the match. As far as we are concerned, however, the matter is now closed, and it is up to us to put things right in the second leg.'

Juventus officials, whose view of the scene in the tunnel was that Taylor had accidentally elbowed Haller as he pushed his way through, were just as anxious to forget the incident, but the whole business left the Derby managerial pair fuming about Schulenburg's refereeing. They were incensed by the bookings that barred McFarland and Gemmill from the second leg because they had also been cautioned against Spartak Trnava, and also by the failure to send off Guiseppe Furino for his persistent fouling of Gemmill. Furino did have his name taken, but, contrary to original belief, was available for the return game at the Baseball Ground.

Gerald Mortimer described McFarland's booking as 'totally absurd'. It was for a clash of heads as the Derby captain went up to challenge Cuccureddu for a high ball. Gemmill was booked for tripping Furino in retaliation after the Italian had smashed an elbow into the little Scot's face – an offence the referee missed. In Derby eyes it looked like a put-up job, suspicions that deepened when it was alleged, as later exposed in the *Sunday Times*, that an unsuccessful attempt was made to bribe the Portuguese referee who was appointed for the second leg.

Thanks to Hector, the Rams' requirement when Juventus turned up at the Baseball Ground on 25 April was a win by 2-0, half of what it would have been if the Italian club had kept their goal intact in Turin. That depended, of course, on no more goals being conceded by the County, which in fact is what they achieved, but events conspired to disprove Brian Clough's claim, linked to his condemnation of the Italians as 'cheating bastards' (a cleaned-up translation), that 'even without McFarland and Gemmill we can still beat this lot and reach the final'.

The two key twists in the tale that were Derby's undoing occurred after a scoreless but breathtaking first half in which even Webster had time to break off from his defensive duties to join O'Hare and Hinton in severely testing Zoff. Several home appeals for a penalty were turned down before, after 56 minutes, referee Lobo finally awarded one for the 25th foul committed by the Italians when Spinosi tripped Hector, but, to the consternation of most in the crowd of nearly 38,500, and above all himself, Hinton dragged his customary powerful spot-shot well wide. When he looked back on his days with Derby County, that was the incident Hinton remembered most clearly with these words:

'It was a nightmare. Friends insisted that I go, as had been arranged, to a Supporters' Club dance the next evening. I was trembling, dreading what people would say. I need not have worried because I was shown the understanding, sympathy and kindness which I had enjoyed since joining Derby County. It was only when I came to Derby that I really began to enjoy my football, even though the ground and facilities left a lot to be desired! It means so much to me now to feel that I was part of Derby's team.'

Demoralising as that penalty miss was, there was another severe blow to come only six minutes later when Roger Davies was sent off. Before the interval he caused the visitors trouble with his close control of the ball at his feet, but after it he lost control in another vital aspect – his temperament. He concluded a series of unsavoury skirmishes with Morini by suddenly hurling himself forward and head-butting the tough central defender, who staggered backwards into the net. Provocation was no excuse, and the referee, who had a clear view of it all, was left with no option but to dismiss him. Next day, a boxing manager named Bobby Thomas offered Davies a new career. He wanted to train him as a heavyweight boxer.

Davies considered himself 'a calm bloke normally', but it was not the first time he had been banished from the field while playing for Derby. That had happened in a reserve match with Stoke when Terry Lees had been carried off after Davies, admitting to losing his head, had turned round and hit him. Brian Clough had fined him a week's wages on that occasion, and the punishment was repeated. 'Disgraceful' was the manager's word for such violent conduct.

In one last desperate attempt to try to salvage something from the European Cup wreckage, John Sims was sent on soon after the reduction to ten men to bolster the attack at the expense of a defender, Peter Daniel, who had done a great job as deputy for McFarland. The end came, however, with no breakthrough, and Juventus would have departed with more than a goalless draw if Boulton had not been on the alert when two of the best chances of the game fell to the Italian champions. Brian Clough, having bemoaned the fact that 'three bad goals' were given away in Turin, now said: 'Our three front-runners were superb, yet we never scored. It's daft.'

My final memory of that match at Derby is a personal one. While I was driving back home to Manchester with my son in the early hours of the following morning we were stopped by a routine police check on the outskirts of Macclesfield. On being asked where we were travelling from, I replied with feeling that we were on our way back from 'the terrible happenings at Derby'. The man in the uniform was immediately agog, but not inclined to approve of either my interpretation of events or my deep concern about them when he was made aware of the exact situation. Clearly, he was no Derby County fan.

Francis Lee celebrates his spectacular winning goal against his old club,
Manchester City, at Maine Road (December 1974)

Charlie George in high-kicking action with Manchester United's Arthur Albiston
(January 1978)

Peter Daniel clears from Liverpool's Keegan at the Baseball Ground (January 1975)

Season 1971-72 group with the club's three trophies.
Back: Stuart Webb, John Sheridan (reserves' trainer), Hinton, Hennessey, Gemmill, Daniel, Gordon Guthrie (physio), Peter Taylor, Sam Longson, Brian Clough, Boulton, Jimmy Gordon (trainer), Brian Newton (youth coach). Front: McGovern, O'Hare, Durban, Hector, Robson, Webster (McFarland and Todd were away on England duty)

> **30** *The Daily Telegraph, Thursday, September 16, 1976*
>
> Soccer—UEFA Cup
>
> # FIVE-GOAL HECTOR EQUALS RECORD IN DERBY DELUGE
>
> By HENRY BEVINGTON
>
> Derby County ...12   Finn Harps ... 0
>
> DERBY COUNTY completely exploited the raw inexperience, lack of skill and tactical naïvety of Finn Harps, their unworldly opponents from Donegal, by scoring 12 times, nine before half-time, in the first leg of their UEFA Cup first-round tie at the Baseball Ground last night.

Team group before the 1976-77 season: Back: Colin Murphy, Gordon Guthrie, George, Rioch, Todd, Boulton, Moseley, Powell, Nish, Thomas, Des Anderson: Front: King, James, McFarland, Gemmill, Newton, Hector, Daniel

Tommy Docherty with chairman George Hardy (left) and secretary Stuart Webb

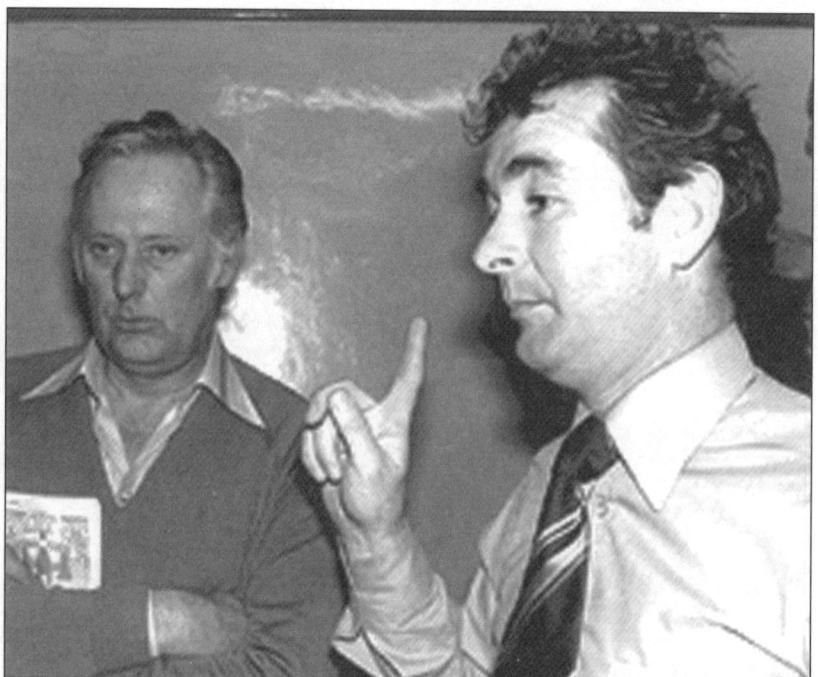

Brian Clough with Peter Taylor

Doyle sent off but Derby title hopes shattered

By DENIS LOWE

Manchester City 4   Derby County 3

HISTORY has recorded Mary Tudor's high opinion of Calais, but Manchester will hardly find a place in the hearts of Dave Mackay and his players after what Derby have suffered at the hands of United and City in successive weeks.

The FA Cup semi-final defeat was followed by one which has surely ended Derby's championship hopes, as City, who had Mike Doyle, their captain, sent off in the 13th minute, emerged narrow but deserved victors from a game which was crazy, controversial and downright cynical in turn.

From *The Daily Telegraph*, 12 April 1976

Colin Boulton is at full stretch to foil an Everton attack at Goodison Park (September 1971)

Charlie George, arms outstretched, congratulates Bruce Rioch, scorer of Derby's first goal in their FA Cup quarter-final victory over Newcastle (March 1976)

Alan Gowling scores Newcastle's second goal in the FA Cup quarter-final at the Baseball Ground, but Derby triumphed 4-2 (March 1976)

Kevin Hector shoots against Burnley at Turf Moor (September 1973)

Liverpool swamp dismal Derby with five goals

By EDWARD GILES

Liverpool 5   Derby County 0

EVENTS at Anfield took their all too predictable course. Liverpool's gallop was hardly likely to be stopped by a struggling, injury-hit club without an away win in the League since last December.

The only surprises, indeed, were that Liverpool led by no more than one goal with almost an hour gone, and still fell short of their seven against Spurs even after Derby had disintegrated.

As it is, the First Division leaders, striding so imperiously along the high road back into Europe, have totted up a dozen goals in their last three games, and have accumulated a goal difference of 29 in dropping only one point out of 20.

For outclassed, demoralised Derby, this was their most crushing defeat of Tommy Docherty's reign. Their manager, now nursing wounded pride as well as two broken ribs and factial cuts, wryly described it as a crash worse than the one he had experienced while driving home the previous night

The author reports for *The Daily Telegraph* on Monday, 16 October 1978 on the match with Liverpool played two days earlier

Derby County: Champions of England 149

The Rams show off the Watney Cup in 1970:
Back: Wignall, Mackay, Webster, McGovern, Hinton, O'Hare, Robson, Green, Carlin.
Front: Durban, Hector, McFarland

John Newman, who briefly followed Colin Addison as Derby's manager

32 *The Daily Telegraph, Friday, October 19, 1973*

Soccer

CLOUGH HITS BACK AT ATTACK BY DERBY CHAIRMAN

By ROBERT OXBY

ON the day English football was expected to take a fresh look at itself, Sam Longson, chairman of Derby County, issued a long and unprecedented statement attacking Brian Clough, the manager, who resigned on Monday, and his assistant, Peter Taylor.

The allegations in the statement were so serious that it is not difficult to predict that there will be an inquiry into the affairs of Derby County by a joint commission of the Football Association and the Football League.

In addition, there is the likelihood of a High Court action. Mr Clough stated last night that he had already taken the first steps to issue a writ for libel and slander against the chairman.

As he dealt with each allegation, Mr Clough demanded: "Why didn't they sack me?—Because according to the statement I didn't break any rule—I broke every rule. According to them, I should be in jail sitting with the train robbers."

Derby County: Champions of England 151

Derby's back four, McFarland, Nish, Powell and Todd, can only look on as Ian Storey-Moore, a player Derby failed to sign, leaps to score for Manchester United at Old Trafford (September 1972)

Roger Davies goes to ground under pressure from Carlisle keeper Alan Ross (April 1975)

Manchester United's Gordon Hill, later to join the Rams, under pressure from Rod Thomas during the FA Cup semi-final at Hillsborough (April 1976)

Brian Clough signs as manager of Derby County, under the eye of chairman Sam Longson (July 1967)

Mike Watterson, third in line after George Hardy in his short-lived stay as Derby County chairman

Rod Thomas and Roger Davies parade the League Championship trophy during the players' lap of honour before the final match of the 1974-75 season against Carlisle

A rare goal from Ron Webster, breaking upfield to head home against Manchester City in December 1971. It was one of seven goals he netted in over 500 appearances

Peter Taylor fires up his Derby players by showing them the anti-Rams headlines, which he has pinned to the notice board.
From left: Walker, Powell, O'Hare, Nish, Hennessey, Daniel, Hinton

Derby County: Champions of England 155

BACK FROM THE BRINK!

DERBY County's players yesterday pulled back from the brink of a strike that could have cost them the sack.

Their first team squad, valued at two million pounds and including four England internationals, changed their minds about handing the club a letter stating they would refuse to report to the ground until 75 minutes before Saturday's home game with Leeds United.

It was the most dramatic day of the many there have been at Derby since the resignation of Brian Clough and Peter Taylor five weeks ago.

On Tuesday night the players prepared and signed a letter which read:

● *We, the undersigned players, refuse to report to Derby County Football Club until 1 p.m., Saturday, November 24, for the following reasons:*
(a) Dissatisfaction with the pesent management.
(b) Reinstatement of Brian Clough and Peter Taylor.●

If they had carried out their threat the players could have been fined, suspended for 14 days or sacked without prejudice to the right of a transfer fee.

BY DAVE HORRIDGE

Derby players call off strike .. and Mackay says: They're a laughing stock

From *The Daily Mirror* (November 1973)

Hector goes up with two Coventry defenders at the Baseball Ground (January 1972)

156   *Derby County: Champions of England*

Past Derby players link arms on the pitch before the concluding match of the 1974-75 championship season

Colin Addison, one of eight Derby managers in eleven years after Brian Clough's stormy departure

Derby County: Champions of England

28 *The Daily Telegraph, Tuesday, May 9, 1972*

DERBY TAKE TITLE AS WOLVES WRECK LEEDS'S QUEST FOR DOUBLE

By DONALD SAUNDERS

Wolves...... 2   Leeds United ... 1

SHORTLY after Leeds had trooped despondently off the pitch at Molineux last night, one point short of the League title, Derby, touring in faraway Majorca, learned they had become champions for the first time in their history.

Though Leeds flogged their weary bodies willingly until the final whistle, they could not quite scale the heights separating them from the double, just 52½ hours after they had won the F A Cup.

Meanwhile, Liverpool's hopes of snatching the championship foundered at Highbury, where Arsenal denied them the victory that would have lifted them to the top of the table on goal average.

So Brian Clough, Derby's manager, now holidaying in the Scilly Isles, will be leading his troops into battle in the European Cup next season.

Peter Daniel with his Player of the Year trophy, 23 April 1975

24 *The Daily Telegraph, Monday, December 3, 1973*

Soccer Commentary

CLOUGH MAY REGRET CRUEL CRITICISM OF PLAYERS IN PUBLIC

By DONALD SAUNDERS

WHEN Brian Clough became manager of Brighton, little more than four weeks ago, he took charge of an indifferent team whose poor home performances had carried them perilously close to the relegation zone.

This morning Brighton are a bewildered rabble, utterly demoralised by the humiliation of F A Cup failure against amateur opponents and the heaviest League defeat they have ever suffered on their own pitch.

And as they seek to regain some semblance of composure, the cruellest words I can remember any manager using to describe his own players boom painfully in their ears.

"This team did not have enough heart to fill a thimble," declared Mr Clough after Brighton had been routed 8-2 by Bristol Rovers on Saturday.

Colin Todd and Liverpool's Kevin Keegan in a tussle for the ball, with Rod Thomas close at hand

Leighton James, accompanied by chairman Sam Longson, is introduced to the Baseball Ground crowd after his £300,000 signing from Burnley (November 1975)

160 *Derby County: Champions of England*

Back-room staff at the Baseball Ground (Colin Murphy, Dave Mackay, Des Anderson, Gordon Guthrie, and Richie Norman)

Roy McFarland, the Derby and England centre-half who became one of the Rams' numerous managers

Soccer stars refuse training

Derby players in revolt over manager

By MATT D'ARCY

DERBY COUNTY players today staged soccer's first-ever revolt. They have refused to train under manager Dave Mackay.

The players are not refusing to play matches. But they will train on their own and will not report at the ground until one o'clock on Saturday, 75 minutes before their home game with League leaders Leeds.

Mackay, who succeeded Brian Clough on October 23, hit back at the players after revealing that some of them had admitted that they were at Brian Clough's house last night.

And Mackay, who may now field the Derby reserve team in Saturday's home match with League leaders Leeds, added:

"The players are making themselves the laughing stock of soccer saying one thing one day and different things the next. They are like a schoolboys' team—not men. I am a man and I like dealing with men, not misguided children."

'Misguided children'

From the *Manchester Evening News* (November 1973)

162 Derby County: Champions of England

John Robertson in action for the Rams after his controversial transfer from Nottingham Forest that caused the split between Brian Clough and Peter Taylor

Frank Wignall scores Derby's second goal in their win at Everton during their first championship season (September 1971)

Archie Gemmill is brought down by Liverpool's Emlyn Hughes, and Charlie George scores from the spot in this 1-1 draw at the Baseball Ground (February 1976)

Colin Boulton (on the ground), Hennessey and Todd are powerless to intervene as Jack Whitham heads the first goal of his Liverpool hat-trick at Anfield (December 1971)

12
Warnings, Discord and Temptations

Brian Clough appeared to be leaving Derby County yet again as the 1973-74 season dawned – this time to take over as anchor man on *World of Sport* for London Weekend Television in succession to Jimmy Hill, who had formerly been a player with Brentford and Fulham, then chairman with the Professional Footballers' Association (the man mainly responsible for the abolition of the maximum wage) and afterwards revolutionising manager with Coventry City. Hill, whose lantern-jawed face remained a familiar sight on the small screen with his switch to the BBC, had left to set up his own television consultancy group and become commercial manager at Fulham, the club he subsequently also served as chairman.

LWT offered Clough £18,000 a year 'to take ten million viewers off the BBC' (Clough's own assessment) in their anxiety to counter Hill's departure to the other channel. Sir John Freeman, the LWT chairman, and Cyril Bennett, LWT's Controller of Programmes, spoke to Clough by phone, and arrangements were made for John Bromley, head of LWT sport, and football commentator Brian Moore to meet him to settle all the details. But Clough was not leaving the Baseball Ground just yet. Sam Longson arranged a compromise, if what turned out to be only a temporary one. The manager was to stay on with the Rams and continue in television as a part-time commentator on soccer.

Clough's new TV job involved a weekly appearance in the *On the Ball* programme, pre-recorded for Saturday lunchtimes, and appearances on the ITV panel which analysed top games. 'This is no different to the amount of television work I have been doing for the last three of four years,' he said. 'It just means I have switched channels.'

Derby's chairman made it clear, however, that his patience was wearing thin. Only two months before the parting of the ways did come about, in the most acrimonious circumstances and in the spotlight of national publicity, he declared: 'If he decides this time that he wants to get out of soccer, to give himself a free platform to speak his mind about the FA, Leeds United, and just about anybody else, then I won't stand in his way.'

As late as the autumn of 1972 Sam Longson had been quoted as saying 'everyone knows I think the world of Brian'. A year made a big difference, however, and from having been an avid supporter of this inspirational but provocative character – to the extent that he had regarded him more like an adopted son than a manager, carried a photograph of him in his wallet, and given him fifty Derby County shares as a Christmas present – he gradually had his enthusiasm eroded to the point where the split was simmering just below the surface. Old Sam had become exasperated by the repeated rumours of Brian's impending departure and increasingly alarmed by his continued outbursts that had attracted admonitions, then dire warnings, from the highest football authorities. The chairman also feared his hopes of getting onto the League's Management Committee would be damaged.

Clough had already complained that the FA and League were conducting a vendetta against him when he gave them serious cause for action by going into print with a call for Sir Alf Ramsey to be disciplined because of his England team selections involving allegedly 'brutal' players. Norman Hunter and Peter Storey were named in the article, but the managers of their clubs, Don Revie and Bertie Mee, refrained from comment. The FA, though unexpectedly deciding that Clough's diatribe did not bring the game into disrepute, joined the League in sending a letter to Derby County, warning that any future outbursts would be regarded as their responsibility.

The reference to Leeds in Sam Longson's statement arose from Clough's comment, also much-publicised, that the Elland Road club should have been relegated to the Second Division instead of having a suspended fine of £3,000 imposed because of their poor disciplinary record in the 1971-72 season. Clough had also criticised the FA Commission's view that Don Revie was not implicated in the matters which brought his club's record before them, adding: 'Some of those who sit in judgment have a vested interest. It is wrong for chairmen and directors of other clubs to be handing out fines.'

Clough made another rod for his own back that contributed to the shortness of his calamitous stay with Leeds United a few years later by making derogatory remarks about Peter Lorimer, one of the Yorkshire club's most popular players, at a dinner in Leeds organised by Yorkshire Television and the Variety Club of Great Britain. The hard-shooting Scottish winger attended as guest of honour and was presented with Yorksport's Sportsman of the Year trophy, but he had left by the time Clough got up to make the discordant speech in which he accused him of falling down 'when he hasn't been kicked', and protesting when he had 'nothing to protest about'.

Harold Wilson, who was between his two terms as Prime Minister, and Sir Len Hutton, the former Yorkshire and England batsman, were among the 500 diners Clough kept waiting while he went to the lavatory before launching into a fifteen-minute tirade of caustic comments, liberally sprinkled with swear words, which the television company said they would censor because of his 'insults and abuse'. Many guests walked out as he was cat-called, booed and jeered. The speech, for which Clough was not paid, was to have been shown on Yorkshire Television three nights later, and then on the national network. After much discussion among the TV controllers it was withdrawn – not specifically on account of its content but because when they looked at it again they found that the Derby manager had turned to the cameramen and said: 'You can switch off now lads. This is not for recording.'

Clough said he was certain he was not rude. He also stated: 'Yorkshire Television wanted someone they could stick on film and steal ten minutes or a quarter of an hour for their Thursday programme. Well, I'm no more interested in what Yorkshire TV requires this Thursday than I am in how Nottingham Pork Butchers went on last Thursday. If in future they want a puppet to get up and say something to please everybody in the room, I suggest they invite Basil Brush.'

The temptation for Clough to go into television full time fed the fact, as he conceded, that working outside the mainstream of soccer had occupied his mind for some while. He said he had even thought about 'packing it in' when Derby won the League title, but after the approach to fill the vacancy left by Jimmy Hill had fallen through he declared himself 'totally and utterly committed to football, with still much for me to do'. At the same time, he was cautious enough to observe that although he would like to see out his contract with Derby, the 4½ years it had still to run in the August of 1973 were 'a long time to commit oneself'.

When asked to comment on an earlier statement that soccer had lost much of its magnetism for him, he replied: 'Ask any manager about the game in mid-January and you'll get the same answer. January is like death. All managers feel run down at this time, but we all get over it.'

To some extent, the jaundiced outlook Clough had on soccer management at one stage was influenced by a rift between himself and Peter Taylor that became public knowledge after the absence through illness of the chairman and assistant manager at the same time had left the manager complaining that he was not prepared to run the Rams single-handed. Taylor was also upset because the row was not kept secret, but said there was no question of their splitting up. 'We've had dozens of rows in our years together,' he admitted, 'but we've always come through them. We've also thrashed this one out.'

Clough could be no other than well aware that speaking his mind got him into a lot of trouble, but he said it was enough for him to know he had been right. He added:

'The strange thing is that it's only now, when we've won championships, that people raise a stink. Nobody cared when we were near the bottom of the Second Division. I used to say just the same things five years ago. Now everybody wants to know what I think and knocks me for thinking it. Anyone who employs me and wants to change me must be nuts. I think my childhood gave me this hatred I have for hypocrisy. We all have to use it sometimes, but it's still the worst of sins. Yet it is something which seems to feed like a disease on football managers. To be a manager you've got to be a bit of everything, and that means that, as well as the good qualities, you've got to lie, do stupid things. The trouble comes when you do one of these things too much. Then you're a bad manager.'

In *The Daily Telegraph*, Bob Oxby recalled: 'I remember being in a boardroom when he was holding forth about everything under the sun. His mother nodded in his direction and made an unmistakable "yapping" gesture. "Been the same since he was 12," she said.'

Of the occasions when there was talk of Clough and Taylor leaving Derby, five firm offers were made for them to do so according to Clough's reckoning – from Birmingham City, Coventry City (twice), Barcelona and the Greek national team. There was also a tentative offer from Keith Collings, then chairman of Sunderland, the club a group of businessmen wanted Clough to manage when, late in 1969, they unsuccessfully sought to oust the board at Roker Park with an offer to put £300,000 into the club on condition that Alan Brown, the former Burnley centre-half who was another to have had a big influence on Clough's disciplinary outlook, was dismissed from his second spell in charge. At other times, after he had left Derby, Clough was twice turned down by Sunderland, the club with which his playing career had been cut short by injury, but he would have been prepared to have considered an offer they wanted to make to him while he was with Nottingham Forest if Stuart Dryden, then chairman at the City Ground, had allowed it. That was when Sunderland were seeking a replacement for another former Burnley player, Jimmy Adamson, who had become one of Clough's managerial successors at Leeds, and banners at Roker Park were urging 'Brian Come Home'.

Back at the start of the 1973-74 season, the impending upheaval behind the Derby County scenes was masked as only one point was dropped, and no goal conceded, in the first three games. Roger Davies, retaining his hold on the No 9 shirt only seven weeks after having a cartilage operation, with John O'Hare on the bench, supplied the pass from which John McGovern first-timed a peach of a winning goal against Chelsea, and on the following Wednesday evening another 1-0 home victory was gained as one of Alan Hinton's free-kick bombshells pierced Manchester City's defence. It was the first time for twelve years that the Rams had won their first two matches of a season.

O'Hare and Davies switched roles for the next game, at Birmingham, which might have had the same result instead of ending in a scoreless draw if, with just under half-an-hour to go, referee John Homewood had not decided against awarding what Clough called 'the most blatant penalty I've seen since I came to Derby'. Kevin Hector, tripped by Kenny Burns as he moved in to shoot, put his hands to his head in disbelief as, instead, a free-kick was given against Derby for something Gemmill said.

The discipline instilled in the Rams' players by good management was commendably demonstrated when they refrained from the deplorable practice, so often seen in soccer in such circumstances, of clamouring around the official in protest. Clough's zest for dealing with those who transgressed – 'the referees' friend', Norman Burtenshaw, a leading match official of his day, called him – dated back to when he was head boy at his Marton Grove school. Ron Smith, one of his fellow pupils, recalled:

'His discipline was rigid. Every day he would haul a crowd of lads out of line to see the headmaster. He was fair, but very, very firm. Some of the lads certainly saw him as a big-head, but whatever you thought it was obvious to everyone that he was different from the rest of us. He stood out.'

While with Forest, Clough, abetted by Taylor, transformed the careers of such 'problem boys' as Kenny Burns, who freely acknowledged that he was 'a changed player', and Larry Lloyd, who, though admitting that he and Clough did not have much in common, said that he would 'run through a brick wall for him'. For all the emphasis on discipline, however, it is a startling fact that five Forest players were ordered off in a short period during 1982 – three of them in pre-season games in Spain. Indeed, for several years the number of Forest sendings-off was unusually high for a club whose manager was such a stickler for requiring his players to behave.

For Derby County, there were to be just nine more games after the draw at Birmingham before their management pair so sensationally walked out. Three of those matches were lost, each without a goal to the Rams, but the four wins included impressive home revenge for a defeat by Liverpool at Anfield, a 6-2 drubbing of Southampton in which Kevin Hector scored the first of his three hat-tricks that season, and, finally, a victory over Manchester United at Old Trafford that hoisted the club to third place in the First Division table.

During that period Clough completed what was to be his last signing for Derby and parted with a player who, though no longer in the first-team reckoning, had rendered superb service over nine seasons, making just over 400 League and Cup appearances and scoring 115 goals. The transfer out, of Alan Durban, came first. The Welshman had evolved from being a ready scorer as an inside-forward in Tim Ward's time to revelling in the most influential years of his career as a midfielder under the supervision of Clough and Taylor. He was fully appreciative of how much the pair had done for him, and paid this especially glowing tribute to Clough:

'Okay, so a lot of players don't really like him. So what? He doesn't want affection – he wants respect. One reason I like the bloke is that when he came to Derby he trebled my wages in five years. Without his influence I'd have been another ordinary Second Division player all my career. Instead, I played at the top and won 27 caps for Wales. Maybe there's a strong element of fear about the way he handles players, but what's wrong with that? People should be on their toes when the boss is around. He's always gone out to buy class players, and when he can't get them he has the ability to get the maximum from the players he already has.'

That fear factor was never more evident than during the first of the two short and stormy spells as manager that Clough endured between leaving Derby and taking Forest to all the game's top honours except the FA Cup. Before player power notoriously booted him out at Leeds, where chairman Manny Cussins contradicted in 44 days his assessment of him as 'the best manager in football', Clough recognised that his Brighton players were 'petrified of me' after they had been knocked out of the FA Cup by the amateurs of Walton and Hersham, then given him 'my worst day in football' by crashing to an 2-8 Third Division defeat, the heaviest at home in the club's history, against Bristol Rovers.

Alan Durban, who captained his country, had a knack of finding space in opposing sides' crowded penalty areas even after dropping back from the attack, and the last two of his four hat-tricks for the Rams came while he was filling the midfield role – in, as already recalled, the defeat of Bristol City at the end of the Second Division promotion season, and an FA Cup-tie against Notts County. He completed the first one in the dying minutes of an away match with Birmingham City, snatching a remarkable 5-5 draw with the club that had also let in five in a game of eight goals at Derby earlier in the same 1965-66 season. The second of Durban's hat-tricks for Derby coincided with the home debut of Kevin Hector, who was the Rams' other scorer in a 4-3 defeat of Huddersfield Town.

For a fee similar to the £10,000 Tim Ward had paid Cardiff City for him, the 32-year-old Durban moved into the Third Division with Shrewsbury Town on 13 September 1973. From being appointed captain and assistant manager, he moved up to caretaker manager when Maurice Evans was sacked as the threat of relegation grew, then was made manager while still playing. It was too late to avoid the drop, but while Evans was back at Reading – managing the club for which he had been a popular player, and soon afterwards guiding them to their first promotion for fifty years before winning the League Cup with Oxford United – Durban missed only two of Shrewsbury's 46 matches, and was their third highest scorer with a double-figure tally, as they went straight back up in 1974-75 as Division Four runners-up to Mansfield Town.

He also guided Shrewsbury to success in the Welsh Cup, making up somewhat for the disappointment of having been omitted by Cardiff from a final in that competition which he had helped them to reach with a 5-0 win. In making more than 170 appearances for Shrewsbury (and scoring 34 goals), Durban exceeded 550 in the League overall and hung up his boots with the rare experience of having played on the grounds of all 92 clubs then in membership. His most astute signing for the Shropshire club was Colin Griffin, a 6ft-tall defender he plucked from Derby County's reserve team. Originally obtained on a month's loan with the object of gaining experience for the Rams' benefit, Griffin did so well in his first League games that he earned a full contract and went on to play for the Town in over 400 more.

With Richie Barker's assistance, Durban set Shrewsbury on course for the further rise to the Second Division they achieved under the direction of Graham Turner, a former England youth international who had found his way to Gay Meadow via Wrexham and Chester, before Stoke City chose him to fill the managerial gap they caused by dismissing George Eastham, short-term successor to the long-serving Tony Waddington, after an FA Cup defeat by Blyth Spartans.

Durban was quite amenable to staying with Stoke, regarding the future there as 'full of promise' after piloting them back to the First Division, when they blocked a Leeds attempt to lure him away to replace Jock Stein, who left to follow Ally MacLeod as manager of Scotland within a few weeks of succeeding Brian Clough at Elland Road. But he was more receptive to the approach Sunderland's millionaire chairman, Tom Cowie, made in the summer of 1981 after failing to persuade Bobby Robson to leave Ipswich. When he was with Cardiff he had been told by Ivor Allchurch, the 'Golden Boy of Wales' who was then at Ninian Park after achieving with Newcastle his ambition to perform on the First Division stage, how special it was to be associated with soccer in the North-East. He was also influenced by the criticism he had attracted, as Stoke found it harder going in the top flight, from fans he had advised to go to watch clowns in a circus if they wanted entertainment.

This hard-headed realist, as he described himself, therefore spurned Stoke's offer of a lucrative new contract and opted to join Sunderland, only to find life up there far removed from being as enjoyable as Allchurch had indicated. In his first season in charge, 1981-82, the then Roker Park club had an even narrower escape from losing their newly-regained First Division status than the one that had cost his predecessor, Ken Knighton, the job, and they had another struggle to survive the following season, his preparations for which included a friendly against Derby County in which he again trod the Baseball Ground turf for a few minutes as a substitute. With no real signs of an improvement, Durban was dismissed two months from the end of his third season on Wearside.

Len Ashurst, a former Sunderland full-back, took over from him, leaving a vacancy Cardiff City filled by themselves appointing one of their past players – Alan Durban. The swap did neither of them any good. Ashurst's number was up when Sunderland were relegated in 1985, soon after losing to Norwich by an own-goal in the League's Milk Cup final, and Durban was discarded by Cardiff after being unable to arrest their nose-dive from Second Division to Fourth in successive seasons, 1984-86.

The way for Durban then temporarily turned out of soccer. He reverted to lawn tennis, at which, with cricket (he had helped his school to win the Port Talbot Junior Festival Cup and played in Glamorgan's second team), he had been an adept player before concentrating on football. He was appointed general manager of the Telford Racquet Centre, and also managed Telford's tennis team in the national league. Later, during the 1990s, he was back with Derby County as assistant manager and chief scout – reunited with Roy McFarland, who was then briefly the club's manager after having left for Bradford City and lifted them from the Fourth Division with the assistance of Mick Jones, a former Derby reserve player. McFarland's return to the Rams, originally as second-in-command after Peter Taylor's surprising emergence from retirement as their manager soon after leaving Forest, was another episode in the club's too-frequent brushes with authority. A sustained charge of poaching (also of Jones, as coach) cost them a £10,000 fine by the League, and £55,000 in compensation to Bradford City.

The player who joined Derby County the week after Durban's move to Shrewsbury was Henry Newton. It was a signing Brian Clough had had to wait six years to make. After shedding the frustration of failing to land Bobby Moore by ending that long quest for Newton with the completion of his £100,000 transfer from Everton at a Stoke hotel, Clough revealed that he had first made an approach for this versatile hard worker within a few days of taking over at Derby.

At that time Nottingham-born Newton was with Forest, whom he had joined early in 1960 after playing for Nottingham Boys. Newton did not then find Derby the big attraction they were so soon to become, but he looked upon them in a very different light when Forest repeated their rejection of another inquiry about him from the Rams before allowing him to move to Merseyside three years later. The player made that clear after he had at last found his way to the Baseball Ground by saying:

'I was very disappointed that Derby didn't sign me in 1970. They were the club I really wanted to join, and for a long time I had regrets about moving to Everton. I have missed three successful years at Derby, but I reckon I've got three or four years left. I couldn't be happier to be joining Derby and moving back among people I know.'

Newton was on the verge of England's 1970 World Cup squad after four appearances in the Under-23 side, but he was never to win the full cap he deserved. The Newton who was chosen for England while with Everton, and who did get to Mexico, was Keith Newton, who cost the Goodison Park club £70,000 less than the £150,000 they paid for his namesake (plus Irish international Tommy Jackson in part exchange) when he joined them from Blackburn.

Neither Newton lived up to expectations at Everton. Keith's career took a down-turn following his return from the World Cup, and after being sold to Burnley (whom he helped to promotion) he criticised manager Harry Catterick for having cramped his style. Henry never properly settled in the North-West, and, beset by a series of injuries, he played only 83 League and Cup games in his three years with Everton before Clough brought him back to the Midlands. Derby's manager found the deal surprisingly simple to complete after making several unsuccessful overtures. Noting that Billy Bingham had made Northern Ireland's Dave Clements his first signing, from Sheffield Wednesday, after filling the vacancy left by Catterick's move into a senior executive role following a heart attack, he phoned to bid again for Newton, and terms were agreed in minutes. Three hours later Bingham and the player were on their way to their rendezvous with Clough, and the final details were swiftly settled.

Bingham, who, like Catterick, was with Everton as both player and manager, said he was sorry to be losing such a very good player, but he now had more midfielders than he needed and felt that the fee was 'attractive enough for a 29-year-old'. Clough enthused:

'The great thing about Henry is that we are buying not just one player but three. He has skill, aggression and character, and he will provide competition for places in midfield, the middle of the defence, and at full-back. I have been sick of getting on the team bus and seeing the same 12 faces. It had even got to the stage when players were not bothering to look at the team sheet when it was pinned up. They will start looking now because, at last, we have done something to open up alternatives. We are keen to buy again to give us an even bigger squad, and I think everybody knows by now that to do this we are prepared to bid beyond the British transfer record.'

Little was Newton, or anybody else for that matter, to know that he would so quickly be caught up in the dramatic developments at the Baseball Ground which were to nullify that promise by Brian Clough to buy boldly for Derby again. Injuries were also to handicap Newton with the Rams, but he made just over 150 appearances for them before Dave Mackay, having obtained his next managerial post at Walsall after his dismissal by Derby, took him to Fellows Park on a free transfer during the summer of 1977. Within a few months, however, Newton had his Walsall contract cancelled as arthritis forced his retirement, and he had to have a hip operation while running a sub-post office in Derby.

With the Rams, he had time for only three games before the stormy exit of the manager and his assistant, but the acute disappointment he felt about that, and the trauma of being caught up in the massive upheaval it caused, were to be offset by the reward of a League championship medal when Derby County topped the First Division for the second time in four years.

Resignations spark Players' Rebellion

'When you have a good manager you don't want to lose him. He got the respect of the players straightaway because he treats the players the right way. If you're wrong he'll tell you. If you've done well he'll tell you that as well. Tactically, he tells you what he wants, and you do that. When you have respect for a manager you want to win games for him. He knows how much the players want him to stay. We would all be devastated if he left.'
David Beckham, talking about Sven-Goran Eriksson, February 2004

On 15 October 1973, two days after Derby County's defeat of Manchester United at Old Trafford with a goal scored by Kevin Hector after only four minutes' play, Brian Clough walked into the weekly board meeting at the Baseball Ground and told the astonished directors that he and Peter Taylor were resigning. Months of growing unrest behind the scenes were about to erupt into a crisis of sensational proportions, unique in English football, with crowd demonstrations, the threat of a players' rebellion, bitter accusations and counter-claims, and writs for libel and slander.

Trouble had been boiling up since Clough's signing of his new part-time contract with London Weekend TV before the start of the season. The breaking point came with a letter to the manager from chairman Sam Longson, his sixth in three months. It was an accumulation of criticisms regarding television in particular and the whole media in general. Derby's directors had become thoroughly alarmed by Clough's continued attacks on soccer's establishment and leading personalities, and by the action they feared might be taken against them by the FA and League in consequence. They also took exception to the fact that Clough's ITV work had made him miss board meetings, and that he had failed to keep to an undertaking not to talk on TV or radio, or have articles appear under his name in newspapers, without their permission.

There was another reason for the final showdown, one not made common knowledge at the time. Clough was not in the habit of going into boardrooms after matches, but Taylor persuaded him that they should go up to the one at Old Trafford because 'winning here doesn't happen very often'. While there, Taylor was beckoned over by Jack Kirkland, who told him to report to him on the Monday to explain exactly what his duties were. Taylor duly did so, but it was a humiliating experience which both he and Clough considered absolutely unnecessary, and his pride was irretrievably hurt. He saw it as the Ord ordeal at Hartlepool all over again, an attempt to get at Clough through himself. In his view there could be no other course but to desert Derby, though on that fateful Monday he went back home and left his pal to resign for both of them.

It was a decision Clough regretted almost as quickly as he had made it. 'Leaving the great players we have on the staff is the most heartbreaking decision I have had to make in my life,' he said, 'but it just has to be. There is too much pride and self-respect for us to remain.' He later admitted: 'I was a fool to have resigned at Derby. I should have suffered the problems and seen off the board, but I thought I could take on the world. I was happy there. We had a lot of success and laughter.'

But there was no going back, literally – although, as we shall be coming to in its proper order, it did at one stage seem certain that he would be. The news of the split spread like wildfire, making the Baseball Ground in Derby's Shaftesbury Crescent the magnet for the national media for some weeks to come. The effect on the players Clough and Taylor were leaving behind was to be the most devastating of all, with the Rams' England men left feeling particularly demoralised as they trained miles away with the national squad for the following Wednesday's match with Poland at Wembley on which World Cup qualification depended.

The gloom into which those absent players were cast by the grim developments at Derby was deepened as England, in whose team Roy McFarland was belatedly joined by Kevin Hector, stumbled off the trail to the next summer's finals in West Germany in being able to do no better than draw instead of gaining the win they required. And that huge disappointment was exacerbated by the ludicrously late introduction of Hector for one of the shortest international debuts on record – with the game inside its last two minutes, during which he still went desperately close to snatching a winning goal. Bobby Moore, who was on the bench that night, recalled that dramatic climax with these words in his autobiography:

'Once Alf agreed I was tearing at Kevin's track suit trousers. Someone else was trying to get his top off. You could feel the seconds ticking away. Racing the clock, we almost threw him onto the pitch. And in the 90 seconds he almost got Alf another knighthood. Alf ended up taking stick for forgetting the time and sending on a sub so late. Kevin might have put us in the finals with his only touch of the ball for England. I think he might have saved us if Alf had acted sooner. It was obvious we needed a left-sided player to go through them. Emlyn Hughes was doing his best from left-back, but, as usual, he was cutting the ball back to his trusty old right foot and losing the angles and chances. It was the beginning of the end of the entire Ramsey regime. Poland went into the finals instead of England.'

Kevin Hector would have been a national hero if his late effort had not been blocked on the line in a packed goalmouth, and he might well also have become an established member of the England team. As it was, he only once more went into action for his country – and that, in their next match, was again as a substitute given precious little time in which to make his mark as Italy held onto a one-goal lead at Wembley. That was also the game in which Bobby Moore last played for England.

Hector had first been strongly tipped for a cap as far back as four years earlier, after taking his goals tally to ten in fourteen games with a couple in the 4-0 defeat of Liverpool in the Rams' first season back in the top division. Brian Clough had then rated him the best striker in England, but had expressed himself 'reluctant to sing the praises of a player in order to get him international recognition'. Hector's representative honours were limited to his appearances in inter-league matches until he was first brought into an England squad the month before the crucial clash with Poland, increasing the Derby contingent to a record four by joining McFarland, Todd (returning from his ban) and Nish among the 22 from whom the team was chosen to meet an Austrian side that was hammered 7-0. As against the Poles, only McFarland made the starting selection. To be overlooked for so long when many experts rated him highly was a grave injustice to Hector, and it was again as only a substitute that, a few months after the conclusion of his abbreviated England career, he was with his three County colleagues in the Football League team that crushed the Scottish League at Manchester City's ground.

Sir Alf Ramsey, who had first blatantly invited criticism over substitutions by seeing West Germany turn a 0-2 deficit into a 3-2 victory after he had taken off Bobby Charlton and Martin Peters twenty minutes from the end of a World Cup quarter-final, was not alone in being taken to task after the Poland game. Brian Clough contradicted popular opinion by calling Tomaszewski, the Polish goalkeeper, a clown. Unorthodox no doubt, brave without question, but certainly no joker as far as England were concerned as he pulled off a spectacular one-handed save from Manchester City's Colin Bell and tipped aside a tricky header from Leeds striker Allan Clarke. Only a penalty by Clarke defeated him, wiping out the lead Domarski gained after an untypical missed tackle by Norman Hunter – the defender, incidentally, Kevin Hector reckoned was the most difficult he ever had to play against.

On the day after his inflammatory after-match comments on television had intensified the already red-hot publicity his resignation from Derby County had attracted, Brian Clough turned up the heat still higher by taking the first steps to issue a writ for alleged libel, seeking damages from the club, Sam Longson, and four other members of the board – Sydney Bradley, Jack Kirkland, Bob Innes and Bill Rudd. This resulted from a statement issued on the club's behalf by the Rams' chairman in which the most serious allegations were that Clough had committed offences connected with expenses, improperly obtained salary increases for himself and Peter Taylor amounting to more than £40,000 in the past year, and threatened to sell a first-team player to provide compensation for their leaving the club. Clough had no real wish to go to court, the directors even less so, and the futility of the legal action he started was underlined when the out-of-court settlement of £17,500 he eventually received, though offsetting his lack of a pay-off, was reduced by lawyers' fees.

Other points in the club's statement included the assertion that Clough 'did not take kindly' to the board's decision, on Longson's recommendation, that the administration of the club should be put in the complete charge of secretary Stuart Webb. Scrutiny of expenses had 'turned out to be a battle between the manager and the board', and there was a genuine fear among the directors that they could be severely censured, and the club expelled from the League, if the manager persisted in his press and television attacks on the FA, League and personnel of other clubs. Letters had been received from the FA and the League about 'the serious nature of these attacks'.

Little had the Derby directors realised what they were letting themselves in for when they had originally been all in favour of their manager's appearances on television, seeing it at that time as good publicity for the club. They had, in fact, insisted that he should accept an invitation to sit on the World Cup panel, only soon to find that he was so much in demand, and so provocative with his remarks, that they felt compelled to view the matter very differently.

The statement made by the club after Clough's resignation also complained about his missing two board meetings through travelling to London for recordings in his new role as a 'freelance commentator' for the *On the Ball* programme broadcast by ITV each Saturday during the season. On this subject, the chairman continued:

'I received a letter from the manager dated September 24, 1973, in which he stated that he had decided that, to avoid any further confrontation or misunderstanding regarding television, radio or newspaper work, he would not utter one single word to any of these media unless permission had at first been obtained. At the present point of time he is already due to appear before an FA Disciplinary Commission on serious charges due to press attacks on the FA, and even as late as last Saturday at Old Trafford he was alleged to have made what is now called 'the Harvey Smith gesture' to Mr Edwards, chairman of United, and to Sir Matt Busby, a director. All in all, I say enough is enough.'

On the day the club's statement was issued, Thursday, 18 October 1973, Clough called a press conference at Derby's Midland Hotel to give his answers to the points raised before leaving to play that night for an Old England XI against a European Past Masters XI in a game held at Birmingham City's ground in aid of a charity to provide football pitches for under-privileged children.

After dismissing the claim that he had objected to the secretary having full charge of the administration as 'too barmy for words', he asked that if he had sought unjustified expenses why was he not in jail? 'Why,' he also demanded, 'do they wait until my resignation before accusing me of being a thief?'

He said that in 6½ years only one of his expense sheets had been rejected, and that was because the club maintained that he had been working for television at the time. The allegation about selling a player to provide for his own compensation he described as 'the selling of your right hand', adding: 'It is striking at the very roots of everything you have ever stood for in your life. To make an accusation like this you have got to have proof. It is criminal. It is in the realms of fantasy. It is too ludicrous even to reply to.'

Clough categorically denied that he and Peter Taylor had used the offer they refused from Coventry City to persuade Derby to increase their salaries. 'My salary was £14,000, and Peter's £8,000. The rest of the money which made up the club's figures we got from incentives through blood, sweat and tears, and now they are trying to hang us.' The alleged V-sign at Old Trafford he shrugged off by saying that if that had been the case 'Sir Matt Busby will be on the phone tomorrow engaging the same QC as me'. He concluded:

'Why didn't they sack me? Because according to the statement I didn't break any rule. I broke every rule. According to them, I should be in jail sitting with the train robbers. Why didn't they put me there? Why didn't they bring in the FA and the Football League on their behalf? I have been told often that I was lucky to have Sam Longson and his millions behind me. But he has never been called upon to put in a penny because the success of the club has been so great, and the finances so sound. The present financial situation at Derby is such that, give or take a few quid, they could go out and spend a quarter of a million and not be in the red.'

How remote that rosy picture now is! Not that a quarter of a million would buy a player of much consequence these days. The prosperous financial position in which Derby County had been placed by Clough and Taylor was made abundantly clear the month after they had left when the club announced a profit of £98,139 on the past season, a healthy advance on one of £27,000 the previous year.

And quite apart from that leaving so much available for buying new players, with a contingency fund of some £300,000, the legacy also included a team of champions, both recent and in the near future, a fine new grandstand and a new training ground.

A sting was injected into the tale of expenses by Clough when he revealed that only the week before the resignations spawned a slanging match he had told the chairman that he and Taylor wanted to go to Rotterdam to see Poland play Holland. Longson, who attended England's match with Poland as a guest of the FA, had given permission, but only if they paid their own expenses. 'I told him that if he was going to be as small as that I would pay my own way, and he immediately replied: 'In that case I withdraw permission for you to go altogether.' We went anyway. We paid our own expenses.'

Clough delivered this other parting shot: 'Our break with Derby County has been caused by others' frustration because we had pulled the club out from nowhere and made it great. Suddenly it was *our* club, not *theirs*. People used to say to the directors: 'Who's running Derby County, Brian Clough or you? Things started to go wrong the day Derby County won their first Football League championship. That was when the directors started basking in the glory of it all and making the mistake that they could keep it up without us.'

An immediate sequel to the split was the formation of a protest movement that sought to co-ordinate the support of thousands of Derby fans with the object of ousting the board and persuading Clough and Taylor to return. It was headed by Don Shaw, a 39-year-old Derby playwright who was a lifelong supporter, and Bill Holmes, a 43-year-old former amateur international who was a manager in industry at Burton-upon-Trent. They had the wholehearted backing of the man who had already resigned from the board – Mike Keeling, who professed that his friend Brian Clough was ready to return 'in certain circumstances', but only if there was what he termed 'a mammoth public outcry'.

The first big attempt to mount that outcry was made by the hastily-formed Supporters' Action Group at the first opportunity – at the Rams' next match, at home to Leicester City on the Saturday. Holmes said he wanted at least 200 volunteers in the morning to offer their services by standing outside the turnstiles to ask fans to sign a petition critical of the board. 'If the fans show their disapproval,' he said, 'I hope the directors will decide to resign and make most of their shares available for thousands of Derby supporters. I know of no-one else in public life who has Brian Clough's honesty, integrity and moral courage. What the board didn't realise, or were not able to cope with, was that they had a genius on their hands, and genius is always coupled with eccentricity and waywardness.'

Shaw, who had forecast that 'this movement will be massive, the whole town is seething with anger', weighed in with: 'This man Clough must not be allowed to go. The board must resign. I talked to Brian this morning [the morning of the match] and he told me his heart was in Derby County, and that he wanted to come back. That's what we all want. That's why we've got to shout for him.'

There was a crowd of more than 34,000 at the game, then the Rams' biggest home gate of the season, but the planned demonstration faded out. In pouring rain, the fans simply left the ground at the final whistle and went home. It was, however, no portent of what was to come in the weeks ahead.

The scenes inside the ground before the kick-off were akin to those of the Roman amphitheatre. Sam Longson presented himself to the crowd in the directors' box five minutes before the teams came out. He stood there, arms upraised, as many fans clapped and cheered him while others jeered. Two minutes later came the dramatic entrance of Brian Clough. Tremendous cheering broke out as he stepped to the front of the main stand near the VIP box. Banners were displayed bearing the words CLOUGH AND TAYLOR IN and LONGSON OUT. From all parts of the ground the chant 'We want Cloughie' roared out. Longson retaliated immediately. He got to his feet again, and the two antagonists stood only some ten yards apart in an undignified gladiator-like duel for public acclaim. Clough won – but not to the extent he would no doubt have expected.

The dethroned manager had no intention of staying to watch the game, and within a few minutes he left the ground in the Rolls-Royce, lent to him by a friend, in which he had arrived. He had an appointment in London that night, to be interviewed on the Michael Parkinson television show. Longson settled down to watch a match that was the best seen at the Baseball Ground so far that season, won deservedly, but by only the odd goal of three, by Derby County. With the diverting preliminaries, it all made for a highly entertaining afternoon, later also appreciated by the millions who saw the televised highlights.

Derby's team, chosen by caretaker manager Jimmy Gordon, was unchanged from the one that had gained the club's first away win of the season in Manchester the previous Saturday. It was greatly to the Derby players' credit, and also to Gordon's for his part in getting them in the right frame of mind, that they put the upheaval of the week behind them to produce the excellent performance that ended Leicester's unbeaten away record. Praise was also due to Derek Nippard, the referee, whose sensible control contributed to the fast and exciting flow of the play. Both teams, too, showed an admirable sporting spirit – reflected in the fact that neither trainer was needed on the field – and so did the supporters of each side on such a potentially explosive occasion. The backing Derby's players were given was especially commendable.

The early goal the Rams required to settle nerves that must have been on a knife edge came in the sixth minute, when Henry Newton set the tempo for his best display since joining the club by beginning the move from which Hinton's curling low centre from the right was slid home by Hector, closing in from the opposite flank. Hector, in the form that might have saved England had he been given a proper chance, almost increased the lead with a courageous diving header among the flying boots, but Stringfellow and Glover had efforts disallowed for offside before Worthington punished Gemmill's misguided pass back into a crowded penalty area by equalising twelve minutes into the second half.

Nothing daunted, Derby were ahead again within six minutes, and again Hinton was the provider. The winger left the beaten Whitworth grounded and crossed a perfect centre that the leaping McGovern met with a gem of a header Shilton was powerless to keep out. The England keeper who was to grace Derby's goal more than a decade later had his work cut out to prevent a heavier defeat, saving well from Davies and Hector (twice) as the Rams ended on a strong note to pull level in the table with Burnley, who lost at Everton – but still four points behind leaders Leeds United.

As the teams trooped off there was scarcely a whiff of the transformation from the exhilaration of victory to the calamitous events that were to engulf Derby County within 24 hours. No sooner had the first venture for a new manager been repulsed by Bobby Robson's unhesitating decision to stay with Ipswich Town than Sam Longson and company were dealt another damaging blow. It came in the form of a letter, handed to the chairman by club captain Roy McFarland. It read:

'During the events of the past week we, the undersigned players, kept our feelings within the dressing room. However, at this time we are unanimous in our support for Mr Clough and Mr Taylor, and ask that they be reinstated as manager and assistant manager of this club.'

The letter, with which it was emphasised Clough had no connection, was signed by all the members of Derby's first-team squad except Henry Newton, who was in Liverpool on personal business that Monday. On the day after resigning, Clough had told Ian Wooldridge in the *Daily Mail* that he would be disgusted if it were true that the players were considering putting in transfer applications out of sympathy. He had said that it would break his heart if they lacked discipline to the extent of becoming a rabble after all he had tried to instil in them while he had been their manager. Now, on being given a copy of the letter received by the chairman, he declared that, whatever happened, he would be grateful to them for restoring his faith in human nature, adding: 'We have made a point of not seeing the players, but we have now arranged to meet them to hear what they have got to say.'

McFarland, speaking on behalf of all the players, said: 'We decided last week that Saturday's match must come first, and we did not intend to do anything rash. After the game we called a meeting. It was made clear that no-one was under any obligation to attend, but everyone was there. It was the same with the letter. We made it a condition that if any player didn't want to sign it, it wouldn't be held against him. There were no refusals. The players did not want to get involved, but we are involved too deeply with these two men – so deeply, in fact, that we could not say in our hearts that we could be behind any other manager, no matter who took over.'

Brian Clough, who on the night before the match with Leicester had addressed a group from the British Institute of Management at the Midland Hotel where he would otherwise have been giving his usual pep talk to his team, responded to the invitation to meet the players by organising a champagne party for them and their wives at a hotel at Newton Solney, a village near Burton-upon-Trent. Clearly touched by the loyalty that was being shown, he said that champagne had never tasted sweeter. After the meeting, McFarland expressed the hope that the stage would not be reached where transfer requests were made, but a revolt was in the offing. Don Shaw prematurely hailed 'a victory for justice', claiming that 'those five directors who tried to hold the town to ransom have got their comeuppance'. He thought the board now had no alternative but to reinstate Clough and Taylor.

A warning note was already being sounded, however, by Cliff Lloyd, secretary of the Professional Footballers' Association, who was keeping in close touch with what was going on. 'I can appreciate the way players are feeling when a manager has been as popular as Brian Clough obviously has,' he said, 'but no doubt they will be aware of their duty to the club and themselves. Their individual reputations are at stake.'

Meanwhile, down on the south coast there was another development that was to be linked with the crisis at Derby. Pat Saward, a former Republic of Ireland international wing-half who had helped Aston Villa to the FA Cup in 1957 and the Second Division title in 1960, was dismissed as manager of Brighton and Hove Albion. After being assistant to Jimmy Hill at Coventry, he had led Brighton to promotion from the Third Division in 1972, earning the reward of a five-year contract, but had been unable to prevent their immediate return there. With results failing to improve, the club's directors had decided he could no longer motivate the side, providing yet another classic case of a manager being sacked only days after being given a vote of confidence.

Circumstances similar to those that were making the Baseball Ground the focus of national attention threatened to erupt at the Goldstone Ground in Hove as the players there also spoke of rallying round their departing manager. Neither was Saward in any mood that he should go quietly. He insisted that he was still in office and intended to turn up for work next day as usual, but it quickly became apparent that his position was untenable.

Events at Derby gave Brighton's chairman Mike Bamber, a 43-year-old property tycoon, a ready target in his quest for a successor, but first the Rams filled their own vacancy with an appointment that was similarly logical, if also a stimulator of some violent reactions. After rumour had suggested a return to the Baseball Ground for Jimmy Hagan, who had handed in his resignation as manager of Benfica only the previous month, and Bobby Robson had reaffirmed his intention to stay at Ipswich by finally signing the ten-year contract the Suffolk club had offered him since an unsuccessful attempt by Everton to tempt him away in the summer, Derby County found the answer to their search just a few miles down the A52. Yet another raid on Nottingham Forest brought the second coming of Dave Mackay, just under a year since his move to the City Ground from Swindon Town.

Mackay had been only a few months off his 37th birthday when, on 14 July 1971, he had breezed into Swindon's County Ground declaring himself 'fighting fit' and ready to play on 'for a couple of seasons at least', after a close season, since leaving Derby, during which he had been on a health farm, played squash and golf, and sweated through numerous road runs. The Wiltshire club's manager at that time was Fred Ford, a cheerful character who had been Bristol Rovers' chief coach when I had got to know him while I was with the *Bristol Evening Post*. Ford, whose playing career had been ended by injury, left Rovers to manage Bristol City, but returned to them as manager before also rejoining Swindon (he had briefly coached there after being dismissed by City).

Ford was gradually phased out after Mackay's arrival, and early in the November Swindon announced that Mackay would take over team selection and discipline 'with a view to management when he decides to give up playing'. Ford left to become Torquay United's coach and assistant manager, then was youth coach with Oxford United until his death at 65 in October 1981.

Swindon ended Mackay's first season with them, his last as a player, in mid-table. He played in 26 of their 42 League games, bowing out as a substitute in a 0-1 defeat at Burnley, and scored his final goal in a 2-2 draw with Millwall. That took him to 551 League appearances, of which 135 were made for Hearts, 268 for Tottenham, and 122 for Derby. Including Cup-ties, he altogether played 318 times for Spurs, and 148 for the Rams. His goals for English clubs totalled 60 – all but nine of them for Tottenham. It was while with Hearts that he first came across Des Anderson, who had then been a Hibernian half-back. After Mackay had moved to Tottenham, Anderson assisted Johannesburg Rangers before returning to England, where he wound up his playing career with Millwall. He was coaching schoolboys in South London when Mackay invited him to join him as his assistant at Swindon – a partnership they were to continue with Forest, Derby and Walsall.

Swindon were down in seventeenth place in the Second Division when, on the first day of November in 1972, Mackay suddenly resigned for 'personal reasons' following his attendance at a board meeting. Financial constraints had frustrated him in his attempts to strengthen the side, and it was to improve the cash flow that he had been given further cause for dissatisfaction by the sale that weekend of Don Rogers to Crystal Palace for £140,000. Mackay had promptly spent £50,000 of that money on Tommy Jenkins, a winger from Southampton, and differences of opinion had arisen over the disposition of the balance.

Mackay accepted the offer to manage Forest the day after quitting Swindon. Only four seasons earlier, Forest had been within sight of the League and Cup double, but since then Johnny Carey, the former Manchester United and Eire captain who had been 1949's Footballer of the Year, and Matt Gillies, who resigned two weeks before Mackay's appointment, had both failed to find the formula for more success. Gates had plunged from the 40,000-plus of their First Division days to as low as just under 6,500, with some 10,000 'floating fans' in the area between Derby and Nottingham having deserted to the Rams. And many of those who had stayed on had been giving the team a hard time, with outbursts of bitter barracking at home games.

Forest finished fourteenth in the Second Division in the only season, 1972-73, they were to end with Mackay as their manager. One of their main weaknesses was emphasised when John Galley, his lone signing of any note at £30,000 from Bristol City shortly before Christmas, topped their scoring list with a mere eight goals. I was in Bristol when Galley went there, and remember him for having done on his debut for City, at Huddersfield, what he had done on his debut for Rotherham, at Coventry – score a hat-trick.

Dave Mackay was driving to watch his youth team play at Northampton when Derby obtained permission from Forest to approach him. On getting back to Nottingham later that night, he arranged to meet Sam Longson and Stuart Webb at the Albany Hotel in the city, and in the early hours of the following morning of 23 October 1973, he agreed to step next day into the void left by Brian Clough. The salary of £20,000 a year, in a contract worth £80,000, was almost double his Forest pay.

Mackay wanted to keep the appointment secret until after Forest had played at home against Hull City the night before he took up the Rams' post ('It would be upsetting for my players at Nottingham'), only for Derby's chairman to jump the gun by announcing it from his Chapel-en-le-Frith home in the afternoon. As a result, the first rumblings of the trouble in store resounded even while Mackay was making his final match preparations as Forest's manager. Shortly before the goalless game with Hull, he was visited by Bill Holmes, who advised him not to take his new job, saying that the situation at the Baseball Ground would resolve itself in Clough's favour by the end of the week, and he was in danger of being the fall guy. Barely was his last match as Forest's manager over than another warning shot was fired across his bow. Roy McFarland phoned to plead with him not to return to Derby.

That call from his successor as the club's captain was what he called 'a real shaker', for he and McFarland had been close friends as playing colleagues. He angrily replied that nobody frightened Dave Mackay off, and next day he travelled to Derby hoping that the situation would sort itself out. 'I had confidence in the Derby players,' he said, 'and I felt they would respect me enough to let the whole thing drop.' Events were quickly to prove him very wrong.

END OF PROTEST AFTER BOARDROOM SIEGE

Brian Clough might have become Nottingham Forest's manager just over a year earlier than he did. Indeed, the man who was appointed to the post after Dave Mackay's departure to Derby was well aware that some in the Forest camp wanted Clough in preference to himself. 'During my interviews at Forest,' said Allan Brown, the cultured former Blackpool and Scotland forward, 'I was amazed when two committee men came up to me and said they wanted Clough there and not me. This had nothing to do with Brian. He wasn't party to it.'

The temptation to go for Clough at that time was offset, however, by the fact that his resignation from the Rams did not recommend him to the majority on the Forest's nine-man committee. 'We were looking for the sort of loyalty Billy Walker gave us for 22 years as manager,' said chairman Jim Willmer. Walker had become as much of an institution at the City Ground as he had been as a player of England standard with Aston Villa, guiding Forest from Third Division to First, and to the FA Cup, before resigning in the summer of 1960. Even then, though feeling jaded, he had continued to serve the club on the committee until ill health had forced him out a year before his death towards the end of 1964.

Oddly enough, Clough found favour with Forest as Brown's successor after having quit Brighton in unhappy circumstances and been soured by the sacking at Leeds that left him thinking seriously about leaving the game for good. The troubled events of those intervening fourteen months led Willmer to declare: 'We think Brian has become a more mature and experienced manager.' It was an inspired change of heart, taking Forest to a glut of trophies, including a League title and the European Cup in two successive seasons, that envious Derby fans justifiably felt could well have been their club's if Clough and Taylor, who rejoined him after staying on for a couple of years as Brighton's manager, had remained at the Baseball Ground.

Forest's choice of Allan Brown was unexpected because, after weeks of speculation linking them with several other prominent figures, he came to them as the manager of a Fourth Division club, albeit one who had guided Bury to the fringe of the promotion race. He provoked some discord in his arrival at the City Ground by trying to persuade Bob Smith, his assistant at Bury, to follow him to Forest, and he left amid further controversy after having fallen out with some of his players he called cheats as the team slipped into the bottom half of the Second Division. Bury won a bitter battle to keep Smith, a former Manchester United junior, by giving him a 2½-year managerial contract worth £12,500 – more than Brown had been paid – and he justified chairman Bill Allen's confidence in him, despite having only five months' coaching experience, by keeping the club on course for promotion. Swindon Town were among the others he later managed, their third in line after Dave Mackay.

Angered though Allen was about Brown's bid to poach Smith, that was nothing compared with the goings-on in Derby. Shortly before learning of Mackay's appointment there, the Rams' players, having received no reply to their letter to the directors, laid siege to the boardroom at the Baseball Ground in pursuing their efforts to get Clough and Taylor reinstated. This followed their meeting, on that afternoon of 23 October, with the outgoing management pair at Archie Gemmill's home.

The players agreed – though Roy McFarland emphasised that 'Brian Clough in no way prompted us in our action' – that a meeting should be arranged with the members of the board. When McFarland rang he was told by an office girl that the directors were at the ground, and the players would be phoned back. Ten minutes later the call came, but McFarland was told the directors had left.

This sparked a unanimous decision to besiege the ground until the meeting was set up. Three directors, Bob Innes, Jack Kirkland and Bill Rudd, were seen there a few minutes before thirteen players arrived shortly after four o'clock, but when they did not show themselves the mood of the players turned from impatience to anger. At 4.30 McFarland hammered on the boardroom door with no response. Half-an-hour later, a light remained shining in the boardroom after assistant secretary John Howarth had locked up the stadium, so the siege became a sit-in. Players took turns in beating on the boardroom door while others strode along corridors searching other rooms before sitting down to eat crisps, doughnuts and pies bought from a nearby shop. Nobody would believe an office clerk's assertion that the boardroom was empty.

The situation bordered on farce when McFarland shinned up a drainpipe to try to peer through a window. Clough's personal assistant, Cliff Notley, turned up several times at the ground, and the protest ended at 7.30pm after he had talked briefly to the County captain. It had lasted three hours and twenty minutes. Police arrived a few minutes before the players ran from a side door through a small group of fans and drove off in their cars. Twenty minutes later, Kirkland and secretary Stuart Webb suddenly emerged and left hurriedly. Kirkland drove away so quickly in his Mercedes that he did not put his lights on.

Alan Hinton warned that 'no-one has even talked about backing down yet', adding: 'We demand to be treated like men and granted a meeting with the men who are supposed to be running this football club. This has not been a light decision, I can tell you.'

Derby's players reported for training at ten o'clock the next morning, and, after meeting Mackay and having a tense confrontation with Sam Longson in the dressing room, asked Clough and Taylor to meet them for lunch. They were ordered not to make any comment to the press, but there was no shortage of off-the-cuff remarks. One international player said:

'We did not want to speak to Mackay this morning, but he just barged his way in. We pointed out that we might not be prepared to play against West Ham on Saturday. Mackay said he might have to play his reserves, and if the club were relegated to the Second Division this season it would not be his fault.'

Clough, who arrived at the Midland Hotel shortly after Mackay had finished his own meal there, claimed – though Longson denied it – that he had been asked by the Derby board under what conditions he and Taylor would return, and had replied that their only stipulation was the removal of the existing directors. Longson hinted he would have wished for a reconciliation, but the circumstances made it impossible. 'Our partnership will go down in history as one of the greatest this century,' he said, 'but it was inevitable it would finish. The players are sad about Brian, but that's only natural because they appear to owe him an allegiance. I cannot argue because he is he best manager England has ever seen.'

Mackay said that if he had been a Derby player he would have led the revolt, but the players had to realise that if he had not come in it would have been somebody else. He intended to talk to each of the players individually in the next few days, believing that they would tell him much more when they were on their own, but they had already appreciated that they could not stick to their threat of refusing to play in the first match for which he was in charge, at West Ham. Mackay pointed out to them that public opinion would be behind him if he were forced to field a patched-up team, though the biggest influence was exerted when Terry Hennessey, their PFA representative, passed on to them Cliff Lloyd's uncompromising directive that they must not put themselves into a breach of contract.

Even so, Hennessey was soon proved mistaken in saying: 'I think this is the end. There is nothing more we can do.' Within hours of having a second meeting with Mackay that lasted almost an hour and led him to understand he had their backing, the militant players sent another letter to the board restating their support for the movement to restore Clough and Taylor. 'I really thought they had come to their senses,' said Mackay, 'but it was now obvious they hadn't. I don't know why they suddenly changed their minds.' He drew some encouragement from the fact that his name was scrawled on the outer walls of the Baseball Ground almost as many times as Clough's, but on the Friday, while he was preparing to take the team to London for the game at Upton Park, Clough and Taylor were still holding court and drinking champagne at the Midland Hotel where they had made their headquarters. Whereas Clough observed that 'you've got to keep your sense of humour, kid,' his successor was certainly not being given much to smile about.

What a deplorable background that all was to the serious business of trying to pick up points, especially as the threat of mass transfer requests still hung in the air. Yet on the day of the match the players, the same ones who had gained the wins against Manchester United and Leicester City, came up trumps. Putting aside their grievances, if only temporarily, they gave one of their most convincing away performances of the season and deserved to come away with another victory instead of having to settle for a scoreless draw. Mervyn Day, an England Youth international goalkeeper who was just embarking upon an impressive career that was to take him to Leyton Orient, Aston Villa and Leeds after more than 200 games for the Hammers, was beaten by a header from his own centre-half, Tommy Taylor, only for Davies to be ruled offside, and he should have been beaten again eight minutes from the end when Hector uncharacteristically made a complete hash of a glorious opening created by Gemmill. The finishing touch to a perfect low centre looked a formality, but Hector ended up alone in the net as the ball slithered wide.

Archie Gemmill was at the peak of his form around this time. Dave Mackay was to admit that he caused him a few problems during his management of Derby County, but emphasised that 'he gave me 100 per cent in every match he played'.

From London, Mackay and his disenchanted men flew to the North-East for Monday's replay of a second-round League Cup-tie with Sunderland, who three weeks earlier had been outplayed for three-quarters of the original match at the Baseball Ground but had scored twice in the last quarter after being fortunate to be trailing by no more than goals netted by Nish and Davies. Defensive errors had let in John Lathan, a reserve deputising for the injured Dennis Tueart, for both those late saving goals, the first of them forced by Boulton's inability to cling onto a firm shot from Billy Hughes, later briefly with the Rams.

At Roker Park, a team that also included another future, but also short-staying, Derby player in Dave Watson, an England centre-half successor to Roy McFarland, found the County, for all their troubles, in a more determined frame of mind and were taken to a second replay after appearing to hold the whip hand despite failing with a penalty. That spot-kick was awarded by referee Ray Tinkler in the twentieth minute when, in Derby eyes, the outrushing Boulton collected the ball fairly at Tueart's feet after

McFarland had under-hit a pass intended for the goalkeeper. Boulton brilliantly saved Tueart's well-struck effort, but the left-winger took only ten minutes to atone by pouncing on the faulty clearance of a header by Watson at a corner to give Sunderland the lead.

Only thirteen minutes were left for play when O'Hare, back on familiar ground, smartly created the equaliser almost immediately after replacing the out-of-sorts McGovern. The scorer was Gemmill, but for whose clearance off the line from teenage full-back Joe Bolton, during a spell of Sunderland's strongest pressure, Derby would have had more than the one goal to wipe out.

So the teams had to try again two days later, also at Roker Park. And that was where results began to go wrong for the Rams' new manager – right from the moment, two minutes after half-time, when Vic Halom, a player Brian Clough had wanted to sign, nodded in the first goal of his hat-trick as Ron Webster collided heavily with a post and had to be carried off to spend the night in hospital with concussion. O'Hare was again sent on as substitute, with Newton switching to right-back. Marking in the reorganised defence was lax when Halom increased the lead with another header, in off an upright from skipper Bobby Kerr's free-kick, and more uncertainty enabled him to complete the scoring as Tueart, breaking through on a misplaced pass by Todd, presented him with a simple tap-in.

It was the fifteenth match in knock-out competitions that Sunderland had played without defeat, including the shock victory over Leeds in the previous season's FA Cup final, since Bob Stokoe had become their manager, but the run ended in the next round at home to Liverpool. Neither, however, was it to be the Merseysiders' year in the League Cup. Out they went in the quarter-finals to Wolverhampton Wanderers, who went on to beat Manchester City in the final. Compensation for that failure by Liverpool, and also for their finishing runners-up to Leeds in the League, came in the FA Cup, which they decisively claimed against Newcastle at Wembley.

Back in the League after their exit from the League Cup, Derby County ran straight into more problems on the field as the discord persisted off it. This was in sharp contrast to their winning of each of their first five home games of that 1973-74 season under Clough, culminating in the 6-2 demolition of Southampton in which Hector's hat-trick was the first in the League for the Rams since Durban's against Bristol City at the end of the Division Two promotion campaign in 1969. That eclipse of the Saints was also the first time Derby had scored so many goals in a League match since April 1963, when Scunthorpe United had been defeated by the same score, and it took Hector, in 287 games, two goals beyond Jack Parry's post-War League scoring record for the club of 105 in 483.

After a narrow defeat in the following fixture at Tottenham, where Hinton and Davies were left out to fit Newton into a 4-4-2 system for his debut, a missed penalty by the recalled Hinton cost Derby their 100 per cent home record in what was to be their last match at the Baseball Ground with Clough as manager – a 1-1 draw with Norwich City in which Newton made a misleadingly unimpressive home debut and Daniel a typically sound 100th full League appearance as deputy for McFarland. At Tottenham, the England centre-half had aggravated a slight knee strain that had been bothering him since a pre-season tournament in Spain.

Now, after the League wins against Manchester United and Leicester City, the draw at West Ham and the League Cup replays at Sunderland, Derby lost their unbeaten home record to Queen's Park Rangers in their first Baseball Ground game with Dave Mackay as manager. A penalty entrusted to Gemmill instead of Hinton was the Rams' only response to the lead the visitors gained through Gerry Francis and Stan Bowles by the 65th minute. It was Derby's first home defeat since losing to Leeds in March, and gave Rangers, London's top team of the moment, revenge for their Cup failure there the month before that.

Some allowance could no doubt be made for the effect the two games played at Sunderland during the week had on Derby's play, yet Mackay said he could not fault the effort shown. Gordon Jago, Rangers' manager, went so far as to say that the Rams were the best side his team had faced that season, but that praise soon faded as two 0-3 defeats, away to Ipswich and Sheffield United, and two home draws, with Leeds and Arsenal, extended the County's winless run under Mackay to eight matches, including the Roker replays, and dropped them from third to ninth in the First Division table.

At a press conference during that depressing sequence Mackay understandably attributed much of the blame to the so-called protest movement. 'Their activities have contributed to our recent poor results,' he said. 'They have unsettled the players and distracted them when they need help to get back their best form.'

The continued strength of the protests was made all too evident even on the day, the first one of November 1973, and two before Derby's home defeat by QPR, when Brian Clough went from being manager of the club that had been third in the Football League to taking charge of one in 63rd place, nineteenth in the Third Division, bogged down by a debt of £200,000. That night, within hours of Clough's agreeing to join Brighton and Hove Albion at £12,000 a year, with Peter Taylor as his assistant on an annual salary of £8,000, and after what Clough called 'weeks of great strain', the pair made an emotional appearance in front of a thousand members of the Derby County Protest Movement at the King's Hall in

Derby. Clough told them: 'This is something totally new to us. It is the first time I have ever been lost for words. We just intended to come along tonight to say thank you and so long. It is very hard for us.'

In the seventeen days since Clough had given up his Derby job the only firm offer he had received had come from Brighton, and he had decided to take it only after some persuasive talking by Taylor and hard bargaining by the Sussex club's chairman, Mike Bamber. One First Division chairman said: 'It seems that none of the big clubs is interested. It could be that he's simply too hot a property to handle.' After all the clamour the appointments aroused, Brighton's first game under Clough was a strangely low-key affair, a scoreless home draw with one of the clubs heading for promotion, York City. It attracted a crowd of 16,017, an increase of almost 10,000 on the previous home match, but 4,000 short of the expected figure.

By the end of that season, after the humiliation of an FA Cup beating by the amateurs of Walton and Hersham, and the club's heaviest home defeat in which all but one of Bristol Rovers' eight goals were shared by the 'Smash and Grab' combination of Alan Warboys (four) and Bruce Bannister (three), only four players remained in the team compared with the one Clough and Taylor had inherited, but in the summer Clough left alone for his ill-fated Leeds venture with Brighton no further up the table than where he had found them. At Elland Road he was to realise that 'anyone following Revie would have a bad time', yet he had already sounded his own prophetic warning: 'I am not equipped to manage successfully without Peter Taylor. I'm the shop front. He's the goods at the back.'

On the Wednesday after Brighton's first game with Clough in control, Derby County's disgruntled fans held another protest meeting, and the players' rebellion persisted for three more weeks. Until the final showdown Mackay showed remarkable tolerance – as most clearly demonstrated when, in an early attempt to clear the air, he called the players into the dressing room, gave each of them a blank sheet of paper, and told them that he wanted all those who were on his side to sign. On his return ten minutes later a few names were missing. One of them was that of Colin Todd, who, according to Mackay, said: 'This is kid's stuff. We don't need to sign to show we're all behind you.' Mackay then asked if they were, and on being given an affirmative answer he tore the papers up and went home mistakenly thinking he had 'finally cracked it'. That very night most of the players went to a party at which they reasserted their backing for Clough and, to make matters even worse, their wives attended a protest meeting in favour of his return.

Even as late as two days before the ending of the rebellion several players and their wives visited Clough's home, and that evening his wife and the wives of Boulton, Davies, Gemmill, Hector, Hinton, McFarland, Newton,

Todd and Webster, plus McGovern's fiancée, attended another protest meeting which was chaired by Michael Keeling, the director who had resigned, and attended by about a thousand supporters. Mrs Clough said it was nonsense to suggest she was leading the players' wives, and that her husband was leading the players. She went further:

'The wives told me they were going to the meeting, and, since I believe they are sincere and right, I went along to support them. I would go again if they asked me. I happen to know that Brian tried to stop the players doing anything rash. To my knowledge he has talked two of them out of putting in transfer requests, and has told them their job is playing and winning for Derby.'

As far as Mackay knew, Clough was back in Derby that day solely to have 'a friendly chat' with him about players who might be available for transfer. He had been given no reason to suppose that the man at the centre of the controversy was in the town for any other reason, and he could not deny that he was disappointed with him 'because he knew it would mean trouble for me when the players were at his house on Tuesday night'. It was the first time, he said, that Clough had ever let him down, but he had no intention of seeking to take any action against him for it.

Clough, however, had already made it abundantly clear that as far as he was concerned the protest movement was a lost cause. 'I don't want to know anything about Derby,' he had said, 'and I am not responsible for what people are saying and doing in Derby. I know nothing about Derby's players going on strike, and to say that I am interested in going back there now is absolute drivel.'

Eight players had, in fact, signed a letter that to some extent amounted to a strike notice because it contained a threat not to report to the ground until one o'clock on the following Saturday afternoon before the home match with Leeds United, the unbeaten First Division leaders. It read:

'We, the undersigned players, refuse to report to Derby County Football Club until 1pm, Saturday, November 24, for the following reasons:

a) Dissatisfaction with the present management.

b) Reinstatement of Brian Clough and Peter Taylor.

But that letter was never handed in. The ending of the rebellion saw to that. The peace formula was finally thrashed out on the Thursday before that deadline, during two hours of negotiations at the Baseball Ground between Dave Mackay and a repentant first-team squad. Roy McFarland, surrounded by team-mates, came out of those talks to announce:

'The nightmare is over. This is the end of the whole affair. We have made up our minds once and for all that we have been in the wrong, and we are giving David Mackay our full backing. We have stopped messing about and we are going to get down to playing football. We hope everything can be forgotten, and all I want to say to the protest movement is: "Pack it in".'

Alan Hinton said they had had no direct contact with the Union's secretary, Cliff Lloyd, and had 'worked it out for ourselves', but a further warning from the PFA that a training boycott or outright strike would be in breach of contract obviously had a big bearing on the players' decision to pull back from the brink. If they had not called off their dispute and trained as usual on the Friday morning they would have been in contravention of Clause Two of the professional footballers' contract, which they were all required to sign. It stated: 'The player shall attend the club ground or any other place decided upon by the club for the purpose of, or in connection with, his training as a player, pursuant to the instruction of the secretary, manager or trainer of the club.'

Stuart Webb had kept the Football League and PFA in daily touch with developments, but matters had not become sufficiently out of hand for Alan Hardaker, the League secretary, to pay his threatened visit to the club. The resolve so typical of Mackay was another important factor in the quelling of the unrest his appointment had aroused. At Forest he had already shown how ruthless he could be with a clear-out of the backroom staff that had included trainer-coach Bob McKinlay, who had been with the club for 23 years, and assistant trainer Frank Knight, whose service stretched back ten years longer than that. Former skipper McKinlay's Forest record of 685 appearances, 614 of them in the League, included a sequence of 265.

On the day Mackay met Derby's players in those conclusive talks he left them in no doubt about his determination to 'fight them to the death'. In having what he described as a 'a real go at them', he castigated them for making him feel he was dealing with 'a schoolboy eleven who are following each other around like sheep'. He said he was sick and tired of hearing that they were putting in transfer requests and strike notices, especially as he had never received anything in writing from them since he had taken over. They were making themselves a laughing stock, saying one thing one day and another the next. He pointed out that he had every right to be angry when he had been so let down, but emphasised that he bore no grudges and made it clear that no disciplinary action would be taken despite all the difficulties he had been caused since his appointment.

Not that those difficulties were confined to the players, for there was a mass exodus of the club's scouts to follow Clough and Taylor to Brighton. That path out of the Baseball Ground was also taken by coaches John Sheridan and Brian Newton, but the vacancies they left were promptly filled as Mackay sent for Colin Murphy and Alan Hill to rejoin him from Nottingham Forest.

Croydon-born Murphy, destined for a hapless spell as Derby's manager after Mackay's departure, was mainly a reserve defender with Crystal Palace before being given a free transfer to Cork Hibernian. After that he moved around the Southern League circuit for some years, gradually turning his interest towards coaching. He followed Des Anderson at Hastings United, then was Gravesend's player-coach under the management of Alf Ackerman, a South African who had Derby County among his clubs as a free-scoring forward, when Mackay invited him to Nottingham. Hill was a goalkeeper with Forest, one of Matt Gillies' best signings at a bargain £12,000 from Rotherham after beginning with Barnsley, until his playing career was ended by a compound fracture of the right forearm for which he underwent five operations.

Sheridan, trainer-coach to the Rams' reserve team, was a player with Notts County and also worked with Clough and Taylor at Hartlepool. He left Derby complaining that 'since Brian and Peter went I have not known where I stood, whether I was wanted or what I was supposed to be doing'. There was, however, no animosity as far as Mackay was concerned. He wished him well, only to have something else to be unhappy about when Sheridan made a statement to the press, under the headline ANOTHER COACH QUITS RAMS, in which he said he did not have a job to go to. 'Of course he had a job to go to,' said Mackay. 'He was going to Brighton. Why didn't he say so?'

Incredible though it may seem, Clough's unequivocal denunciation of any further connection with the County, coupled with the players' overdue acceptance of Mackay's appointment, did not deter Keeling from trying to carry on with the protest. 'We will continue with our petition for the reinstatement of Mr Clough,' he said, 'and will march through Derby before Saturday's game with Leeds, even though the players have decided to take no action.' It was such a forlorn gesture that plans for demonstrations inside the ground that day were abandoned, and in the match programme this warning was given:

'Our former manager, Mr Brian Clough, should concentrate on his Brighton club and players, and ensure he has said his last farewell to his former playing staff at Derby. Mr Clough insists that the gathering of our players and their wives at his home this week was no more than a farewell, and we have no evidence to suggest otherwise. Several of our players have told manager Dave Mackay in front of his assistant, Des Anderson, that Mr Clough invited them and their wives to his house by telephone, and when they got there other players and their wives were also there. The facts are that on the same night the wives attended a protest meeting, accompanied by Mrs Clough, and the next day the alleged players' strike got under way. Mr Clough would now probably agree that it would be better for him, the players, Derby County and Brighton, were he not to expose himself to speculation by consorting with his former staff.'

But, successful as he was to be, Mackay never escaped from the shadow of Clough. And neither had the last been heard of the 'Bring Back Clough' campaign.

Two Riochs and three van Goghs

Defeat for Derby County in four of the six matches they played under Dave Mackay's management before the ending of the rebellion, with the two others drawn, made a mockery of his prediction, on taking over, that 'this team is capable of winning the League and both Cups this season'. The players' demeanour during that period was more accurately summed up when one of them parodied a Cup-winning captain by lifting an empty tea urn above his head and saying: 'Without Brian this is all we'll win this season.'

The spirited manner in which they then tackled the formidable task of trying to check the steamroller advance of their hoodoo team Leeds gave Mackay some justification, however, for asserting that 'if we could play those matches again I think the results would be different because of the changed attitude of the team'. They were unable to prevent the Yorkshire club equalling the longest post-War unbeaten start to a season that had ended for Arsenal at the Baseball Ground after seventeen games in 1947, but they did the next best thing in holding them to a no-score draw – the same outcome of the Cup match Clough's Brighton team played that afternoon as their shock prelude to the replay humiliation at the hands of the amateurs of Walton and Hersham. The Rams did most of the pressing in the second half against Leeds, enlivened by the substitution of Davies for O'Hare to combat Gordon McQueen's height advantage, but some fine goalkeeping by David Harvey denied them the goal that would have made history repeat itself.

Leeds' inexorable progress to the League title was not checked until their thirtieth match, which they lost by 2-3 at Stoke, though they were defeated in two other competitions along the way – at Ipswich in the League Cup, and, in a major upset, at home to Second Division Bristol City in an FA Cup replay.

Burnley had gone thirty League games without defeat in winning the First Division championship of 1920-21, but only after losing each of their first three matches. Leeds therefore set a record for being unbeaten from the beginning of a season that was equalled by Liverpool in 1988, then surpassed by Arsenal, who went right through 2003-04 without defeat in the Premiership and extended that unbeaten run to 49 games before losing at Old Trafford. It was also at the Baseball Ground that Liverpool matched Leeds' achievement, foiled of victory by a spectacular late equaliser by Derby's Liverpool-born full-back Michael Forsyth, but they were also beaten by the odd goal next time out – at the home of their Everton neighbours.

During the week in which Derby's players finally agreed to toe the line, Dave Mackay made his first signing for the Rams by going back to Swindon to pay £80,000 for Rod Thomas, the tall full-back who had played more than 300 games for the Wiltshire club since joining them from Gloucester City in 1964, and had missed only six with Wales since making his full international debut in a scoreless draw at Belfast's Windsor Park in the spring of 1967. Besides being a key member of the team that shocked Arsenal to win the League Cup, he had taken part in all but two of Swindon's matches during the 1968-69 season in which they were promoted from the Third Division as runners-up to Watford.

To the thirty senior caps he won while with Swindon, after playing six times at Under-23 level, Thomas was to gain nineteen more as a Derby player, making him at that time his country's most-capped defender – and there would have been more but for his being left out of several games because the Wales manager, Mike Smith, decided to experiment with a redesigned back four that included the more attack-minded Leighton Phillips, of Aston Villa. As a defender, Thomas could not resist saying he was 'surprised, and a little puzzled to be the only one left out because we have not been getting enough goals'.

Despite his imposing record, Thomas was not immediately guaranteed a first-team place with Derby County. When Ron Webster anxiously asked Mackay where he now stood, he was assured that he would remain in the side as long as his form justified it. Consequently, the Welshman had to wait to be a regular choice until Webster damaged knee ligaments in an FA Cup replay against Orient just beyond the halfway mark in the club's second League championship season of 1974-75. In the meantime, Thomas was confined to eight First Division appearances – two of them as deputy for Webster, one at centre-half before Daniel settled there in McFarland's absence, and the five others at left-back when Nish was out injured.

While Thomas was kept on the sidelines in 1973-74 Webster played so well that he was chosen as the Rams' Player of the Year by nearly 12,000 votes in a total of 25,000. He also had his wife to thank for that because it was she who urged him to battle on when he contemplated retirement on finding himself only fourth in line for the right-back position after Clough, preferring Powell, had left him out early the previous season. He had not wanted to finish struggling in the Third or Fourth Divisions ('I've got better things to do'). Having battled back to display some of the best form of his career, this unsung one-club man, the only Derbyshire-born player to appear regularly in the club's first Division One title team, was left wondering as he received his award: 'How did I come before all the international stars in this great team of ours?' He answered his own question by saying: 'I might be short of some of the ball skills of the rest, but boy, do I fight.' Modest to a fault, he said there really was no Player of the Year – 'We're a team.'

Once allowed a run in the side, Roderick John Thomas went on to make more than 100 appearances, beginning with a half-century sequence, before fading out as Webster made a final comeback. Both then fell victims of the Tommy Docherty clear-out that followed Colin Murphy's short troubled stay as manager after Mackay's dismissal. Thomas returned to Wales, transferred for £10,000 for Cardiff City, with whom he won his fiftieth and last cap against Czechoslovakia in Prague in November, 1977. Webster wound up his playing days in the United States with Minnesota Kicks, where he had previously been on loan during the English close season. Both also had a final spell with Derby County – Webster as youth coach for four years up to late 1982, Thomas, who ended his playing career at Newport after going back to Gloucester, as the Rams' Director of Football for seven months in 2003.

The appointment of Thomas as a link between the board and the training ground was strongly criticised because fans found it hard to understand why such a position needed to be created, especially as the Rams were then around £30 million in debt, and he left abruptly when his post was declared redundant after a boardroom coup. Despite the club's desperate financial situation, it did not take the new directors long to change tack by appointing a Director of Football of their own.

Thomas made a competent First Division debut on the last Saturday of 1973 as deputy for Nish, who had been handicapped by a leg injury for most of a drawn Boxing Day match at Stoke, but it unfortunately coincided with Derby's first defeat in six games since the end of the rebellion. They conceded two goals, one of them a penalty, at Everton before Hector, in his 301st League appearance for the club, made their lone reply by scoring for the first time in ten weeks (his last goal had been in the home win against Leicester) three minutes from time. That was an unusual lean spell for Hector, for whom the season turned out to be an indifferent one by his standards, yet he still finished way ahead as the side's top scorer with nineteen goals – his biggest tally for one season in the First Division. The patchiness of his displays was reflected in the fact that nine of them came in three matches, with hat-tricks at home against Burnley and Sheffield United as well as Southampton.

One particularly sad feature of the game at Goodison was that John O'Hare was carried off with an ankle injury a quarter of an hour from the end, never to play in Derby's first team again. Having no longer been a regular choice since the start of the season, he was back at the head of the attack only because of injury to Davies, in whose place for the last half-hour at Stoke Jim Walker also had his final experience of League life with the Rams.

The substitute for O'Hare at Everton was Steve Powell, who had been expressing his startling maturity for a seventeen-year-old in midfield instead of defence until breaking a bone in a foot during a home draw with Norwich early in October. His re-establishment in the starting eleven opened the exit door for another player who had been an important contributor to Derby's rise under Brian Clough. John McGovern, ousted by Powell at No 7, was rated the County's outstanding player by Dave Mackay when recalled at No 11 for a home match in which the double was completed over Newcastle, but he was given only one more first-team chance, in a narrow defeat at Maine Road by a makeshift Manchester City side deprived of Law, Lee, Marsh and Summerbee, before accompanying O'Hare for their reunions with Clough at Leeds and Nottingham Forest. After adding 335 appearances for Forest to his 240 with Derby, McGovern was player-manager at Bolton, then set out on travels that included spells as assistant to Peter Shilton at Plymouth and joint manager with Archie Gemmill at Rotherham.

With Hinton out of favour after an FA Cup replay failure at home to Coventry, Jeff Bourne was switched to play on the left wing for the last fourteen games of the 1973-74 season. This, following straight on from nine League and Cup appearances as a central striker, was the only settled spell this neat young player was given in Derby's first team, so keen was the competition for places to become because of other major signings Mackay made. He would not have started that one but for the injuries to Davies and O'Hare that let him in for a New Year's Day home match with Birmingham City. In five years with the club, he had previously played only twice in the First Division – as Gemmill's deputy at the end of the 1970-71 season – and he had been substituted in the second of those matches.

Although less effective when moved to the flank, Bourne certainly looked the part in scoring six goals in five successive games at centre-forward. After getting the one that saved a point against Birmingham, besides hitting a post with a header, he added a couple to Hector's three in a 5-1 home win over Burnley, then was on the mark again in a draw at Chelsea that Derby were lucky to gain because the referee was not alone in being deceived by the quickness of Nish's hand, not Boulton's, as the ball was fisted over the County's crossbar. Bourne's two other goals in that sequence complemented a hat-trick (Gemmill's), in the 6-1 FA Cup replay victory at Boston that exactly avenged the Rams' humiliating home defeat of eighteen years before, but Coventry then dashed dreams of Wembley by narrowly winning a replay.

Bourne's inability to sustain a claim to a regular first-team place after that season meant that most of his subsequent senior appearances for Derby County were made as a substitute – most notably, as to be recalled later, on the European stage – but he gained the confidence to make a bigger impact at League level elsewhere through playing with some scoring success in American soccer on loan to Dallas Tornado in the summer of 1976.

Shortly before the following season's transfer deadline he linked up in Crystal Palace's attack with David Swindlehurst, a lofty striker who made a £400,000 move to Derby, after first being on loan, towards the end of the 1979-80 campaign in which the Rams lost the First Division status they had held since the Clough era. When Palace rose in 1977 from the Third Division, Bourne made a creditable contribution with nine goals in the London club's last fifteen games of the season, bearing out Palace manager Terry Venables' estimation of him as 'a player with the skill and experience to weld our youngsters together up front'.

Venables, the former Chelsea, Tottenham, QPR and Crystal Palace player who alone represented England – whom he also managed – at five international levels, reckoned he had got a bargain at £30,000, but Bourne scored only one more goal in seventeen further League appearances for Palace, and he had his contract cancelled before Venables also led the Selhurst Park club up to the First Division in 1978-79. Apart from six months with Sheffield United, Bourne spent the rest of his playing career back in the United States, shared between Dallas Tornado, Atlanta Chiefs, Seattle Sounders and Wichita Wings, before returning near his Derbyshire roots for a short spell as coach at Gresley Rovers.

The regular place Bourne held in Derby County's team for the second half of the 1973-74 season was indicative of Dave Mackay's aim not to let it become a closed shop. The new manager's belief in current form rather than reputation enabled this young man who had been for so long overlooked to be persevered with, even when those for whom he had originally deputised were fit again, and the competition for places was stepped up, pushing even Henry Newton into the background for a while, when the next big venture into the transfer market was made. This new arrival, costing £200,000 from Aston Villa, was Bruce Rioch, a forward turned midfielder who was born of Scottish parents at Aldershot while his father, an accomplished athlete, was stationed there in the Army.

The transfer helped to turn Villa's operating loss of nearly £7,000 into an overall profit of almost £125,000, and showed a handsome profit on the £110,000 they had paid during the 1969 close season to sign Rioch from Luton Town with his younger brother Neil, who had limited first-team opportunities before going into American football with Portland Timbers.

Covetous eyes had been on Bruce Rioch since his 24 goals had helped Luton to the Fourth Division championship in 1967-68.

In a sense, Derby, like Luton and Villa, had two Riochs. One was the attack-minded packer of a fearsome shot, all the more remarkable for the fact that he underwent cartilage operations on both knees, who gave Mackay the extra scoring power he wanted from midfield. That Viking-style version, dubbed Eric Bloodaxe by Roy Christian, one of the broadcasters of running commentaries on home matches to local hospitals, outscored the recognised strikers with fifteen goals (twenty including cup-ties) in the club's second championship side of 1974-75, and he altogether netted 48 in 139 matches before being sold by Colin Murphy to Everton for £180,000, to help raise money for a new striker, Derek Hales, soon after doing half Derby's scoring as a forward in an 8-2 demolition of Tottenham. (Hales, a black-bearded striker, joined Derby for £330,000 while Colin Murphy was still only caretaker manager. He scored just seven goals in thirty games for the Rams before Tommy Docherty, another in the quick-changing line of men at the County's helm, sold him to West Ham for £110,000.)

The other Bruce Rioch who played for the Rams was a £150,000 pale imitation noted more for getting the wrong side of management and referees than for his forthright football and goals (only six in 45 more games) after being recalled from an unhappy year on Merseyside by Docherty.

When Dave Mackay was at Goodison Park for what proved to be his last match as Derby's manager, he was asked by Everton's Billy Bingham if he would part with Rioch, Archie Gemmill or Colin Todd – in that order. He replied that he would consider letting one of them go only in exchange for Bob Latchford, a centre-forward who was to play a dozen times for England. That did not appeal to Bingham, but shortly after Mackay had left Derby the Everton manager phoned him at home and asked which of the three Rams players he had inquired about he rated best. 'Rioch' was the prompt reply. So the deal was done, but it was undermined when Bingham was sacked only a few weeks later as Everton slumped into the bottom half of the table, and Rioch, who had been far from keen on the move because he had business interests in Birmingham, became even more eager for a return to the Midlands when his wife failed to settle in the North-West.

The granting of that wish made Rioch what Jeff Farmer told his *Daily Mail* readers was 'lot No 127 in the remarkable catalogue of Docherty's 16 years of trading in soccer's transfer market', with 61 players signed and 66 sold at an average annual deficit of just under £30,000. Docherty, whose many clubs gave rise to his stock joke that he had more of them than golfer Jack Nicklaus, was with Aston Villa when he first signed Rioch, who might have risen to international rank with England instead of Scotland if the interested Don Revie had not been in Cyprus the weekend he was snapped up by Willie Ormond, the former Hibernian winger who followed Docherty as Scotland's manager, when Chelsea's David Hay dropped out to have an eye operation. Rioch, told he would never play for Scotland after quitting their squad for a World Cup qualifying game to play for Villa in a League Cup-tie, went on to total two dozen appearances for his adopted country, eighteen of them while with Derby. What was more, he became Scotland's first English-born captain.

Docherty enthused about his 'three midfield van Goghs' in linking Rioch at Derby with Don Masson, another Scotland cap, and Gerry Daly, whose £175,000 transfer from Manchester United was the last big splash Murphy was allowed to make in the transfer market and temporarily made him Ireland's most expensive footballer. Daly got off to an impressive start with the Rams, who were at the bottom of the table when he arrived, but he was dismayed to find Docherty following him to the Baseball Ground after, as he put it, they had 'failed to see eye to eye' at Old Trafford. How distorted the manager's comparison with the celebrated Dutch painter was so swiftly to prove! Rioch and Masson were big disappointments both before and after going to Argentina for the 1978 World Cup finals, and the disillusioned Daly left for Coventry City complaining about wasted years in a struggling team after a further change of manager had brought in Colin Addison, yet another who found the task of arresting Derby's decline well beyond him.

Masson was rated 'world class' by another Scotland manager, Ally MacLeod, and hailed as 'perhaps the best passer of a ball in Notts County's history', but he never reproduced for the Rams the form that had helped Notts from Fourth Division to Second, and QPR to runners-up in the First, before returning to Meadow Lane as player-coach. On top of that, he was fined £500 by Docherty for a meal he did not eat (he failed to turn up to dine with the other players before a match after being transfer-listed), and was suspended by him for two weeks for remarks in Sunday newspaper articles which the manager regarded as an insult to Derby County and their supporters. Docherty said it was a particularly disgraceful thing for a professional to say that he would be quite happy to pick up his money in the Reserves until his contract expired. Masson was also cast out by Scotland for 'having admitted giving false information to our medical officer on a most important issue'.

Rioch was twice sent off and twice loaned out during his second spell at Derby, and had rows with both Docherty and Addison. He reached his lowest point with the Rams early in 1980, when he spoke up forcefully on behalf of David Langan, an Eire full-back who was ordered straight back home by Addison after turning up late for an FA Cup-tie with Bristol City under the suspicion that, restless for a move, he had deliberately missed travelling with the team to avoid being cup-tied. Rioch was also told to leave, and the weakened Rams crashed to a 2-6 defeat. Soon afterwards, with Derby heading out of the First Division, Rioch was freed to Seattle Sounders before embarking upon an often-fraught managerial career back in England.

He resigned from his first post in that role, at Torquay, after being involved in a training-ground incident that left one of his players requiring hospital treatment. At Middlesbrough, where he had Colin Todd as his assistant and David Nish as coach to the youth and reserve teams, he survived a lock-out when the Official Receiver was called in and piloted the re-formed club from Third Division to First. That made him the first manager to take Boro to promotion in two successive seasons, yet it all counted for nothing when one prompt relegation and a slump towards another brought about his dismissal. There had also been discord in the camp, given a public airing when the latest of his dressing-room bust-ups with Peter Davenport resulted in the former Forest, Manchester United and England striker being banned from the stadium and training ground for a fortnight.

Rioch next managed Millwall and Bolton, where he was rejoined by Todd, before having the shortest stay by an Arsenal manager – 61 weeks from filling the vacancy caused by George Graham's sacking in a 'bungs' scandal to being replaced by Arsene Wenger. He then became assistant at QPR to Stewart Houston, a former Scotland full-back who had been his assistant at Highbury. After that he spent less than two years managing Norwich City and only eight months at Wigan, resigning from both, and had temporary charge of Gresley Rovers in the Dr Martens League.

Such a chequered existence seemed highly unlikely when Rioch first settled in as a Derby County player. He was not seen at his best until playing a prominent part in the club's second League championship side, but there was reason to regard him as something of a lucky talisman from the last Saturday of February in 1974 on which he made an encouraging debut even though he did not meet his new team-mates until the previous evening because they had only just returned from a week's training break in Majorca. Four goals in a win at Norwich were riches indeed considering that Derby had netted a mere six in their last fourteen away First Division matches, if devalued to some extent by the defensive flaws in a home team for which relegation was looming.

Rioch's reputation for hard shooting made him an automatic acceptor of the penalty-taking responsibilities after that game at Carrow Road. He made no mistake with his first spot-kick for the Rams, despite which West Ham held them to their fourth draw in six home games, but he failed with the next, in a 0-4 drubbing at Wolverhampton, and was third time unlucky at Coventry – but thankful to see Hector score the winning goal from the rebound when the brilliant Bill Glazier beat the ball away.

The award of another penalty, for handball, in the last match of the season, at home to Wolves, found Rioch reluctant to try again, so, after what Gerald Mortimer called 'a swift *ad hoc* committee meeting' the job was entrusted to Roger Davies. Not a wise decision in view of the fact that the mercurial centre-forward, though by then an England Under-23 international after having been sent on as a substitute with the two goals already scored in a defeat of Scotland at Newcastle, had found the net only three times in his last two dozen League outings. Sure enough, he also failed. His kick lacked power and the grateful Gary Pierce did not have to perform any heroics to save. Failure to convert four of the last five penalties was an unwelcome contrast to the prime of Alan Hinton, fallible as he also could be from the spot.

This latest one, however, did not stop the Rams rounding off an eventful season with the flourish for which Dave Mackay had hoped. Goals from Hector, with a header from a corner-kick Nish placed to him with unerring accuracy beyond the far post, and Powell, a real stunner of a shot from an opening Nish and Hector created, brought speedy revenge for the heavy defeat in the abject display given at Molineux. More importantly, aided by Sheffield United's unexpected victory at Ipswich, it guaranteed a final third place in the First Division – and with it a return to European competition in the UEFA Cup. Such a reward could scarcely have been anticipated during those first few turbulent weeks of Mackay's management.

To finish so high in the table, if as many as nine points behind second-placed Liverpool, was also quite an achievement in light of Derby's undistinguished away record. They had only four wins to set against ten defeats on their League visits, and their goals total on their 21 travels was a paltry twelve – the lowest number in the division, shared by the bottom club, Norwich, and superior in the whole League only to the eight of Oxford United, who narrowly escaped relegation from Division Two, the ten of Workington, one of the four clubs that had to seek re-election to the Fourth Division, and the eleven of Darlington, who just avoided being among them.

At home, Derby countered their susceptibility on opponents' grounds by gaining thirteen victories, a total exceeded in the First Division only by Liverpool's eighteen, but they frittered away points after leading in five of their seven drawn League matches at the Baseball Ground. Against Manchester United, they squandered a two-goal advantage. Missing the calming influence of Todd in that match, they were pegged back in the second half by a shot from well outside the penalty area and a misdirected centre that went in off the far post.

Those slip-ups, however, could not disguise the transformation brought about after Mackay had at last been accepted by his players. Of their last 25 League fixtures of the season, Derby lost only five. The scoreless home draw with Leeds which began that improvement was followed by the visit of Arsenal in which McFarland's early goal was the first one scored in open play for the Rams in six successive League matches, only for another of their players to be responsible for the late equaliser as Newton turned the ball past Boulton in attempting to intercept a shot from John Radford that was going wide. Then, at the ninth attempt including the Cup replays with Sunderland, came the first win under Mackay. In his words: 'We went to Newcastle and they murdered us, but somehow we sneaked a 2-0 victory and that seemed the turning point.'

Against a side weakened by injuries and the suspension of Jimmy Smith, the Rams were kept in the game mainly by the brilliance of Boulton, and McFarland's unwitting deflection past a post of a fierce shot from Terry McDermott, before Davies put them ahead with a header from McGovern's centre six minutes before half-time. It was the first goal by a Derby forward since Hector's against Leicester seven weeks earlier. Not until the same late stage of the second half was the elusive victory clinched as a typical Hinton hammer blow crowned a Nish-Gemmill move.

The goal-shyness that bedevilled Derby so often away from home that season threatened to scupper their chances of re-entering European competition as they suffered three of those five after-rebellion defeats in the last six matches, all without scoring. The Rams produced one of their worst displays since returning to the First Division in the midweek mauling at Molineux, but gave a creditable account of themselves despite their 0-2 defeats at Elland Road and Highbury. They often outplayed Leeds, Bourne going close three times and Hector hitting a post in injury-time; against Arsenal they were doubly out of luck in seeing a Davies shot bounce out off the bar and then conceding a controversial penalty as referee Ted Wallace rejected heated protests that McFarland had handled accidentally.

Alan Ball's conversion of the spot-kick early in the second half gave the Gunners a grip on the game that Charlie George, who was to be another Mackay signing for the Rams, tightened with the second goal before limping off. Then, however, came the concluding win over Wolves that ensured European entry, Hector scoring his fifth of the seven goals Derby registered in offsetting those away lapses with full points from each of their last three home matches.

Regardless of the revival that lifted the team into the top three, there was an average drop of 5,000 in attendances at the Baseball Ground which showed that the loss of Brian Clough still rankled among a good many, and, although some of the defectors were won back as results improved under Mackay's direction, gates generally remained below what they had been during the previous years of plenty. For example, a comparison of the size of home crowds in the two First Division title seasons shows that they exceeded 30,000 at seventeen of the 21 matches in 1971-72, but in only six in 1974-75. And whereas nine of the seventeen were recorded before Christmas, all half-dozen on the second occasion did not come until the New Year as the title race was hotting up – three of those against Liverpool, Leeds and Manchester City, clubs that could be expected to be among the main attractions in any case, and another as the winning of another championship was being celebrated on the final day.

In the season that preceded the regaining of the title, Mackay failed with his first bids to boost the side's striking power before landing another major coup just in time for the opening of the next campaign. Peter Osgood, who went to Southampton for £275,000, rejected Derby after Chelsea had agreed to a £300,000 deal that would have involved Roger Davies, valued at £125,000, going in part-exchange; Sunderland decided it was a better proposition to part with Dennis Tueart (and Micky Horswill) to Manchester City in exchange for Tony Towers instead of accepting Mackay's cash offer for the winger; and Duncan McKenzie left Forest for Leeds after Derby's new manager had given way to the old in declining to go beyond his valuation of £200,000.

The player who was brought in was precisely the type the team needed, an ebullient character of experience and class whose uplifting influence on the field and off transformed him from arch enemy into favourite son in the eyes of Derby fans as the Rams regained the League title.

Francis Henry Lee, a £100,000 bargain from Manchester City, relished that change of heart. As he put it: 'They used to hate me here when I visited the ground with City. I was more than an enemy. I was a bit of an extrovert on the field, and I could practically touch the animosity wafting over from the terraces. All that changed when I joined Derby. The fans switched straight onto my side, and I got along with them famously.'

FRANCIS LEE GIVES LIFT TO ANOTHER TITLE

Franny Lee entered First Division football with his home club Bolton Wanderers on 5 November 1960, at the age of sixteen. At 3.15pm by the clock on the front of the Burnden Park stand he headed the first of the 229 goals he was to score in exactly 500 League appearances – past Bert Trautmann, German-born goalkeeper of Manchester City, the club with which Lee spent what he had good reason to look back upon as 'seven fabulous years'.

During that time this dynamic, stocky battler helped City, who paid Bolton £60,000 for him in October 1967, to win the League championship, FA Cup, League Cup and European Cup-Winners' Cup. It was one of the greatest periods in the Maine Road club's history, masterminded by the managerial partnership of Joe Mercer and Malcolm Allison that blended Lee's bustling style with the other attack-minded talents of Colin Bell and Mike Summerbee. Those three were the key men in a team that was one of the most entertaining in the country – if, like Leeds, also frequently niggling and over-inclined to pester referees.

In 1971-72 Lee was the First Division's top scorer with 33 goals, plus two in cup-ties. A record fifteen of them came from the penalty spot. 'Lee One Pen' was a familiar Chinese-sounding sight on scoresheets, one that not a few opponents looked at sceptically because of his propensity to take a tumble in the area. Some cynics regarded him as the best English diver since Brian Phelps, a British highboard champion. In 320 League and Cup games for City Lee notched 143 goals, and he also introduced a refreshing air of enterprise into the England line-up, scoring ten times in 27 matches without the aid of penalties (Geoff Hurst and Allan Clarke converted the kicks awarded when he played). He took part in all but one of England's World Cup games in Mexico in 1970.

All was unchecked progress for Lee until shortly after he had scored one of the goals that defeated Derby County's coming champions towards the end of April in 1972. Early the following month he was suddenly taken ill after returning to his magnificent 360-year-old thatched-roof home at Westhoughton from a business trip to Liverpool. Pale and groggy, he feared he was having a heart attack as his wife Jean drove him to Bolton Royal Infirmary, but, fortunately, it was found to be simply physical and mental exhaustion. As managing director of F H Lee (Paper Converters) Ltd, a firm manufacturing a number of household products from an old cotton mill off the Darwen road just north of Bolton, he had been leading, as his brother Arthur, a partner at the waste-paper factory, saw it, 'an extremely busy life outside football, continually involved in business interests and charity appearances.' For five years his working day had stretched to eighteen hours, often seven days a week – something he vowed never to repeat after making a full recovery.

Besides carrying that burden of responsibility, and on top of a demanding season in which he had been a City ever-present in both League and Cup, Lee was preparing to play his fourth match in five days, a benefit for his City colleague Alan Oakes, when he suddenly complained of feeling dizzy. Two of those games were also benefits, the other an international at Wembley in which he scored England's only goal in a defeat by West Germany. According to Malcolm Allison – by then in the first of his two spells as City's team manager following the switch to general manager by Joe Mercer, who was shortly to leave for Coventry – that failure against the Germans was 'the last straw' for Lee, who, said Allison, was already 'very depressed about City losing the First Division championship'. It also proved to be the end of Lee's international career. He had to pull out of the return match with West Germany, drawn in Berlin a few days after he was taken ill, and he was not called on again.

Back to fitness, Lee resumed his habitual role as City's leading scorer in each of the following two seasons, jointly in the League with Rodney Marsh in the first of them and despite having his appearances restricted by knee trouble in the other, but life at Maine Road was never the same for him after Allison, feeling that he could no longer motivate his players, moved on to Crystal Palace. During Ron Saunders' short stay as manager after Johnny Hart's even shorter one, due to illness, as Allison's successor, Lee complained of being 'used like something in a game of monopoly', and near the end of it, in April 1974, he regarded his proposed transfer to Birmingham City as an insult. It had been suggested that money from the sales of Lee and Summerbee, who was wanted by Leeds but a year later ended up at Burnley, would go towards the purchase from Hull City of Stuart Pearson, who instead became a £200,000 signing by Tommy Docherty for newly-relegated Manchester United and helped them to prompt promotion.

Another change of manager seemed certain to ensure the continuance of Lee's career with City when his old team-mate Tony Book was promoted from having been Saunders' assistant and declared: 'The Birmingham business is in the past, and I've got no thought about wanting to sell him.' Within a week of that statement, however, a prediction that Lee would be on his way when his contract expired at the end of June was shown to be not all that wide of the mark when he was transfer-listed early in August after being in dispute with the club over a new contract. City had an additional four-year option on his services, but Lee was in no mood to accept the new terms offered. He put his point of view uncompromisingly:

'Up to the time City wanted to sell me to Birmingham last season I was easy-going about such things as football contracts. Now, after being upset by that proposition, I am looking at the whole thing in a more businesslike way. City would have made a profit on me, and if I had gone to Birmingham or any other club I believe I could have got better terms than at Maine Road. If City want me to play for them they can pay me more money to do it, or transfer me. Every player in the country must have been affected by inflation, and I reckon my pay is now worth only about half of what it was when I signed the contract that has just run out.'

With no improved offer on the table, Book took the decision to put Lee on the list 'in the best interests of everybody', but he admitted to being 'a bit of a sentimentalist' and, having played in the same team as Lee for several years, said he was bound to feel a tinge of sadness now that the sturdy little striker was leaving. They had first met when on opposing sides early in their careers in an FA Cup-tie between Bolton and Bath City. Before that game a member of the Bolton training staff had been sent to spy on Bath and reported back: 'They've got an old full-back who is very dodgy. Play on him and it should be easy.' Book, who soon afterwards was taken by Malcolm Allison from Bath to Plymouth, and then to Manchester City when near his thirtieth birthday, made that report itself look dodgy as Bolton were lucky to escape with a draw (they won the replay).

Contrary to reports that had been circulating, Book, who played more than 300 games for City despite his late entry into League football, emphasised that he was under no financial pressure to sell after taking over as the club's manager. Indeed, only 24 hours before Lee left he paid West Bromwich £250,000 of City's money for Asa Hartford, the Scottish international midfielder whose stamina belied the fact that two years earlier his £170,000 move to Leeds had been called off after a routine medical examination had revealed a heart condition, albeit a minor one.

City recouped £100,000 of that outlay on Hartford on 14 August 1974, when Dave Mackay pulled off another of his astute deals, one that was to have a crucial bearing on the title race of the coming season, by persuading Lee to move to Derby County. Not that much persuasion was needed. Lee saw it as a good move, also recognising that, apart from the deadlock over terms at Maine Road, City felt it was time to buy new players and make changes. 'When they want you to go, you go,' he said.

The Rams' arrangement, to allow Lee to combine business with what he still saw as the pleasure of playing, was for him to go to Derby on Tuesdays, spend two nights at the Midland Hotel, travel back north on Thursday afternoons, and return to Derby on Fridays. Mackay maintained that good professionals could be treated in this way, adding: 'Francis is in a similar position to myself when I came to Derby from Tottenham. I used to travel up for one day a week, and it worked out. In fact, I liken Francis to myself in many ways. I was 33 when I came to Derby and Francis, as a striker, is 30, so that's about even. And I'm looking to Francis to be able to lift the front men they way I managed to lift them in defence.'

Mackay was not to be disappointed. Lee brought much-needed aggression into the Derby attack as well as goals – though, unfortunately, too much aggression on one occasion we shall be coming to during his second season with the club – and he was also an important influence in the dressing room with his cocksure outlook. He did not score on his quietly encouraging debut for the Rams away to Everton three days after signing, but neither did anybody else as a point was deservedly extracted from a club who were to be among Derby's strongest rivals for the championship almost to the death.

Lee opened his account with the goal that earned another draw, against Coventry, at the Baseball Ground on the following Wednesday evening, and by the time, in mid-October, he took his total to seven by scoring the brace that gave Derby their first away win of the season, ending Sheffield United's unbeaten home record in the League, he was having to revise the target of fifteen he had set himself. He seemed well on course to surpass that total when, playing as well as he felt he had ever done in his career, he got into double figures by the end of November, earning the *Daily Mirror* accolade as Footballer of the Month and a cheque for £100, but had to be content with sixteen – still no bad return on Mackay's investment – after missing eight successive games because of injury throughout March and into early April.

Of those goals, one stood out, to join the others of which he had a special memory – the decider in the 4-3 win at Newcastle United that clinched the First Division title for Manchester City in 1968, the goal against Tottenham Hotspur that put City into the FA Cup's last four on their way to their Wembley defeat of a Leicester City side captained by David Nish in 1969, and the penalty that gave City the European Cup-Winners' Cup against the Poles of Gornik Zabrze in a Vienna downpour in 1970. Lee added to that list, most appropriately back at Maine Road, on the last Saturday of 1974. 'Just look at his face,' screamed commentator Barry Davies on television that night as the delighted Lee buried the winner into the far corner of his old club's net with a spectacular 65th-minute shot after turning away from three defenders and cutting in from the left towards the edge of the penalty area. It inflicted Manchester City's first home defeat of the season, much to the mortification of Lee's ten-year-old son Gary, an avid City fan:

'There he was [said Lee] with his City scarf on. He just won't support any other club. My wife Jean has told me that when Colin Bell equalised Gary was jumping up and down with delight in the stand, but he was upset when I scored straight after. It was like a dream come true, scoring one like that. I got a marvellous reception from the City crowd too. It was like a Roy of the Rovers thing to score in this game.'

Bell's classic goal wiped out the deserved first-half lead Henry Newton gave Derby with a spectacular shot into a top corner of City's net. It was Newton's first goal of the season, and, curiously, the two others he was to score during it came in the next two First Division games – another stunning opener in a home defeat of Liverpool in the 400th League appearance of his career, and the only one, also splendidly taken, of a hard-fought match at Wolverhampton.

The return encounter with Wolves, on a Wednesday evening in April just over three weeks before the final day, coincided with Lee's comeback after recovering from his injury – and he celebrated by nudging in a 69th-minute winner that lifted the Rams to the top of the table for the first time that season with the unexpected assistance of Luton Town. While Wolves were again making the Rams battle for victory, far from as co-operative as they had been in enabling Derby to become champions three years earlier by beating Leeds, relegation-bound Luton dimmed Everton's title hopes with a 2-1 home win. This was how the top teams then stood:

	P	W	D	L	F	A	Pts
DERBY	39	20	9	10	66	49	49
Liverpool	39	18	11	10	55	37	47
Everton	39	15	17	7	52	39	47
Stoke	39	17	13	9	64	46	47
Ipswich	38	21	4	13	58	39	46
Middlesbrough	39	16	12	11	51	38	44

Derby's home match with Wolves also coincided with the reappearance of Roy McFarland, who had been mainly a spectator since suffering his serious Achilles tendon injury in the 36th minute of England's defeat of Northern Ireland at Wembley the previous May. He had been hoping to return two months earlier, but had injured his other ankle in a third-team try-out. Though making his first-team comeback wearing the No 3 shirt in place of Nish, who had hobbled off with a groin injury at Middlesbrough the Saturday before, he operated in his usual position in central defence with the faithful Daniel at left-back for the one match Nish missed.

McFarland reclaimed No 5 for the remaining three games, in which Derby again did not concede a goal in holding onto top place, and that summer he was among the 35 players called to a get-together by England's manager, Don Revie. The following October he ended an absence of fourteen matches from the national side with a recall against Czechoslovakia in Bratislava, but in both that game, which was lost, and when he won his next cap, in a defeat by Scotland at Hampden Park, he had to be substituted, and he played only twice more for England after that. Following his reappearance against the Republic of Ireland, in a drawn match at Wembley, he bowed out as Italy won a World Cup qualifier in Rome in November 1976.

McFarland still had plenty to offer Derby County, who were fortunate to have such a reliable deputy during his absence for most of their 1974-75 championship season. Peter Daniel did so well, in fact, that he was elected the club's Player of the Year by supporters. Colin Todd, the national Footballer of the Year by the votes of his fellow professionals, ran Daniel mighty close in the club poll, but when it was suggested to him that a recount was needed, and that it might turn out to be a joint award, he sportingly said: 'Give it to Peter on his own. He deserves it after all he had done for the club this season.'

It was a typically generous gesture by an immaculate defender who scarcely put a foot wrong that season. Three days after Derby had become assured of the title, Todd was also elected Footballer of the Year by *Daily Express* readers, narrowly beating Alan Hudson and Kevin Beattie, whose respective clubs, Stoke and Ipswich, were other strong contenders for the championship during one of the closest campaigns on record, the leadership constantly changing. With the *Express* award went a £500 cheque which, with the trophy, was presented to Todd by Jocelyn Stevens, deputy chairman and managing director of Beaverbrook Newspapers, before the Rams' final match against Carlisle at the Baseball Ground.

Todd was an excellent role model not only for his outstanding ability. His team-mates also looked up to him for being punctual, tidy, well-dressed, modest and polite. He had dreamed of being in the limelight since the days when he had idolised Ivor Allchurch and Len White at Newcastle, but had not started to blossom until Brian Clough, as Sunderland's youth team coach, had moved him into defence. He rose to the first-team captaincy at Roker Park at the early age of twenty, but according to Gerry Francis rejected the chance to be England's skipper. Francis, while with QPR, said he knew that 'two other players, Colin Todd and Colin Bell, were asked before me if they'd captain England, but refused'. Francis felt honoured to take over the job from Alan Ball, but it did not take him long to appreciate why it was not one coveted by others. 'I must confess,' he also said, 'that I thought I'd made a mistake soon after accepting when I started taking stick on away grounds in club matches. People were so quick to get at me, just as they had been to other England captains before me.'

On moving to Derby, Todd was at first inhibited by the big fee paid for him and slow to realise his full potential. 'Brian and I showed him the way of life,' said Peter Taylor. 'He used to lack ambition, and we had to tell him how good he was. We told him: "You're big. Think big".' It also helped Todd to come out of his shell, as he expressed it, because with Derby he was in one of the most successful teams in the country.

After England's defeat of West Germany, then the world champions, in 1975, Don Revie paid Todd the highest of tributes in likening him to the acknowledged master of the free, defensive sweeper's role, Franz Beckenbauer. 'Todd gives the ball so early, the moment a pass is possible, that the receiver gains several extra yards,' said Revie. 'Not a split second is wasted in running with the ball, and his accuracy is tremendous. When he comes forward, the same as Beckenbauer, he is fast and decisive, rarely losing possession to put his team in trouble.'

Peter Daniel, who benefited from having Todd alongside him, received his Player of the Year award, the Jack Stamps Trophy, during County's annual dinner, at Bailey's night club in the town, on the Wednesday evening of 23 April 1975, on which the Rams were confirmed as champions by Ipswich's failure to gain the victory at Maine Road that they needed, as the only remaining rivals, to take the issue right to the season's finale on the coming Saturday. Manchester City drew 1-1 with the Suffolk challengers, and one of the first telegrams to congratulate Mackay and his men came from their captain, Colin Bell, whose fourth-minute goal against Ipswich was equalised by Bryan Hamilton in the 66th. As the result from Maine Road was announced Mackay's wife Isobel flung her arms around his neck and kissed him. He confessed that he felt like crying and also admitted:

'Sitting through that meal was worse than being at the match. It is a tremendous moment. Quite fantastic. I'm the sort of man who lives for the present. This has to be the greatest moment of my life, irrespective of what I achieved as a player with Hearts and Tottenham. When I returned to Derby I said that if I didn't win something with this club within two years then I didn't deserve to be a manager. Winning the Cup is OK. Playing in Europe is OK. But winning the League is very difficult. This is the real accolade, and that's why I'm so proud. We tried to do it our way, and that meant playing attacking, entertaining football. It is one thing to win a title, but it is even better to do it in a way which entertains the fans. The Derby players are a great bunch, and this season has been a terrific team effort. They have always played the way I wanted to play, and any misunderstandings or bad feelings of the past had disappeared long before we started this season. We have pulled together.'

Mackay joined the select band of men who have played in and managed championship-winning teams, fifth behind Ted Drake, Bill Nicholson, Alf

Ramsey and Joe Mercer. Since then the list has been added to by Bob Paisley, Howard Kendall, Kenny Dalglish and George Graham. But, like Brian Clough in 1972, Mackay was denied the Manager of the Year award, which went to Ron Saunders, whose Aston Villa team paired the winning of the Second Division title with the League Cup. When Derby were champions under Clough, Leeds United's close approach to the League and Cup double made Don Revie the Manager of the Year, but Nottingham Forest's League title and League Cup win earned Clough the premier honour in 1978 – and a year later, when Forest finished runners-up to Liverpool, he received £500 and an inscribed silver salver as 'consolation prizes' after seeing the top award go the Anfield club's manager, Bob Paisley, for the third time in four seasons.

Mackay professed to having never lost confidence in Derby's ability to come out on top again, yet they made one of the poorest starts by any eventual champions, sinking as low as fourteenth in the table after winning only one of their first seven League matches. There were four other distinct periods of the 1974-75 season in which their prospects looked decidedly dicey. Firstly, on successive Saturdays in late October they gave an abject performance in losing in chilly Cumberland to Carlisle United, deceptive early table-toppers in what was to be their only experience of First Division football, then lost their unbeaten home record to Middlesbrough, who that April had stormed to promotion even more decisively than Derby had done five years earlier.

The manager missed the match with Middlesbrough. He was at his Nottinghamshire home at Burton Joyce, recovering from cuts and severe bruising suffered in a car accident the previous night. He had returned home from Derby County's annual meeting, and was on his way to join his players at their overnight accommodation when his Mercedes struck a road sign on the Borrowash by-pass between Nottingham and Derby. Debris struck another car, but its driver was unhurt. Mackay managed to drive back home, but the doctor who was summoned to give him treatment immediately ordered him to bed. 'When I look at the car I feel I'm lucky to be alive,' said the Rams' manager. 'I feel faint every time I move.'

A week later, his team gave him just the tonic he needed. They bounced back from those damaging defeats by laying their Leeds bogy, a late goal by Lee snatching their first points at Elland Road since their return to the First Division.

The next qualms arose from two more consecutive League defeats in the lead-up to Christmas, straight after their exit from European competition. Everton wrested the leadership from Stoke by benefiting from Derby's defensive slackness to win by an only goal on the Baseball Ground's apology for a pitch, and a week later the Rams lost by the same score away to Luton Town, who, like Carlisle, were heading for immediate relegation. It was only the second victory of the season for Luton, whose team contained two players who were to find their way to Derby – Steve Buckley (the one lasting legacy Tommy Docherty left the Rams) and Paul Futcher.

Those setbacks dropped Derby to tenth in the table, and, although they were still just five points behind leaders Ipswich, they were only six ahead of twentieth-placed Carlisle, who sprang the biggest surprise of the day by recovering from a two-goal deficit to beat Everton at Goodison. Again, however, the County pulled themselves together, gaining four wins in a row that included Lee's heroics in Manchester and a home success against Liverpool in what Mackay regarded as their most important game of the season.

The defeat away to Queen's Park Rangers that followed was not the next serious check because the 1-4 margin made it look a lot worse than it was. Derby, encouraged by an early lead, had much the better of the play until conceding a second goal, hotly disputed for offside, ten minutes from time. Don Givens then did what Kevin Hector had done for Derby in the match between the clubs at the Baseball Ground – completed a hat-trick. Dave Sexton, manager of the London club, said it was a very tight game that he thought would result in a draw until those last ten minutes, 'but we were able to catch them when they came out looking for an equaliser.'

After a home victory against Arsenal in which the Gunners had two players, Alan Ball and Bob McNab, sent off, the Rams' chances of regaining the title took another knock with a 0-3 slip-up on a raw night at Ipswich while Everton, then the favourites, and Leeds were other winners. Once more the Rams rallied, beating Tottenham and Chelsea (their first win at Stamford Bridge for 23 years), only to falter seriously for the fourth time by dropping both points to Stoke as conditions at the Baseball Ground became even more appalling, mud seeping over the players' boots.

The see-saw state of the title race intensified three days later as Stoke themselves lost ground in a home defeat by Ipswich and Everton were beaten at Middlesbrough. Worse still for Stoke, they were deprived of Denis Smith, their commanding centre-half, who broke a leg – their fourth player to be sidelined by such a serious injury that season. Everton, who had also been weakened by injury to a key man, Colin Harvey, then led by three points from Ipswich.

On the following Saturday, while Everton were recovering to force a draw in their crucial clash at home to Ipswich, Derby County revived once more with their fourth League victory at Newcastle in six seasons. That left the Rams, although in seventh place, only one point behind each of the five clubs immediately above, with a match in hand over all of them, but five points behind Everton, who had also played one game more. The Merseysiders, with seven fixtures to fulfil to Derby's eight, still seemed unlikely to be caught, but they promptly wobbled again by losing as heavily at Carlisle, by 0-3, as Derby had done. It was one of the oddities of such an unpredictable season that Carlisle, who finished four points adrift in last place, took maximum points from Everton and all but one against Derby.

As is customary, much depended on the Easter games, and the Rams rose to the occasion with five-goal blasts at home to Luton and away to Burnley. The defeat of the Bedfordshire club was a personal triumph for Roger Davies, who did all of the Rams' scoring and, as Mackay readily pointed out, would have doubled it to equal the ten-goal League record of Derbyshire-born Joe Payne (for Luton, against Bristol Rovers, on Easter Monday in 1936) if it had really been his day. The facts clearly fitted the manager's view. Besides doing the hat-trick in 33 minutes and netting twice more in the last dozen, Davies had two 'goals' disallowed, a fierce drive brilliantly stopped by goalkeeper Keith Barber, a header cleared off the line by Steve Buckley, and registered a series of other near-misses. The ball, thrown to him by referee Ray Tinkler as he was given a standing ovation at the end, was autographed by both teams.

Hughie Gallacher, the dynamic little Scot who had his peak years in English football with Newcastle and Chelsea before joining Derby, had been the last to score five times in a League game for the Rams – at Blackburn in 1934 – but Dave McCulloch, another Scottish international centre-forward, had done so during a wartime match with Mansfield. There had been three earlier instances, by Sandy Higgins, Johnny McMillan and Jim Moore, and Kevin Hector was to join the list in a UEFA Cup-tie.

Davies had previously scored only six goals in that 1974-75 season – four of them in the first seven games – and he felt that he should at least have reached another half-dozen against Luton, matching the club record for one match set by Steve Bloomer against the Wednesday (as the Sheffield club was then officially known) in 1899. Davies said:

'I was disappointed when one of my goals was disallowed, as I did not handle the ball on purpose. It was an accident. The other disallowed goal was a fair offside [though one report described it as "marginal"]. My only previous hat-trick in senior football was against Spurs in the Cup. Strangely enough, before the game with Luton Kevin Hector asked me how long it was since I had scored a hat-trick. I told him I had never got one for Derby in the League, and it was a job for me to remember when I had last scored two in one game – against Birmingham last year. Kevin said I must be due for a hat-trick, and perhaps it could be today. But five – it's unbelievable. The first one gave me most pleasure because it's been so hard to get goals. I haven't even been getting them in five-a-side games.'

Perhaps the changed playing conditions at the Baseball Ground had something to do with it. The pitch was transformed into firmness after three weeks without rain, and while much of Britain was being either rained on or snowed on that Saturday, the Derby groundsman had to do some watering. Or, more likely, Davies owed his regained scoring touch to extra work he had been doing with Des Anderson in training, plus the shooting practice he had put in with Bruce Rioch and Alan Hinton.

He scored one more goal in the 5-2 win at Burnley two days later, though that was his lot for the season. Hector led the way with two goals that afternoon, and next day Rioch scored a brace in a hard-earned 2-1 home victory against Manchester City which lifted the tiring Rams into third place, behind Ipswich and Everton only on goal-average. Then, after a last-minute goal by Hector had snatched a priceless point in what Dave Mackay termed the Great Escape at Middlesbrough, and Lee's goal against Wolves had taken Derby to the top, Rioch again came up with the winner as West Ham became the sixteenth losing visitors of the season (including cup-ties) to the Baseball Ground. Crucial as those goals by Rioch were, the strength of his finishing, so welcome after the scoring shortage from midfield since Alan Durban's departure, was most vividly demonstrated that season at St James' Park, where he finished off Newcastle United in storming style after a run almost half the length of the field.

Rioch joined Todd, Nish, Gemmill (an inspiring captain in McFarland's absence), Hector and Lee as obvious big-name successes in the Derby lineup, but, of their comparatively unsung colleagues, vital contributions were also made by Boulton, Webster, Thomas, Newton and Hinton in addition to Daniel and Davies.

Boulton was initially one of the players who most resented Dave Mackay's appointment. He said it was 'like the end of the world' when Brian Clough left, and he had a habit of looking away when Mackay entered the room. During one practice match, he was chased over the field by Mackay after the manager had overheard him complain to the coach, who was refereeing, that Mackay had been awarded a free-kick only because of who he was. 'I don't often lose my temper,' said Mackay later, 'but this time I completely lost control. All I wanted to do was catch him and kick him.'

Not behaviour befitting a manager, admittedly, but it was typical of Mackay that he did not let personal feelings warp his judgment in choosing the team, enabling Boulton deservedly to be an ever-present member of a title-winning side for the second time, and the air was eventually cleared between the two when they both spoke their mind in a big argument in the manager's office. At the end of it, Boulton held out his hand and said: 'I am looking you straight in the eyes now.' The goalkeeper was well rewarded for his consistent service with a testimonial match just two days before Derby were confirmed as champions.

Webster, an ever-present until injured shortly after Christmas, received a silver salver to mark his 500th appearance in the Boxing Day home defeat of Birmingham. Newton, settling in after Steve Powell, unlucky with injuries, had at first taken over in succession to McGovern, made a surprisingly early return, missing only three matches, after needing eight stitches in an ugly gash below his right knee, suffered at Newcastle, which Mackay, not without personal experience of serious injury, said was the worst he had ever seen.

Hinton, like Powell, did a good job without being a regular choice. Brought back when Lee was injured, he gave the attack extra width, showed much of his old skill, and used the ball immaculately. Indeed, he returned with such enthusiasm that there was the intriguing sight of Tottenham's Ralph Coates wagging a finger at him and telling him not be to so rough. With Lee fit again, Hinton was back on the bench for the last four games, and found it a far bigger ordeal watching rather than playing. 'It was absolute murder,' he said after fretting through the penultimate match against Leicester City in which Filbert Street's biggest League gate of the season, swollen to 38,943 by the strong support from Derby, saw a frenetic scoreless draw. Swansea referee Tom Reynolds prolonged the agony by allowing almost four minutes of time added on for stoppages.

Leicester brought out the champagne to celebrate having escaped relegation. For Derby, the point at first appeared to be just a useful one that kept them in the running, but as the results of the other games came through they realised that only Ipswich could still catch them. Liverpool were beaten at Middlesbrough, and Everton threw away another two-goal lead in losing at home to Sheffield United.

So to the final Saturday, on which Derby's midweek clinching of the title through Ipswich's draw at Maine Road brought out many of their missing 'supporters'. The top attendance of the season at the Baseball Ground, 36,882, turned up for the gala occasion. And the second championship was not the only cause for celebration. After that concluding game with relegated Carlisle, work began on digging up the much-maligned pitch in preparation for laying a new one in time for the following season. Pieces of the old turf still with at least a semblance of some grass were sold off to the public as mementoes. Ten years later, BBC Radio Derby brought out an audiotape, *The Derby County Story*, on which one enthusiast told of how he had bought a section containing a penalty spot but had been unable to keep it for long. His dog ate it – without, apparently, suffering indigestion.

Before the kick-off against Carlisle there was a nostalgic parade of former players, ten of whose careers with the club had started during the period between the two world wars: George Thornewell and Sammy Crooks (that era's main holders of the right-wing position), Freddie Knowles, Harry Bedford, Dai Astley, Jack Howe, Tim Ward, Jack Stamps, Freddie Jessop and Jack Webb. Then came five who first played during the 1939-45 War: Tommy Powell, Jack Parr, Billy Townsend, Jim Bullions and Peter Doherty. And after them a representative selection of those had followed, including Johnny Morris, Paddy Ryan, Reg Matthews, Ray Young, Willie Carlin and Terry Hennessey.

Also on parade were Peter Daniel, Steve Powell and Ron Webster, out of the side with injuries, and members of the Rams' nursery club, Holme Valley Blues, who brought with them a cup won in Paris. The only pity was that one of the sixteen players who had shared in the championship success was missing. Jeff Bourne was required to play for the Reserves at Hillsborough.

The Derby team took the field to a flourish of trumpets and a guard of honour provided by the visiting players. The First Division trophy was presented to Archie Gemmill by Sam Bolton, a League vice-president, and the ritual lap of honour was made to the ear-splitting accompaniment of songs, chants and countless ovations.

Then came the let-down, though nobody seemed to care overmuch. The anticipated slaughter of the division's bottom club by the new champions failed to materialise. The match was a sad anti-climax, a boring goalless draw. With the pressure off, Derby were unable to raise their game, though Hinton, on for Lee, almost broke the deadlock with a vicious cross shot that severely tested goalkeeper Alan Ross. Dave Mackay regretted that 'after all the fun we turned it off when we should have turned it on, but I'm not going to complain after such a magnificent season'. Indeed not. The stuttering start had been more than counter-balanced by a flourishing finish, with only one defeat in the last dozen games from which nineteen points had been gained out of 24.

This time there was no Central League title to go with the big one, but the Rams Reserves did the next best thing in finishing just one point behind Liverpool's champions under the guidance of Colin Murphy (they were third in each of the next two seasons). Success on such a scale justified the prediction Sam Longson had made after some semblance of order had been restored after the colossal upheaval caused by Brian Clough's departure and Dave Mackay's return. Puffing a Havana cigar and with a recharged champagne glass in hand, the venerable chairman had hailed 'the start of a new era at Derby' after, in November 1973, the club had won the *Daily Express* five-a-side championship before a sell-out crowd of 8,000 at Wembley's indoor arena, beating a young Glasgow Celtic side 3-1 in the final with a hat-trick from David Nish. (Kevin Hector received the five-aside trophy from Sir Max Aitken, chairman of Beaverbrook Newspapers. The other members of the Derby squad were Boulton, Gemmill, McGovern, Nish, and Todd. They reached the final by defeating Middlesbrough 3-0, Manchester United 2-0, and Chelsea 2-1.)

The big drawback with the 'new era' was that it did not last very long, ending with another traumatic disruption that was to lead the club back to the Third Division into which they had first floundered so soon after winning the FA Cup for the first time. For the moment, however, the Rams had every reason to celebrate, with this supreme tribute from Mackay ringing in their ears: 'This is the best team I have been associated with – and I include the Spurs double side.'

DROUGHT DAMAGE TO NEW PITCH AT BASEBALL GROUND

The drought during the hot summer and autumn of 1976 caused excessive damage to the new £40,000 pitch at the Baseball Ground, and extensive repairs had to be carried out during the 1977 close season. The remaining root fibre was rotovated, and the whole area re-seeded with deep-rooted grasses possessing maximum wear toll.

The major cause of waterlogging on the replaced pitch had been its inability to drain. As well as installing a new drainage system, the contractors, Chipman Ltd, of Horsham, Sussex, had put in a predominantly sandy mix for the new soil. This had dried quickly in any case, so an automatic sprinkler system had also been provided to keep all the top soil fully moistured so that the deep-rooted rye grass could bed in to a depth of its accepted growth rate of half an inch a day.

Regulations during the drought meant that water had to be used sparingly, however, and after a complete ban irrigation was allowed only to surface depth. Consequently, the roots of the new grass went sideways instead of down, in search of moisture, leaving a dense mass of shallow surface grass with roots an inch deep rather than the intended six-inch minimum.

As soon as the pitch was used again at the start of the 1976-77 season, wear was not confined to a loss of just grass but also of large divots and root material, which were torn away.

A Cup Clash of 18 Penalties

Two trips to the South Coast had sharply contrasting outcomes for Derby County as they embarked upon their three-track Cup trail in the 1974-75 season which they would end up as League champions.

Drawn away in the League Cup to Portsmouth, former League champions who had become struggling members of the Second Division soon bound for the Fourth, they gave their best performance since Dave Mackay took over as manager in storming to a 5-1 victory. It was a triumph of teamwork, with the Rams firmly in charge from the tenth minute in which Kevin Hector spectacularly opened the scoring with a scorching right-foot drive from just under thirty yards out.

The next three goals were also something special. On the half-hour, Franny Lee twisted in mid-air to smash the ball home from close range after it had hit him as Roger Davies volleyed goalwards from a corner taken by Bruce Rioch. Then, in the first five minutes of the second half, Rioch rounded off a flowing right-wing move he had begun with a pass out to Davies, just beating Lee to slotting home the resulting low cross, and Hector clinically applied the finishing touch to Lee's pulled-back pass from the left.

Soon afterwards, Derby were temporarily put out of their smooth stride by an injury to Ron Webster, who was carried off after an elbow in the face had knocked him out in an accidental collision, and about twenty minutes later, in the seventieth, Portsmouth reduced their arrears with a goal made by a perfectly-timed through pass by Bobby Kellard. The scorer, with a neat left-foot shot just inside Colin Boulton's far post, was Peter Marinello, the winger who had misguidedly been hailed as the new George Best when signed by Arsenal from Hibernian for not much less than £100,000. Webster's place was taken by Henry Newton, but, fortunately, the full-back was not seriously hurt and he was back in action for the next League game three days later.

The scoring at Fratton Park was completed nine minutes from time in a fortunate manner. Davies, displaying the nifty close control that on another occasion had commentator David Coleman likening it to threading a needle, worked his way into the penalty area before slipping a pass to Lee, whose powerful shot cannoned into the net off Welsh international Phil Roberts as goalkeeper David Best went the other way. There might have been more goals as Derby, having recovered their poise, continued to dominate the closing exchanges, but Hector was denied a hat-trick by a clear offside decision, and Lee brought out the best of Best with almost the last kick.

The ease with which Portsmouth had been dispatched gave Derby County every reason to suppose they would progress further in the competition when the third-round draw paired them with Southampton, also then a Second Division club, even though they had to travel to The Dell. Southampton had won only once at home in the League that season in five attempts – against Portsmouth, and that by only the odd goal – and they had looked far from impressive in losing away to Nottingham Forest in their most recent match. Furthermore, they had managed just the one goal in labouring to the defeat of Notts County that had earned them a visit from Mackay's men. One of manager Lawrie McMenemy's critics loudly invited him to resign as he walked to his seat on the touchline bench before the kick-off against the Rams.

But how fickle was form to prove! And how forewarned it was found Derby should have been by the presence in Southampton's attack of Mike Channon and Peter Osgood, players of the highest calibre. Channon did the hat-trick, and Osgood was one of the other scorers, as the Rams, outfought and humiliated, were counted out by five goals to nil only three days after giving one of their best away displays of their championship-winning season in twice coming from behind to force a deserved draw in a match at West Ham that was a splendid advertisement for the game at a time when it was haemorrhaging support largely because of increasing hooliganism. It was Derby's heaviest defeat since their thrashing at Leeds by the same score two years before almost to the day, and they had again lamentably failed to do what they had not done for four years – get past the League Cup's third round.

Between those highs and lows down in Hampshire, Derby got off to an encouraging start in the UEFA Cup with a comfortable 6-2 aggregate win against Servette, who had qualified for European competition by finishing third behind Zurich and Grasshoppers in the Swiss League. Servette's total of thirteen national titles was second only to Grasshoppers' sixteen up to that time, but they were swept aside at the Baseball Ground before the Rams eased up in the last half-hour after forging four goals ahead.

The first one came in the twelfth minute, when Hector headed in from a free-kick by Nish for a foul on Daniel. Lee then had an acrobatic overhead kick cleared off the line, and Newton a well-struck volley beaten out by goalkeeper de Blaireville, before the lead was increased by Daniel's first goal in senior soccer – a header from a centre by Webster. There was the touch of the master craftsman as Lee turned smartly after receiving a pass from Gemmill with his back to goal to give the Rams a three-goal cushion two minutes from the interval, but the *pièce de résistance*, to use a phrase appropriate to the opposition, was Hector's second scoring effort early in the second half. Although off balance when the ball reached him from Nish, he quickly brought it under control, neatly evaded a couple of tackles, and placed his shot to perfection.

Soon afterwards, in the 54th minute, Hinton was given a fond reception when restored to the side for the first time that season, as substitute for Newton. He showed flashes of his old form, but the change disturbed the rhythm that had so clearly given the Rams the upper hand, and Servette grasped the opportunity to cut the deficit, through Petrovic, with what they hoped might prove to be a vital away goal.

Those hopes were further raised in the return leg in Geneva a fortnight later when, not long after Nish had cleared off the line, the expected opening onslaught culminated in a second Servette goal. Player-coach Sundermann, who at Derby had been the rarity of a substituted substitute after only a dozen minutes on the pitch, took a corner-kick which eluded Derby's defenders, and the ball dropped conveniently for Martin to score with a first-time shot.

Derby were still behind on the night at half-time, but Hector gave signs of what was to come – first by having a goal narrowly ruled out for offside, then by hitting the bar. Daniel also went close to the equaliser that Lee snapped up in the first minute of the second half as fumbling by de Blaireville offered him a simple chance. With their overall three-goal advantage restored, the Rams asserted themselves as Servette lost impetus, and in the 72nd minute Hector headed a goal that was as much of a gift as Lee's after de Blairville had failed to hold one of Rioch's free-kick bombshells and Bourne's follow-up shot. It was not all Derby at that stage, however, and Boulton had to be alert to make two excellent second-half saves from Guyot, deflecting the ball against an upright off his fingertips on the second occasion.

Some of the Swiss tackling, benefiting from the leniency of the Austrian referee, was so over-zealous that even Hector, not easily provoked, was stung into a booking for throwing the ball at the worst offender, Morganegg, after one of the more vigorous fouls. Most physical damage was done to Newton, whose shin took the force of the first kick substitute Barriquand delivered after Sundermann had again withdrawn from the action. Two stitches were needed in the cut that opened the flesh down to the bone, but the indomitable Henry was fit to continue at West Ham on the following Saturday.

The victory clinched in Geneva's Stade des Charmilles left Derby County as England's sole UEFA Cup survivors. Ipswich Town went out to Twente Enschede, Stoke City to another Dutch club, Ajax of Amsterdam – both on the away-goal rule after two drawn games – and Wolverhampton

Wanderers to the Portuguese side Porto after finding a 1-4 deficit from the first leg just too big to overcome. In European competition the Rams now shared English interest with Leeds, who went on to be runners-up to Bayern Munich for the European Cup, and Liverpool, who scored an aggregate of twelve goals without reply from the Norwegians of Stromsgodset in the first round of the Cup-Winners' Cup, but were then also to join the vanquished, conceding a costly equaliser to Ferencvaros at Anfield before playing a scoreless draw in the return leg in Hungary.

Derby County's next European opponents were Atletico Madrid, the previous season's beaten European Cup finalists, and conquerors of KB Copenhagen in the first round of the UEFA Cup with a 4-0 home win after losing 2-3 in Denmark. A more skilful side than Servette, they put themselves in a seemingly formidable position by drawing 2-2 at the Baseball Ground, leaving the Rams needing either a victory in Spain or a draw of at least 3-3. Neither of those tremendous tasks was accomplished, yet it was Derby who progressed after one of the most dramatic matches ever seen at the impressive, but on that occasion only half-filled, Vicente Calderon stadium.

Both legs of this pulsating tie ended with penalties – two bizarre ones at Derby, and an incredible sixteen more in the shoot-out after extra-time in Madrid. In the first match Nish equalised with a half-hit hook shot two minutes after Ayala, the stocky, bow-legged Argentine World Cup striker, had given Atletico a thirteenth-minute lead with a dipping 25-yard volley, and that was how the score stood until the last dozen minutes during which both sides scored from the spot and Hinton, on as substitute for Bourne, so nearly snatched a winner by hammering the ball against the inside of the far post.

Robert Helies, the French referee, had an excellent game until, in the 78th minute, he completely misinterpreted a save at the feet of Garate, who pushed the ball too far ahead of him after breaking clear down the middle and appeared to fall over Boulton as the goalkeeper came out to gather the ball. Derby's heated protests being of no avail, Atletico hurriedly brought on Luis, their 36-year-old penalty expert, in place of Leal, and he readily restored the visitors' lead with his first kick. Nine minutes later, one controversial decision was neutralised by another as the referee again pointed to the spot when Lee gained possession with his back to goal and fell as if he had been shot as Dillario Eusebio (not to be confused with the Benfica wizard) closed in. Rioch made no mistake with his trusty left foot to bring the scores level again, though the Madrid club's two away goals made it look a lost cause for the Rams.

It took only four minutes of the second leg for the tie to drift still further away from them. The referee, this time a German named Biwersl, ruled that Gemmill, whose 200th game for Derby was one of his greatest, had fouled Ayala, and Luis punished slack marking by a defence deprived of the injured McFarland and Todd with a header from Adelardo's free-kick. Lee and Rioch missed chances to reply before half-time, but Atletico themselves had two good scoring opportunities, and also had appeals for a penalty against Webster rejected, before Rioch renewed hope with a firm 54th-minute shot from an opening created by Davies following a Hector centre.

Ten minutes later, Derby went ahead for the first time. Hector chested down an accurate centre from Gemmill and as his shot hit the net a chorus of whistling broke out from the Spanish fans among the 35,000 spectators, coupled with calls for the dismissal of coach Juan Carlos Lorenzo. Both sides then had further escapes, Newton going closest with a shot that shaved a post, before Atletico again scored from a free-kick, harshly awarded against Newton for handling. This was entrusted to Luis, who lived up to his reputation as a dead-ball specialist with a brilliantly-executed swerving kick into the top corner of Boulton's net from some 25 yards, making the score 4-4 on aggregate.

The last chance of settling the contest in normal time fell to Davies, back in European football after the suspension incurred by his sending-off against Juventus. He ran right through the home defence from the halfway line, but goalkeeper Reina ran out to block his shot. So to extra-time, and more near-misses before it was all down to penalties.

Both teams had one failure in the original spot-kick decider of five to each side. Successful kicks by Rioch and Hector were cancelled out by Luis and Ayala, but Reina then dived to his left to foil Davies. Salcedo, who had come on as a substitute after an hour's play, put Atletico 3-2 ahead, only for full-back Capon to scoop his shot over the bar after Nish had kept the Rams in the reckoning. Lee and Irureta made it 4-4 on penalties, which took the contest into sudden death. Conversions by Gemmill and Newton were countered by Benegas and Garate, after which Powell, who had a great game as deputy for Todd, scored what was to be the decider. The sixteenth kick was taken by Eusebio, and Boulton made the most important save of the match by diving to his right to push the ball against an upright. Eusebio, following up, slipped the rebound into the net, but too late to count. Derby were through 7-6 on penalties.

Boulton, hero of the hour in his testimonial season, had gone into that match recognising that he was playing for his first-team future. He had originally been dropped for the previous Saturday's League game at Leeds, but had preserved his ever-present record in another title-winning side by being reinstated 24 hours later after a long discussion with Dave Mackay. That was the visit to Elland Road in which the Rams so unexpectedly ended their run of bad results against the Yorkshire club with a late winning goal by Francis Lee, and Boulton responded to his reprieve by keeping his goal intact with what the manager described as 'an immaculate performance'. The grateful goalkeeper said afterwards:

'I talked the boss into playing me at Leeds and giving me another chance. He took a gamble because I had chucked in three goals in both our previous League games. To keep my place I have got to produce my peak form consistently from now on.' Which he did.

For their dramatic defeat of Atletico Madrid against all the odds, Derby's players were rewarded by a bonus of only £50 a man. Whereas Atletico were playing for £1,000 each, and every member of Leeds' European Cup squad was earning £750 for beating Ujpest Dozsa, the Derby players were limited by contracts they had signed before the start of the season. Mackay explained: 'I cannot alter bonus clauses in contracts, even though the lads deserved it. But I don't believe that there are many players who are motivated by money. My players couldn't have given more, or played better, in Madrid if they had been on £5,000 a man. There is no point in comparing our bonus scale with other teams. We are only beginners in Europe, and, maybe, when we have had the experience and success of a club like Leeds we will be paying bigger bonuses.'

Derby's UEFA Cup bonus was on a sliding scale, increasing round by round, and it was set to rise above £1,000 if they won the trophy. That, however, was not to be. Two substitutions dragged them back from the brink of defeat in the home leg of their third-round tie with Velez Mostar, a Yugoslav team of ball-playing skills and a touch of steel, but this time penalties went against them as they conceded two in the return match – the decider a hotly-disputed award only five minutes from time.

On the Baseball Ground gluepot, Derby were behind from only the second minute. Franjo Vladic, a blond Yugoslav international with a permanent limp, struck the ball into the corner of the net from fifteen yards after Todd had lost his footing in the clinging mud in attempting to deal with a cross from skipper Jadra Topic. And that was how the score stayed until shortly after Dave Mackay had made those inspired substitutions – Bourne for the tiring Davies in the 59th minute, Hinton for Lee, hampered by a groin strain, in the seventieth.

Hinton had the misfortune to be shown the yellow card for entering the field before the referee signalled for him to do so, but he promptly shrugged that off as he and the combative Bourne provided the thrust the Rams had still been lacking despite improving as the game progressed. Battling through snow flurries that made the already unpleasant conditions even more difficult, Derby at last drew level after 74 minutes, when Bourne steered home Hector's crisp centre. Six minutes later they were ahead, the crowd brought to their feet by one of Hinton's specials, a glorious left-foot shot taken in superb style on the turn after good work by Rioch.

An infringement by Hinton denied Hector a goal almost immediately afterwards, but three minutes from the end Bourne widened the advantage to 3-1 from Gemmill's low centre. Velez, who earlier had three players booked by the East German referee, lost not only the match but also their heads in those closing stages, brawling and body-checking culminating in the last-minute sending-off of their giant centre-back, Ahmed Gladovic, for butting Bourne in the face. Just before the final whistle, Nish was charged off the pitch and crashed against the boundary wall below the directors' box. He lay on the track for three minutes after the end of the game before being helped off for treatment, and although his injuries fortunately proved no worse than a sprained ankle and damaged fingers, he missed the next three League games besides the second leg in Mostar.

Dave Mackay considered himself 'lucky' with the substitutions, saying that 'when a manager does this sort of thing he is either a hero or a clown', but it was not alone for making them that he showed commendable foresight. Before being sent on, Bourne and Hinton spent ten minutes back in the dressing room to have the good warm-up their manager deemed necessary after both had been feeling the cold while sitting on the bench.

The only disappointment after such a rousing rally was that the crowd numbered not much more than 26,000, with many no doubt deterred by the bitter weather as well as the increased admission prices. That was some improvement on the attendance at the home game with Servette (17,716), but below the gate for the visit of Atletico (29,347).

Spectators were still sparser, about 15,000 of them, for the second leg at Mostar's small and mist-shrouded Gradski stadium, where Derby were up against it from the eleventh minute in which Gemmill conceded a penalty by bringing down winger Vukoje in attempting to retrieve a ball he allowed to get away from him when he had plenty of time in which to have cleared. Boulton got a hand to Primorac's spot-kick, but could not keep the ball out. Twenty minutes later the overall scores were level, but Velez in front on the away-goals rule. From a corner taken by the influential Vladic, Boulton's punched clearance sent the ball straight to Pecejl, who blasted it straight back past him through the crowded goalmouth.

Six minutes into the second period, the home side went into a 3-0 lead, 4-3 ahead in all. Todd was penalised for a foul when Hallhodszic clearly dived. Vladic took the free-kick from some 25 yards out, and although Boulton did well to touch the ball onto the crossbar it bounced down and trickled into the net off the goalkeeper's back.

Another substitution by Mackay then quickly led to another Rams revival. In the 55th minute he sent on Davies in place of Bourne, and with his second touch the lanky striker headed down Newton's left-wing cross for Hector to force his way past two defenders before levelling the aggregate with a strong shot that nullified Velez's away goal. As before, the Yugoslavs were badly rattled, resorting to obstructive tactics as increasing pressure left Derby desperately unlucky not to regain an overall advantage. Newton hit a post with one hefty shot, then put another narrowly over the bar, and Hector was foiled by a clearance off the line.

With seventeen minutes left Mackay tried another substitution, Hinton for Lee, but there was to be no repeat rescue act. With extra-time looming came the controversial decision by Dutch referee Charles Corver that cost Derby County a place in the last eight. He pointed to the penalty spot when a shot from Vukoje struck Todd on the upper arm – on the shoulder according to Todd – at such close range that the Derby defender had every justification for saying that he could not get out of the way. Mackay later advised Corver to watch the television film to prove the referee wrong in his belief that 'the ball was played by Todd's wrist'. The resulting conversion that prevented the Rams proving Mackay's other claim that 'we would have done them in extra time' was thumped home by Bajavic, a World Cup striker.

Next day, Derby sent an official protest to UEFA, asking for an annulment of the match at Mostar. They alleged that Corver was biased towards the home team and also committed several technical errors – most glaringly in permitting the County to kick-off at the start of each half. Those objections were rejected, and so was the appeal they lodged. But Velez, who went out to Twente Enschede, of the Netherlands, in their quarter-final after winning the first leg, did not escape some punishment. They were fined £500 because a number of their fans set off firecrackers during the home leg against the Rams. Twente defeated the Italian giants Juventus in their semi-final, but lost 1-5 at home to the German club Borussia Moenchengladbach in the final after coming away from the first leg in Dusseldorf with a goalless draw.

Having been banished from two cup paths, Derby County were in danger of being knocked straight off a third when they went two goals down in their third-round FA Cup-tie with Orient, a side then struggling in the Second Division after going close to promotion the previous season. Orient went into the match with only sixteen goals behind them in two dozen League games, yet they breached Derby's defence after only thirteen minutes and scored again three minutes later.

The first goal was beautifully hit by Derek Possee, a former Tottenham winger who had cost Crystal Palace more than £100,000 but had left them for Orient on a free transfer. The manner of the finish offset the luck of the ball landing at his feet from a clearance by Newton after Boulton's indeterminate punching-out of a free-kick awarded against Todd for obstruction and pumped upfield by Phil Hoadley, another former Palace player. Hoadley again strayed from the efficient job he did of policing Lee by combining with Possee to create the chance smartly accepted by a third ex-Palace player, Gerry Queen, whose involvement in shocks of a very different kind while with the Selhurst Park club had given a national newspaper sub-editor the opportunity he eagerly grabbed of putting up the headline: QUEEN IN PUNCH-UP AT PALACE.

Derby very nearly conceded another goal to Queen, his header bouncing off the top of their crossbar, before, in the absence of the injured Hector, relief came from a most unlikely source. Colin Todd, so constantly the Rams' saviour in defence, turned rescuer in attack by celebrating his 200th game for the club by scoring both goals that averted humiliation in giving them a second chance at the Baseball Ground four days later. Fortune smiled on him as deflections of his shots deceived goalkeeper John Jackson, yet another player previously with Palace. The first one rekindled hope before half-time, from a free-kick tapped short and square to him by Gemmill after Bourne had been obstructed, but only seven minutes were left when he equalised from a cut-back centre by Rioch. By that time Bourne had made way for Hinton, who was then the only player still in the First Division who had won an England cap while Walter Winterbottom was in charge of the national team.

How close the Rams came to an early exit was also emphasised by the two big escapes they had between those goals. A shot by Barrie Fairbrother struck a post, and there were strenuous appeals for a penalty when Possee sprawled under challenges from Daniel and Webster. Referee Crabb decided he had dived, a decision that left Orient manager George Petchey bemoaning the fact that 'our luck in this game was about the same as it has been all season'.

It was much the same story in the replay, with Derby making extremely hard work of getting through in the heavy going of a liberally-sanded pitch. They once more soon fell behind, and did not score their winning goal until two minutes from the end. As in the first meeting, Orient seriously troubled their defence, though Newton did well on switching to right-back after a knee ligament injury, suffered some fifteen minutes earlier, had forced Webster off just before the half-hour. Hector was again missed up front, but the Rams' main weakness was in midfield. Bourne looked uncomfortable on having to drop back there in Newton's place, and Rioch lacked consistency.

Derby were too busy looking for offside when Fairbrother moved onto a long pass from Tom Walley, a former Arsenal midfielder who had been capped by Wales while with Watford, to give Orient a fifth-minute lead, but

Lee side-footed an equaliser from Bourne's low centre within a minute. Fairbrother did appear offside when he was allowed to close in on a Possee pass near the end, and Boulton had to move smartly to block his shot. Home nerves continued to jangle until a neat interchange of passes between Nish and Davies set up Rioch to emerge from one of his periods of anonymity with the late winner, a typical Bruce blaster.

The draw for the fourth round was again kind to Derby, giving them a home tie with Bristol Rovers, who that season only just escaped relegation back to the Third Division. The Rams did manage to make their higher status and ground advantage tell, if with some more difficulty, and at that stage they were in the reckoning for two trophies – in the FA Cup's last sixteen for the fifth time in six seasons, and fifth in the First Division, only two points behind leaders Everton with nine of their last sixteen League matches at home. And they then also still had hopes of a third string to their bow – the hearing of their ultimately unsuccessful UEFA Cup protest that was not due, in Switzerland, until midway through the following month of February.

The head groundsman and his staff had their work cut out over the weekend on which most of the other fourth-round ties were played in order to get the Baseball Ground pitch playable for the Rovers' visit on the Monday night, and their efforts were rewarded as Boulton marked his record-breaking 247th game in Derby's goal by remaining unbeaten while Hector and Rioch found the target at the other end. Hector opened the scoring in the sixteenth minute after Davies had turned neatly on a long throw-in by Thomas to supply the centre that was nudged in at the far post, but Rovers stayed in the hunt until eight minutes from time, when Rioch thumped in a penalty awarded for a foul on Gemmill.

Indeed, the outcome might have been very different if the Bristol club had not been denied the penalty their manager, Don Megson, thought should have been given in the first half. He was convinced that Bruce Bannister was held to prevent him reaching the ball before Boulton. The narrowest of several squeaks the Rams had after that came when their goalkeeper was hurried into a first-time clearance as a Todd back-pass stuck in the mud. The ball hit Rovers' substitute, Chesterfield-born Dave Staniforth, on the head and cannoned back over the bar.

In though Derby's luck was that night, it was most definitely out when, at home again, they faced Leeds United, the club that had so often had the beating of them, in the fifth round. At the time the draw was made Leeds, like the Rams, were not sure of staying in it. They had still to get past Wimbledon, then a Southern League side, who survived to force a shock goalless draw at Elland Road when their goalkeeper, Dicky Guy, saved a penalty taken by Peter Lorimer, possessor of one of the hardest shots in the game, in the 82nd minute. The replay was due the night after Derby had disposed of Bristol Rovers, but had to be postponed because of a waterlogged pitch. Then there was a further delay of a fortnight to release four Leeds players – David Harvey, Billy Bremner, Gordon McQueen and Joe Jordan – for Scotland's match with Spain in Valencia, where a goal by Jordan earned a 1-1 draw.

So it was not until 10 February, two days after Leeds had drawn 0-0 in the League at Derby for the second successive season, that the Yorkshire club finally ousted Wimbledon in front of a crowd of more than 45,000 at Crystal Palace's Selhurst Park ground. They won unconvincingly through an own-goal. A second-half shot by Johnny Giles was diverted past Guy by Dave Bassett, the chirpy cockney character who had joined Wimbledon, whom he was also to coach and manage, after being with Walton and Hersham when they embarrassed Brian Clough and Brighton during the season following their victory in the Amateur Cup final.

Leeds had been knocked out of the League Cup by Fourth Division Chester, and were to finish that season only just above halfway in the First Division, but when it came to revisiting the Baseball Ground in the FA Cup they yet again made the Rams feel fated to fail. As in the quarter-finals two years before, they won there by an only goal, and, as against Wimbledon, it was an opponent who scored it. Even Jimmy Armfield, Brian Clough's successor as their manager, said that he felt desperately sorry for Derby.

A repetition of the recent League stalemate between the clubs looked likely until seven minutes from the end, when David Nish, otherwise as immaculate as ever, made the costly mistake that let Leeds through to a quarter-final against Ipswich which they lost in a third replay at Leicester. The cross Eddie Gray put over after attacking down the Leeds left with his brother Frank did not look particularly threatening until it caught Nish in two minds as he was distracted by Duncan McKenzie's approach from behind him at the far post. In deciding to play for safety, he tried to put the ball behind for a corner, but it bobbled up and looped off his shin over Boulton's head into the net. The sympathetic Dave Mackay was reminded of the winning goal he had conceded to Queen's Park Rangers in similar circumstances at the same stage of the competition five years before.

The injustice of Nish's unfortunate error was underlined by the fact that Derby County's goalkeeper had been given so little to do in comparison with his opposite number, David Stewart, whose excellent display as a short-notice deputy for David Harvey, who had been badly injured in a car crash, prompted Armfield to dash onto the pitch to congratulate him at the final whistle. Yet the Rams could have equalised only two minutes after falling behind. Davies, on as substitute for Bourne, feebly prodded the ball wide when Rioch cut it back to him, thus prolonging the dearth of goals from a Derby centre-forward that then stretched back more than two months.

Stewart, who, like Harvey, played for Scotland (he saved a penalty when he gained his only full cap in a narrow defeat away to East Germany), made most of his saves from the busy Lee, a danger man Leeds fans made a target for the beer cans that came over from their section of the terraces in the early minutes of a match the players contested in a spirit that, by contrast, was commendably sporting. McQueen, though troubled by cramp towards the end, was outstanding at the heart of the resolute Leeds defence; Todd and Thomas were in top form for Derby, but Gemmill, starting a two-game suspension, was missed.

As when they won the First Division title three years earlier, the disappointment of FA Cup defeat left the Rams free to concentrate on the League, whereas Ipswich Town, who were to be the last of their challengers for the championship, had the distraction of their seven-hour quarter-final marathon with Leeds, followed by their first appearance in the semi-finals that ended in replay defeat by West Ham under the handicap of injuries to key players Allan Hunter, Kevin Beattie and David Johnson.

Though also failing to add that year to their League title triumph of 1962, Ipswich gained Cup compensation in 1978 with victory over Arsenal at Wembley. For Derby County, major honours have remained elusive since their second First Division championship success of 1975 – at first only just out of reach, but disappearing over the horizon under the weight of the huge financial losses incurred through the fall (along with Ipswich) in 2002 from the Premiership to which they had risen in Jim Smith's first season as manager six years before.

REAL DAZZLERS REACH EUROPEAN PINNACLE

Derby County entered the final month of what was to be Dave Mackay's second and last full season as their manager, 1975-76, still with hopes of landing the League and Cup double, but shortly after successive 1-1 draws with three of their main rivals for the championship, Manchester United, Liverpool and Leeds, it all started to unravel for them from the 21st minute of a home midweek match with Stoke City.

It was then that Charlie George dislocated a shoulder in falling awkwardly as he unnecessarily challenged Denis Smith when the Potters' pivot was clearing a ball he already had well under control. A Rioch penalty salvaged another share of the points, but the season had prematurely ended for George, the Rams' leading scorer and Midlands Player of the Year, just half-a-dozen games from the First Division finishing line. With him went those dreams of the double he had helped Arsenal to attain. Memories remain crystal clear of the devastating right-foot drive with which he scored the extra-time winner for the Gunners' newly-crowned champions against Liverpool at Wembley, and of the sight of him lying back full length on the turf, with arms outstretched above his head, as team-mates rushed to celebrate with him.

Derby's chances of emulating that double triumph were smartly shattered by the two Manchester clubs as George was confined to the role of spectactor with his left arm tucked Napoleon-like inside his sweater. United repeated the two-goal margin of their 1948 FA Cup semi-final defeat of the Rams at Hillsborough; City as good as put paid to a retention of the League crown with a win by the odd goal of seven at Maine Road despite being reduced to ten men by the early sending-off of their captain, Mike Doyle. Derby tailed away to finish fourth, seven points behind Liverpool's champions.

The 24-year-old Charlie George, like Francis Lee the year before, was an eve-of-season bargain signing. 'We stole the man,' Des Anderson cheerfully declared when Arsenal accepted a fee of £90,000 after news of a snag in Tottenham's negotiations for the player had brought Mackay hurrying back from his holiday in Scotland to complete the deal.

George, of the flowing locks and abundant ability, was an Arsenal local boy who made good. Born not far from the Highbury ground, he was taken on as an apprentice straight from school in May 1966. Within two years he turned professional after scoring a stack of goals for the club's youth and reserve sides. His development avoided an expensive dip into the transfer market, making manager Bertie Mee suddenly realise that 'in George we had a youngster with all the flair and instinct of the truly great and gifted player for whom we had been searching'.

In those early days, though, this precocious find's volatile temperament made him inclined to be difficult to handle. After one game against Chelsea at Highbury he was roundly condemned by the national press, and some of the visiting players warned him that if he persisted in hurting other professionals he would eventually 'be taken on by someone who is bigger and stronger'. That, in fact, is what happened as he came in for a lot of rough treatment from defenders who provoked him into retaliation, and a consequent piling-up of penalty points, after a first season with Derby in which, prior to injury, he played 46 games without a booking and became a big favourite among Rams fans with his exquisite passing and penchant for scoring spectacular goals. From that encouraging new start, which, in his words, 'worked wonders' after he had thought seriously about giving up football because, handicapped by injuries, he had no longer been sure of a regular place in Arsenal's first team, he deteriorated into beginning the following 1976-77 season as he was to end it – with one of his four sendings-off while with the Rams. He became so disillusioned after Mackay's sacking as the team struggled that he was openly disdainful of Murphy and showed such a lack of interest that there was some talk of his malingering.

He answered that accusation by saying he should, with hindsight, have rested instead of trying to play on while suffering from 'a bit of slipped disc trouble' that had compelled him to sleep on a hard board for a month, but he had already been given something he considered more unjust to protest about. Having had to wait until only a few weeks before his 26th birthday to add what was to be his only senior England cap to his five Under-23 appearances, he had the mortification of being substituted by Gordon Hill, the winger who was briefly to join him at Derby, as England, also including McFarland and Todd, laboured to a 1-1 draw with the Republic of Ireland at Wembley. Not much more than a year later George cast himself into the international wilderness. Ron Greenwood, the former West Ham manager who had succeeded Don Revie in the England job when Brian Clough had been the people's choice, explained that his 'B' squad for the first match at that level for 21 years, against West Germany at Augsburg, comprised players on the fringe of full selection, but George, his earlier treatment still rankling, rejected the invitation to join it.

Dave Mackay left Derby describing George as his 'finest signing – an even better player than I had originally believed'. Tommy Docherty arrived thinking he was 'a villain who would be down the road in no time', only quickly to acclaim him as 'a hell of a bloke'. George regained his best form after recovering from injuries suffered in a car accident, yet he was made available for transfer soon after another of his dismissals, in a defeat at Bolton. Forest were first in the field, but, in a reversal of the Henry Newton episode, George's move to such close neighbours was blocked by the Derby directors. He was also forbidden to join West Bromwich, a club he had earlier rejected, but a 0-5 trouncing at Liverpool, from which he was carried off with a knee injury, proved to be his last for the Rams before the drawn-out saga of his £350,000 move to Southampton was finally resolved near the Christmas of 1978.

His service with the Saints was interrupted by problems with both knees and a foot, a month's loan to Forest during which he helped to beat Barcelona in the European Super Cup, a lawn-mower accident that cost him the index finger of his right hand, and a scuffle with an *Eastern Daily Press* photographer at Norwich for which he was fined by magistrates, suspended for a week, and fined, by Southampton, and reprimanded by the FA. In September 1981, after adding 52 games and fourteen goals for Southampton to his 179 and 49 for Arsenal and 136 and 54 for Derby, he was transferred to Bulova for £50,000, but fans threw missiles and lit bonfires the second time his debut for that Hong Kong club was delayed by a back injury, and his contract was cancelled after only seven games. His style of play did not suit coach Ron Wylie, a former Notts County, Aston Villa and Birmingham player who afterwards had an unrewarding experience as manager of West Bromwich Albion.

Back in England, George joined Bournemouth on a non-contract basis and played twice for them in the Fourth Division before he was offered the chance to turn out for Derby again by John Newman, a former Birmingham wing-half who for eight frustrating months replaced the dismissed Colin Addison after having given up successful management of Grimsby Town to become his assistant at the Baseball Ground. News of George's return sparked a mini-boom in the Rams' new public issue of 60,000 shares at £10 each which were part of a £350,000 survival scheme, but the comeback lasted only eleven games, from the last of which, at Oldham, he dropped out with a groin strain on the penultimate Saturday of the 1981-82 season. Derby's financial situation had become so dire, soon to put them on the brink of extinction, that they could not afford to keep him. He later rejoined Arsenal as a match-day host.

As George stepped off the Derby stage, so did another who had been one of the club's favourite sons – in a fitting blaze of glory. Kevin Hector, ditched by Docherty and accused by him of being greedy in prevaricating over a move to Mansfield, had been brought back to the Rams by Addison after making one appearance for Burton Albion following his return from playing in Canada with Vancouver Whitecaps, but he had not been a first choice since George's return. Now, at 37 the sole survivor of the championship years, he was recalled for the final match of the season as relegation threatened, and rounded off his County career by scoring the winning goal against a Watford side already assured of promotion to the First Division. A year later Derby again won their last match when in danger of the drop back into Division Three, but they were unable to save themselves the season after that. The non-League clubs in the Derby area Hector assisted after leaving the Rams for the second time included Belper Town, whom he helped to the Northern Counties East League title in 1984-85. Away from football, he became a postman.

For Charlie George, the impression was left that, in common with several other gifted players the game has produced, he did not fully do himself justice overall, but Derby fans at least had the satisfaction of being treated to some of his finest displays. Those began, after the Rams' warm-up friendlies in preparation for the 1975-76 season in Holland and Scotland (where they lost to an only goal in front of a 44,000 crowd at Celtic Park in Glasgow), with the Charity Shield match at Wembley in which the reigning League champions met the FA Cup winners, West Ham, on a sweltering Saturday in early August.

It was only the second time that this annual fixture had been held at the famous stadium, and also the second appearance there by Derby. Having missed the County's FA Cup defeat of Charlton Athletic 29 years earlier while on National Service in the RAF, I was grateful for the chance to be in the crowd of just under 60,000, along with my son. The outcome was a 2-0 win for Mackay's all-star cast, gained with a performance unanimously acclaimed. The *Daily Mail* report stated that 'the overall impression was so devastating that the odds of 5-1 against Derby retaining the League title look an open invitation to make money'. The *Sunday Mirror* declared that 'Derby set the standard for a new season with an hour of glowing football.' In *The Daily Telegraph*, Bob Oxby wrote:

'Seldom has a side flowered so excitingly at Wembley. To see a side of West Ham's flowing skills reduced to something close to ineptitude was to understand the prodigious depth of talent Mackay and his predecessor, Brian Clough, have assembled. The most significant and, indeed, symbolic display was that of the former *enfant terrible*, Charlie George, now a model of courtesy and liquid grace. His passing recalled the half-forgotten geometry of a Haynes or a Mannion.'

The match was played in a commendable spirit by both teams, in marked contrast to the deplorable scenes, building up to the dismissal of Billy Bremner, the Leeds captain, and Liverpool's Kevin Keegan, that had disfigured the Shield's first staging at Wembley the previous year, but, regrettably, the same could not be said of the behaviour of some West Ham followers. Forewarned by the trouble supporters of the London club had caused at the FA Cup final, police were there in force, and their speedy removal of the ringleaders averted an escalation of violence, and a repeated pitch invasion, after brawling on the terraces had preceded a hail of bottles and cans flung from the stands. Even then, mounted officers were needed afterwards to break up disturbances outside the stadium.

On the other hand, Derby's fans, greatly to their credit, earned high praise. 'They were impeccable,' said Len Went, the Wembley spokesman, 'and they will be welcome back at any time'. Not for eighteen years, however, were the Rams to have their next opportunity – and then, in the First Division only because that is what the Second Division had become with the formation of the Premiership, they lost to Cremonese in the Anglo-Italian Cup final. A year later, in 1994, they were back at Wembley for the Division One play-off final, but failed again – beaten after leading by Leicester City, who had been losers on each of their six previous appearances there (in four FA Cup finals and the play-offs of 1992 and 1993).

In 1975, however, the Rams were rampant, worthy winners of a Shield which they, as champions for the first time, and Cup holders Leeds had opted out of competing for in 1972 (when Manchester City defeated an Aston Villa team that included Bruce Rioch with a goal by Franny Lee). Despite a temperature that at pitch level touched the upper nineties – we were still dealing in Fahrenheit then – Derby's players paced themselves perfectly against West Ham, content to keep control for much of the second half without striving to increase the lead they gained with goals by Hector and McFarland after twenty and 44 minutes. It was long-overdue revenge for the 2-5 semi-final defeat by the Hammers in 1923 that had cost the County the chance of taking part in the first FA Cup final to be staged at Wembley.

McFarland, back at the stadium for the first time since the injury, while playing for England, that had kept him out of most of the Rams' second title season, played down suggestions that he had been worried about returning there by saying:

'A lot of people tried to build it up, but to me it was just another game. I have played at Wembley often enough, and the fact that I was injured there did not make it any more difficult. I wasn't injured by Wembley. I happened to fall awkwardly, and that caused the tendon trouble. One reporter even asked if I would go to the spot where I went down, but I never even considered it. I played four games at the end of last season and proved to myself that I was fit. This match was just a natural extension of my return, without the pressure of a League game.'

Impressive as Charlie George was that day, one of his displays for Derby stands out above all the rest. It came at the Baseball Ground on the night of October 22, 1975, when the eclipse of the mighty Real Madrid raised the Rams to the pinnacle of their European achievement. George augmented a hat-trick with the perfection of his passing in the defeat of one of the most famous teams on the Continent, by the astounding margin of 4-1, that demonstrated the incredible advance Derby County had made since their wilderness seasons of the 1950s in the old Third Division North at a time when the Spanish giants they had now vanquished clamped a hold on the European Cup that was to last for the competition's first five finals.

Disillusionment for Derby was to come in front of a 120,000 crowd that packed the Estadio Santiago Bernabeu for the return leg of this second-round tie, but for a fortnight they and their fans had one of the most famous victories in the club's long history to relish. To quote just one of the headlines that heralded it: DERBY REAL DAZZLERS.

To qualify for that epic encounter Roy McFarland and his men overcame an away deficit to knock out the Czechoslovak champions Slovan Bratislava. As when they visited Spartak Trnava for the first leg of a European Cup quarter-final three years earlier, they came away just one goal to the bad, but on this occasion, though leaving it late, they widened the winning aggregate by scoring three at home without reply instead of edging through with two. Transfer-listed Jeff Bourne brought more width to the attack when he replaced the injured Newton eight minutes before the interval, and on the stroke of half-time he equalised with a shot that curled in off an upright. That, however, was how the score stayed until the last dozen minutes, during which Lee netted twice, two minutes either side of having a penalty-kick saved. Full-back Elefant was not as cumbersome as his name implied, but he was at fault in enabling Nish, who had earlier hit a post with the aid of a deflection, to get in a shot which rebounded off the goalkeeper for Lee to settle nerves with his second goal.

So to the magical night of the Real turn-up. George took the main plaudits with his three goals (two of them penalties) and all-round excellence, but for Archie Gemmill it was also something special because, at the age of 28, his typically industrious and inspiring performance earned him a recall to the Scotland team from which he had been excluded for more than three years. Dropped after being in the side beaten by England at Hampden Park on 27 May 1972, he was brought back at the Glasgow stadium for a European Championship game against Denmark on 29 October 1975, a week after Derby's defeat of the Spanish champions. Again he was on the winning side, by 3-1, with Bruce Rioch scoring one of the goals. Gemmill had almost given up hope of playing for his country again. He said:

'I had not heard a whisper from Scotland since Willie Ormond became manager, and it was clear it had become a bit embarrassing for him to call me up after making it clear for so long the he didn't fancy me. I feel I've been playing well ever since I came to Derby five years ago. Perhaps playing against people like Netzer and Breitner in European games has helped me to prove it because the likes of Netzer don't like people who are as busy as I am on the pitch.'

From being an international outcast, Gemmill became Scotland's captain, forming with Rioch and Don Masson a midfield that was described in many quarters as 'the best in Europe', but he then fell out of favour again after Ally MacLeod had succeeded Ormond. When he regained a place in the side, and with it the captaincy, for a World Cup trial against Bulgaria at Hampden Park early in 1978, by which time he was with Nottingham Forest, it was only because Rioch, who had taken over as skipper, and Masson, his deputy, were both unavailable.

Gemmill recognised that 'if we had a full team I wouldn't have been playing', yet he did well enough, also scoring from a penalty in a 2-1 win, to retain his place, and in June that year he enjoyed one of the supreme moments of his career when he waltzed through the Dutch defence to score a marvellous goal during the World Cup finals in Argentina.

Scotland, who were Britain's only representatives, were 3-2 winners of that match, Gemmill also scoring one of their other goals from the penalty spot, but they were unable to achieve the three-goal winning margin that would have qualified them from their group instead of Holland. Feeble displays in their previous two games undermined their challenge. They came in for a great deal of criticism after a shock 1-3 defeat by Peru, Masson failing with a penalty, and they disappointed again in a 1-1 draw with Iran. It was an embarrassing let-down after all their confident talk in the build-up, and their gloom was deepened when Willie Johnston, the West Bromwich and former Rangers winger, was jettisoned from the squad, and banned for a year by FIFA, on being found guilty of taking an illegal stimulant. To top it all, Holland, runners-up to Peru in the group, went on to reach the final, in which, though beaten, they forced Argentina to extra-time.

Gemmill again lost his place in the Scotland team the following year, and his cap career really did seem to be over after he had dropped into the Second Division with Birmingham. But once more he came back. With Colin Todd again among his team-mates in a side assembled by Jim Smith, a future Derby manager, he helped Birmingham to promotion, and another Scotland manager, Jock Stein, restored him to his country's captaincy for a European Championship game against Portugal in Glasgow in March 1980. What was more, Stein showed his confidence in him by allowing him complete control on the field. 'I've told Archie he can make switches – before half-time if necessary,' he said. 'He still has a lot to offer this side.'

There were eight more Scotland games for Gemmill to come. And there might well have been more if he had not got the wrong side of Stein before a World Cup qualifier against Israel at Hampden Park in April 1981. After playing for Birmingham at Leicester he drove north to join the Scotland squad through some of the foulest weather of that spring, and it was past midnight when he parked his car at their headquarters at Troon. What happened next is best told in his own words, as expressed to Richard Bott in the *Sunday Express*:

'When I got there some of the lads were sitting around and they wanted me to ask Jock Stein if we could go out for a few drinks. I said: "There's no way he'll let you out." But they kept on at me, and, since I was team captain, I said I would go and ask Jock. He went berserk. I told him it was only because we respected him so much that we'd asked his permission. If it had been anybody else the lads would have gone out anyway. To this day I'm convinced that making that request turned Jock Stein against me. I think he felt I should have been man enough to tell the lads there was no way they could go out. He left me out of the team for the Israel game and I was never picked again. There is no sentiment in football, none at all.'

Maybe not, Archie, but was it any wonder that Stein jibbed at the thought of his players going out for a few drinks *after midnight* with an important game coming up? There could be no reasonable complaint in those circumstances about the reaction of the great man, whose sudden death just over four years later, on collapsing soon after a drawn game with Wales in Cardiff, shocked the whole of football.

Discarded by Scotland though he was, Gemmill had not also been lost to Derby County – to the extent, after Peter Taylor had made him his first signing on rejoining the Rams as manager, of ending the 1982-83 season with the *Sunday People-Rediffusion* £1,000 merit prize as the top Second Division player, and being voted the Rams' Player of the Year in 1984. It had been the first of the many transfers Tommy Docherty conducted for Derby that had taken Gemmill away – and, twisting the knife for the club's fans, to arch rivals Nottingham Forest at that. Gemmill would have gone there earlier if Colin Murphy, uneasy occupier of the manager's chair between the tenures of Mackay and Docherty, had been able to exchange him for Tony Woodcock, a striker who blossomed to England level under Brian Clough's direction, but Docherty did not want to lose the little Scot, then in his 31st year, and he compelled him to forfeit £6,500 for the privilege of playing again for Clough.

Before completing that deal, in exchange for John Middleton, an England Under-21 keeper, and £25,000, Docherty insisted that Gemmill put his strongly-expressed wish to leave Derby in writing, thus depriving him of the five per cent signing-on levy. The manager said that Derby's supporters deserved an explanation, and he wanted to make it clear that, while delighted to acquire Middleton, the sale of Gemmill was not his idea.

He continued: 'The situation was created by Gemmill, who told me he wanted to leave. When I came here I told him that I admired him as a player and as a person, and that I wanted him to stay and play his heart out for Derby, as he always has. But he said he didn't want to play for Derby again in any circumstances. I told him to put it in writing and he could go. Obviously, he didn't fancy that idea, but I made it clear he had two choices – write out a transfer request and go to Forest without a signing-on fee, or stay with Derby. I insisted on a written transfer request to cover myself and the directors. I think it's only fair that the supporters should know the real position, and not blame us for getting rid of Gemmill. He was on a contract at Derby which was staggering – guaranteeing a very good wage up to 1981, and a testimonial at the end of it. People in his position can't have their cake and eat it. When I was a player I would have paid money to join some clubs.'

The two-way transfer worked very much to Forest's advantage, even though Clough was to regret not keeping Gemmill for more than two years before allowing him to move to Birmingham City for £150,000. During that time the 5ft 5in powerhouse gained a third First Division championship medal in 1978, then helped Forest to retain the League Cup, with a Wembley win over Southampton in 1979, after having been unavailable for the previous year's final success against Liverpool, in a replay, because he had already played in that season's competition for Derby.

In 1977-78 Gemmill was runner-up for both the PFA and Football Writers' Association Player of the Year awards – to clubmates Peter Shilton and Kenny Burns respectively – and in the following season, when Forest were second to Liverpool in the League, he took part in the European Cup run but missed the defeat of Malmo in the Munich final after being substituted in the first-leg semi-final against FC Cologne.

Middleton, who had lost his place in Forest's first team with the £270,000 signing of Peter Shilton from Stoke, played in eighty League and Cup games for Derby, but was forced to retire in 1980 by a persistent shoulder injury. His arrival brought down the curtain on Boulton's outstanding County career, even though 'Bernie' had been showing no sign of decline. After a short stay with Tulsa Roughnecks, Boulton was given a free transfer by the Rams at the end of the 1977-78 season and he re-entered American football for what proved to be an unhappy spell with Los Angeles Aztecs. Having become unsure of his position there, he found he had been signed by San Jose Earthquakes when he tried to obtain his release, and it required the assistance of the FA and FIFA to make him a free agent again. Colin Murphy then took him to Lincoln, but he was playing only his seventh game for the Imps, at Crewe, when a serious injury prevented him staying in the side that went on to win promotion from the

Fourth Division. He did not play in League football again, and his contract was cancelled early in 1982.

Archie Gemmill had reached the age of 35, and acquired the nickname 'Silver Fox' because of his dark beard and greying hair, when Peter Taylor brought him back into the Derby fold on an eighteen-month contract in November 1982. He came from Wigan, where he had agreed to rejoin his former Forest clubmate Larry Lloyd, then the Lancashire club's player-manager, provisionally just for one month, after teaming up in the North American League with Jacksonville Teamen. 'When I came back from America,' said Gemmill, 'I spent five weeks waiting at my home in Derby for an offer from the First or Second division. I didn't get one. Larry, who had been chasing me since Birmingham gave me a free last March, called me again and said: "You might as well come and play for us. It's better than sitting on your backside watching the telly or doing the garden".'

Gemmill, who was to make a third comeback at Derby – as overseas scout while Jim Smith was manager, after also returning to Forest, as coach, and having a couple of years as joint manager with John McGovern at Rotherham – was an inspirational figure in the Rams' successful fight against relegation in 1983, but he subsequently fell out with Taylor and was unable to help to avert the drop the following year after being restored to the team by Roy McFarland.

Memories are still cherished of Gemmill's busy-bee version of an emergency centre-forward, only a few weeks after fracturing his skull in a collision during a six-a-side training game, in an emphatic win against Manchester City that helped to avert relegation and was completed by a penalty Gerry Daly was able to take only after groundsman Bob Smith had been summoned with his tape measure to repaint a spot lost in the Baseball Ground mud. If any other displays are to be singled out from the many of excellence Gemmill gave during the 404 games he played in his two spells with Derby County, they must surely be those he produced against sides from Madrid – in the away UEFA Cup-tie with Atletico, and in the home European Cup clash with Real.

'Magnifico' was the word Atletico's coach, Juan Carlos Lorenzo, had for him after the dramatic match in the Spanish capital that has already been recalled. Against Real at Derby, he tormented Gunter Netzer and company from as early as the tenth minute in which he was at the heart of the sweeping move that ripped the visitors' defence apart for George to score a spectacular opening goal. Todd, also in tremendous form, flung a glorious crossfield ball out to Nish after collecting a throw-in on the Rams' right flank, near the halfway line, and from the full-back's pass Gemmill delivered a hard and low centre which George, running across the face of the goal on the edge of the penalty box, met first time with a left-foot volley of such power and accuracy that Miguel Angel had not the ghost of a chance of saving.

Five minutes later, after Lee and Rioch had gone close, Derby were two up. Lee was bowled over by the tough little Camacho, and George again left the goalkeeper groping with his first penalty-kick for the Rams. It was then, however, that Real demonstrated their strength of character. In the 25th minute, they hit back through Pirri, who found plenty of time and space to chest the ball down and place his shot into the corner of the net from the veteran Amancio's perfect chipped pass, and on the half-hour they were unlucky not to be awarded a penalty themselves when Roberto Martinez sprawled into the box on being tackled from behind by Thomas. The Russian referee ruled that the offence had occurred just outside the area, and gave a free-kick which was blocked.

Having survived that scare, Derby restored their two-goal advantage two minutes before half-time. McFarland completed one of his surging runs upfield with a pass to Nish, whose drive from some 25 yards sped too fast for Angel's dive. In the second half Angel made one breathtaking save from Rioch and two of little less quality from Lee, but in the 65th minute fortune again favoured the Rams when Real were denied a second goal on the intervention of another Russian official. The impressive Pirri again popped the ball into the net, but was flagged offside by linesman Bakhramov, the man who had confirmed England's crucial third goal in the 1966 World Cup final by deciding that the ball had bounced over the line off the crossbar from Geoff Hurst's shot.

Real protested bitterly – and again also to no avail – when Derby went further ahead with twelve minutes left. The Madrid aristocrats had not been all that satisfied with the award of the first-half penalty to the Rams, but they were positively livid when another one was given against them. Hector did make a meal of falling under Netzer's tackle just inside the area, but referee Ivanov shared the general view that he was clearly pulled down. George promptly thumped home his third goal, and a minute later, having suffered a knock early in the second half, retired from the action with Hector as Davies and Bourne were sent on as substitutes.

It was evident that, even with a three-goal cushion, Derby would face a huge task in the return leg – and so it proved, though not until extra-time did they concede the goal that knocked them out by 5-6 on aggregate. They went into the Bernabeu cauldron without not only Lee, suspended after his sending-off against Leeds (more about that in the next chapter), but also the injured Rioch. And that was not the limit of their problems. McFarland, limping along on one good leg, was not passed 'fit' until just before the kick-off, and Newton joined him in needing attention from the club doctor, who was flown out to Madrid for that special reason, before being put into the starting line-up despite doubts that he, too, would last the full distance.

Both did manage to get through the two hours, if with great difficulty, and in those circumstances it was a wonder that McFarland, in particular, was able to play so magnificently. Powell was another who was short of full fitness, and he would have been replaced shortly after Real's killer goal in extra-time if Bourne had not been a more pressing case. Bourne, substitute for Hector, who played in midfield throughout his 75 minutes on the pitch, was down requiring attention, injured in a tackle by Camacho, just as Powell was about to be taken off, and had to be carried away on a stretcher with a cartilage problem.

As if their injury worries were not enough to contend with, the Rams were up against it from the third minute. The last thing they wanted was to concede an early goal, yet that is precisely what they did as Real so swiftly started to right what they regarded as the wrongs of the Baseball Ground. A well-judged pass by Netzer was headed down for Martinez to tuck the ball away, and Derby were in danger of being overwhelmed by the series of attacks that early strike encouraged. Gradually they got to grips, only for all the hard work of preventing further setbacks before the interval to be undone by the concession of two more goals in the first ten minutes of the second half. Martinez scored again after Boulton had beaten away two close-range shots from Santillana, who five minutes later planted a firm header into the net from a free-kick curled in towards the far post by Netzer.

That put Real level 4-4 on aggregate, but Derby, true to Dave Mackay's natural instincts, responded by stepping up attacks in which McFarland and Todd joined, and in the 63rd minute this enterprise was rewarded. The skipper, linking up with Gemmill, pushed a pass to George, who eluded three tackles before regaining the overall lead by unleashing another of his specials, a humdinger of a shot that hit home off the underside of the bar.

As time ticked away it began to look as if the Rams would reach the quarter-finals after all, and only five of the ninety minutes were left when victory was snatched from them by the penalty that took two tired teams into the extra period. Amancio was ruled to have been brought down by Thomas after fastening onto a penetrating pass from Netzer, and Pirri calmly planted the spot-kick past Boulton.

The decisive moment came in the 100th minute, just as Derby were showing signs of lasting the pace a little better. And the goal that settled this dramatic tie was a most fitting one. Santillana chested the ball down, flicked it over his head, then drifted between McFarland and Newton before slotting in a neatly controlled shot. Even then, though, three centres from Hinton, Bourne's replacement, almost turned the game back Derby's way. Davies only just failed to get on the end of the first one at the far post, Benito flicked the second one clear with his head in the nick of time, and McFarland shot over after Nish had created the chance from the third.

Real squeezed through their quarter-final against Borussia Moenchengladbach on away goals, drawing 2-2 in Germany and 1-1 at home, but were then held to another 1-1 draw in Madrid by Bayern Munich and lost the return leg 0-2. Bayern beat St Etienne 1-0 in the final at Hampden Park.

GEMMILL BANNED IN IDENTITY MIX-UP

Archie Gemmill was the victim of an amazing identity mix-up while playing for Scotland in a World Cup qualifying match against Czechoslovakia in Prague on 13 October 1976.

Millions of television viewers saw Andy Gray, the Aston Villa striker, and Czech defender Anton Ondrus ordered off during the 0-2 defeat that ended Scotland's unbeaten run of nine games, but in his report to FIFA the Italian referee, Alberto Michelotti, stated that he had sent off No 10 Gemmill 'for punching an opponent after he had been kicked', and that Gray was one of four Scottish players he had booked (Gordon McQueen, Martin Buchan and Willie Donachie were the others).

Consequently, Gemmill was at first suspended from Scotland's next three games by FIFA, but then cleared to play against Wales the following month after the Scottish FA had pointed out that a mistake had been made. The investigation carried out by FIFA revealed that the referee had mixed up the numbers worn by Gemmill (10) and Gray (11).

Dave Mackay's Biggest Disappointment

Bitterly disappointing as Derby County's European Cup defeat in Madrid was, they had to endure another setback in the 1975-76 season that hit Dave Mackay even harder. This was how he looked back on it:

'Of all the disappointments I have had in my career – and I haven't had that many – our defeat by Manchester United in the FA Cup semi-final at Hillsborough was the biggest of all. I just could not believe that a team of our talent and calibre could play so badly on the day. Of course it was my job to pick the boys up off the floor, but, for once, I was on the floor too! I couldn't pick myself up.'

The run to the last four of the competition kept hopes of the League and Cup double alive until they disintegrated three weeks from the end of the season as the Rams began to go back as a team after the injury to Charlie George against Stoke that Mackay described as 'the most crucial blow we suffered'. Up to then they had shrugged off another early exit from the League Cup and the steep dip from glory to gloom against Real Madrid to look fully capable of a third First Division title and a second winning of the FA Cup.

The League Cup got off to a stuttering start at home to Huddersfield, the once proud League champions of three successive years who had tumbled from First to Fourth Division in four seasons. Terry Gray's header on the half-hour wiped out the fourteenth-minute lead gained by Bruce Rioch, and a replay was only eleven minutes off when George nipped in to bury Hector's low centre. The draw then sent the Rams to Middlesbrough, where they were distinctly unlucky to be knocked out by an Alan Foggon goal that came as late as the 82nd minute. Immediately afterwards the ball somehow stayed out as George's shot freakishly bounced clear off a post when the ball's flight suggested that it might just glance in.

Slightly astray though the player Arsenal had so misguidedly discarded was on that occasion, he was firmly back on the goal standard the next time he did Cup battle for the County. The third-round FA Cup-tie with Everton at the Baseball Ground was only three minutes old when George reacted quicker than anybody else to ram home another ball that rebounded off an upright, from a shot by Roger Davies. Shortly after the hour he scored again, with a shot, from a pass by Davies, that clipped the far post on its way in. Everton replied through Garry Jones, who just got the final touch to a Hurst free-kick headed on by Kenyon, but they never seriously threatened an equaliser.

Merseyside's other giants were the next vanquished visitors. Liverpool arrived as leaders of the First Division towards the end of January, but departed with no answer to the goal Davies scored six minutes after the 67th in which he was sent on in place of Leighton James, the 22-year-old Welsh international winger who had become the Rams' first £300,000 player when signed from Burnley late in November. James had himself been the substitute in his debut for Derby, which unfortunately coincided with a defeat at Birmingham that cost the Rams the First Division leadership on goal average to Queen's Park Rangers, against whom he was on from the start as Rioch's 100th League goal earned a draw at Loftus Road the following Saturday. Mackay then had such a wealth of forward talent at his disposal that he could afford to leave out Hector, the scorer of more than 200 goals in his career, to make room for the newcomer, but the 'King' was soon brought back at centre-forward in preference to Davies, who lacked confidence after a cartilage operation, when Lee dropped out with a knee injury.

With Thomas, Lee, Hector, George and James on the books, Derby evoked memories of the Arsenal side of the 1930s in which the presence of Jack, James and John was said to have been welcomed by an old lady who liked to hear the players called by their first names. It is scarcely stretching a point to say that Leighton James arrived at the Baseball Ground after being as important to Burnley as Alex James, one of the 'Wembley Wizards' who crushed England 5-1 at Wembley in 1928, had been to Arsenal. Fast and tricky, with two good feet and a ready eye for goal, he became, at eighteen, the Lancashire club's youngest player to be capped when Wales put him on their left wing for a Nations Cup game against Czechoslovakia in Prague in 1971, and he went on to play 53 more times for his country – thirteen of them while with Derby.

James left a rugby-playing grammar school in South Wales to become an apprentice at Turf Moor, and he considered himself lucky to learn his football under the management of Jimmy Adamson, a wing-half in nearly 500 games for Burnley and the 1962 Footballer of the Year. Adamson, who, remarkably, never won a full England cap, and who later spurned the opportunity to manage the national team, encouraged James to take players on. 'He used to tell me,' the Welshman recalled, 'that even if I lost the ball nine times I would keep it in the tenth and win the game for us.' Burnley fans so delighted in his skill, which had been the main driving force behind the club's return to the First Division, that they felt betrayed when he put Dave Mackay on his trail by asking for a move as soon as success dried up at that Lancashire outpost and announcing publicly that the only other club he wanted to play for was Derby County. They gave him a right roasting when he returned with the Rams less than two months after deserting them, provoking his perfect response of scoring one of the goals that took away both points.

With Derby, however, it was not as frequently as could have been wished that he fully lived up to his Burnley reputation, though he remained a regular choice until quickly falling out of favour when Tommy Docherty became manager. He was off-loaded to QPR in a straight swap for Don Masson after making ninety appearances for the Rams in which he scored 21 goals. 'The Doc didn't fancy me,' James was to say later. 'Fair enough, that was his right, but I had two years left on my contract. I should have stayed and tried to ride out the storm. My big regret is leaving Derby.'

That exchange deal, in which both players were valued at £180,000, backfired completely on Derby when Masson's failure to fit in led in less than a year to his return to Notts County on a free transfer. For James, too, it did not turn out well. He played fewer than thirty League games for QPR, but was spared a Daly-type situation with Docherty in being sold back to Burnley for £165,000 before that man of many clubs took the same route out of Derby. After Burnley's drop into the Third Division in the 1979-80 season he justified Swansea's £130,000 investment in him by top-scoring when they reached the First Division for the first time, only to be paid what he called 'the biggest insult' in being given a free transfer as relegation swiftly loomed amid troubles behind the Vetch Field scenes.

His next stop was at Sunderland, then managed by Alan Durban, and he was valued there as both left-winger and youth coach until Durban's dismissal put him on collision course with the new manager, former Sunderland full-back Len Ashurst. Another free transfer left him complaining of hearing about it only by a letter from the secretary, but admitting that he had for long been too outspoken for his own good. 'It took me an awful long time to realise that I was better off not trying to fight everyone else's battles,' he said, 'but there are no grey areas with me. My biggest problem is being a perfectionist.'

Invited to Gigg Lane by Martin Dobson, a former Burnley clubmate who was Bury's player-manager, James was an ever-present in the team that climbed out of the Fourth Division in 1984-85. He then went to Newport as player-coach before joining Burnley for a third time and helping them to a last-day escape, at the expense of Lincoln City, from becoming the first club to lose their place in the League, of which they were founder members, under the new ruling that the bottom club in Division Four had to give way automatically to the champions of the Vauxhall Conference. While Burnley narrowly defeated their Orient visitors, Lincoln lost at Swansea and were pipped on goal-difference by an equaliser Torquay scored against Crewe in the injury-time caused when one of their defenders needed attention for a bite from a dog that had strayed onto the pitch.

It was the fourth time Lincoln had fallen from the League, but Colin Murphy took over as their manager and guided them straight back – also with a victory on the final day.

In his third spell with Burnley, James combined coaching of the youth team with increasing his total of League appearances, shared between seven clubs, to more than 650, and took his overall goals tally into three figures. Afterwards he was coach to the youth and first teams with Bradford City, for whom he was also caretaker manager before the appointment of Frank Stapleton, the former Arsenal, Manchester United and Eire centre-forward (and Derby player on loan), who had Colin Todd as his assistant. (After returning to Derby, first as assistant to Jim Smith in November 2000, then briefly as manager, Colin Todd rejoined Bradford City as assistant to Bryan Robson, the former Manchester United and England captain, in November 2003, then succeeded Robson as manager the following June.) James was briefly manager of Morecambe when he finally went out of the Football League – after changing his mind about accepting the Weymouth post 'for personal reasons' on the day Len Ashurst was temporarily made that club's consultant manager.

When James was taken off in Derby County's fourth-round FA Cup-tie with Liverpool in 1976, Roger Davies was just about the last man the Merseysiders wanted to see in his place. It was because the gangling striker had been so effective in previous games against them that Dave Mackay chose him as substitute ahead of Hector, and the decision paid off as Davies began and ended the move that propelled the Rams into the last sixteen for the sixth time in seven seasons. It also put them back in the winning groove at the Baseball Ground at the first opportunity after Tottenham's League victory a fortnight earlier had ended their sequence of fifteen home successes spread over four competitions.

Derby appeared assured of a comfortable passage into the quarter-finals for only the second time since 1950 when, in being drawn at home for the third time, they were paired with Southend United, a struggling Essex club for which relegation to the Fourth Division awaited. Once more, however, it was by only one goal that they progressed, and that would not have been enough but for a brilliant late save from Ron Pountney by Graham Moseley, who kept his place for the rest of that season, and the first fifteen games of the next, after Colin Boulton had harshly been adjudged the chief culprit for the 2-3 home defeat by Spurs. The Rams were also grateful to avoid a replay when, greatly to Southend's anger, Alan Moody had a goal disallowed for offside.

Davies was on from the start that afternoon, with Lee relegated to substitute, but he had to be replaced for the second half after injuring an ankle when, in trying to turn to get in a cross shot, he fell over a photographer's camera case. He left with the satisfaction of having again begun the move that led to the vital goal. His pass up the left sent James clear, and – despite George being offside – Rioch recovered to smash the ball into the roof of the net after being unable to connect with the centre at his first attempt.

With their hoodoo team Leeds no longer in the way, having succumbed at Elland Road to a goal scored for Crystal Palace by Dave Swindlehurst, a future Derby player, the Rams' prospects of appearing in their fifth FA Cup final, and their first for thirty years, became brighter still when they were again drawn at home in the quarter-finals. They were back to facing First Division opposition in Newcastle United, but Dame Fortune still smiled on them in the important matter of team selection. Whereas Rioch returned refreshed from a two-match suspension, completed in the nick of time, and James passed a late fitness test, the visitors from the North-East were compelled by injury and illness to call on their third-choice goalkeeper, Eddie Edgar, and a pair of young reserves, full-back Ray Blackhall and midfielder Ray Hudson, in the absence of Mike Mahoney, Willie McFaul, Irving Nattrass and Tommy Craig.

Furthermore, depleted Newcastle turned up only a week after having their confidence dented by defeat at the hands of Manchester City in the League Cup final. In those unhappy circumstances they earned high praise for the spirited manner in which they forced Derby to step up their tempo, especially after falling two goals behind in the first fifteen minutes. Rioch scored both of them. In only the fourth minute his well-placed drive rounded off a flowing move that also involved Thomas, Hector and George, and he increased the lead with the fiercest free-kick I have ever seen, a full-blooded blast of awesome power I rate with a header by Tommy Lawton, for Notts County against Nottingham Forest, as a prime example of spectacular finishing. Sitting in the Ley Stand, I was right behind the flight of the ball as it zoomed through the shell-shocked defensive wall after George had been brought down just outside the Newcastle penalty area. Since taking longer than expected to get off the mark, in view of his scoring success of the season before, Rioch had regained his touch in getting six goals in as many games, and he ended second only to George in the Derby list with seventeen including cup-ties.

Between those broadsides against Newcastle, Malcolm ('Supermac') Macdonald had a goal ruled out for illegally bundling the ball out of Moseley's hands, and United's determination to try to salvage something from a disintegrating season (they were in the lower half of the League table) was further demonstrated soon afterwards when Derby's lead was halved. The scorer, after Blackhall's low cross had bounced favourably to him off George, was Alan Gowling, whose alertness and stamina belied the fact that he had spent most of the week in bed with bronchitis. Gowling, who was to total thirty for the season, also obtained Newcastle's second goal, stretching out a long leg to prod the ball in when Tom Cassidy drove it goalwards from Stewart Barrowclough's pass twelve minutes from the end, but by then Derby were comfortably in front with two more goals, scored in five minutes just after the hour.

Newton notched the first of them with a stunning curling shot from just outside the penalty area after Macdonald had headed out a corner by Nish. George grabbed the other, sinking to his knees in celebration after Hector, back to his best since being out of the first-team reckoning for nearly a dozen matches in mid-season, had deceived the defence with a nifty back-heel. Smiles were transformed to sadness for Newton, however, as he limped off with a quarter of an hour to go, Davies contriving a couple of glaring misses as his substitute, and the former Forest man therefore missed the semi-final against Manchester United along with George, who was kept out by the dislocated shoulder he suffered during the intervening home League match with Stoke.

As Tommy Docherty, the Manchester club's manager, observed, the clash of two of the First Division's leading sides at Hillsborough was worthy of being the final. The pairing of Southampton and Crystal Palace in the other semi-final at Stamford Bridge certainly paled by comparison, but what a shock there was in store for Docherty and his men after the Hampshire underdogs from the Second Division had denied Palace the privilege of being the Third Division's first finalists. Victory at Wembley was what Southampton had been waiting for ever since their defeats in the finals of 1900 and 1902.

That United should be the Saints' opponents instead of Derby was one of the biggest lost opportunities in the Rams' long history, a sorrowful repeat of the two-goal margin by which they had also been beaten in the semi-final between the clubs at the same ground in 1948. On that former occasion they had at least scored, a brilliant opportunist goal by Scottish international Billy Steel, in losing 1-3. This time the score was 2-0, both goals coming from Gordon Hill, who, in following Docherty and Daly from Old Trafford a couple of seasons later, was to be as big a let-down with Derby as he had been a lively eye-catcher with United, but David Nish did have what would have been an equaliser controversially disallowed.

Derby were behind from as early as the twelfth minute in which Todd was left stranded by an inaccurate return pass from Davies after rashly straying too far upfield. Brian Greenhoff, whose elder brother Jimmy left Stoke to join him in the United team later that year, sent Hill through the gap, and after slipping the ball to Gerry Daly the former Millwall winger had ample time to curve a superb shot past Moseley when the Republic of Ireland international rolled an inviting pass back to him.

Nish, who, along with McFarland, was at the top of his game in Derby's defence, had his moment of misfortune in the second half when he decided to try to beat United's offside trap on his own. He lobbed the ball over the defenders in front of him and ran through to put it into the net, only to hear a blast on referee Jack Taylor's whistle because his forward colleagues had not moved back in time. Whether or not they were interfering with play was a moot point.

After that there was precious little sign of the Rams pulling level, and seven minutes from the end the outcome was put beyond all doubt. A wasted free-kick by Nish gave Manchester United the opportunity to launch another attack in which Steve Coppell, Docherty's other perceptive wing signing from the Third Division (Tranmere Rovers), was stopped only by a tackle for which Powell was penalised. Hill took the free-kick, and the hapless Powell had the added frustration of deflecting it beyond Moseley's reach. 'You only paid £70,000 for me,' Hill told Tommy Docherty afterwards, 'while Derby paid £300,000 for Leighton James. Can I have the balance?'

As if being so summarily knocked off the road to Wembley at the penultimate stage was not enough of a shattering blow, headlines the next day made the most unwelcome reading in drawing graphic attention to the unpleasant nature of some of the exchanges. Bruce Rioch was the main target of the criticism. Stuart Pearson, the centre-forward who played for England after being plucked out of the Second Division with Hull City, branded him 'a coward' after an ugly flare-up between them in the seventieth minute. This was how Pearson viewed it:

'Rioch had just done Sammy McIlroy, and I went over to have a word with him about it. I was going to say "Don't be stupid," but before I could say anything he whacked me. I know I was out of order to have a go at him soon afterwards, and I deserved to be booked. But Rioch should have been sent off. He did Sammy again in the last minute, and we have a World Cup final referee who claims he didn't see either incident. I thought Rioch had broken my cheekbone and it is very sore – just like toothache. Only cowards do things like that.'

Pearson was booked for going over the top at Rioch, whereas the Derby player was merely admonished by Jack Taylor, a respected referee who had made history at the 1974 World Cup final by awarding a penalty to Holland within seconds of the kick-off against West Germany – a setback the host nation had shrugged off by going on to win after equalising from another penalty. Taylor, a Wolverhampton butcher, explained Rioch's escape from severe punishment in the FA Cup semi-final by saying: 'Players were making certain allegations about incidents after the ball had gone. I didn't see them. I consulted my linesman, and he said he was following the play and had seen nothing. The United player who was injured lost his head and I had to book him.'

Dave Mackay also said that he had not seen the incident, nor was he given the opportunity to do so in the edited recording of the match shown that night on television. In common with the referee and the FA, therefore, Derby County did not take any action against Rioch. The Derby manager acknowledged that 'there were one or two bad tackles in the second half, but they were mainly due to frustration'. He added: 'We didn't play well, and got what we deserved.'

The assault by Pearson on Rioch left the Rams' midfielder with a badly swollen knee that forced him to drop out of the Scotland squad for the following Wednesday's game in Glasgow against Switzerland. He was again lucky not to be at least cautioned for his last-minute foul on McIlroy, and when the final whistle blew he was chased by a United fan as he ran towards the tunnel. 'Rioch was rattled,' said McIlroy, 'but he's the sick one. We're at Wembley.' Some years later, Rioch told Tony Hardisty in a *Sunday Express* interview:

'I bitterly regret some of the things I did as a player. Yes, there were times when I was dirty, when I did some shameful things. And I have no excuse about that incident at Torquay. I lost my temper and hurt somebody. It left me with no choice but to resign. The only thing I can offer in mitigation is that I love the game of football with a passion.'

Francis Lee was a central figure in another unsavoury incident involving Derby County in the 1975-76 season. The Rams' home game with Leeds should have been best remembered for the perfectly-struck left-foot swerving shot with which Roger Davies gave the Rams a 3-2 win two minutes from time in his 100th League appearance – his fourth successive game as a substitute after taking over in the first half when Rioch went off with an injured ankle. Instead, all was overshadowed by the punch-up between Lee and Norman Hunter for which both were ordered off. The trouble began shortly before the interval when referee Derek Nippard, a Bournemouth policeman, awarded a controversial penalty, converted by George, after Lee had fallen spectacularly over Hunter's leg. It looked – as Leeds vehemently claimed and television's all-seeing eye did nothing to contradict – like one of the dives for which Franny was so notorious, and it set the simmering scene for the flare-up that broke out seven minutes into the second half.

Lee was stung into retaliation when Hunter clattered into him with a late challenge, and Hunter responded with a blow to Lee's lip that caused a cut requiring four stitches. Both were banished after being pulled apart by players of each side, but as they were leaving the field Lee suddenly started another fight from which they again had to be separated. As Dave

Mackay saw it, 'Hunter appeared to start it, but Lee certainly finished it. I think the second flare-up came after Lee realised the extent of his injury. I still maintain Lee was totally innocent until after he had been sent off.'

It was the fourth time two players had been ordered off in a match at the Baseball Ground. Jack Hope, a forward Derby signed from Crook Town, and Patrick Hunt, a Burnley centre-half, had been dismissed during a reserve match in 1929, Johnny Morris had been sent packing with Portsmouth's Jimmy Scoular in 1950, and the Arsenal pair earlier in 1975.

Lee claimed extreme provocation at the FA commission hearing, but he received the severer punishment of a four-game suspension and £250 fine because only the second bout of fighting was taken into consideration, despite the fact that it would not have happened without Hunter's original punch. The first incident had already been automatically dealt with by a one-match ban and accumulation of twelve penalty points for both players. Hunter, who said he acted only in self-defence when attacked as they were going off, was therefore effectively given just the one-match suspension. He did also miss three more games, but that was a cumulative punishment because his disciplinary points had reached twenty.

Lee, who was fined two weeks' wages, approaching £400, by Derby, said it was 'the worst thing that's happened to me in almost 16 years of League football'. He added: 'It's not the money aspect that hurts me most, though this business has cost me around £650 in club and FA fines. I'm coming towards the end of my career, and the danger is people might remember me just for this and think "He was a violent, vicious player". But I've never thrown a punch at anyone before in my life, and I've taken a hell of a lot of stick from many defenders without reacting.'

Derby County also had good reason to feel hard done by because Lee's one-match ban for the original incident, in which he was the injured party, meant that he was automatically barred, in the FA's words, 'from the next recognised first-team match.' And that match just happened to be the second leg of the European Cup-tie with Real Madrid for which one of the Spanish club's players would still have been available if he had been similarly suspended.

Injury as well as suspension compelled Lee to miss much of the first-team action from shortly before Christmas until the Rams' last five matches of the season. He was not among the scorers when that late sequence began back at Maine Road in the 3-4 defeat that virtually ended hopes of retaining the League title, but he netted twice in the next game, salvaging a home point against Leicester with an astonishing overhead kick in the last five minutes that Dave Mackay rated 'the best goal I've seen at this club', and, made captain for his farewell appearance on the final day, he rounded off his sixteen years of top football, in his 500th League game, in storybook style by grabbing two more goals in the last 56 seconds of a 6-2 win at Ipswich.

He could not have wished for a better way to go out after having already announced his intention to retire, on completing his two-year contract, to concentrate on his flourishing paper converting business at Egerton's Deakins Mill. Peter Walters, who refereed the match, was also ending his League career.

Lee remembered that game not only for its personally happy ending. 'I bought a couple of bottles of champagne to celebrate,' he said, 'but the team's bus broke down after we had stopped for an evening meal, and I didn't get home until nearly five o'clock on the Sunday morning.'

The two points Derby took home from Ipswich secured the final fourth place that made them sure of competing in Europe (in the UEFA Cup) for the fourth time in five seasons. It was their biggest win of the season, and they achieved it with an experimental formation in which Jeff King, a young Scot signed by Dave Mackay from Albion Rovers for £7,000 in the spring of 1974, but recently out on loan to Notts County and Portsmouth, made a startlingly impressive League debut as deputy for Leighton James, who, along with Rod Thomas, was away in Zagreb, in the Welsh team beaten by Yugoslavia.

King had been an unused substitute at home against Arsenal the previous season, and had played for the senior side in friendly matches besides travelling into Europe as a member of the squad. Well as he played at Ipswich, however, he was to have scant scope for developing his career with Derby. After being unsuccessfully sought by Huddersfield Town and having a spell at Walsall while Dave Mackay was in his next managerial post there, he found more expression for his talents in helping Sheffield Wednesday out of the Third Division in 1979-80 and Sheffield United out of the Fourth in 1981-82.

Ron Webster was recalled in place of Thomas against Ipswich, with Steve Powell also at the back, Colin Todd in midfield, and Bruce Rioch switched into the attack until further demonstrating his versatility by filling in at centre-back when McFarland had to limp off twenty minutes from time.

Dave Mackay was to regret that he did not tempt Lee out of retirement. It was certainly not for want of trying. He made a couple of attempts, the second of them only just before he was sacked, but by then Lee had bought a new factory and his business, in which he was employing 150 people, was demanding too much of his time for him to consider any of what he estimated as 'around 30 offers from League clubs to crackpots to play again'. Two years later, by which time his number of employees had risen to 275, he moved with his wife Jean, son Gary and daughter Charlotte into a fifty-acre farm, bordering on the Cheshire stockbroker belt of Wilmslow. From there he directed the development of a stud farm. While with Derby he had been the joint owner of a racehorse with Rod Thomas, and his interest in that sport soon spread to riding in point-to-point races as he kept fit, losing weight after leaving the Rams, by playing cricket and squash. 'When I was playing soccer I would finish training and feel ravenous. Now I eat more normally.'

As owner of a farmhouse that more closely resembled a manor with its fifteen rooms and five baths, plus three Mercedes and a Range-Rover, Lee had come a long way since progressing from part-time labouring and lorry driving, through the ownership of launderettes and hairdressing salons, to the directorship of his tissue-paper firm. Right from being a sixteen-year-old apprentice at Bolton he had concentrated on safeguarding the lifestyle he built up from professional football with occupations outside the game. 'I could have stayed on for a few more seasons, but at 33 I felt the time was right to quit,' he declared in making what was an almost complete break from soccer, apart from playing in a few charity games and watching a handful of live matches, until his short-lived return to Manchester City as chairman in the 1990s.

Lee's departure from Derby was soon followed by that of two other forwards, Roger Davies and Alan Hinton. The 1975-76 season had been a disappointing one for the 25-year-old Davies, with only a dozen games in the starting line-up and sixteen appearances as a substitute, and he moved to Bruges, the Belgian champions, for a fee of £135,000 after going in to see Dave Mackay to sort out where he stood. He did not ask for a transfer, but he was put on the list after they had agreed that he would probably be better off if he could get a move to another club. Mackay then went off on holiday, so the negotiations were concluded by Des Anderson, who said that Bruges were the first club to make a firm offer close to their valuation.

Davies helped his new club to a League and Cup double, but was then at odds with their coach, Ernst Happel, after being dropped from the team that played against Derby in Roy McFarland's testimonial match in November 1977. Matters came to a head when he was told to train with the Reserves, and he walked out after Happel had refused to offer an explanation. Tommy Docherty, by then manager of the Rams, was keen to bring him back to the Baseball Ground when Bruges agreed to release him, and Davies also relished the prospect of renewing a partnership with Charlie George. But it was Leicester City who paid about £160,000 to restore him to English football – and it was against Derby that he re-entered it in a drawn game at Filbert Street.

With four goals, one of them a penalty, in fourteen First Division games – a meagre tally that still made him the team's joint leading scorer –

Davies did little to improve a Leicester attack that had cobbled together only seven in the previous eighteen, and relegation was inevitable as a mere five wins were set against 25 defeats. Early in the following 1978-79 season Davies reappeared at the Baseball Ground as a substitute in a League Cup-tie won by Derby, and after only eight other games and no more goals he was off to American football with Tulsa Roughnecks. From there, in the autumn of 1979, he did rejoin the Rams, only to be on his way out again shortly before they, too, lost their First Division place. The 23 appearances and four goals of his comeback increased his totals for the club to 144, plus 22 as sub, and 44 goals.

Back he went to the United States, with Seattle Sounders and Fort Lauderdale Strikers, before making Burnley and Darlington his last League clubs. He did not get into Burnley's first team, and he played only ten times in Darlington's, scoring one goal, before having his monthly contract cancelled in February 1984. After that he was with two clubs in the Burton district, Gresley Rovers and Stapenhill. As Gresley's player-manager he followed David Nish, who, his effectiveness diminished by three operations on his right knee, had made the last three of his 237 appearances for Derby as a substitute before also moving to Tulsa. On being replaced by Frank Northwood, Davies stayed with Gresley as player-coach for a few months before parting company towards the end of 1985.

Alan Hinton, released without a fee on his head in recognition of his service to the club, was one of seven players given a free transfer by Derby County at the end of the 1975-76 season in which he made the last four, all as a substitute, of his 319 appearances for the Rams. Football had come to have little meaning for him. He and his wife had lost their son Matthew with cancer, and he could no longer see the point of kicking a ball around. 'One day we went to hospital with the boy. It was something trivial we thought, and then his doctor was telling us our boy was going to die. Soccer seemed utterly pointless.'

He turned out once more at the Baseball Ground, however – on 9 October 1976, in his testimonial game against a Great Britain XI managed by Tommy Docherty. Nearing his 34th birthday, and less than a year since appearing in front of a European Cup crowd of 120,000 in Madrid, he prepared for that match by playing for Borrowash Victoria, the club near his home at Ockbrook on the outskirts of Derby, after politely refusing offers from, among others, Nottingham Forest, Notts County and Sheffield Wednesday. Then he found some kind of rehabilitation in Dallas, Texas. 'The Dallas Tornado coach, Al Miller, rang me, suggesting that a new environment might help both me and my family. It did, slowly.'

From there he moved to Vancouver, where, as player and assistant coach with the Whitecaps, he became an instant success with the pinpoint accuracy of his crosses. In 1978 he set a North American Soccer League record for 'assists' to scorers, his thirty beating the total achieved by no less than Pele and George Best, and before joining Tulsa Roughnecks as head coach later that year he helped Tony Waiters to build the foundations for the Whitecaps' 1979 Soccer Bowl triumph.

Hinton next went to Seattle, where, in being named NASL Coach of the Year with the Sounders in 1980, he paid tribute to the influence of Brian Clough by saying: 'Cloughie is considered an eccentric by many, but really his work couldn't be more sound. He taught me that always you have to answer for yourself, whether you're a player or a coach. Once at Derby I failed to appear at a charity cricket match. I told some of the lads I couldn't make it. There was a good reason. After training the following morning, Cloughie came up to me and said: "You're fined £50." Then he took me to his office, poured me a scotch, and said: "It's not the fine, son, it's the idea that individuals always have to think of their responsibilities".'

Hinton signed a three-year contract with Seattle that paid him a minimum of £50,000 a year. The Sounders were then drawing crowds of up to 30,000 at the massive Kingdome, a civic facility they shared with the baseball Mariners, the basketball Sonics and the American football Seahawks. Hinton saw, however, that there was much to be done in North American soccer, and he had a particular dislike for the play-off system. In one of his seasons with the Sounders, they lost a play-off on a penalty shoot-out after scoring more goals than Los Angeles in the two games. Even the LA coach, Rinus Michels, was embarrassed.

The NASL folded not long after Hinton had rejoined Vancouver Whitecaps as their head coach. He then moved into the Major Indoor League with Tacoma Stars, but soon afterwards left soccer to help his wife run a real estate business in the United States. He still has a soft spot for Derby County, and it was on one of his return visits to this country that I had the pleasure of meeting him at Pride Park. I could well appreciate why the late Billy Wright, the former Wolves and England captain who was chairman of his testimonial appeal, had admired him for 'his quiet reassuring manner, and for just being a helluva nice bloke'. How Derby could do with a winger of his ability these days – although, as Peter Taylor had predicted, he was never fully appreciated by many Rams supporters until after he had left.

The Vote of Confidence that never came

On the face of it, Derby County treated Dave Mackay shabbily when they dispensed with his services on Thursday, 25 November 1976, in the fourth month of his fourth season as their manager. In the previous three seasons, after all the acrimony stirred up by Brian Clough's departure, he had guided the Rams to final positions of third, first and fourth in the First Division, and to their first FA Cup semi-final for 28 years.

But, sadly, that was not the whole story. Since the repeated Hillsborough defeat by Manchester United that had stirred the bring-back Clough brigade and other militants into clamouring for a change of management, Derby had been in serious decline. After that demoralising Cup exit only three wins had been gained in eighteen League games, and in going without a victory through their first eight First Division matches of the new season they had equalled their worst start since 1920 – a run that had led to the relegation they were now not to escape until the final fixture. On top of that, they had been knocked out of the UEFA Cup and been taken to two replays in narrowly accounting for three clubs from lower divisions in the League Cup.

Nor was even that all. There had also been strong criticism of playing tactics, inadequate training, a failure to sign new strikers of proven ability at the highest level, and allegations of a lack of discipline both on and off the field. Injuries had complicated Mackay's attempts to improve results, but he had never fully come out from the long and dark shadow cast by Clough, and several players – the Clough faction in particular – had failed to give him the support he had been entitled to expect. One of those who did support him put it this way:

'Dave Mackay stood for a lot of the good and important things in football, but he fell down on some of the basic rules and standards necessary in the running of a club. It's been known that discipline was lax, and when things went wrong he was unable to protect himself and the team by normal disciplinary measures which shield a club from public pressure, from the misinterpretation of facts. Some of the players have not helped as much as they might have done when they could have shown courage on the field. The shadow of Clough has always been in the background hanging over Mackay, even after we won the championship. If he tried things which didn't come off there was criticism.'

Mackay conceded that he was not as strict a disciplinarian as Clough. 'We were different types. Clough ruled the club with a rod of iron, and some of the things he said to the other blokes when I was a Derby player made me cringe. I'd have told him what I thought if he'd said anything like that to me, but he never did.' Mackay treated his players the way he had always been treated at Tottenham, but maintained that they all knew he would not stand for liberties. He fined them £1 a minute up to half-an-hour if they were late for training, but never made that generally known. Players were warned on foreign trips that they would have to pay for any damage they caused. It cost Rod Thomas £80 when he accidentally broke a plate-glass window playing snooker in Spain.

After his dismissal, Mackay told the *People* newspaper: 'Generally speaking the Derby players were a well-behaved bunch. And, despite the rumours which swept through Derby earlier this season when results were going wrong, they aren't drinkers. It's hardly a secret that I like a drink after a match. It was always "open house" in my office at Derby every Saturday night after a home game. But it wasn't my social habits or lack of discipline that cost me the Derby job. It was the fact that the team was struggling at the wrong end of the table, and that I'd never crawled to the board. Like the players, I always told the directors just what I thought.'

And there lay the crux of his problem. A new power had arisen in the Derby County hierarchy. George Hardy, a wealthy man of property and scrap metal who drove a Rolls-Royce GH 2000, joined the board as a firm follower of the 'Bring Back Clough' movement, and his influence began to grow as the team's fortunes faded. He became a vice-chairman who gradually pushed Sam Longson into the background, and began to question the management in leaning more and more to the view that Clough should come back. It was said that players were visitors to his home and were asked for their views on the manager and the way he was running the club. Mackay was to come to realise that he should have been more of a diplomat, especially where Hardy was concerned.

One bone of contention concerned the board's instruction to cut down on expenses when the team travelled to away games. Mackay ignored it, and also argued with the directors to get improved bonuses for the players. Eventually, he arranged a meeting with Hardy and the players to sort things out, and it was not until then, only two weeks after the board had insisted there was no more money, that they obtained the increases they had been seeking.

On the playing side, the main worries switched from a defence that in 1975-76 had kept only thirteen clean sheets in 53 games, and conceded nearly thirty more goals than Liverpool's champions, to an attack that failed to score in eight of the first thirteen League matches played in the 1976-77 season before Mackay lost his job. The departure of Davies and Lee was keenly felt, especially when George (through suspension) and Hector (flaked ankle bone) were also out of the side. Bruce Rioch had to be moved into the front line to fill one of the gaps in a scoreless home draw with Middlesbrough, and in the next game, also at home and also without a goal, Jeff Bourne was called upon perhaps earlier than he would have liked against Manchester United after having only just returned from his summer on loan to Dallas Tornado.

Bourne, who was to have few other chances before his move to Crystal Palace, damaged a thigh muscle within a few minutes and soon had to be replaced by Eric Carruthers, a fair-haired Scot who had been sidelined by a serious knee injury soon after being signed for £15,000 from Hearts in the spring of 1975. Carruthers was unable to regain the level of fitness the First Division demanded, and that was his only first-team appearance for the Rams before having his contract cancelled. He moved to South Africa with the Arcadia Shepherds club of Pretoria.

The match with Manchester United was tainted by one of the worst instances at Derby of the hooliganism that was then rife in British soccer. Violence reached frightening proportions as brawling fans of both teams invaded the pitch and afterwards fought in the adjoining streets. There were more than sixty casualties, including three policemen who were taken to hospital, and about twenty arrests were made. Stuart Webb, the Rams' secretary, deplored 'the bad image it gives football in the eyes of millions at a time when a lot of money and effort is being spent on improving the game'. The attendance topped 30,000, but Webb claimed that 3,000 Derby season-ticket holders were among the club's supporters who stayed away because they feared the hooligan minority that followed Manchester United around would bring trouble, and he doubted that many of them would be keen to come back unless some drastic action could be taken to resolve the problem.

As Dave Mackay pointed out, however, there was a limit to how much could be done. 'No matter how tough you are,' he said, 'there's no way a few men can stop a mob on the rampage.' Tommy Docherty, the United manager who was so soon to be Derby's, commented: 'If that's what happens when we draw 0-0, what will those idiots do when we lose?' He was in favour of bringing back the birch.

And Manchester United were not alone in being saddled with these soccer savages. For those whose homes were in the streets of terraced houses in the immediate area of the Baseball Ground – many of them in Shaftesbury Crescent directly opposite the main stand – match days had become a regular living hell as fans stormed past. They had to board up their windows, move their cars off the street, and lock up their pets. Women took tranquillisers to cope with the strain; children often hid under beds and tables.

One man told of how he stood in fear as morons crashed against his bolted front door, trying to get inside. Another spoke of standing behind his door, poker in hand, as the mob ran riot outside. 'If I return at lunchtime on a match day,' said a third, 'I have to ask police permission to get to my house. Then we go out, and we wait at least a quarter of an hour after the game before returning home. Every home game puts us in a state of siege.' There was also one householder who had the window of her little daughter's bedroom broken by a missile. Matters had come to such a pass that families had planned to barricade the streets on match days, but had refrained from doing so after being advised against it by the police.

Women of the district demonstrated outside the Baseball Ground when, during the week following the horrific scenes on the day of Manchester United's 1976 visit, a top-level inquiry was held there involving the FA chairman, Professor Sir Harold Thompson, Football League secretary Alan Hardaker, high-ranking officials from the Ministry of Sport, and senior police officers. A three-point plan was drawn up:

1 Harsher penalties for offenders;
2 Ban reimposed on football specials;
3 Fencing-in of pitches (The fences came down after the Hillsborough disaster of 1989)

The FA blamed neither Derby County nor Manchester United for what had happened, and the Rams took stringent action to try to ensure there would be no repeat of such mayhem when the Old Trafford club revisited the Baseball Ground a year later. They did what they had considered doing for their home match with United in 1975 – they banned their supporters from the stadium. Admission was limited to Derby season-ticket holders and possessors of vouchers issued at the previous home game. Consequently, the gate was down to not much more than 20,000, who saw United win by an only goal, but the ban was welcomed by the Minister for Sport, Denis Howell, and the FA secretary, Ted Croker. United also raised no objection. Their secretary, Les Olive, said: 'They are no doubt doing what they think is right, and we just have to accept it.' Not until 1983, when Derby were back in the Second Division, was there another 30,000-plus crowd for a Manchester United visit – for a fifth-round FA Cup-tie the Rams also lost 0-1.

Back in 1976-77, Derby County had quite enough disciplinary trouble on their hands without having to contend with the hooligan element among supporters. Starting with a pre-season tournament during which Archie Gemmill was sent off against Athletic Bilbao, there were four cases in that period of one of their players being given his marching orders.

Charlie George was the miscreant in two of them – beginning the season as he was to end it in being banished for violent conduct – and Leighton James talked himself into the other dismissal in the penultimate match.

Another discordant note was struck when Dave Mackay refused to travel to Tyneside for the opening fixture of that season because the board would not pay a loyalty bonus for Roy McFarland – a decision they retracted the following week. The point the Rams brought away from Newcastle would normally have represented a satisfying start, but it was blemished not only by George's indiscretion but also by remarks James made to the referee at the final whistle which stung a police sergeant into pinning the Welshman against the wall as he made his way up the tunnel and admonishing him for using obscene language. It also set the pattern for the bleak winless sequence in which Mackay's already considerable troubles were racked up another gear by a request for a transfer from Colin Todd, who did not relish the midfield role to which the hard-pressed manager had shifted him.

When Todd's turn came for talks Mackay had with each player about the club's poor start to the season, he said that, at 28, he felt he needed a move for the security of his family. On the Friday, the first day of October, when that shock news broke, Mackay called all his players together and told them they must tackle their problems 'in a manly fashion'. Next morning, he read newspaper reports that the whole club was unhappy and unsettled, and he was therefore not in the best of moods when he left for London to check on Arsenal striker John Radford in a reserve game at Crystal Palace. It was scarcely the right atmosphere for seeking a first League victory of the season that afternoon at the eighth attempt on a ground, Birmingham City's, where, in any case, the Rams had not won for 28 years. And so it proved, though on an even bigger scale than Mackay had feared possible.

By the time he had driven up the motorways to St Andrew's, Derby were right up against it, and they went in at half-time 1-3 down. When he got to the dressing room he told Todd to get changed because he was sending on the substitute. At the final whistle, with the score 1-5, Mackay, in his own words, was 'boiling over', with Todd the chief target of his tirade:

'I called Colin everything. Perhaps it was just as well that he never argued or yelled back at me. He just shrugged his shoulders and took it all. I left the dressing room still raging, and chairman Sam Longson tried to calm me down. I said: "Mr Longson, if it was left to me Todd would never play for Derby again".'

Back at the Baseball Ground, Mackay met with the players about the Todd business in particular and the dire performance of the whole team in general. When the meeting ended, Todd followed the manager into his office and said that he would not want to leave Derby if he could be assured of a contract that would secure his future. That was a matter for the board, but Mackay replied that he was fully in favour of it, and after the pair had consulted with George Hardy (then still the vice-chairman but already the real authority) Todd withdrew his transfer request on reaching what he termed 'a gentleman's agreement' under which 'Derby will look after me when my present contract runs out at the end of the season'.

Though incensed by the earlier attitude of the player who had been at the heart of two championship teams, Mackay had long had the highest regard for the ability of Todd, who, after all, had produced the best football of his career under his management. He appreciated that the temporary move from Todd's favourite position in central defence had been at the root of the friction, but he was not alone in making that decision. Don Revie had also switched him from there – to full-back, where he had played some of his early games for the Rams – and that change had cost him caps.

Within a few hours of the solution to the Todd problem, Derby were back on the winning path in a League Cup replay against Notts County at Meadow Lane. Despite again being without McFarland and Hector, whose injuries had kept them out of the debacle at Birmingham, and also Newton, who became a casualty in that game, they repeated the 2-1 margin of their only previous victory of the season, in the same competition at Doncaster of Division Four, with a couple of Rioch goals. They were to need another replay to get through the next round by the same score against a Brighton side heading up from the Third Division under the management of Alan Mullery after Peter Taylor's departure to rejoin Brian Clough with Nottingham Forest, but then, after Mackay's own exit, out they went, also by 1-2, to Bolton Wanderers, who that season only just missed the promotion they were to gain as Second Division champions a year later.

From looking strong candidates for relegation after the Birmingham blitz, the Rams exceeded all expectations by building on their improved form against Notts County with a stunning first win of their First Division season in their next outing. By eight goals to two they shattered a Tottenham team plunging towards the bottom of the table, though there was little indication of the landslide to come as Spurs recovered from going two down in the opening five minutes to trail by only 2-3 at the interval.

It was a day to remember for Bruce Rioch, scorer of four of the goals, in his literally striking guise, against the Northern Ireland colossus Pat Jennings, then one of the best goalkeepers in the world and the reigning PFA Footballer of the Year. But other outstanding displays were given by George, who embellished his two goals (one from a penalty) with the vision and scope of his passing, McFarland, whose dominant form ensured his recall to the England team for what, unfortunately, was to be his final cap in a defeat in Rome, and Leighton James, on one of the infrequent occasions when the Welsh winger spectacularly did the simple job for which Mackay had signed him – getting to the by-line and crossing the ball as he had done with Burnley. The bullet-like header with which Rioch completed his hat-trick from one of James's centres was the highlight of the afternoon.

Special praise was also due for the young Irishman who filled the midfield vacancy left by Rioch. Tony Macken had been in title-winning teams in Northern Ireland and the Republic, but mainly kept in the background since being signed by Mackay from Waterford for £30,000 in the 1974 close season – loaned out first to Portsmouth and then to Washington Diplomats and Dallas Tornado in the United States. In this match against Spurs, however, he showed why he became one of the then record Derby players selected for their country during that 1976-77 season (George, Gemmill, McFarland, Rioch, Todd, James, Thomas and Daly were the others. Eleven Derby men were capped in 1997-98). Macken's first-team opportunities dried up soon after Mackay left, but the pair were quickly reunited at Walsall, for whom Macken made almost 200 appearances before going back to the Republic of Ireland. He became player-manager of Drogheda United and was later assistant manager of Shamrock Rovers.

Todd and Thomas were Derby's other scorers against Tottenham, for whom Steve Perryman and Keith Osgood replied. Osgood, a former England Youth international, later joined the Rams for £150,000 while Colin Addison was their manager, but they recouped only £20,000 when he returned to London with Orient.

To score so many goals in one First Division match was staggering enough, yet while Derby were struggling along in the League they served up an even more remarkable achievement by gaining the biggest victory in a history dating back to 1884. Admittedly, the opposition was of only the modest variety, mid-table Finn Harps from the Republic of Ireland, in the first round of the UEFA Cup, and skipper McFarland accepted that 'we know that even if we win by 10-0 the public will say: "So they should".' But, roused by Dave Mackay's demand for a big improvement, the Rams went two goals better than that, falling just one short of the record 13-0 victory by an English club in European soccer achieved by Chelsea against Jeunesse Hautcharage, of Luxembourg, in the Cup-Winners' Cup in 1971. And there might well have been more. The framework of the visitors' goal was hit five times, and the referee rejected two penalty appeals. My old friend Mike Carey, reporting for *The Daily Telegraph* under his assumed name of Henry Bevington, remarked that the organisers of the Golden Goal were in danger of going out of business. They had to pay out £250 on the first half alone.

Kevin Hector indulged himself by equalling the record of five goals scored by two other English players in a European match – Ray Crawford, in Ipswich's 10-0 defeat of Floriana, of Malta, in the European Cup in 1961, and Peter Osgood in that big win by Chelsea ten years later. Hector had previously scored five goals in a 7-2 win by Bradford against Barnsley.

George and James both netted three times against the Harps, and Rioch was the other player to beat the hapless Gerry Murray, one of the most diminutive of goalkeepers. Again the crowd was disappointingly small, only 13,353 bothering to turn up.

Macken and King, who replaced Todd for the second half, found places in the Derby line-up, which was: Moseley; Thomas, Nish, Rioch, McFarland, Todd, Macken, Gemmill, Hector, George, James. With Colin Boulton on loan to Southampton, and Steve Bowtell (borrowed from Margate) ineligible, there was an interesting choice of goalkeeper among the Derby substitutes. Nottingham-born Steve Cherry, then only a month past his sixteenth birthday, was not required on that occasion, but he was to get near a century of first-team appearances before leaving for Walsall, and in 1982-83 he was the Rams' Player of the Year. After Walsall he was with Plymouth Argyle and on loan to Chesterfield, then returned to his home city to join Notts County, whose goal he guarded in more than 300 matches. He made the last of nearly 550 League appearances in Mansfield Town's first game of the 1998-99 season.

With Derby so far ahead, it was scarcely surprising that they lacked urgency for the return UEFA Cup-tie at Ballybofey, and they made hard work of progressing by 16-1 on aggregate. Hector, needing four more goals to set a record for a Football League player over the two legs of a European match, had to be content with two, both scored in the first half-hour. George scored the other two in the last ten minutes. It was a sad trip to Eire for McFarland, who gave Harps their goal with an over-hit lobbed back-pass after just fifteen seconds, then had to go off with a strained hamstring with the game only just more than a quarter of an hour old.

Derby's fourth venture in a European competition, to which they have dismally drifted far away from adding, then had only two more games to go. Wary of what had happened in Madrid, Dave Mackay contradicted his customary bold approach in preparing for the second-round visit to AEK in Athens. Ever since being a member of the Hearts team that had scored 132 goals in winning the Scottish First Division title by thirteen points from Rangers in 1957-58, he had been a firm believer in attacking, adventurous football, and he condemned European competition for forcing him to abandon that refreshing outlook. After defeat in Athens he stated:

'We went to Greece for a result to get us through, and although we lost 2-0 I was satisfied we had the right formation and the right attitude. It is a terrible thing for football, but experience has taught me that there must be a systematic approach for the away game in two-leg competitions. I will never change my well-known beliefs for any game in English football, but I can't afford to make Derby the exceptions in Europe. It is a pity because European football should offer all the best things in the game, but nobody comes to the Baseball Ground planning to entertain the crowd. Our thinking must be just as ruthless when we go abroad.'

Mackay's tactics might well have paid off if Derby had accepted the two good chances they had to score before Walter Wagner, a German-born striker who had formerly played for Eintracht Frankfurt, struck twice in three minutes just after the hour. Thomas was unable to get in a telling shot when Rioch's centre, driven in low, found him at the far post, and George unwisely preferred placement to power from an opening created by King, the substitute when Gemmill had to go off with hamstring trouble.

Derby's hopes of still getting through were raised in the return leg when George, who struck the bar as early as the sixth minute, halved the deficit eight minutes into a second half for which Mackay took the gamble of having four up front and only three at the back by replacing Thomas with Macken. But George, feeling the recurrence of a groin strain, had to go off after 69 minutes – just as Powell conceded the free-kick that was bent round the defensive wall for the equaliser on the night which restored the Greeks' two-goal advantage overall. And that was the start of a devastating burst of three goals in sixteen minutes that made Rioch's neat finish from Hector's centre just before the end of no consequence. AEK, with just four good strikes on goal – the other thudded against the crossbar – were winners by 3-2, and 5-2 on aggregate.

The Athens club squeezed through the next round against Red Star Belgrade when Wagner scored the vital away goal, then accounted for another English side, QPR, only after a penalty shoot-out. That took them to a semi-final with Juventus, whose 5-1 aggregate win led to the Turin team's first European trophy after losing their three previous finals – but only by virtue of the away goal they scored against Athletic Bilbao.

In the League, Derby County's slide continued even after the trouncing of Tottenham that had been expected to signal an upturn in their fortunes. Indeed, in their very next First Division match, three days after the Athens leg of the UEFA Cup-tie, they gave another insipid display in losing by an only goal away to Stoke City, a club destined to go down with Spurs. After the match – which Gemmill missed through injury, ending a run of 82 appearances – the players and Des Anderson stayed in the dressing room discussing what had gone wrong, and when Dave Mackay entered he found Charlie George the man most upset. 'We were rubbish,' George told him. 'You ought to say so.'

While Mackay insisted there was no crisis at the Baseball Ground, the storm clouds gathering over his head were made all too obvious at a bitter annual meeting early in November. His policies were strongly criticised, and he looked shaken when George Hardy told shareholders: 'We are not asleep to your fears.' The only comfort for the manager was that a renewed 'Bring Back Clough' move was defeated. Only two more wins were to be gained, however, before the axe fell – one in the League at home to lowly Bristol City (for whom Norman Hunter made his debut back at the Baseball Ground almost exactly a year after his notorious punch-up there with Francis Lee), the other in the League Cup replay with Brighton. The manner of those victories was far from reassuring, and in then losing feebly at Everton the Rams failed to benefit from having had a fortnight away from the First Division fray through postponements before midweek international fixtures. A team devoid of Nish, McFarland and George succumbed to one goal fortuitously deflected in off Powell's boot and another given away by defensive errors.

That defeat left Derby down in nineteenth place, and five days later Mackay and Anderson were sacked at a board meeting which lasted four hours. The day, Thursday, 25 November 1976, began eventfully enough for the doomed manager. He helped rescue casualties from a car crash outside the training ground and drove them to hospital in his Mercedes.

At the meeting, the usual manager's report was the second item on the agenda, after the approval of a proposal that chairman Sam Longson should become president. But there was also an ominous item No 9 – to discuss the manager. Mackay did not wait for them to get around to that. When item No 2 came up he asked the directors for a unanimous vote of confidence. He sensed what the outcome might be, but he wanted them to come out in the open about it. Instead, they insisted that he left the room while they talked it over, and nearly two hours went by before he was recalled.

'It's bad news,' he was told. They said the vote against him was unanimous, though Sam Longson was later to leave no doubt that he was against the sacking. Unfortunately for Mackay, however, the old man no longer held sway. The hint that he had been dislodged from the driving seat had been there for all to see when Hardy had appeared on the pitch before the home leg of the UEFA Cup-tie with AEK to cheer-lead the crowd. Mackay acknowledged the support he had been given by Longson, whereas he 'threw in a few home truths' at the other board members, Hardy in particular, after telling them he was not going to let them take the easy way out by acceding to their request that he resign. 'Old Sam has done a marvellous job for Derby,' he said, 'but I think he's now at an age when the chairman's job is too much for him. I'm sorry he was still officially in the chair when

I was sacked. It means I can never help him to realise his greatest ambition of seeing Derby play in another Cup Final at Wembley.'

Mackay also stood up to the board when they originally offered to give him just one month's salary as a not-so-golden handshake. At £15,000 a year, that worked out at only about £1,200 before tax. Realising that he was ready to go to law to get what he felt he deserved, the directors eventually reached a settlement whereby he received a £5,000 pay-off, plus his salary to the end of the season, and the Mercedes.

Perhaps Mackay might have survived if he had had a hard disciplinarian as his lieutenant, but Des Anderson was of the same free-wheeling mould. There was also the fact that Mackay lost a great ally when Franny Lee retired. Lee commanded instant respect, and if he suspected a colleague of not pulling his weight he was not slow to let him know about it. Someone close to Derby County was said to have told Lee that his return could have kept Mackay and Anderson in their jobs.

Another important influence on the casting out of a manager whose record with the club won widespread praise before the rot set in was the extent to which money became the subject of dressing-room disharmony. New signings, especially when they did not readily fit in, caused some unrest when they earned more than established members of the side, and reference has already been made to Todd's having to be placated with the promise of an improved contract.

As captain, Roy McFarland insisted, however, that player power had not forced Mackay out. 'There has been no sinister dressing-room influence on what the board have decided,' he declared. 'The feeling among the players this morning was one of sadness, because farewells are always sad. When I heard the news I had the same feeling in the pit of my stomach that I experienced when Cloughie left, but we soldier on. Obviously the players must take some responsibility for the fact that we are fourth from bottom in the First Division. That must reflect on the team as well as the management.'

McFarland had been one of Mackay's closest friends, dating back to their early playing days together when they had both been billeted by the club at the Midland Hotel, but he was one of the four members of the Derby team for whom Mackay did not have a parting handshake. In an exclusive article for the *People* newspaper, Mackay wrote:

'The day I left Derby for good the first-team players were sitting in the coach outside the Baseball Ground. I climbed aboard to shake hands for everything they'd done for me in my three seasons at Derby. All of them, that is, except four. And, to upstage the rumour-mongers, I'll name the four – Colin Boulton, Archie Gemmill, Roy McFarland and Colin Todd. I didn't feel I owed them anything. Not even a handshake. I've never been two-faced. I've always said what I think and expected the same treatment from others. Those four know that, and I'm sure they got the message.'

Mackay found himself out of a job for the first time on being booted out of the Baseball Ground, and nearly four months went by before he went from having aimed at regaining the title of the First Division, at the outset of that 1976-77 season, to taking on the task of trying to keep Walsall in the Third – a sphere of the League new to him in his 26 years as player and manager. Walsall, fourth from the foot of the table when he joined them, finished fifteenth, six points clear of the relegation cut-off. During the summer his recruits included, on free transfers, Henry Newton from Derby (though he was soon forced out by his hip problem), Middlesbrough striker Alf Wood, and Stoke winger Jimmy Robertson, a former Scottish international who had been one of his team-mates in Tottenham's FA Cup-winning side of ten years before. Two more men from Derby, Macken and Moseley (on a month's loan) followed, and Walsall ended Mackay's first – and last – full season with them sixth from the top, only three points behind Preston, occupiers of the third promotion place.

Shortly before the 1978-79 campaign opened, Mackay was tempted away to manage the Arabic Sporting Club in Kuwait at an annual salary of more than £40,000. Des Anderson also left Walsall, but, having recently taken over a public house in Derby, decided not to accompany him. Instead, Mackay was joined in the Middle East by Neil Martin, the former Coventry and Forest striker (scorer of the winning goal in Brian Clough's first match as the Nottingham club's manager) who had been Walsall's reserve coach. The managerial vacancy at Walsall was briefly filled by Alan Ashman, previously a player with Carlisle and Forest, and manager of Carlisle and West Bromwich Albion, who had been scouting for Manchester United since being Workington's last manager in the Football League. He later assisted John Newman at both Derby and Hereford.

After also working with success in Dubai for the Alba Shabab club, Dave Mackay had his last managerial posts back in England with Doncaster Rovers and Birmingham City. Doncaster were already in deep trouble when he joined them, and he was unable to save them from relegation to Division Four before resigning midway through the 1988-89 season 'on a point of principle'. At St Andrew's he joined a club that had just had a change of ownership and whose relegation to the Third Division for the first time had been confirmed only a few days earlier – on 15 April 1989, the date of the crowd disaster at the FA Cup semi-final between Liverpool and Nottingham Forest at Sheffield Wednesday's ground.

Birmingham ended his first season with them in seventh place, immediately below the play-off places, but they were down to fifteenth when he again resigned towards the end of January in 1991. After opening with four victories they had gained only three more in 21 games in Division Three and their latest setback, a 0-3 home defeat by Cambridge United which Mackay described as 'pathetic,' had provoked fresh demonstrations by supporters.

Mackay went on to have more success abroad with the Zamalek club in Egypt, but as far as soccer in England was concerned it was a most inappropriate end to the career of one of the footballing greats of the twentieth century. It is good to know, however, that he has retained a close regard for Derby County. In recent years he and Des Anderson have been regular spectators at Pride Park, the Rams' home since 1997.

Hapless short reign of 'an Apprentice'

The news that so many Derby County fans had been yearning for was emblazoned across the sports pages of the national papers on Tuesday, 22 February 1977. Brian Clough was coming back to the Baseball Ground!

George Hardy, who had been a dismayed season-ticket holder in the Ley Stand when his favourite manager had quit the club, made no secret of the fact that Clough was the man he wanted when Dave Mackay was sacked, but at that time, as a comparatively new director, he did not have sufficient clout to sway the issue. As he said, 'decisions of that nature are always made by the board as a whole.'

So the 33-year-old Colin Murphy was provisionally promoted to caretaker manager on the strength of his work as coach with the second team over the three years since he had followed Mackay from Nottingham Forest. Murphy, who then lived with his wife Judith, a teacher, and their fourteen-month-old son Benjamin at the Derbyshire market town of Melbourne, had also had his coaching talent recognised by the FA with his appointment as an instructor at one of their full-badge courses in the 1976 close season.

After being allowed to sell Bruce Rioch to Everton and buy Derek Hales from Charlton while still only in temporary charge, Murphy was officially made manager of the Rams on 6 January 1977, even though they were continuing to struggle for First Division survival, down in sixteenth place. He was given a salary of £15,000 a year, but without a contract. 'Colin does not need a contract,' said Hardy, who did not think they were worth much. 'His security lies in the results he achieves.' Murphy claimed that his appointment was a dramatic breakthrough for coaches in English soccer, though he left himself wide open to being challenged for his statement that 'people have believed for too long that only good players make good managers'. There have, in fact, been a good many good players who have not made good managers.

Hardy asserted that Murphy did not live in daily fear of the sack, yet here, only 46 days after he had been installed in the job, were those headlines heralding the return of Clough, along with Peter Taylor as his assistant, while Derby County floundered immediately above the relegation zone after successive defeats by Manchester United, Leeds and Liverpool. At a meeting hastily convened on the Monday morning after the failure at Anfield had deposited the Rams in nineteenth position, Derby's directors deliberated for three hours before deciding, by five votes to one, to ask

Nottingham Forest for permission to approach their manager. The dissenter was the 76-year-old Sam Longson, who was still the chairman but because of ill health had surrendered much of his power and responsibility to Hardy. Longson walked out of the meeting saying he was 'dead against' the idea.

At 4.20pm on that eventful day, talks between Forest's chairman, Brian Appleby QC, their vice-chairman, Stuart Dryden, and Clough led to permission being given for Derby to make their approach, and at 7.45pm Clough and Taylor met Hardy in a private room at the Riverside Inn at Burton-upon-Trent. Just over two hours later Hardy announced: 'We are confident of receiving the answer we want from Brian tomorrow.'

Word of this soon got around, and next day fans queued outside the ticket office at the Baseball Ground. Some wanted to know if any season tickets were left; others asked about buying season tickets for the following season. For Murphy, who cancelled that day's training, it was, as he understated it, 'a very difficult situation.' Hardy, boisterously confident of getting his man, said: 'I'm sorry Colin Murphy finds himself in this position, but life is cruel and the nice guys suffer most. Colin is one of the nicest men I've ever met, a man of integrity and moral fibre.' When Murphy was seen walking from his office to the boardroom a voice was heard from among a group of some thirty reporters, saying: 'Kiss me goodbye, Hardy.'

Clough and Taylor arrived at Forest's ground at 11 o'clock that Tuesday morning to find more than 300 supporters waiting outside, some close to tears. Fathers of schoolboys and apprentices signed by the pair phoned begging them to stay, but it was not until after the manager and his assistant had met Appleby, Dryden and committee member Derek Pavis that there was the first sign of a hitch in the proceedings. In a telephone call to Derby, Clough advised that a press conference arranged at the Baseball Ground should be delayed.

Appleby had to leave the meeting to go to Nottingham Crown Court to defend a man accused of the manslaughter of his wife. When the case was delayed on a technicality he dashed back across the city to add his considerable weight to trying to persuade Clough to stay. Meanwhile, Clough and Taylor went into a private room to discuss the matter between themselves.

At 2.30pm Hardy returned from lunch with three other Derby directors. 'Has he arrived yet?' he asked the waiting pressmen. 'No? Well, it shouldn't be long now.' It was not. At three o'clock Clough left Nottingham for Derby in a car driven by Jimmy Gordon, who had rejoined him as trainer with Forest after filling in with a job as a storeman at the Rolls-Royce works in Derby on leaving Leeds in Clough's wake. Taylor drove home. While Clough was on his way Dryden issued a statement that 'Brian and Peter have told us they will see out the full period of their contracts'. That meant they would be remaining at the City Ground for at least more than three years. Clough's current four-year contract dated back to the previous June.

Unaware of this, about a hundred cheering fans were waiting outside the Baseball Ground when Clough arrived. 'Good old Brian,' said one, 'Welcome home,' another. Clough looked pale and tense as he went straight to the boardroom. Half-an-hour passed before, at 4.20pm, Clough and Hardy came out and confirmed to the press that Forest would be keeping their manager after all. The 'sick and bitterly disappointed' Hardy, who also failed to persuade Francis Lee to make a playing comeback, said that the question of money had not entered into it, and he certainly did not see this as any gesture of revenge against Derby County.

As Brian Appleby saw it, the refusal to switch clubs meant that Clough and Taylor had proved they were men of integrity. He also emphasised that 'Brian has never made any financial demands on this club since his arrival'. Clough, who had come over to give Hardy his decision face to face, rather than just phoning, said he would have walked out and joined Derby if Forest had mentioned a financial settlement or increase. He was not a penny better off for deciding to stay. In admitting it was not the happiest day of his life, he added:

'I have not changed my mind about wanting to be Derby's manager. I have wanted it so much it's unbelievable. There was nothing more I wanted in life than managing players like Roy McFarland and Archie Gemmill again. When I was approached yesterday I was so flattered, so elated – every possible emotion. This is why it has taken me so long to say "No". There was never a time when I felt I wouldn't be joining Derby right until the last moment this afternoon. I have wanted the job every single minute of every single day since I left over three years ago, but despite that I have been extremely happy at Forest, and being happy is one of the secrets of life.'

The reason for his dramatic turnabout was that he came to appreciate the over-riding consideration was the debt he owed Forest for having brought him back into soccer in the first week of 1975 after he had been out of it for four months on leaving Leeds without receiving another offer. He was especially grateful to Stuart Dryden. 'He was the man who came for me when I was out of work. I always remember things like that.' Dryden, who succeeded Appleby as chairman at the end of the 1977-78 season, observed that 'it would be fair to say their decision to stay hinged on my talks with them'.

Sam Longson insisted that he had not stood in the way of Clough's return before negotiations broke down. This is what he had to say from his Chapel-en-le-Frith home following his standing down as chairman at a board meeting held three days after the one at which it was agreed to seek permission to approach the Rams' former manager:

'I did not resign the chairmanship. I was asked to retire, and this I agreed to do. I feel that the present board have given the impression that my position was the stumbling block to Brian Clough's return. This is not the case. I had previously offered to retire as chairman and to continue as life president in order to avoid any personality clash or any kind of unpleasantness. Now I no longer have any say in the matter. My opposition to having him back is not personal. That doesn't come into the reckoning. What happened in the past is gone and forgotten. I just believe it is wrong for us to try to pinch a manager from a neighbouring club. The decision to go for Clough was taken without my knowledge, but I am in no way elated at the news he is not coming. I think George Hardy was trying to do his best for the club, and I also think Brian Clough is the only man in the country who could sort Derby out. But I know him more than anybody else. We had problems with him before, and we don't want the same sort of problems again.'

On his way out of the Baseball Ground after delivering the shattering news of his refusal to return, Clough knocked on the door of Colin Murphy's office, shook hands, and went in for a five-minute chat. He wished him well, and advised him to make sure of getting a contract. About a couple of hours later, Murphy and Dario Gradi, whom he had taken on as his assistant six weeks earlier, were summoned to the boardroom by George Hardy and accepted the offer of written contracts until the end of the calendar year. The four other directors present at the board's embarrassing climb-down included Bob Innes, who became vice-chairman when Hardy officially took over as chairman that week, but not Sam Longson, who had been absent from the ground all day. The Italian-born Gradi, the FA's staff coach in the London area before helping Chelsea to develop their youngsters, had been brought in by Murphy from managing Sutton United, the club for which he had played in their FA Amateur Cup final defeat by North Shields in 1969, and with which he had earned one England amateur international cap.

Murphy, who had been given to understand that he would probably have been kept on in some minor capacity if Clough and Taylor had been reappointed, explained his decision to shrug off the humiliation and strain he had been put through by saying:

'I had a written agreement before any of this blew up, and now certain adjustments are to be made. It has nothing to do with salary. I'm well paid, but I want certain safeguards, and the board have agreed to tailor the agreement to my needs. It took more courage to stay and start again than it would have to tell the board to "get lost" and walk out. I know what people are saying, but to walk out was the easy thing to do. It takes courage to stay and face the music. I mean to ensure Derby remain in the First Division, and a number of well-known managers have phoned to say they think I'm right. I know I am putting the future of myself and my family on the line, but I believe I have a future. I feel stronger as a manager and a man after this experience. The board have always let me do what I wanted, although I have given way on some matters because I'm sensible. But there is no way I would still be here if I hadn't clarified a few things.'

Incredibly, however, Murphy had barely uttered those words than one Derby official was quoted as saying 'we're still in there battling', and declaring himself willing to bet a fiver that Clough would be back at Derby within ten days. It took an unequivocal statement by Brian Appleby to scotch such talk, and also the speculation which persisted throughout the rest of that week in the press. 'I would like to make it clear once and for all that the matter is closed,' he said, emphasising that Forest would not give permission for any club to approach Clough and Taylor at any time during their current contracts, which then ran to April 1980.

At the time he was originally appointed as Derby's manager, Colin Murphy asserted that he had 'tremendous confidence' in his ability to get the right response from the players, but Sam Longson had already done much to undermine his authority by demeaning him as 'an apprentice'. Before going off for a five-week winter break in Cyprus, the deposed chairman made another contribution to the air of discord, in his new capacity as president, by leaving behind a letter in which he called for Hardy's resignation and proposed the return of Mackay.

The lack of the right attitude in the team came not only from the strong pro-Clough faction, but also from those who had been dismayed to see Mackay leave. Charlie George was prominent in the latter group, and caused particular problems for Murphy. The absence of respect from that quarter was exposed when, during a replayed Cup-tie against Blackpool, George shouted abuse at Murphy that could clearly be heard in the front rows of the Baseball Ground's main stand. The situation between the two deteriorated to such an extent that an incident at the Raynesway training ground during preparations for the 1977-78 season resulted in Murphy suspending George for one week, fining him, and placing him on the transfer list for 'a breach of club discipline'.

In view of all the difficulties the rookie manager had to face, it was remarkable that in the season he took over Derby progressed as far as the quarter-finals of both the League Cup and FA Cup in addition to escaping relegation. The League Cup run ended with a dismal display at home to Bolton Wanderers, then third in the Second Division. The other mirage of Wembley dissolved at Goodison Park as the Rams meekly surrendered to an Everton side supposedly wearied by their then undecided involvement in a League Cup final that went to two replays before they yielded by the odd goal of five to Aston Villa after extra-time at Old Trafford. It was also in a replay, over the other side of Manchester at Maine Road, that Everton were FA Cup semi-final losers to their Liverpool neighbours, whose defeat by Manchester United beneath the celebrated twin towers then cost them a League and Cup double.

In the League, Charlie George's growing discontent was reflected in the dwindling of his goals to a mere five from 29 games. He totalled one more than that in the two knock-out competitions, but, although his opportunities for scoring were slightly reduced by the short-lived experiment of trying him in midfield, the disturbing fact remained that in the First Division he did not add to the goal he scored in a home win as far back as the end of October against Bristol City, companions in distress. In the last match of the season, a scoreless home draw with Ipswich that was such a contrast to the high-scoring game between the clubs at Portman Road the year before, he gave a display that was the most disinterested I have ever seen from any Rams player – until, that is, ten minutes from time when he was suddenly galvanised into an action for which he was sent off. Dave Mackay had blamed the First Division hatchet men for George's deteriorating disciplinary record, but on this occasion the provocation was an innocuous foul by John Wark, a coming Scottish international who was to become a key member of the powerful Liverpool line-up. In not unnaturally trying to defend himself, Wark was not a little unlucky to be also ordered off.

Leighton James, though still not slotting in as efficiently as the big fee splashed out on him warranted, ended that season as Derby's top scorer in the League with nine goals, and the shortcomings of the rest were emphasised when Gerry Daly, a midfielder who did not come into the team until early March, was the next highest with seven – four of which were penalties. When Daly made his debut the Rams were at the foot of the table after five League defeats in a row. With his deft displays a crucial influence, they lost only two of their remaining seventeen First Division matches and finished fifteenth, three points clear of the drop. Murphy, at last feeling safer in his job, even spoke of getting back into Europe as he prepared that summer for what he felt was going to be 'a really good season'. He was given a vote of confidence by the board, and said he felt as if a noose had been removed from his neck when Hardy came back from a Mediterranean cruise to announce that Derby County had no interest in Tommy Docherty, or any other manager. Docherty had just been dismissed by Manchester United after confessing to a love affair with Mary Brown, wife of the club's physiotherapist, and leaving his own wife to set up home with her in the Derbyshire village of Charlesworth.

'Now is the time to end all rumours and speculation,' stated the Rams' new chairman. 'We passed a vote of confidence in Colin before I went on holiday. What more can we say or do to get the message across?' Murphy expressed his relief by saying:

'I have had the stigma of being on trial publicly removed, and now I will not have to put up with every other manager being linked with my job. Derby County have elected to keep me, and this latest expression of confidence changes a few things. I know I have been manager in terms of picking and organising the team, but there's only one way to run this club – and if anybody here does not like it they are quite welcome to get out. Now I can walk around without wondering what people are thinking. It changes my authority, and I am in a position to be a great deal firmer with players. Last season I decided to tread warily in the interests of survival. I want only players who will be disciplined and who will work hard on behalf of Derby County. The attitude, work-rate and discipline of the players in pre-season training has been absolutely tremendous, and I'm not going to let any one incident, or any one individual, whoever it may be, affect the players' chance of success, which they richly deserve.'

The one big exception to the rosy picture Murphy painted of the players' attitude was Charlie George, for whom Derby had been open to offers for several months. And as for all those unreserved reassurances, well, Murphy was only six games into the new season when they were completely contradicted. Out he went – and, surprise, surprise, in came Docherty, who would have taken over even earlier if Hardy and company had not had to wait until Manchester United's agreement to pay him £50,000 for the unexpired portion of his contract with them. Even then, his acceptance of the Rams' three-year deal worth about £75,000 was complicated by the fact that he had pledged to start a two-year coaching appointment the following January with Lillestroem, the Norwegian champions. At the Baseball Ground, therefore, he embarked upon his ninth managerial post (there were to be half-a-dozen more) under the threat of being sued for breach of contract, though he insisted that the Norwegian club's president, Einar Kroken, 'aware that I would prefer to stay in England, told me to go ahead and take the job with Derby.'

It was with great reluctance that the other Lillestroem officials eventually withdrew their objections. 'There's a great danger when you go abroad that you become forgotten,' said Docherty. 'Anyway, how could I ignore a club like Derby?'

The new, and more substantial, rumours that Docherty was on his way were circulating as Colin Murphy, not yet told of developments, but fearing the worst, took his seat in the directors' box alongside George Hardy, only a few yards from where the vultures of the press were sitting, for a home match with Leeds in which the Rams were seeking their first League win of the season after three defeats and two draws. Heads turned to see if it was Docherty when late-comers arrived in the main stand, but he did not turn up until after the game in which Derby – from whose team the costly Hales had been dropped by Murphy, never to appear in it again – had to settle for a third draw as the visitors from Yorkshire took advantage of McFarland's missing most of the second half with another pulled hamstring by recovering from a two-goal deficit in the last quarter of an hour. The elusive victory was snatched away with only two minutes left.

Hales's place at the head of the attack was taken by Billy Hughes, an experienced forward Murphy had signed from Sunderland, originally on a month's loan just before the season started, and then for about £30,000 – quite a reduction on the offers of £200,000 from other clubs that had been rejected only a year earlier. Hughes, who had played in the same Sunderland youth team as Colin Todd, coached by Clough, had scored 74 goals in 286 League games since making his first-team debut at the age of eighteen early in 1967, but in the past season he had been unable to regain his place after asking to be omitted because of loss of confidence and form.

A Scottish international along with his brother John, of Glasgow Celtic, if only through a lone cap as a substitute against Sweden, he had been in the Sunderland team that shocked Leeds in the 1973 FA Cup final, and he again enjoyed himself against them by increasing the lead Gemmill gave Derby in the first half. His 65th-minute header opened his League account for the Rams, though he had netted twice in a pre-season 4-2 home win against the Dutch club Nijmegen after accompanying his new clubmates to Belgium for a tournament in Bruges. By early December he was Derby's top scorer with eight First Division goals, yet in the same month – at about the time Kevin Hector went to Vancouver Whitecaps – he was sold for £45,000 to Leicester City, in whose attack he briefly linked up with Roger Davies.

That deal was one of the first of the many that Tommy Docherty conducted during a tempestuous reign with the Rams that was to last for only one full season after the one in which he replaced Murphy, and included his suspension for a week by the club because of 'possible repercussions' after the sensational collapse of his libel case against Granada TV and the former Manchester United player Willie Morgan with his confession to telling 'a pack of lies'. Docherty said he had to give the transfer of Hughes 'a great deal of thought' when Leicester inquired about him, but he had no such reservations in parting with Hales. After watching the misfiring striker play for the Reserves he offered to lend him to any club, feeling that 'it would be unfair to ask anybody to pay a fee for Hales at this stage', but only a few days later – and just ten after taking over – he sold him to West Ham for £220,000 less than the £330,000 the player had cost when bought from Charlton in the face of competition from Sunderland, Tottenham, West Ham and the Belgian club Anderlecht.

The hirsute Hales, a piratical figure with his black beard and mass of hair, spent less than a year with the Hammers before rejoining Charlton for £75,500 and helping them out of the Third Division for the second time in his career. Whereas he scored only seven goals in thirty first-team games for Derby, he totalled 168 in 368 during his two spells with the Athletic before ending his League career with Gillingham, under his twelfth manager. In his post-Rams period, he achieved some unwanted notoriety in temporarily having his Charlton contract terminated after starting a fight during a match with team-mate Mike Flanagan, for which both were sent off, but, to this day, greying, beardless and thinning on top, he remains a legendary figure at the Valley, where supporters voted him the club's first 'Hall of Fame' winner.

Billy Hughes's career, which had already been checked by the double fracture of his right leg while with Sunderland and then his relegation to their second team in the North-Eastern League to the detriment of his testimonial season, failed to pick up again after reviving with the Rams. He followed a spell on loan to Carlisle by joining in the exodus to the United States, but San Joe Earthquakes sent him home after only one game without giving him a reason.

Hughes had a few offers from clubs in the lower divisions when he returned from America, but the 'something better' for which he hung on never came along, so after going on the dole, an experience he found 'degrading and humiliating', he entered the public-house trade, beginning at the Rising Sun in Derby before going back to the North-East. Up there he found what he called his 'football replacement' by managing the Stressholme Golf Club near Darlington.

On the afternoon of Derby's game against Leeds in which Hughes impressed as the replacement for the discarded Hales, Tommy Docherty had been planning to watch Mick, the eldest of his three sons (he and his wife Agnes also had a daughter) play for Sunderland against Bolton until he saw a flashed item on television suggesting that he was to be appointed as the Rams' new manager. He received a phone call from that quarter soon afterwards, and a car was sent to fetch him to Derby, where he first looked in at the Midland Hotel to make a phone call of his own – to Norway.

Colin Murphy had argued that it was fair to judge him only when he had completed his rebuilding of the team, claiming that 'we're very close to producing a young, vibrant side that can play for the club for the next seven or eight years'. But he was not to be granted even seven or eight weeks from the start of that season. He left the Rams' dressing room after the match with Leeds just as copies of the local football paper arrived, and as he walked towards the boardroom he could not avoid seeing the banner headline: DOCHERTY SET TO TAKE OVER. The official confirmation came at 5.40pm in a BBC interview George Hardy gave to Stuart Hall. I was among those who attended the subsequent press conference at which the chairman said Murphy took the news 'like the gentleman he is'.

Docherty, who, Hardy also said, 'has had a somewhat chequered career, but obviously has qualities we admire,' stated his willingness to employ Murphy as his assistant, but the deposed manager decided to look elsewhere. His route out of Derby took him, like Brian Clough, along the A52 to Nottingham – not back to Forest, but to Notts County, where he spent a year as assistant to Jimmy Sirrel (later a Derby chief scout) before returning to management in his own right with Lincoln City. 'Nothing could be harder than the inferno I walked through at Derby,' he said as he accepted a two-year contract in succession to Willie Bell, a former Leeds and Scotland full-back who had left to become a minister with the Campus Crusade for Christianity in the United States, but Lincoln ended the 1978-79 season where he had found them – at the foot of the Third Division.

Nothing daunted, Murphy led them back up two years later, entertaining and bemusing the frequenters of Sincil Bank with his strange brand of soccerspeak in his programme notes along the way. He twice crossed swords with Derby County (losing away, but drawing at home) in Division Three, to which the Rams had just made their further descent, before leaving 'by mutual consent' at the end of the 1984-85 season in which Lincoln went close to another relegation.

Murphy was then twice manager of Stockport, either side of being paid £25,000 for a year's coaching in Saudi Arabia, before rejoining Lincoln and promptly rousing them to regain, as 1987-88 champions of the GM Vauxhall Conference, the League place they had lost in pitching up at the bottom of the Fourth Division the season before. His subsequent moves took him to Leicester City as youth coach, Luton as assistant manager, Southend United as manager, Shelbourne, as the Irish club's fourth manager in just over a year, back to Notts County as general manager after a consortium taking over Cardiff City had wanted him as their manager, and then to Vietnam as the third man to be national coach there in six months.

He chose Vietnam from the number of offers he received through a London-based company that head-hunted for football associations in Europe and Asia because, having been a manager in every division of the Football League, he was 'fed up with driving up and down the motorways week in, week out'. But within a few months he resigned for 'personal reasons'. He had found out why previous coaches there had complained of a lack of co-operation, poor living and working conditions, and dismal team displays. Back in England, he shared in another promotion, from the Third Division, as assistant with Hull City to Peter Taylor, the former Crystal Palace, Tottenham and England forward who had been one of his successors at Southend.

With Colin Murphy out of the Derby door went Dario Gradi, who wasted little time in snapping up Alan Cork, a Derby-born Rams reserve, on a free transfer after becoming manager of Wimbledon, midway through their first season of League membership, when Allen Batsford resigned because of a personality clash with his chairman, Ron Noades.

Cork, like Phil Boyer, was a striker who made good elsewhere after failing to get into Derby's first team. He had spells with Lincoln, Sheffield United and Fulham, but became best known as one of the original members of the Wimbledon 'Crazy Gang' that soared, after a couple of false starts, from Fourth Division to Premiership. He was also in the side that caused one of the biggest FA Cup final upsets by beating Liverpool at Wembley in 1988, and he altogether exceeded 400 appearances for Wimbledon, scoring nearly 150 League goals, before retiring from playing in 1995 because he 'couldn't cope with training any more; it was driving me mad'. After that he was youth development officer at Fulham, and set up their School of Excellence before becoming assistant manager to Micky Adams. He followed Adams to Swansea in 1997, took over as manager when Adams walked out after only thirteen days on finding that money promised for new signings was not available, but was sacked eight months later and rejoined Fulham as a scout.

Dario Gradi guided Wimbledon to their first promotion to the Third Division in 1979, and although promptly relegated they bounced straight back at the end of the 1980-81 season during which he left to succeed Malcolm Allison as manager of Crystal Palace. The Selhurst Park club were going through one of their leanest times, and after being unable to stop them slipping out of the First Division in the short time available to him he lasted only ten months in the job as results continued to disappoint. He was then Orient's youth team coach before joining Crewe Alexandra in June 1983, and, after threatening to leave when fans barracked him as the team struggled, he settled in to become the longest-serving contemporary manager after first Brian Clough, at Forest, and then Joe Royle, at Oldham, had left their posts. His durability earned him a place in the National Football Museum's Hall of Fame.

The buying and selling of players was 'meat and drink' to Tommy Docherty, and after taking over from Murphy he wasted no time in negotiating the first of just over forty transfers, either in or out, he was to conduct in almost twenty months as manager of Derby County. And there might have been even more. Fran O'Brien, whose brother Ray was later taken on loan from Notts County by Peter Taylor, was to have accompanied winger Gerry Ryan from Bohemians, but failed a medical. The £250,000 transfer of Steve Sims, an England Under-21 centre-back, from Leicester City broke down for the same reason, though Leicester's contradiction of that verdict was borne out when Sims went on to play more than 300 games with Watford, Notts County and Aston Villa.

Another proposed deal went seriously awry when Frank Blunstone, the former Chelsea and England winger who had followed Docherty from Manchester United as his assistant, was severely censured, warned as to his future conduct, fined £500 and ordered to pay the costs, amounting to about £300, of a joint FA and SFA commission in Glasgow for making an illegal approach to Dave Narey, the Dundee United and Scotland defender he accosted at Brusssels airport while the player was travelling back from a European match. There was also a complaint from Bristol City concerning their centre-half, Gary Collier, but Derby were cleared of any wrong-doing on that occasion.

Two Manchester United players, Stuart Pearson and David McCreery, a Northern Ireland international, were others denied to Derby. Dave Sexton, Docherty's successor at Old Trafford, had already had more than enough departures from his staff to the Rams with Blunstone, Gordon Hill and a couple of young midfielders, Jonathan Clark and Ray Storey.

Despite all the unsettling comings and goings, Derby finished Docherty's first season with them only just below halfway in the table, and George Hardy publicly complimented him on the success of his first year with the Rams. Fans, too, waved banners in support at the only game the team played during Docherty's club-imposed ban after the collapse of his court case in November 1978, but how quickly it was all to change as the team plummeted towards relegation. There were ugly scenes when the 1978-79 season was wound up with a home defeat by Middlesbrough which left Derby thankful that Leeds had ensured their safety by beating QPR, who went down with Birmingham and Chelsea, the night before.

Hundreds of irate fans were loud in their displeasure as they swarmed in front of the main stand at the final whistle. I was among those in the press box who had to duck to avoid inaccurate missiles – clods of turf from the pitch, stones and even metal objects – that were aimed at the adjoining seats occupied by the directors. 'We hate the Doc,' they chanted. 'What a load of rubbish.' It was to be Docherty's last match as the Rams manager. No fewer than 29 players had been called upon that season – and Steve Buckley, the £163,000 full-back from Luton who had been missed by the Rams while with Burton Albion, was the only one with an ever-present record. He was to become the only player in the club's history to complete two separate centuries of consecutive League appearances.

No Taylor-made answer as problems mount

Rejection by Brian Clough, after so much confidence had been expressed about luring him back, hit Derby County hard as the teams he and Dave Mackay had built to become League champions were ripped apart in the course of two relegations that returned the Rams to the outposts of the Third Division under the weight of a debt that so nearly drove them out of existence. And what made it even worse for the club's suffering fans was that in the meantime Clough kept Nottingham Forest among the leading teams in the land.

Not that the last had been heard of a proposed return by Clough. The 1981-82 season in which Colin Addison joined the list of deposed Derby managers was less than a month old when there was talk of Clough and Peter Taylor being poised to return if a consortium of powerful businessmen could pull off a shares coup at the Baseball Ground.

Addison, a former York, Forest, Arsenal and Sheffield United forward who had guided League newcomers Hereford to promotion in 1972-73, taken Durban City to the South African title, and gained other managerial experience at Newport in addition to being assistant at Notts County and West Bromwich, had appeared a promising choice, after rejecting offers from Sunderland and Cardiff, when brought in following Tommy Docherty's return to the QPR club from which he had resigned within a month in 1968 because of a disagreement with chairman Jim Gregory.

'It was by mutual consent that I left Derby,' said Docherty, 'and I left as good friends.' But there was one irritant. He and Mary Brown were expecting a child, and, commenting on Derby's cancellation of the insurance on the Mercedes car they had bought him, he said: 'I think it is very small-minded and petty, especially considering they know Mary is pregnant.' There was also an unpleasant sequel when dealings between the Rams and the North American Soccer League came under scrutiny during a police investigation into the club's affairs. Stuart Webb cut short a holiday in Majorca to assist the inquiry, and Docherty was called back for questioning, but the police were unable to unearth anything convincing to warrant a prosecution and after eighteen months it was decided there was no case to be answered.

Under Docherty, things went from bad to worse for Derby after a dramatic improvement in his first season, and the relegation he had then only just avoided, putting his job in jeopardy in any case, could not be prevented by Addison. Furthermore, heavy expenditure, notably more than £1 million on Barry Powell, Alan Biley and David Swindlehurst, put the Rams in a parlous financial position.

So it was that millionaire Doug Ellis, looking for a way back into soccer after being ousted as Aston Villa's chairman, held several meetings with Clough and Taylor in which they were joined by Stuart Webb, who had by then temporarily left the Rams to concentrate on his travel business, and Stuart Dryden, who had been followed as Forest's chairman by Geoffrey MacPherson. Ellis, who was Webb's guest in an executive box hired for a Rams' home match, was said to be seeking more than 3,000 of the club's shares from the Bass Brewery at Burton-upon-Trent, in the belief that this would give him the leverage to gain a place on the County board. Derby's chief shareholder, John Kirkland, was a close friend of Webb and a keen advocate of Clough.

The Rams' directors had known of Ellis's interest for some time – as had Addison and his assistant John Newman, who were also wary of the rumours linking him with the reinstatement of Clough and Taylor not only in their managerial roles but also possibly as major shareholders. The threat posed by Ellis was believed to be at the root of Derby County's decision to launch their £350,000 survival scheme, followed by the announcement of a new public issue of 60,000 shares at £10 each.

These developments came at a time when there was much speculation about the position at Forest concerning Clough and Taylor, whom Ellis had previously tried to lure to Aston Villa. There had been an uneasy truce between Clough and a section of the Forest committee ever since Dryden, a close friend, had been ousted after his appearance in court on a charge of giving the Post Office false information, and of obtaining money by deception, in his running of a sub-post office at the Nottinghamshire village of Ruddington. Dryden had been found guilty and sent to prison for six months.

It was no secret either that Clough was unhappy about the size of Forest's crowds after the club's failure to win a major trophy or gain a place in Europe in the 1980-81 season, whereas he knew full well that fans would flock to the Baseball Ground if he were to return there. He also deplored the bad behaviour of some Forest supporters, threatening to close the Trent End terracing if it persisted. Taylor was understood to have become as disenchanted as Clough with the atmosphere at the City Ground, but thought they should 'stay to battle it out', and suggestions of their sharing in an Ellis coup died out when 'Deadly Doug', as one of his managers, Ron Atkinson, tagged him, faded from the Derby scene, soon to embark upon his third reign as Villa chairman.

Clough's name was inevitably again linked with Derby County, with talk of his being tempted back to take total control, when Addison's bold assertion that 'I certainly do not fear the sack' was refuted within two days by his dismissal towards the end of January in 1982. A source close to the Derby board said that 'Brian has already been sounded out and indicated he would be very interested indeed'. It was suggested that he had for long seen a managing directorship as 'the rightful reward for a top manager', and that he did not believe he would ever be offered such an opportunity with Forest, even though their coming change from being a private club, run by a committee, to a public company would enable them to appoint a paid managing director under new concessions by the FA.

Peter Taylor had already said he would see out the remaining eighteen months of his Forest contract, no matter what Clough did, and the optimism emanating from Derby was also swiftly discounted by Clough, whose contract had the same distance to run. From Majorca, where he was about to end a winter break, he said: 'I am not going to become Derby County's manager again. I have not had secret talks with them. I will not be applying for the managing director's job. That is my answer to speculation that I am about to return to the Baseball Ground. I have only ever applied for one job in my life. That was for the England job, and I won't be doing that again.'

Clough has been called 'the greatest manager England never had', but he would have been a certainty to succeed his arch rival Don Revie in that post if many experienced observers and most members of the general public had had anything to do with it. Peter Swales, then chairman of Manchester City and one of the officials charged with appointing the new England manager, freely conceded that 'public opinion forced us to give Cloughie an interview', and Sir Bert Millichip, another of those on the special sub-committee, was only too aware that 'Mr Clough was always the public's choice'. But there was never the slightest chance that someone so strong-willed, outspoken and contentious would be chosen, even though Swales also said that 'the Cloughie interview was something different, the greatest interview I was ever associated with. It was really good enough to have got him the job'.

Sir Harold Thompson, the FA's chairman in those days, was no admirer of Clough, and, according to Swales, 'he was raring to get at him and read the riot act to him.' But he was completely taken aback when Clough breezed in on the stroke of the appointed hour of 9am, looked at his watch, and said: 'I hope if I get this job I don't have to come in at nine o'clock on a Monday morning' (with a few expletives thrown in). 'That really floored Sir Harold,' said Swales. 'From then on Cloughie was most charming. He dominated the meeting and got on top of Sir Harold.'

'I just told them exactly the truth, that I was the best man for the job,' Clough said afterwards. 'They were worried that I was possibly going to take over the FA, which I would have done. I couldn't have stood for committees, and meetings with people who didn't have the remotest idea about football.'

Bobby Robson, then manager of Ipswich Town, and Lawrie McMenemy, manager of Southampton, were also interviewed by the committee, the other members of which were Sir Matt Busby (Manchester United), Dick Wragg (Sheffield United) and Dick Speake (Kent FA), but Ron Greenwood, West Ham's general manager and former team manager, had already been put in temporary charge of the England team until the appointment was made and he was confirmed in the post after avoiding defeat in his three matches as caretaker.

Other paths to international management were also blocked for Clough. In 1985 he was on the short list for the Republic of Ireland post that went to Jack Charlton, but Nottingham Forest refused to allow him to be interviewed for it. Just over two years later he was keen to accept the Welsh FA's offer of the part-time management of their national team ('I wanted a crack at the World Cup'), but again Forest's permission was withheld and the job went to Terry Yorath, one of the players who had been at Leeds during Clough's troubled short stay there.

So Clough had to make do at country level by accepting Greenwood's invitation to become part-time joint manager with Ken Burton of the England Youth squad, which included Steve Cherry, only for Burton to resign after the Atlantico Cup had been won in Las Palmas on the first occasion Clough and Taylor, who was taken on as coach, were involved. Burton said there had been no clash of personalities or ideas on how the squad should be run, but he felt it wrong that Clough should run the team on a match-days only basis. In less than a year, the Forest pair also quit, forced into deciding to devote their undivided attention to 'the far more important business' of managing their club. For the first time during their City Ground collaboration, Forest finished what was to be their last season together, 1981-82, in the bottom half of the table (though only just), and went straight out of the FA Cup at home to a Wrexham side heading down to the Third Division.

The reunion at Nottingham of the partnership that had revitalised the Rams came about as the result of a chance meeting similar to the one that had led to Taylor's becoming manager of Burton Albion. Taylor took his family on holiday to Majorca during the 1976 close season and bumped into Clough on the sea front at a part of the island popular with the footballing fraternity for summer breaks. Taylor, who also saw Des Anderson out there, had not been in touch with Clough since the previous Christmas, and they had time for only a quick chat during which his old side-kick, realising how miserable Taylor felt about having just missed promotion with

Brighton, invited him to meet him later for a longer talk. The upshot was Taylor's acceptance of Clough's invitation to go with Forest on their pre-season trip to Germany, and his subsequent agreement to throw in his lot with him again. He said:

'I reasoned I had failed at Brighton. The chairman, Mike Bamber, backed me to the hilt and gave me money to spend, but I didn't quite make it. For someone like me who has to win I felt I must go. That's all there was to it, and anybody who suggests I was tapped is a liar. Mike Bamber was genuinely distressed, but I like to think I left the club in a better state than I found it. My time there also helped to restore my faith in directors.'

The Anglo-Scottish Cup was Forest's first prize under the Clough-Taylor regime, but that was very small beer compared with what was so speedily to come. In the three seasons from 1977 to 1980 Forest were not only First Division champions but also won both the League Cup and European Cup twice in succession, besides beating Barcelona to lift the European Super Cup which they almost retained later the same year in losing to Valencia only on the away-goals rule. Forest also went 42 First Division games unbeaten, 51 without defeat at home (a run ironically ended by newly-promoted Brighton, who were at the bottom of the table), and trounced a depleted Ipswich side by the biggest margin, 5-0, in the annual Charity Shield match for ten years.

That deeply purple patch was prefaced in 1976-77 by promotion, if by only just scrambling into third place, to the First Division as Derby County narrowly avoided relegation from it under the management of Colin Murphy. The tempo, however, was too torrid to be sustained. Taylor was tired and depressed by the time, in May 1982, he told Clough he was going into retirement, uncomfortably conscious of the fact that some misfiring outlays on costly strikers had tarnished his Midas-like image as a recogniser of top talent. 'I have been in football for 36 years,' he said, 'and it is having its effect on me now.' His health had caused some concern since a heart attack as far back as the early 1970s, and his family's constant changes of home — well into double figures with his move from Brighton — had also taken their toll.

Yet, only six months into his retirement, Taylor was immediately interested in returning to the Baseball Ground when Addison's successor, the luckless John Newman, was also dispensed with by Derby. Clough consulted Taylor, whom he had already failed to persuade to rejoin Forest, about the possibility of their getting back together with the Rams, and after deciding against it he said he 'would have been less shocked if I had been run down by a car' when Taylor agreed to take the job himself, becoming Derby's sixth manager in as many years. Clough was having his differences with the Forest board ('they've been treating me like a rookie 30-year-old manager'), but he had a good working relationship with Fred Reacher, then the vice-chairman, and he was also deterred from leaving by the loyalty of fans at the Trent end of Forest's ground. 'They are the most foul-mouthed supporters in the land,' he said, 'but they are tremendously loyal to me – and I do mean me, not the club.'

Clough considered that Taylor 'must be crackers' for tackling 'a tremendously difficult task' at Derby, but at first his old partner looked like making a big success of it, once the unpleasant business about the alleged poaching of Roy McFarland and Mick Jones back from Bradford City had been got out of the way at considerable expense to the Rams. Mike Watterson, a snooker entrepreneur who had only recently become Derby's third new chairman since George Hardy (the two others were Richard Moore, an accountant who ran a knitwear and hosiery business at Long Eaton, and Bill Stevenson, a heating and ventilation engineer from Belper), threatened to drag the League 'through every court in the land even if it means liquidating our club' before having to accept the findings of the first case brought under Regulation 80 that had been introduced to 'give some teeth' to the gentleman's agreement covering attempts to induce another club's employee to break a contract. He could not say, however, that he had not been warned.

Graham Kelly, the League secretary, sent a letter, 'a warning shot across their bows' as he termed it, in which he drew attention to the regulations about illegal approaches, and Jack Dunnett, the League president, phoned Bradford City's ground to speak to Watterson before talks were opened with McFarland, who had kept a house in Derby since the Rams had given him a free transfer, and a silver tray as a memento of his fourteen seasons as a County player, at the end of the 1980-81 season.

Watterson emerged from the four-hour League inquiry complaining of 'a frame-up with the outcome clearly premeditated'. He added: 'We were led to believe the Commission was an inquiry into an alleged breach of regulations, with possibly a hearing to follow. Obviously, our manager Peter Taylor would have been a very relevant witness in our defence, but, unfortunately, he was not present. One of the reasons for that was because we thought we were on a fact-finding mission – only to discover ourselves to be in court. We were hung, drawn and quartered. Our barrister [Derby and Bradford City both included a lawyer in their five-man delegation] ripped every opposing argument to shreds, yet the Commission chose to ignore the fact.'

Bradford City's claim for compensation, in addition to the League fine of £10,000, was originally for £200,000, but Derby County had difficulty enough in meeting the £55,000 to which it was reduced by the League's valuation. 'You cannot strip the shirt off a naked man,' said Watterson in maintaining that he was not going to put up the money, nor did he intend asking other members of the board to do so. The answer was to split the payment into instalments, and after the first £20,000 had been handed over the amount left was about what Derby would have been allocated from that season's League fund. The League management committee saw the handing of that sum straight to Bradford City as the solution.

Peter Taylor believed that the timing of the appointments – McFarland as assistant but with the official title of team manager, and Jones as coach, both on a three-year contract – underlined Derby's straight dealing because they were made on the day the posts were advertised. 'I saw no point in hanging around once I knew that Roy and Mick were available,' he said. 'It would have been easy to have delayed things until after the Commission had met, but that would have been a sham – and we have nothing to hide.'

Bob Martin, the Bradford club's manager, saw it all very differently, as was to be expected of an angry man who had just seen his team, well placed in the top half of the Third Division and through to the quarter-finals of the League Trophy competition, abandoned only two days after reaching the second round of the FA Cup, and two days before 'the biggest game in our recent history' – a League Cup replay in which they lost at Old Trafford after having held the might of Manchester United to a goalless draw.

Derby County had just hit rock bottom in Division Two when Taylor rejoined them, and they promptly crashed to a fifth successive defeat in a League (Milk) Cup-tie at their bogy Birmingham ground during which Steve Powell and John McAlle, a Newman signing from Wolves, were ordered off. A more miserable start for Taylor could hardly have been visualised, but he brought about a remarkable improvement with a side into which he introduced Archie Gemmill, Bobby Davison, an £80,000 striker from Halifax Town who was to be the Rams' top scorer for four consecutive years, Paul Futcher, a £115,000 defender from Oldham, Paul Hooks, who cost £60,000 from Notts County, and the former Forest king-pin Kenny Burns, on loan from Leeds and subsequently signed on a free transfer. From New Year's Day until the beginning of May the Rams lost only one of eighteen League games, and although they did not escape from last place until the end of March, they avoided relegation in the amazingly exalted final position of thirteenth – their highest all season – and, above all, they knocked Nottingham Forest, then fourth in the First Division, out of the FA Cup.

Forest were outplayed, even though the second goal, by Ilkeston-born Andy Hill, in Derby's first win in the competition for five years was not scored until the last minute. Gemmill, man of the match, netted the first with a wonderful curling free-kick beyond the clutches of Steve Sutton, a

Derbyshire-born goalkeeper who had been missed by the Rams as a schoolboy but was to play for them later, before limping off to a standing ovation with a pulled hamstring. 'Losing at Derby was a terrible blow to the club and me,' said Brian Clough. 'I have never known the feeling to linger so long. I could not read a newspaper. I could not watch television.' Victories for Forest on each of their next four visits to the Baseball Ground made up for all that.

Another late goal, by Kevin Wilson, an Addison find from Banbury after having trials with Sheffield United and Stoke, put paid in the next round to Chelsea, a club Wilson was to join after becoming a Northern Ireland international with Ipswich. It was greeted, as had been a late penalty equaliser by Gemmill in the previous home League game against Leeds, by a barrage of seats thrown onto the pitch by aggrieved visiting supporters – hooliganism that cost Derby £7,500-worth of sponsorship and brought them stern warnings from the FA. The Rams were narrowly beaten by Manchester United when again drawn at home, but that disappointment was transformed into delight by the avoidance of relegation which, with the sale of £400,000-worth of season tickets, Taylor rated 'equal to winning the European Cup'.

For the second consecutive season Derby entered their final game still not sure of safety, though the outcome of other matches again ensured they would have escaped in any event. Their Fulham visitors needed a win to reach the First Division in the hope that Leicester City, rivals for the third promotion spot behind QPR and Wolves, would be unable to beat Burnley at Filbert Street, but the points went to the Rams through a classic volleyed goal by Davison. It came a quarter of an hour from the end of what would have been normal time if Darwen referee Ray Chadwick had not been forced to abandon play 78 seconds early by his reckoning when fans around the touchline encroached onto the pitch. The League's rejection of Fulham's protest that the result should not be allowed to stand sent Leicester up after being held to a scoreless draw, and was generally accepted outside Craven Cottage as a fair decision considering that, on the clocks of neutrals, the Baseball Ground game had lasted 94 minutes with the allowance of a mysterious amount of stoppage time.

That, however, was a good as it got for Peter Taylor. Like Newman after warding off relegation, he was unable to see out another season as the Rams' manager. His slide down the slope to a sacking started during the summer when Watterson resigned after only seven months as chairman, declaring that Taylor had 'become uncontrollable'. The FA Cup again brought some unexpected welcome relief, this time with a run to the quarter-finals, but in the League it was downhill all the way for Taylor from the first day of the 1983-84 season on which the unimpressive form shown in the warm-up friendlies was ominously confirmed in a 0-5 trouncing at Chelsea.

Nine weeks later, with Derby next to the bottom of the table with the worst goals-against record in the League, there was talk of Watterson, then Chesterfield's vice-chairman, being ready for an amazing comeback as chairman of the crisis-torn Rams. He still had a twelve per cent shareholding in Derby County, with £20,000 on loan to the club plus cash guarantees, and his master plan was said to have been agreed in principle with John Kirkland, his successor as chairman at the Baseball Ground, as the price for saving Derby from new threats of bankruptcy. Kirkland admitted the club's players were owed a fortnight's wages.

Under the Watterson plan Taylor was to be dismissed along with McFarland, Jones and chief scout Ken Gutteridge, and Watterson was insisting on massive economies in the playing staff. Stuart Webb, who had returned to the club and become chief executive, and fellow director Trevor East were not expected to survive a boardroom shake-up, with Brian Henton, a former Grand Prix racing driver, and Geoff Glossop, a local computer millionaire, lined up as replacements, both promising to inject £50,000 into the club. But the players were paid, Derby's directors decided to try to survive with their own money-raising scheme after first trying to work out a financial agreement involving the City Council and County Council, and Webb did not only, like East, survive as a director, but also became chairman. The frustrated Watterson filed writs to recover £33,000 owed to him in loans and guarantees.

The Rams were not alone in their plight. Bradford City, Bristol City, Charlton, Crystal Palace, Preston, Swansea and Wolves were also flying distress signals. Aston Villa, recent European champions, and newly promoted Leicester City, reported huge losses. Over at Forest, financial problems forced Brian Clough to shelve his aversion to live televised matches and allow his club's UEFA Cup-tie with Celtic to be broadcast live in Scotland.

By the beginning of 1984 Derby's debt had risen towards £1½ million (a very real threat to their existence then, but dwarfed by the £30 million and more to which it soared with their fall from the Premiership in 2002) and Watterson felt moved to stir up further controversy by saying: 'At the final count I must hold myself responsible because I made the biggest mistake of my life in signing Peter Taylor. When I joined the board in November 1982, there was a definite cash flow problem. During the last close season Taylor was getting out of hand, offering money for players without checking whether he had that money. I did my nut. I resigned, but I still have a substantial stake in the club. I think the basic problem has been caused by the thoroughly irresponsible way the club has been run at director and managerial level for the past six years.'

Derby's directors sprang to Taylor's defence with a specially prepared statement in which they stood by the contracts Watterson had granted the manager and his backroom staff, and they unanimously felt that Taylor, 'with his vast experience at all levels in the game is the man for the job.' They were soon to take a very different view, however, as the return to the Third Division loomed ever nearer and the club went perilously close to being driven out of business.

Early in February Derby County were served a winding-up notice by the Inland Revenue, who were owed £129,000, and they faced a petition to that effect after hopes of an arrangement with a Hong Kong-based multi-national conglomerate had been dashed. It was then that the publishing tycoon Robert Maxwell appeared on the scene. Foiled in his attempt to merge Oxford United, of which he was chairman, with the Reading club under the name of Thames Valley Royals, and also thwarted in making offers for the control of first Birmingham City, then Manchester United, he was still keen to help even after the High Court judge had refused to approve his take-over bid for the Rams.

After the winding-up petition had three times been adjourned, Maxwell's agreement to buy the Baseball Ground from the National Westminster Bank for £300,000 aided the clearing of the tax debt as Stuart Webb's untiring efforts to save the club at last bore fruit. Within days, Derby County Council bought the Baseball Ground and leased it to Maxwell, who received rent from the club. Maxwell, who was to meet a mysterious death by drowning off his yacht, became an unpopular chairman after Webb had stepped down to vice-chairman, imposing a block on costly transfers and rarely being seen at the ground. He was succeeded as chairman by his son Ian before the Maxwell dynasty was bought out by money from the sale of internationals Dean Saunders and Mark Wright to Liverpool in 1991. Webb became managing director and associate director, but again left the Rams in the early 1990s.

Preliminary settlement was reached for a 50p in the pound payment to unsecured creditors, 75 per cent of whom accepted to clear debts of £275,000. Next day, 4 April 1984, Taylor left the Rams, 'by mutual consent,' after being called into lunchtime discussions with the re-formed board chaired by Webb, who, ironically, had been instrumental in bringing him out of retirement.

This came in the wake of a defeat at Barnsley in which, under the handicap of having Burns sent off in his first match as the club's signed player, Derby conceded five goals in one game for the third time that season, and shortly after the freakish ending of the welcome diversion of the FA Cup run. After accounting in the third round for a Cambridge team booked for last place in the Second Division, the Rams remained so consistently fallible in the League that Taylor conceded that his own men would be the underdogs when they were drawn at home against Telford United, the last non-League side left in the competition.

He took them off for training at Scarborough in the hope that the sea air would stir up the blood, but his worst fears were desperately close to being realised as a hat-trick by Davison, who earlier in the season had been dropped for literally missing the bus, to a match at Blackburn, by oversleeping, enabled them to squeeze through by the odd goal of five. Indeed, the visitors from the Alliance Premier League were right out of luck when the ball rolled along the Derby goal-line before bouncing out off the far post, and they left convinced they should have been awarded a last-minute penalty. They also thought the Rams' third goal should have been disallowed for offside.

Andy Garner, a Derbyshire lad from the Alfreton area who had first played for the Reserves two years earlier at the age of fifteen, made an impressive senior debut in the next round as Derby reached the last eight for the first time since 1977 with a much livelier display. First Division Norwich City would have been beaten by more than 2-1 but for the brilliance of a man who almost missed the match through illness – Chris Woods, the former Forest goalkeeper who went to play nearly fifty times for England. Garner, strongly built and skilful but somewhat lacking in pace, was to score some valuable goals in Derby's 1985-86 Third Division promotion season (during which Telford were hit for six when back at the Baseball Ground for another FA Cup-tie), and one of the most notable of them came at the home of his next club, Blackpool, where he became a big favourite.

The pairing with Plymouth, a lowly Third Division club, in the quarterfinals raised the Rams' hopes of a place in the semis, even though they had to travel to Devon and, on top of the increasing threat to their existence, continued to be haunted by the prospect of relegation that made Peter Taylor admit to feeling 'staggered, sickened and frightened'. He told Mike Beale in the *Sun*: 'Over the past three months I have certainly found out who my real friends are. I'm staggered at the number of people queuing up to kick us in the teeth. The hostility to a club in our position is frightening.'

Another alarming possibility arose – that Derby County would be kicked out of the Cup without getting to Plymouth. They had already been overdue in paying Telford their share of the gate, and when the same thing happened to Norwich, and the Rams also delayed sending in their share to the FA pool, an official warning of expulsion was issued. Those outstanding dues from Cup receipts were settled with only hours to spare.

With that worry out of the way, even the supreme contradiction of reaching Wembley as a club newly consigned to Division Three became a

Taylor-made prospect for Derby County, provided that they could survive being wound up, when an astounding late save by Steve Cherry ensured a goalless draw at a Home Park ground into which nearly 34,500 were packed – Argyle's biggest crowd for nine years. But the replay was a bitter let-down for the Rams, offsetting the relief of the first adjournment of the winding-up petition with which it coincided. They were beaten by a goal that made Plymouth the first Third Division team to reach the last four since Crystal Palace in 1976, and only the sixth in League history. And it was scored in what for them was a most deplorable manner – direct from an inswinging corner-kick taken by left-winger Andy Rogers after eighteen minutes.

There was also only one goal in Plymouth's semi-final at Villa Park – but it went to Watford, who lost to Everton in the final.

After their sorry Cup exit, Derby went through three more League games without a win before that fateful board meeting at which Taylor bowed out. Stuart Webb, who had taken over as chairman from John Kirkland only three hours earlier, said that 'we have all made sacrifices these past few months, but Peter Taylor has made the biggest sacrifice of all. In light of the club's financial difficulties, he has accepted a nominal amount of compensation'. This was believed to be about £5,000, whereas the two years remaining on his contract were worth just over £40,000. Taylor revealed the heartache behind his agreement to stand down after seventeen months in charge by saying:

'I was getting a lot of stick, and the adverse publicity was affecting my family. The noose around my neck was the length of contracts players were on when I came back to the club. There were six players in the side against Barnsley last Saturday I have tried to get rid of at some time or other. I have to admit that inside I am shattered. My main problem has not been the money the players were earning, but the length of their contracts. I've no serious complaints, though. I was allowed to do my job without interference, and given money to spend.'

Roy McFarland, as acting manager, was left with nine matches in which to try to pull Derby out of the mire. It was a hopeless task, but he made a good stab at it with wins in each of the last four games at the Baseball Ground, which seven previous visitors had left with all three points. Away from home, however, there was only a draw at mid-table Leeds to set against four defeats, and the Rams needed the miracle that never came when, on the penultimate Saturday, a Newcastle side inspired by Kevin Keegan but so soon and so sensationally to lose their manager, Arthur Cox, to Derby County, celebrated promotion by sending them packing from St James' Park with four goals to which there was no response.

On the following Wednesday Archie Gemmill, who had been restored to the team after his tiff with Taylor, made an emotional Baseball Ground farewell as two Davison goals against Portsmouth earned the Rams a fourth successive home victory for the first time in six years. A booking for protesting too much about not being given a penalty was just an over-enthusiastic side-issue in a typically wholehearted display by the busy little Scot, but it was a great pity that he should mar his last match for Derby at Shrewsbury in the final match of the season three days later by misfiring when he did have the chance to score from the spot even though Davison was outside the area when brought down by goalkeeper Steve Ogrizovic. The two other penalties Harrogate referee David Hutchinson awarded that afternoon, from both of which Shrewsbury scored in their 3-0 win, were also contentious.

Having returned to Forest as a coach, Gemmill was near his 39th birthday when he diverted from supervising the juniors in the Nottingham Thursday League to make a playing comeback with the Reserves for a game against Leeds in which sixteen-year-old David Carlin, son of Willie, made his debut at right-back. Five years later, in 1991, Gemmill was suspended as coach to the second team when Clough returned from holiday to find that in his absence the Central League title had been thrown away through the loss of three matches out of four. On reinstatement, he stayed on Forest's coaching staff for three more years before again leaving the club and going into joint management with John McGovern at Rotherham.

When Gemmill ended his Derby playing days there was a distinct possibility that McFarland would be going too, for, although the former England centre-half was on a short list of four for the vacancy left by Taylor, there was every indication that the appointment would go to someone from outside. So it proved, with Cox brought in after a breakdown in his negotiations for a new contract at Newcastle, but McFarland was asked to stay on as his assistant and accepted with 'a certain sense of relief about not being required to leave along with Peter because he brought me here and I must obviously share responsibility for our poor results.'

There was an unpleasant sequel when McFarland needed a police escort in the face of a hostile reception when he returned to Valley Parade for a match in which Derby were beaten by Bradford City, but on a happier note he was in charge of the Reserves when the Rams became the first Third Division club (though they were promoted that season) to win the Central League title in 1986.

The Cox-McFarland partnership prospered with two promotions before Cox, whose nine-year reign was the longest by a Derby manager since George Jobey, resigned because of severe back trouble soon after another promotion had been missed in the 1991-92 play-offs. McFarland then finally, but first temporarily, became manager in his own right, but his hold on the post deteriorated from the tentative to the precarious when, in the autumn of 1994, another boardroom power struggle ended in victory for the club's new owner, Lionel Pickering, who had made his millions from the sale of the Trader group of free newspapers he had built up in the Derby area after his return from working as a journalist in Australia. Brian Fearn, the successor to Ian Maxwell, was ousted as chairman when Pickering won a crucial poll at an extraordinary meeting of shareholders after being beaten on a show of hands, and he failed in the High Court to take out an injunction forbidding Pickering to use his decisive 78 per cent shareholding.

McFarland's relationship with Pickering had become strained since the Rams' defeat by Leicester City in the previous season's Division One play-off final, and it became worse when he backed the sale of striker Paul Kitson to Newcastle against Pickering's wishes. He was allowed to see out his contract, but learned it would not be renewed after Derby had been beaten by Southend in their last home match of the 1994-95 season. The Rams had revived from languishing in the bottom half of the table for much of that campaign, winning five games in a row at one stage despite the selling of £6½ million-worth of players to ease the financial problems, but another defeat in their final fixture, at Watford, left them in ninth place, ten points away from the play-offs. 'This has been a difficult decision,' said the new chairman, 'but the board has given him his chance over the past two seasons. Gates are down, and the fans do expect Derby County at least to make the play-offs.'

So McFarland, not long turned 47, ended an association with the club that had lasted for 28 years apart from his eighteen months as Bradford City's player-manager. In seeking his successor, the Rams were refused permission by Manchester United to approach Steve Bruce, then skipper at Old Trafford, and they twice interviewed Brian Horton, a promotion winner with Brighton and Hull, before appointing Jim Smith to his ninth managerial post in 26 years. The popular 'Bald Eagle' had been chief executive of the League Managers' Association for the three months since his dismissal by Portsmouth, with whom he had suffered the double whammy of missing the FA Cup final in a penalty shoot-out with Liverpool and promotion to the Premiership in a play-off against Leicester City. He transformed the Rams into a Premiership force in his first season, and enjoyed several years of further success before over-staying his welcome as, under a debt of calamitous proportions, the club plunged into another decline that also ejected Lionel Pickering from office.

The next managerial door opened to Roy McFarland with his link-up at Bolton with Colin Todd that lasted only six months before his sacking as scapegoat for the Wanderers' immediate relegation from the Premiership. He then worked as northern scout for Glenn Hoddle during the former

Tottenham midfielder's spell in charge of the England team before piloting Cambridge United to promotion to the Second Division and the last sixteen of the FA Cup.

Life in the higher League sphere was far from comfortable, however, and near the end of his second season of struggle he was dismissed on the same late February day in 2001 that Bruce Rioch resigned at Wigan. McFarland next managed Torquay United, but he resigned from there in less than a year over the decision, as part of an economy drive, to release David Preece, who had followed him from Cambridge as player-coach. The diminutive Preece, a former England 'B' midfielder, had shared some 500 appearances between Walsall and Luton before costing Derby County £75,000 after failing to agree terms for the renewal of his contract with the Hatters, but he turned out in only fifteen first-team game for the Rams – three of them as a substitute – and then found his way to Cambridge after being loaned out to Birmingham and Swindon.

From Torquay Preece moved to Telford United, then of the Nationwide Conference but soon to go into liquidation, as assistant to Mick Jones, for whom there had been no room in the new Derby set-up following Taylor's exit. After having a constant battle under the threat of bankruptcy as manager of Halifax Town on leaving the Rams, Jones reached Telford via Peterborough (where he was briefly team manager when Noel Cantwell, the former Eire full-back to whom he had been assistant, was made general manager) and Notts County, with a spell scouting for Blackpool intervening.

As a player, Jones had made up for not getting into Derby County's first team by being in Fourth Division championship sides with Notts County and Peterborough United. After that he had taken over as manager of Kettering Town at a time when they were threatened with closure, and in one season, 1978-79, had guided them to the FA Trophy final, in which they lost to Stafford Rangers, and to runners-up behind Worcester City in the Premier Division of the Southern League. That had led him to two seasons as manager of Mansfield Town, during which he had been unable to avert relegation from the Third Division before joining McFarland as Bradford City's coach.

On his return to Notts County, he was coach and assistant to manager Neil Warnock when the Meadow Lane club gained promotion to the First Division through the 1991 play-offs, but both were dismissed as poor results persisted after prompt relegation.

For Roy McFarland, the path in management led back to Derbyshire with Chesterfield, where Arthur Cox had been one of his predecessors.

The Break-Up of a Big Friendship

Peter Taylor was on holiday back in Majorca when he died on 4 October 1990, at the age of 62, halfway through the sixth year of his second retirement after leaving Derby County for the last time. He went to his grave without being able to resolve the big bust-up that had stung Brian Clough into vowing he would never have anything to do again with the man who for so long had been his partner and biggest friend.

Until then the worst of their differences had occurred during what Taylor called the 'Black October' of 1980 in which Nottingham Forest were knocked out of the European Cup, lost heavily to Watford in the League Cup, and were caught up in controversy over transfer deals involving the departure of one striker, Garry Birtles, to Manchester United, and the arrival of another, Peter Ward, from Brighton as his replacement. But there had been nothing to compare with the row that blew up between them when Taylor signed John Robertson for Derby County behind Clough's back.

After the repairing of the rift arising from the Ward deal, completed as Clough changed his mind about disagreeing with Taylor's high assessment of the player, Taylor asserted that their friendship would 'weather any storm'. When Taylor left Forest, Clough dismissed gossip that their relationship had been fractured with a typically forthright comment: 'Fall out? That's crap.' But the Robertson affair proved both of them very mistaken to believe that nothing could ever happen to cause an irreparable split. In the remaining seven years before Taylor's death they exchanged what Clough called in his autobiography 'just a few brief words on the telephone', and he could not even remember what they were about.

Robertson had his career transformed by Clough and Taylor. Scruffy, overweight and out of form, he was on Forest's transfer list when Clough took over at the City Ground. 'You're a tramp, lad – a boozer and a bloody disgrace,' the outspoken manager told him the first time they met. Clough appreciated, however, that here was a player who had not realised just how good he could be, and he gave him a hard time in stirring him out of his lethargy. 'I hated him at first,' Robertson said later. 'Then I saw why he was having a go. He wanted to gee me up.'

The outcome was a revelation, given added impetus after Taylor turned up. Switched to the left wing, the slimmed-down Robertson rose to play for Scotland and become one of the finest players ever to wear a Forest shirt – scorer of the winning goal in a European Cup final, and an indispensable member of the team that carried the club through the most prosperous period in its long history.

Robertson was out of contract and in his thirtieth year when Taylor sought him for Derby, but Clough felt confident of keeping him after, as he said, offering a three-year deal worth £900 a week. It was therefore with fierce resentment that the first Clough learned of losing his man was in a phone call from his wife while he was taking a break from football by walking the Pennine Way for a children's charity. He felt so strongly about not having heard about it first from Taylor that he called him 'a rattlesnake' in a highly-critical newspaper article. Taylor retorted by describing that outburst as 'poisonous, vicious and disgraceful', adding that it was 'the sort of thing I have come to expect from a person I now regard with great distaste.'

Robertson said he had decided to move to the Baseball Ground because, contrary to what Clough had claimed, Forest would not offer him a three-year contract. He was reported to be getting £500 a week from Derby, who also had to pay Forest £135,000 – a transfer fee, set by tribunal, which caused the Rams to be temporarily barred by the League from buying other players for getting behind with the instalments. The financial depths to which Derby had descended were also made clear when FIFA banned Yugoslav-born Yakka Banovic, an Australian international goalkeeper, from continuing to play for them until they had paid the Melbourne club Heidelberg United the last instalment on his £40,000 transfer fee. Debts had piled up more because of Colin Addison's big spending than that of Tommy Docherty, who had not been excessively in the red despite the proliferation of his deals that had made a much-weakened Derby County more like Debris County according to the sick joke that went around, and Peter Taylor had shown a loss of more than a quarter of a million pounds on his dabbles into the transfer market.

Banovic, a spectacular performer unfortunate to be cast into a side on the slide, played fewer than forty times in the Rams' first team before returning to Australia. Neither did the money spent on Robertson bring the hoped-for dividends, making his move as unproductive as those involving Birtles and Ward. Birtles cost Manchester United £1,250,000, but rejoined Forest for £275,000; Forest paid £400,000 for Ward, but let him go back to Brighton on loan before he was sold to Seattle Sounders, who suffered a financial collapse while still owing £70,000 of the £100,000 fee.

Robertson underwent a cartilage operation early in the year he joined Derby, and he needed another one after having to be substituted in only his fourteenth League game for the Rams. That ended his international career, in which the last two of his 28 appearances for Scotland were made as a Derby player. On his return to fitness the task of putting some spark back into an ailing team was beyond him, but he was a regular choice in the following 1984-85 season back in the Third Division before returning to Forest on a free transfer. He was afterwards with several non-League clubs before scouting for Norwich and assisting his former Forest clubmate Martin O'Neill at Glasgow Celtic.

In his second spell with Forest, Robertson added only a dozen games, one of them as substitute, to just over 500 he had played before going to Derby, but Brian Clough really hit the jackpot in his post-Taylor period with the acquisition of such players as Stuart Pearce, Des Walker, Neil Webb and his own son Nigel, who between them totalled nearly 180 England appearances, plus a young Irishman, Roy Keane, who went on to win all soccer's top honours with Manchester United.

Clough's other signings for Forest during that time included Colin Todd, who had preferred Everton to Southampton when controversially transferred out of Derby by Tommy Docherty for £300,000. Todd had been welcomed by the Goodison club's manager, Gordon Lee, as 'the sort I would like my lads at Everton to grow up like', but the move had not worked out well for him. Lee upset him by switching him to full-back, but recouped his outlay when Todd rejoined Archie Gemmill at Birmingham City. It was after three seasons at St Andrew's, during which he helped in promotion from the Second Division but, most un-Todd-like, was twice ordered off, that he was brought back into the Clough fold – and in only the second of fewer than fifty games for Forest he was sent off again. He joined Oxford United's final push to the Third Division title in 1984, then followed a summer with Vancouver Whitecaps by making the last three of his career total of nearly 780 League and Cup appearances with Luton Town.

Ronnie Fenton, Peter Taylor's successor as Forest's assistant manager, had originally been recruited by Brian Clough to ease the workload of Jimmy Gordon (who retired in 1980, five years before his death in Derby at the age of eighty) after turning down the chance to become No 2 to his successor as manager at Meadow Lane, Jimmy Sirrel – the post that went to Colin Murphy. Clough also took Alan Hill from Notts County to work on the youth and scouting side, and made Liam O'Kane, the Irishman who had filled the gap at the heart of Forest's defence left by Terry Hennessey's transfer to Derby, coach to the first team.

In Clough's remaining eleven seasons at the City Ground after losing Taylor, Forest three times ended third in the First Division, were twice losing semi-finalists and once beaten finalists in the FA Cup (the one big trophy to elude him), again twice winners of the League Cup in successive years, and once losing finalists. They also won the Simod Cup, as the Full Members Cup had been renamed, the Zenith Data Systems Cup, and the final, if on penalties, in the Mercantile Credit Football League Centenary Festival at Wembley. Clough, having become the first manager since Herbert Chapman to win the First Division title with two clubs, also became the first to complete a domestic cup double when Forest, 4-3 winners against Everton after extra-time, added the Simod Cup to the League Cup in 1989, and he was in line for a unique treble until Liverpool won the replayed FA Cup semi-final after the Hillsborough disaster.

In the end, however, Clough went on too long, and he lost his golden touch as his addiction to alcohol took its toll. He did suggest he would retire at fifty, recommending either Fenton or Orient manager Frank Clark as his successor, but, with Forest frequently fearing that he would be leaving as rumours of other openings for him circulated, he went eight years beyond that age before stepping down in favour of Clark, the former Newcastle full-back whose playing career he had revived, at the end of the 1992-93 season.

For much of his time with Forest, Clough refrained from the frequent opinionated utterings in public that had stirred up so much controversy at Derby, but he still went close to being charged with bringing the game into disrepute by making derogatory remarks about the chairmen of Football League clubs, and also had to apologise to Manchester United for criticising them on the *Saint and Greavsie* Show conducted by Ian St John, the former Liverpool and Scotland forward, and Jimmy Greaves, the sharpshooter who had graced the attacks of Chelsea, Tottenham and England. Otherwise, Clough's TV image was kept alive more by impressionists such as Mike Yarwood than by himself. He told Doug Weatherall, of the *Daily Mail*:

'I have turned down a lot of things. I have no desire, and see no sense, in talking to journalists and TV. For six months I used to get up at half-past five on a Sunday morning to go to London for the *Big Match* programme. It's ridiculous when you think about it. *London Weekend* asked me to go on TV for a period of three or four months, and Forest were keen for me to do it, but Barbara, my wife, said: 'In no circumstances.'

Clough's brushes with Forest's board were an unsettling factor, and towards the end of his reign his increasingly eccentric ways did seem to some to be more of a liability than an asset, with supporters beginning to question a few of his team selections. He signed what was to be the last extension of his contract in November 1992. It was for twelve months, but although he indicated that he would like to carry on until his sixtieth birthday that was never a serious possibility as his deteriorating health, all too apparent from his blotched countenance, cost him his hitherto sure touch. Throughout that season – the first in the Premiership which Derby County missed also entering as inaugural members with their defeat in the play-offs

– his team laboured in the depths of the table, and at one stage he was so confused that he attempted to send on as a substitute a player he had pulled off in the first half.

There were still about eight weeks of the season to go when Forest's board decided, by five votes to two, to part with him, and Fred Reacher, then the chairman, said it was one of the saddest days of his life when he announced the retirement of the League's then longest-serving contemporary manager on 26 April 1993, during the week preceding the club's last home game of the season.

Defeat in that match, and with it relegation, was the harshest possible way in which to go out, all the more so for a man who had brought so much footballing glory to Derby and Nottingham. In an emotional City Ground farewell, the playing of *Memories* and *My Way* over the public address system fittingly set the scene for the visit of Sheffield United. Forest kicked off still with a faint mathematical chance of staying up, but it faded on the half-hour when Glyn Hodges curled his shot beyond the reach of goalkeeper Andrew Marriott, and it disappeared midway through the second half as the unmarked Brian Gayle completed the scoring with a header from Charlie Hartfield's cross. Another defeat in their final fixture at Ipswich a week later, Clough's 1,184th as a manager, left Forest firmly anchored at the foot of the table – four points behind Middlesbrough and nine adrift of Crystal Palace, the two other clubs that went down.

In his retirement, continuing to live in the Derby area, Brian Clough took up the big challenge of trying to control his drinking habits. He finally accepted that he had a drink problem after collapsing and being taken to a clinic towards the end of 1996. In his autobiography *Walking on Water* he admitted that alcoholism had cost him the ability to manage properly in his final season, that he had spent time drinking when he should have been doing other things. 'If you do something to excess something has to suffer somewhere,' he said, and it caught up with him at the beginning of 2003 when he had to have a liver transplant to save his life. The operation was carried out at the Freeman Hospital in Newcastle-upon-Tyne after he had met the National Health Service's two most essential criteria for a transplant – he was undergoing counselling for reformed alcoholics, and tests showed that he had not had an alcoholic drink for the past six months.

'He is very lucky,' his consultant Derek Manas said afterwards. 'He had only weeks or months to live. I would have been worried if we had waited another two months. Now he is being his old self, teaching us all how to play golf and telling us what, and what not, to do.'

Cancer was also found during the operation, however, and it was that, of the stomach, which caused his sudden death at Derby's City Hospital in September of the following year at the age of 69, leaving his family expressing their 'heartfelt thanks' to the relatives of the liver donor 'for allowing Brian to have 21 months of health and happiness'. Only a few months earlier he had attended his European Cup teams' 25-year reunion dinner. He had mellowed in his later years, and he deeply regretted that the split between himself and Peter Taylor had never been healed. He tried to make up for that by attending his old partner's funeral at the packed St Peter's Church in the Nottinghamshire village of Widmerpool, a short walk from the Taylor home, and dedicated to him the autobiography he wrote with John Sadler. It bore this inscription:

'Still miss you badly. You once said: "When you get shot of me there won't be as much laughter in your life." You were right.'

The tributes paid to Brian Clough at the time of his own death were glowing and extensive, justly hailing him as one of the finest managers soccer has ever known. Nigel Doughty, Forest's chairman at that time, said that Nottingham had become synonymous with Robin Hood and Brian Clough. Jeremy Keith, Derby County's chief executive, described him as 'our club's greatest-ever manager, and, in the eyes of Rams supporters, the best the world has ever seen'. As Bertie Wooster said of Jeeves, he does indeed stand alone, especially as Robin Hood has now been controversially replaced by the letter 'N' as the Nottingham symbol, and attention drawn to the claims for him as a Yorkshireman.

Of course, like all of us, Brian Clough was not perfect, but it was unfortunate that five years into his retirement he should have been a central figure in the FA's inquiry into alleged illicit payments after Alan Sugar, while Tottenham's chairman, had said in court, during his dispute with Terry Venables over control of the London club, that Clough 'liked a bung'. Clough strongly denied such allegations ('asking me what it's like to make money out of transfers is like asking: "What's it like to have VD?" I don't know. I've never had it'), but he would have faced misconduct charges if the FA had not decided that it would not be in the best interests of the game to pursue them after receiving medical advice concerning his deteriorating health.

Clough never had bestowed upon him the knighthood so many so vehemently felt he deserved, but honours aplenty came his way. He was appointed OBE; granted the freedom of the cities of Nottingham and Derby; had a grandstand named after him at the City Ground and a bronze bust of himself erected in the reception area there; received an honorary degree from Nottingham University for his services to football and the city; and had a reception suite for VIP visitors at Derby County's Pride Park named after him.

Those, in addition to his Manager of the Year award and numerous Manager of the Month accolades, were just some of the distinctions that came to him in his lifetime, quite apart from all the prizes his teams gained. His death brought more as committees at the two 'unfashionable' clubs he had taken to the heights in the East Midlands got down to deciding upon further lasting recognition.

On the night of Thursday, 21 October 2004, Derby and Forest fans came together in the crowd of some 11,000 who braved torrential rain, gusting winds and biting cold to mourn and pay their respects at a special memorial service that was switched from Derby Cathedral to Pride Park because of the large number who wanted to attend. Many more would have been present but for the vile weather. Not all who had obtained tickets ventured out.

Pictures from Brian Clough's playing and managerial careers were shown on the screen that displayed team information on match days, to the accompaniment of songs by Frank Sinatra, one of his favourite performers. The invited guests included Sir Bobby Robson, Sir Trevor Brooking, MPs and civic dignitaries, along with many of the footballers who had played for him at Derby and Nottingham. The funeral service was conducted by Father Frank Daly, and moving tributes were paid by Martin O'Neill, the Celtic manager who had been a prominent member of the Forest team, World Cup referee Clive Thomas, Yorkshire and England cricketer Geoff Boycott, Mrs Barbara Clough, and son Nigel.

'I was asked by someone,' said Martin O'Neill, 'if I could sum Brian's genius up in three words. I said he would have been insulted if he had been summed up in three volumes. No-one will ever eclipse his deeds and triumphs.'

The fact that the man affectionately known as Old Big 'Ead (his own interpretation of his OBE award) was mourned at both ends of the A52 linking Derby and Nottingham made it a most fitting suggestion in the view of a great many that his memory should be honoured by the renaming of that fifteen-mile stretch of tarmac as Brian Clough Way.

GUIDE TO SEASONAL SUMMARIES

Col 1: Match number (for league fixtures); Round (for cup-ties).
e.g. 4R means 'Fourth round replay.'

Col 2: Date of the fixture and whether Home (H), Away (A), or Neutral (N).

Col 3: Opposition.

Col 4: Attendances. Home gates appear in roman; Away gates in *italics*.
Figures in **bold** indicate the largest and smallest gates, at home and away.
Average home and away attendances appear after the final league match.

Col 5: Respective league positions of Derby and opponents after the game.
Derby's position appears on the top line in roman.
Their opponents' position appears on the second line in *italics*.
For cup-ties, the division and position of opponents is provided.
e.g. 2:12 means the opposition are twelfth in Division 2.

Col 6: The top line shows the result: W(in), D(raw), or L(ose).
The second line shows Derby's cumulative points total.

Col 7: The match score, Derby's given first.
Scores in **bold** show Derby's biggest league win and heaviest defeat.

Col 8: The half-time score, Derby's given first.

Col 9: The top line shows Derby's scorers and times of goals in roman.
The second line shows opponents' scorers and times of goals in *italics*.
A 'p' after the time of a goal denotes a penalty; 'og' an own-goal.
The third line gives the name of the match referee.

Team line-ups: Derby line-ups appear on top line, irrespective of whether they are home or away. Opposition teams are on the second line in *italics*.
Players of either side who are sent off are marked !
Derby players making their league debuts are displayed in **bold**.

Substitutes: Names of substitutes appear only if they actually took the field.
A player substituted is marked *

N.B. For clarity, all information appearing in *italics* relates to opposing teams.

LEAGUE DIVISION 1

Manager: Brian Clough

SEASON 1971-72

No	Date	Att	Pos	Pt	F-A	H-T	1	2	3	4	5	6	7	8	9	10	11	12 sub used
1	H MANCHESTER U	35,386	7 *10*	D 1	2-2	0-2	Boulton *Stepney*	Webster *O'Neill*	Robson *Dunne*	McGovern *Gowling*	Hennessey *James*	Todd *Sadler*	Gemmill *Morgan*	Wignall *Kidd*	O'Hare *Charlton*	Hector *Law*	Hinton *Best*	
	14/8						Scorers, Times, and Referees: Hector 50, Wignall 60 Law 15, Gowling 25 Ref: D Pugh											
							After a thunderstorm dies down, Denis Law volleys United ahead and Alan Gowling dives to head a spectacular second. Clough's half-time pep talk is effective, Hector lashing in a loose ball. Hinton's cross is headed against the bar by O'Hare and Wignall swoops to net the rebound.											
2	H WEST HAM	30,783	6 *22*	W 3	2-0	2-0	Boulton *Ferguson*	Webster *McDowall*	Robson *Lampard*	McGovern *Bonds*	Hennessey *Stephenson*	Todd *Moore*	Gemmill *Ayris**	Wignall *Best*	O'Hare *Hurst*	Hector *Taylor*	Hinton *Robson*	Howe
	18/8						Scorers: O'Hare 2, Wignall 8 Ref: J Hunting											
							Derby get off to a storming start. O'Hare beats Bobby Moore in the air and his header crosses the line before being thumped clear by Frank Lampard. A slick move involving four colleagues sets up Wignall to head home. Derby ease up after this and the Hammers go close to scoring.											
3	A LEICESTER	35,640	3 *12*	W 5	2-0	0-0	Shilton	Webster *Whitworth*	Robson *Nish*	McGovern *Kellard*	Hennessey *Sjoberg*	Todd *Cross*	Gemmill *Farrington*	Wignall *Brown*	O'Hare *Fern*	Hector *Sammels*	Hinton *Glover*	
	21/8						Scorers: Hector 63, Hinton 66p Ref: R Challis											
							Peter Shilton has a fine game for the newly-promoted Foxes. His resistance is finally broken when Webster's centre is flicked home by Hector. Then Graham Cross handles in a scramble and Hinton tucks in the penalty. It is Jimmy Bloomfield's men's first league defeat in seven months.											
4	A COVENTRY	27,752	3 *15*	D 6	2-2	0-1	Boulton *Glazier*	Webster *Smith*	Robson *Cattlin*	McGovern *Mortimer*	Hennessey *Blockley*	Todd *Barry*	Gemmill *Young*	Wignall *Carr*	O'Hare *Joicey*	Hector *Hunt*	Hinton *McGuire*	
	24/8						Scorers: O'Hare 53, Wignall 84 Joicey 40, Hunt 57p Ref: J Taylor											
							McFarland stumbles and Brian Joicey gets through to beat Boulton. O'Hare finishes off a move to level matters. Joicey seizes on McFarland's slack back-pass, but is hauled down by Boulton; Ernie Hunt converts the penalty. Wignall saves the day, heading in a late corner.											
5	H SOUTHAMPTON	28,498	4 *7*	D 7	2-2	1-0	Boulton *Martin*	Todd *Kirkup*	Robson *Fry*	McGovern *Fisher*	Hennessey *McGrath*	Todd *Gabriel*	Gemmill *Paine*	Wignall *Channon*	O'Hare *Stokes*	Hector *O'Neil*	Hinton *Jenkins*	
	28/8						Scorers: McGovern 39, Hector 62 Stokes 70, Gabriel 82p Ref: N Burtenshaw											
							Good work by Todd and Gemmill ends with McGovern's fine finish. Hector adds another after a series of corners. Ted Bates' team fight back and Bobby Stokes scores after Terry Paine 'nutmegs' McFarland. Jimmy Gabriel, who had earlier hit the crossbar, nets after Todd's handball.											
6	A IPSWICH	18,695	2 *9*	D 8	0-0	0-0	Boulton *Best*	Todd *Hammond*	Robson *Harper*	McGovern *Morris*	Hennessey *Bell*	Todd *Jefferson*	Gemmill *Robertson*	Durban *Mills*	O'Hare *Clarke*	Hector *Hamilton*	Hinton *Miller*	
	31/8						Ref: K Walker											
							Opposing centre-forwards Frank Clarke and Wignall both go agonisingly close to opening the scoring. Wignall thinks he has done so from Hinton's pass, but the effort is disallowed. Bobby Robson's side are generally second best, although Derek Jefferson's header flies just over.											
7	A EVERTON	41,024	3 *18*	W 10	2-0	1-0	Boulton *West*	Webster *Scott*	Robson *Newton K*	Todd *Kendall**	McFarland *Kenyon*	McGovern *Darracott*	Gemmill *Husband*	Durban *Ball*	Wignall *Johnson*	Hector *Hurst*	Hinton *Morrissey*	Royle
	4/9						Scorers: Hector 18, Wignall 72 Ref: A Oliver											
							Howard Kendall's misplaced pass allows Hector through to open the scoring. Kendall departs injured, and when Jimmy Husband also goes off Harry Catterick's side are down to ten men. Dominant Derby deserve their second goal, Wignall hitting the bar, but converting the rebound.											
8	H STOKE	32,545	2 *12*	W 12	4-0	2-0	Boulton *Banks*	Webster *Marsh*	Robson *Pejic*	Todd *Bernard**	McFarland *Smith*	Gemmill *Lees*	Durban *Mahoney*	Durban *Greenhoff*	Wignall *Ritchie*	Hector *Dobing*	Hinton *Haselgrave*	Stevenson
	11/9						Scorers: Todd 29, O'Hare 31, Hinton 48, [Gemmill 89] Ref: E Wallace											
							Gordon Banks has an altercation with a photographer at a corner and is then beaten when the flag-kick finds Todd unmarked. O'Hare heads in Hinton's free-kick soon after. Hinton continues the punishment after the break and the fourth is a gem, Gemmill's rocket ending a slick move.											
9	A CHELSEA	42,872	3 *15*	D 13	1-1	1-0	Boulton *Bonetti*	Webster *Boyle*	Robson *Harris*	Todd *Hollins*	McFarland *Webb*	McGovern *Hinton M*	Gemmill *Cooke*	Wignall *Baldwin*	O'Hare *Osgood*	Hector *Hudson*	Hinton *Houseman*	
	18/9						Scorers: McFarland 32 Baldwin 67 Ref: R Nicholson											
							Todd and McFarland look immaculate in defence and the latter gets forward to fire home a shot on the turn. Charlie Cooke's cross produces a superb equaliser from Tommy Baldwin. Dave Sexton's side press hard near the end and Peter Osgood's effort hits the bar in the dying seconds.											
10	H WEST BROM	30,628	3 *17*	D 14	0-0	0-0	Boulton *Cumbes*	Webster *Hughes*	Robson *Wilson*	McGovern *Cantello*	McFarland *Wile*	Gemmill *Kaye*	Durban* *McVitie*	Wignall *Brown*	O'Hare *Gould*	Hector *Hope*	Hinton *Hartford*	McGovern
	25/9						Ref: D Nippard											
							The Rams dominate, forcing 21 corners to Albion's nil. It is largely dull fare for home fans and efforts by McFarland are the closest they get to a goal. Jeff Astle is missing because of an appendix problem and on a rare Albion raid Asa Hartford beats Boulton, but the effort is disallowed.											

308

#		Date		Res															
11	A	NEWCASTLE	3	W	1-0	Boulton	Webster	Robson	Hennessey	McFarland	Todd	McGovern	Durban	O'Hare	Hector	Hinton
	2/10	32,077	18	16		McFaul	Craig	Ellison	Gibb	Howard	Clark	Barrowc'gh	Tudor	Macdonald	Nattrass	Hibbitt

Hinton 61
Ref: R Kirkpatrick

Derby are mostly on top but fail to beat Willie McFaul for an hour. With Malcolm Macdonald lying injured and Derby complaining about a foul on Webster, the ref waves play on and Hinton scores. Sheffield United lose elsewhere, so Derby are the only unbeaten side in the division.

| 12 | H | TOTTENHAM | 4 | D | 2-2 | Boulton | Webster* | Robson | Todd | McFarland | McGovern | Gemmill | Durban | O'Hare | Hector | Wignall |
| 9/10 | 35,744 | 7 | 17 | | Jennings | Evans | Knowles* | Mullery | Collins | Beal | Pearce | Perryman | Chivers | Peters | Gilzean | Pratt |

Todd 67, McFarland 84
Chivers 54, Pearce 88
Ref: C Smith

An excellent see-saw contest against Bill Nicholson's men. Martin Chivers nods the first with Alan Gilzean looking offside. Todd races upfield to volley in Hector's pass and his partner McFarland heads in a Hector corner. Near the end Jimmy Pearce forces the ball in after a scramble.

| 13 | A | MANCHESTER U | 4 | L | 0-1 | Boulton | Todd | Robson | Hennessey | McFarland | McGovern | Gemmill | Durban | O'Hare | Hector | Hinton |
| 16/10 | 53,247 | 1 | 17 | | Stepney | O'Neill | Dunne | Gowling | James | Sadler | Morgan | Kidd | Charlton | Law | Best |

Best 52
Ref: P Partridge

New United boss Frank O'Farrell receives the monthly manager's award before kick-off. The leaders dominate and George Best nets after a Bobby Charlton shot is blocked. Alan Gowling and Brian Kidd hit the bar and Hennessey goes close to an undeserved equaliser near the end.

| 14 | H | ARSENAL | 2 | W | 2-1 | Boulton | Webster* | Robson | Todd | McFarland | McGovern | Gemmill | Durban | O'Hare | Hector | Hinton | Powell |
| 23/10 | 36,480 | 8 | 19 | | Wilson | Rice | Nelson | Kelly* | McLintock | Roberts | Armstrong | George | Radford | Kennedy | Graham | Simpson |

O'Hare 10, Hinton 44p
Graham 29
Ref: W Hall

A stirring Rams display ends the Gunners' winning run. O'Hare shrugs off Sammy Nelson to grab the lead. George Armstrong's corner is converted by George Graham against the run of play. Pat Rice's tackle on Hector provides a controversial winning goal from the penalty spot.

| 15 | A | NOTT'M FOREST | 2 | W | 2-0 | Boulton | Webster | Robson | Powell | McFarland | Todd | McGovern | Gemmill | O'Hare | Hector | Hinton |
| 30/10 | 37,170 | 20 | 21 | | Hulme | O'Kane | Fraser | Chapman | Hindley | Richardson | Lyons | McKenzie | Buckley | Robertson | Storey-Moore |

Hinton 58p, Robson 79
Ref: D Smith

Todd hauls down Duncan McKenzie, but Ian Storey-Moore's header seems to have crossed the line when Sammy Chapman handles it clear, but the penalty is given anyway. Storey-Moore clatters the bar with a fine shot before Robson hits Derby's second.

| 16 | H | CRYSTAL PALACE | 2 | W | 3-0 | Boulton | Webster | Robson | Todd | McFarland | McGovern | Durban | Wignall | O'Hare | Hector | Hinton |
| 6/11 | 30,388 | 22 | 23 | | Jackson | Payne | Wall | Goodwin | Bell | Blyth | Tambling | Craven | Hughes | Wallace | Taylor |

Bell 3(og), Wignall 49, Hector 88
Ref: E Jolly

A great start as Bobby Bell's back-pass goes beyond the reach of the stranded goalkeeper John Jackson. Hinton's corner is headed firmly home by Wignall. With two minutes left, Hector adds the finishing touch to a comfortable win. Soon after this game Wignall moves to Mansfield.

| 17 | A | WOLVERHAMPTON | 2 | L | 1-2 | Boulton | Webster | Robson | Todd | McFarland | Hennessey | McGovern | Gemmill | Hector | Hinton |
| 13/11 | 32,957 | 12 | 23 | | Parkes | Shaw | Parkin | Bailey | Munro | McAlle | McCalling | Hibbitt | Richards | Dougan | Wagstaffe |

O'Hare 26
Richards 33, 75
Ref: D Laing

John McAlle inadvertently deflects the ball away from his keeper, allowing O'Hare to nod into an empty net. Boulton dashes out recklessly, misses the ball and John Richards bags an equaliser. A drive by Kenny Hibbitt gets away from Boulton and Richards has another easy task.

| 18 | H | SHEFFIELD UTD | 2 | W | 3-0 | Boulton | Webster | Robson | Todd | McFarland | Hennessey | McGovern | Gemmill | O'Hare | Hector | Hinton |
| 20/11 | 35,326 | 5 | 25 | | Hope | Badger | Hemsley | Flynn | Colquhoun | Hockey | Woodward | Salmons | Reece | Currie | Scullion |

Hector 2, Hinton 14p, 72p
Ref: V Batty

Hennessey's deflected through pass sees Hector snap up an early opening goal. O'Hare's header is kept out by John Flynn's arm and Hinton blasts in the penalty. John Harris's side accept that decision, but argue fiercely when Ted Hemsley is penalised for a second Hinton spot-kick.

| 19 | A | HUDDERSFIELD | 3 | L | 1-2 | Boulton | Webster | Robson | Todd | McFarland | Hennessey | McGovern | Gemmill | O'Hare | Hector | Hinton |
| 27/11 | 15,329 | 17 | 25 | | Lawson D | Clarke | Hutt | Jones | Ellam | Cherry | Mahoney | Smith S | Worthington | Lawson J | Chapman |

McGovern 76
Worthington 64, Lawson J 75
Ref: G Hill

Todd slips in the mud and Dennis Clarke's cross is converted by Frank Worthington. Les Chapman's low cross is headed in by a diving Jimmy Lawson. McGovern halves the deficit, cracking Hector's pass into the roof of the net. Hector miskicks when presented with a chance to level.

| 20 | H | MANCHESTER C | 2 | W | 3-1 | Boulton | Webster | Robson | Todd | McFarland | McGovern | Durban | Gemmill | O'Hare | Hector | Hinton |
| 4/12 | 35,354 | 3 | 27 | | Corrigan | Book | Donachie | Doyle | Booth | Oakes | Summerbee | Bell | Davies | Lee | Mellor |

Hinton 23p, Webster 36, Durban 38
Lee 66p
Ref: W Johnson

Ian Mellor trips McGovern and Hinton's penalty flies past Joe Corrigan. In a two-minute spell, Hinton crosses set up goals for Webster and Durban. Rampant Derby are pegged back after the break when Mike Summerbee is hauled down by Robson and Francis Lee nets the spot-kick.

| 21 | A | LIVERPOOL | 4 | L | 2-3 | Boulton | Todd* | Webster | Hennessey | McFarland | McGovern | Durban | Gemmill | Hinton | Hinton | Walker |
| 11/12 | 44,601 | 5 | 27 | | Clemence | Lawler | Lindsay | Smith | Ross | Hughes | Keegan | Hall | Heighway | Whitham | Callaghan |

O'Hare 42, 49
Whitham 14, 44, 53
Ref: C Howell

In an Anfield thriller, O'Hare twice equalises before big Jack Whitham – in a rare appearance for Bill Shankly's side - completes his hat-trick against a reorganised Rams defence. Robson is absent for the only time this season. Todd departs in the second-half after breaking his nose.

LEAGUE DIVISION 1
Manager: Brian Clough
SEASON 1971-72

310

No	Date		Att	Pos	Pt	F-A	H-T	Scorers, Times, and Referees	1	2	3	4	5	6	7	8	9	10	11	12 sub used
22	H	EVERTON	27,895	3 *18*	W 29	2-0	0-0	Hinton 49, 56 Ref: B Daniels	Boulton West	Webster Wright	Robson McLaughlin	Hennessey Kendall	McFarland Lyons	McGovern Newton H Husband	Durban Husband	Gemmill Ball	O'Hare Royle	Hector Hurst	Hinton Whittle
								Gordon West allows Hinton's free-kick to slip though his hands shortly after the break. Then West stands no chance as Hinton cuts in from Hector's pass and blasts in a cracking drive that delights home fans with its sheer power. O'Hare and McGovern star in a well-deserved win.												
23	A	LEEDS	44,214	5 *3*	L 29	**0-3**	0-2	Gray 6, Lorimer 21, 58 Ref: A Morrissey	Boulton Sprake	Webster Madeley	Robson Cooper	McFarland Bremner	McFarland Charlton	Hennessey Hunter	McGovern Lorimer	Gemmill Clarke	O'Hare Jones	Hector Giles	Hinton Gray
								Eddie Gray and Billy Bremner swap passes and the winger nets a low drive. Things get worse as Peter Lorimer's downward header bounces up and hits Boulton on the arm before trickling into the net. Gray carves an opening for Lorimer to bag the third. Tony Bailey makes his debut.												
24	H	CHELSEA	33,063	4 *10*	W 31	1-0	0-0	Gemmill 84 Ref: T Dawes	Boulton Sherwood	Webster Mulligan	Robson Harris	Todd Hollins	McFarland Dempsey	McGovern Webb	Durban Garland	Gemmill Kember*	O'Hare Osgood	Hector Hudson	Hinton Houseman	Cooke
								Chastened by Brian Clough's tongue-lashing after the Leeds defeat, Derby struggle to overcome a side well marshalled by David Webb. Last week Webb played in goal against Ipswich, but this time he unluckily deflects Gemmill's shot past debutant Steve Sherwood for the winner.												
25	A	SOUTHAMPTON	19,321	4 *18*	W 33	2-1	1-1	O'Hare 44, Durban 88 O'Brien 13 Ref: A Oliver	Boulton Martin	Webster McCarthy	Robson Fry	Durban Stokes	McFarland Gabriel	Todd Byrne	McGovern Paine	Gemmill Channon	O'Hare Davies	Hector O'Brien	Hinton Jenkins
								After a corner, Gerry O'Brien nets his first Saints league goal. Robson is prominent in a fine move that yields O'Hare's equaliser. A great shot by Durban gives Eric Martin no chance. This win puts pressure on leaders Manchester U, who today dropped misbehaving star George Best.												
26	A	WEST HAM	31,045	4 *12*	D 34	3-3	1-1	Hinton 5, Durban 60, Hector 87 Lampard 43, Robson 47, Brooking 80 Ref: J Thacker	Boulton Ferguson	Webster McDowall	Robson Lampard	McFarland Bonds	McFarland Taylor	Todd Moore	McGovern Redknapp	Gemmill Best	O'Hare Hurst	Hector Brooking	Hinton Robson B
								Hinton capitalises on Tommy Taylor's early error. Bobby Moore's free-kick is converted by Frank Lampard. Bryan 'Pop' Robson shoots the Hammers ahead but Durban pounces when McFarland's flick is parried. Trevor Brooking's late goal is cancelled out by a fine Hector header.												
27	H	COVENTRY	29,385	3 *17*	W 36	1-0	0-0	Robson 46 Ref: H New	Boulton Glazier	Webster Smith	Robson Cattlin	McFarland Machin*	McFarland Blockley	Todd Parker	McGovern Young	Gemmill Carr	O'Hare Chilton	Hector Rafferty	Hinton Mortimer	McGuire
								On a blustery day, Derby work hard to beat a jinx and finally record a Division One win over the Sky Blues. Man-of-the-match Gemmill seizes on Wilf Smith's poor pass and sets up Robson, whose crisp shot beats Bill Glazier. Elsewhere, Manchester City hit five and go top of the table.												
28	A	ARSENAL	52,055	3 *4*	L 36	0-2	0-1	George 44, 84p Ref: K Burns	Boulton Wilson	Webster Rice	Robson Nelson	McFarland Kelly	McFarland McLintock	Todd Simpson	McGovern Armstrong	Gemmill Ball	O'Hare George	Hector Kennedy	Hinton Graham
								Derby have the upper hand early on in muddy conditions, but just seconds before the half-time whistle Charlie George dives to head a beauty from George Graham's cross. Boulton brings down George six minutes from time and the scourge of Derby bags his second goal from the spot.												
29	H	NOTT'M FOREST	31,801	3 *22*	W 38	**4-0**	2-0	Hinton 34, 49, O'Hare 38, Hector 63 Ref: R Matthewson	Boulton Barron	Webster Gemmill	Robson Winfield	Durban Chapman	McFarland Hindley	Todd Cottam	McGovern Lyons	Gemmill O'Neill	O'Hare Cormack	Hector Richardson	Hinton Storey-Moore
								Mediocre Forest somehow hold on for 34 minutes until Hinton's delicate chip beats Jim Barron. McGovern sets up O'Hare, who fends off challenges before sliding the ball in. A foul on O'Hare sees Hinton crack the free-kick home. Hector completes the rout after a poor clearance.												
30	H	WOLVERHAMPTON	33,456	3 *7*	W 40	2-1	0-1	Hinton 50p, McFarland 64 McCalliog 7p Ref: R Challis	Boulton Parkes	Webster Shaw	Robson Taylor	Durban Hegan	McFarland McAlle	McGovern Munro	Todd McCalliog	Gemmill Hibbitt	O'Hare Richards	Hector Dougan	Hinton Wagstaffe
								Constant rain makes the notorious Baseball Ground pitch worse than ever, but both sides produce good football. Boulton brings down Derek Dougan for Jim McCalliog to net an early penalty. Frank Munro fells Hector for the equaliser and McFarland forces the winner from a corner.												
31	A	TOTTENHAM	36,310	3 *5*	W 42	1-0	0-0	Hinton 86p Ref: A Morrissey	Boulton Jennings	Webster Evans	Robson Knowles	Hennessey Holder	McFarland England	Todd Beal	McGovern Gilzean	Gemmill Perryman	O'Hare Chivers	Hector Peters	Hinton Morgan
								On a bitterly cold day, Derby's defence holds firm and the travelling fans get something to celebrate in the dying minutes. An unlikely mix-up between experienced duo Pat Jennings and Mike England sees Hector pulled down by the keeper. Hinton's spot-kick wins two valuable points.												

Match 32 — H 18/3 LEICESTER — 34,019 — 2 W 3-0 — 16 — 44
O'Hare 17, Durban 67, Hector 86
Ref: V James

Derby: Boulton, Webster, Robson, McFarland, Todd, Durban, McGovern, Hennessey*, O'Hare, Hector, Gemmill — Walker
Leicester: Wallington, Whitworth, Nish, Cross, Manley, Woollett, Fern*, Sammels, Weller, Birchenall, Glover — Lee

Derby bounce back from their midweek FA Cup defeat despite the absence of injured Hinton. Durban's superb pass sets up O'Hare for the first goal. Durban nets a flicked header after a Walker corner to make amends for a bad miss earlier. Gemmill puts Hector clear for a clinical finish.

Match 33 — H 22/3 IPSWICH — 26,738 — 2 W 1-0 — 15 — 46
Hector 15
Ref: E Wallace

Derby: Boulton, Webster, Robson, McFarland, Todd, Durban, McGovern, O'Hare, Hector, Hinton*, Gemmill — Walker
Ipswich: Best, Mills, Harper, Hunter, Jefferson, Morris, Robertson, Miller, Beffit*, Mills, Whymark — Lambert

With Allan Hunter and Derek Jefferson back-pedalling desperately, Boulton's huge downfield punt bounces nicely for Hector to tuck the ball past David Best. A great tackle by Todd prevents Trevor Whymark equalising just moments later. A late shot by Hector cracks against the bar.

Match 34 — A 25/3 STOKE — 33,771 — 2 D 1-1 — 15 — 47
Durban 51 — Greenhoff 48p
Ref: R Kirkpatrick

Derby: Boulton, Webster, Robson, McFarland, Todd, Durban, McGovern, O'Hare, Hector, Hinton, Gemmill — Walker
Stoke: Banks, Marsh, Jump, Smith, Bernard, Bloor, Conroy, Greenhoff, Ritchie, Dobing, Burrows

Todd brings down Harry Burrows and Jimmy Greenhoff nets the spot-kick. Walker is impeded 20 yards from goal and Durban bends in the free-kick brilliantly. Brian Clough is left furning when Hector is penalised for bundling the ball out of Gordon Banks' grasp and into the net.

Match 35 — A 28/3 CRYSTAL PALACE — 21,158 — 2 W 1-0 — 19 — 49
Walker 33
Ref: C Nicholls

Derby: Boulton, Webster, Robson, McFarland, Todd, Durban, McGovern, Hennessey, Hector, Hinton, Gemmill — Walker
Crystal Palace: Jackson, Payne, Goodwin, Kellard, McCormick, Bell, Craven, Queen, Wallace, Taylor, Tambling* — Wall

Hector has an early shot blocked on the line and then deputy penalty-taker Gemmill fires a spot-kick wide after Sam Goodwin fouls O'Hare. Hennessey's shot is parried by John Jackson to Walker, who shoots the Rams ahead. Lowly Palace fight gamely but are out of luck tonight.

Match 36 — H 1/4 LEEDS — 39,450 — 1 W 2-0 — 3 — 51
O'Hare 16, Hunter 69(og)
Ref: D Smith

Derby: Boulton, Webster, Robson, McFarland, Todd, Durban, McGovern, Gemmill, Hector, O'Hare, Hinton — Walker
Leeds: Sprake, Reaney, Cooper, Bremner, Charlton, Hunter, Lorimer, Clarke, Madeley, Giles, Gray

An epic win in a tense top-of-the-table clash, with Leeds weary from playing the previous day. Johnny Giles has a goal disallowed and Paul Reaney heads a Gemmill shot off the line. O'Hare heads in Durban's cross and the points are safe when a rebound goes in off Norman Hunter.

Match 37 — H 3/4 NEWCASTLE — 38,119 — 1 L 0-1 — 11 — 51
Cassidy 71
Ref: R Tinkler

Derby: Boulton, Webster, Robson, McFarland, Todd, Durban, McGovern, Gemmill, Hector, O'Hare, Hinton — Walker
Newcastle: McFaul, Craig, Clark, Gibb*, Howard, Moncur, Barrowc'gh, Green, Macdonald, Tudor, Reid — Cassidy

Having gone top on Saturday, this Easter Monday game is an anticlimax despite Derby dominance. Gemmill's effort hits a post and rolls along the line. Sub Tommy Cassidy nets after Boulton blocks a Malcolm Macdonald effort. McFarland played on with five stitches in a forehead cut.

Match 38 — A 5/4 WEST BROM — 32,439 — 1 D 0-0 — 17 — 52
Ref: R Challis

Derby: Boulton, Webster, Robson, McFarland, Todd, Durban, McGovern, Gemmill, Hector, O'Hare, Hinton — Walker
WBA: Osborne, Nisbet, Wilson, Suggett, Wile, Robertson, Hope, Astle, Brown A, Brown T, Hartford — Cassidy

In high winds and on a bumpy pitch, good football is at a premium. Derby stay top and are worth their point, although Don Howe's side go closest to a winner. The recalled Jeff Astle misses a good chance from Ally Brown's pass and a penalty appeal is turned down after a scramble.

Match 39 — A 8/4 SHEFFIELD UTD — 38,238 — 1 W 4-0 — 10 — 54
Gemmill 12, Durban 18, Hector 65, (O'Hare 82) Hope
Ref: J Taylor

Derby: Boulton, Webster, Robson, McFarland, Todd, Durban, McGovern, Gemmill, Hector, O'Hare, Hinton — Walker
Sheffield Utd: Hope, Badger, Hensley, MacKenzie, Colquhoun, Salmons, Woodward, Scullion, Dearden, Holmes, Ford

The title race hots up even further with all four serious contenders winning today. Gemmill nets the first goal after John Hope misses a cross and then Durban heads in a swirling corner. Hinton's cross allows Hector to head his 200th league goal. Hector sets up O'Hare for the fourth.

Match 40 — H 15/4 HUDDERSFIELD — 31,414 — 1 W 3-0 — 21 — 56
McFarland 15, Hector 21, O'Hare 51
Ref: J Yates

Derby: Boulton, Webster, Robson, McFarland, Todd, Durban, McGovern, Gemmill, Hector, O'Hare, Hinton — Walker
Huddersfield: Lawson D, Clarke, Hutt, Smith, Ellam, Cherry, Hoy, Jones, Worthington, Lawson J, Chapman

Relegation-bound Huddersfield fall behind to McFarland's header from a corner. Hector knocks in a simple goal when the ball cannons to him off Roy Ellam and O'Hare heads in a Hector cross. With Leeds in FA Cup action and Manchester C drawing, Derby are now three points clear.

Match 41 — A 22/4 MANCHESTER C — 55,026 — 3 L 0-2 — 1 — 56
Marsh 25, Lee 67p
Ref: N Burtenshaw

Derby: Boulton, Webster*, Robson, McFarland, Todd, Durban, McGovern, Gemmill, Hector, O'Hare, Hinton — Hennessey
Man City: Corrigan, Book, Donachie, Doyle, Booth, Jeffries, Lee, Bell, Summerbee, Marsh, Towers

The mercurial Rodney Marsh plays a blinder and this amazing title race takes another twist. Marsh cracks a wonder goal and is bowled over by Hennessey for Francis Lee's penalty. City have now completed their fixtures and the title can now only be won by Derby, Liverpool or Leeds.

Match 42 — H 1/5 LIVERPOOL — 39,420 — 1 W 1-0 — 4 — 58
McGovern 62
Ref: C Thomas

Derby: Boulton, Powell, Robson, McFarland, Todd, Durban, McGovern, Gemmill, Hector, O'Hare, Hinton
Liverpool: Clemence, Lawler, Lindsay, Smith, Lloyd, Hughes, Keegan, Hall, Heighway*, Toshack, Callaghan — McLaughlin

A win is essential and the crucial goal comes when Durban dummies Gemmill's pass and McGovern nets. A great team display, including by the 16-year-old Powell, secures victory. The Rams return to the top but must now wait for the outcome of Liverpool and Leeds' final games.

Home 33,155 / Away 35,473 / Average 34,314

LEAGUE DIVISION 1 (CUP-TIES)   Manager: Brian Clough   SEASON 1971-72

                                                                                                                                                    312

League Cup			Att		F-A	H-T	Scorers, Times, and Referees	1	2	3	4	5	6	7	8	9	10	11	12 sub used
2	H	LEEDS	34,023	3 D 2	0-0	0-0	Ref: B Homewood	Boulton *Harvey*	Webster *Reaney*	Robson *Yorath*	Todd *Bremner*	McFarland *Charlton*	Gemmill *Hunter*	Durban *Lorimer*	Wignall *Clarke*	O'Hare *Belfitt*	Hector *Giles*	Hinton *Madeley*	Walker *Madeley*
							Derby pound away at the Leeds defence but Jack Charlton is in dominant form. Hector, Hinton, O'Hare and Durban all go close, but Leeds end the stronger side and nearly snatch a win when Billy Bremner's dangerous chip is dealt with by Webster with Peter Lorimer waiting to pounce.												
2R	A	LEEDS	29,132	3 L 5	0-2	0-1	Lorimer 34, 63 Ref: B Homewood	Boulton *Sprake*	Webster *Reaney*	Robson *Cooper*	Todd *Bremner**	McFarland *Charlton*	Gemmill *Hunter*	McGovern *Lorimer*	Wignall *Yorath*	O'Hare *Belfitt*	Hector *Giles*	Hinton *Madeley*	Hinton *Mann*
							A first defeat in 12 games this season thanks to goals in each half by hot-shot Peter Lorimer. Billy Bremner and Archie Gemmill have a grim battle in midfield and, after one clash, the Leeds skipper goes off to have five stitches put in a leg injury. Scotland boss Tommy Docherty looks on.												

Texaco Cup

1:1	H	DUNDEE UTD	20,059	2 W	6-2	2-0	Dur 12, Hec 25, Wal 46, O'H 49, Hin 73, Gordon 50, Rolland 59 [Robson 82] Ref: G Hartley	Boulton *Mackay*	Webster *Gray*	Robson *Cameron*	Todd *Smith W*	Hennessey *Smith D*	McGovern *Henry*	Bourne *Watson*	Durban* *Reid*	O'Hare *Rolland*	Hector *Rolland*	Hinton *Copland**	Walker *Devlin*
							The Tangerines' defence looks shaky a second-half goal-glut. Hinton's drive quells a mini-revival, Robson's solo rounding things off nicely. The Tangerines' defence looks shaky but O'Hare flicks over Don Mackay for Durban to head home. Hector heads a second. Sub Walker lashes home with his first touch to spark a second-half goal-glut.												
1:2	A	DUNDEE UTD	6,000	3 L	2-3	2-1	Hinton 3, Butlin 18 Copland 40,67, Devlin 60 Ref: E Thomson (Derby won 8-5 on aggregate)	Boulton *McAlpine*	Daniel *Rolland*	Robson *Cameron*	Hennessey *Markland*	Bailey *Gray*	Gemmill *Henry*	McGovern *Traynor*	Wignall *Reid*	Butlin *Copland*	Walker *Devlin**	Hinton *White*	Hinton *Smith*
							Hinton nets a long-range drive and Butlin swivels neatly to beat the advancing Hamish McAlpine. Despite being six goals adrift, the home side rally impressively. John Copland heads home Sandy White's cross and Alan Devlin nets a crisp shot. Copland's winner salvages Scots' pride.												
2:1	H	STOKE	21,487	4 W 9	3-2	2-0	O'Hare 10, 38, Hector 50 Mahoney 64, Smith 87 Ref: N Burtenshaw	Boulton *Banks*	Daniel *Marsh*	Lewis *Pejic*	Hennessey* *Smith*	McFarland *Bernard*	Todd *Bloor*	Wignall *Mahoney*	Powell *Stevenson*	O'Hare *Greenhoff*	Hector *Jump**	Hinton *Haslegrave*	Bailey *Jackson*
							O'Hare goes round Gordon Banks to net a well-taken goal. Hennessey departs injured and Stoke get back into the tie. Two headed goals give them real hope for the return.												
2:2	A	STOKE	23,461	2 D 10	1-1	0-0	Wignall 60 Smith 86 Ref: J Hunting (Derby won 4-3 on aggregate)	Boulton *Banks*	Webster *Marsh*	Robson *Pejic*	Todd *Bernard*	Hennessey *Smith*	McGovern *Bloor*	Durban *Haslegrave*	Wignall *Mahoney*	O'Hare *Conroy*	Hector *Eastham**	Hinton *Jump*	Stevenson
							Wignall bamboozles Gordon Banks with a shot that spins over the England keeper on the hour mark. Tony Waddington's men only hit back in the closing stages, Denis Smith's speculative 20-yarder flying past Boulton. It is too little too late and Derby play out the final minutes easily.												
SF	H	NEWCASTLE	20,201	2 W 19	1-0	1-0	O'Hare 25 Ref: C Thomas	Boulton *McFaul*	Webster *Craig*	Robson *Clark*	Todd *Nattrass*	McFarland *Burton*	Hennessey *Howard*	McGovern *Barrowc'gh Green**	Wignall *Macdonald*	O'Hare *Tudor*	Hector *Hibbitt*	Hinton *Hibbitt*	Gibb
							Treacherous conditions make life difficult for both sides, but O'Hare shows rare balance on the frosty pitch, collecting a pass and sweeping in a fine goal. When skilful Tony Green departs with a stomach upset, Newcastle's threat fizzles out. Hector's late effort bobbles narrowly wide.												
SF	A	NEWCASTLE	37,140	2 W 19	3-2 aet	0-1	Walker 73, McGovern 102, Todd 116 Macdonald 44, Barrowclough 60 Ref: F Nicholson (Derby won 4-2 on aggregate)	Boulton *McFaul*	Todd *Craig*	Webster *Clark*	Hennessey *Nattrass*	Bailey *Burton*	Daniel *Howard*	Durban *Barrowc'gh Green*	McGovern *Macdonald*	O'Hare *Macdonald*	Hector *Hibbitt*	Hinton* *Coulson**	Walker *Gibb*
							Joe Harvey's men stun Derby as clinical finishes by Malcolm Macdonald and Stewart Barrowclough turn the tie upside down. Walker then converts Durban's cross to force extra-time. McGovern swings a corner straight into the net before Todd pops up to clinch a place in the final.												
F:1	A	AIRDRIE	16,000	4 D	0-0	0-0	Ref: W Anderson	Boulton *McKenzie*	Webster *Jonquin*	Robson *Clarke*	Todd *Menzies*	Daniel *McKinlay*	Hennessey *Whiteford D*	Parry *Wilson*	Hennessey *Walker*	O'Hare *Busby*	Butlin *Jarvie*	Hinton *Cowan**	Walker *Whiteford J*
							The Broomfield Park battle is a hostile reception. The Diamonds are bottom of their league but have bags of enthusiasm and physical endeavour. Todd and Gemmill are magnificent in the heat of the battle. Butlin goes close with a volley after seizing onto Boulton's long punt.												
F:2	H	AIRDRIE	25,102	3 W	2-1	1-0	Hinton 40p, Davies 51 Whiteford 78 Ref: J Taylor (Derby won 2-1 on aggregate)	Boulton *McKenzie*	Powell *Caldwell*	Robson *Clarke*	Durban *Menzies*	Daniel *McKinlay*	McGovern *Whiteford D*	McGovern *Wilson*	Butlin *Walker*	Davies *Busby*	Hector *Jarvie*	Hinton *Cowan**	Jonquin
							With key men unavailable, Derby are under-strength but good enough to withstand Airdrie's physical challenge. Home fans jeer Jack Taylor for being far too lenient. Hinton nets after Hector is hacked down and debutant Davies heads a second. Derek Whiteford slots in a consolation.												

FA Cup

3	H	SHREWSBURY	4	W	2-0	0-0	Hector 69, 85							
	15/1	33,463	3:7				Ref: B Homewood							
		Boulton	Webster	Robson	Durban	McFarland	Todd	McGovern	Gemmill	O'Hare	Hector	Hinton		
		Mulhearn	Brown	Fellows	Moore	Holton	Bridgwood	Roberts	Andrews	Wood	Moir	Groves		

Derby are well on top, but struggle to find a way past Ken Mulhearn. The Shrews' leading scorer, big Alf Wood, causes Derby major concerns and twice goes close with headers in the second period. Harry Gregg's men crumble in the final 20 minutes as Hector pounces to bag a brace.

4	H	NOTTS CO	3	W	6-0	2-0	Robson 19, Hector 44,							
	5/2	39,450	3:2				[Durban 56, 58, 74, Hinton 64p]							
							Ref: A Morrissey							
		Boulton	Webster	Robson	Durban	McFarland	Todd	McGovern	Gemmill	O'Hare*	Hector	Hinton		
		Brown	Brindley	Worthington	Carlin	Stubbs	Jones	Nixon	Bradd	Hateley	Masson	Cozens	Powell	

Ex-Ram Willie Carlin gets a warm welcome, but Derby show no mercy during the game. After Gemmill sets the tone by hitting the bar early on, Jimmy Sirrel's side take a pounding and have no answer to the incoming tide. O'Hare goes off hurt after a clash with ex-Ram Mick Jones.

5	H	ARSENAL	3	D	2-2	0-1	Hinton 46p, Durban 88							
	26/2	39,622	4				George 40, 80							
							Ref: P Partridge							
		Boulton	Webster	Robson	Durban	McFarland	Todd	McGovern	Gemmill	O'Hare	Hector	Hinton		
		Wilson	Rice	Nelson	Kelly*	McLintock	Simpson	Armstrong	Ball	George	Kennedy	Storey		

Eddie Kelly departs early with an injury, but the champions go ahead via Charlie George. Pat Partridge ignores a trip on Gemmill by George Graham, but agrees Peter Simpson's tackle on O'Hare is a penalty. Durban thrills home fans with a late leveller after George had struck again.

5R	A	ARSENAL	3	D	0-0	0-0								
	29/2	63,077	4			aet	Ref: P Partridge							
		Boulton	Webster	Robson	Durban	McFarland	Todd	McGovern	Gemmill	O'Hare	Hector	Hinton		
		Wilson	Rice	Nelson	Storey	McLintock	Simpson	Armstrong	Ball	George	Kennedy*	Graham	Radford	

A fine display by the defence, particularly McFarland and Todd, frustrates a huge Highbury crowd. The touts are out in force, asking £20 for £1 seats. After histrionics in the first tie, Charlie George is subdued, on the same day that the FA announce an inquiry into an article he wrote.

5	N	ARSENAL	3	L	0-1	0-1	Kennedy 4							
2R	13/3	40,000	8				Ref: D Smith							
	(at Filbert Street)													
		Boulton	Webster	Robson	Durban	McFarland	Todd	McGovern*	Gemmill	O'Hare	Hector	Hinton		
		Wilson	Rice	Nelson	Storey	McLintock	Simpson	Armstrong	Ball	George	Kennedy	Graham	Hennessey	

A McGovern blunder in the opening minutes proves decisive. Instead of feeding the available Hinton, he chooses to pass back to Boulton, only for the ball to deflect off Todd into the path of grateful Ray Kennedy. Hinton nearly forces more extra-time but Bob Wilson makes a fine save.

Odds & ends

Double wins: (5) Leicester, Everton, Nott'm F, Crystal Pal, Sheffield U.
Double losses: (0).
Won from behind: (3) Southampton (a), Wolves (h), Newcastle (a) (Tex).
Lost from in front: (2) Wolves (a), Dundee U (a) (Tex).
High spots: The club's very first League championship triumph.
Winning the Texaco Cup – the first 'major' cup triumph since 1946.
The superb form of defensive kingpins Todd and McFarland.
Alan Hinton's spectacular long-range shooting.
The tension-packed 1-0 victory over Liverpool on the final day.
Low spots: The continuing poor state of the Baseball Ground pitch.
The Easter Monday flop at home to Newcastle.
The defeat at Maine Road in April, which jeopardised the title bid.
The 0-3 thumping by Leeds in December.
Losing to a soft goal after 300 minutes of Cup action against Arsenal.
Player of the Year: Colin Todd.
Ever-presents: (1) Colin Boulton (+ Kevin Hector in league only).
Hat-tricks: (1) Alan Durban (v Notts Co, h, FAC).
Opposing hat-tricks: (1) Jack Whitham (v Liverpool, a).
Leading scorer: (20) Alan Hinton.

League table

		P	W	D	L	F	A	W	D	L	F	A	Pts
				Home					Away				
1	DERBY	42	16	4	1	43	10	8	6	7	26	23	58
2	Leeds	42	17	4	0	54	10	7	5	9	19	21	57
3	Liverpool	42	17	3	1	48	16	7	6	8	16	14	57
4	Manchester C	42	16	3	2	48	15	7	8	6	29	30	57
5	Arsenal	42	15	2	4	36	13	7	6	8	22	27	52
6	Tottenham	42	16	3	2	45	13	3	10	8	18	29	51
7	Chelsea	42	12	7	2	41	20	6	5	10	17	29	48
8	Manchester U	42	13	2	6	39	26	6	8	7	30	35	48
9	Wolves	42	10	7	4	35	23	8	4	9	30	34	47
10	Sheffield U	42	10	8	3	39	26	7	4	10	22	34	46
11	Newcastle	42	10	6	5	30	18	5	5	11	19	34	41
12	Leicester	42	9	6	6	18	11	4	7	10	23	35	39
13	Ipswich	42	7	8	6	19	19	4	8	9	20	34	38
14	West Ham	42	10	6	5	31	19	2	6	13	16	32	36
15	Everton	42	8	9	4	28	17	1	9	11	9	31	36
16	West Brom	42	6	7	8	22	23	6	4	11	20	31	35
17	Stoke	42	6	10	5	26	25	4	5	12	13	31	35
18	Coventry	42	7	10	4	27	23	2	5	14	17	44	33
19	Southampton	42	8	5	8	31	28	4	2	15	21	52	31
20	Crystal Pal	42	4	8	9	26	31	4	5	12	13	34	29
21	Nott'm For	42	6	4	11	25	29	2	5	14	22	52	25
22	Huddersfield	42	4	7	10	12	22	2	6	13	15	37	25
		924	227	129	106	723	437	227	106	129	437	723	924

Appearances / Goals

	Lge	Sub	LC	Sub	FAC	Sub	Tex	Sub	Lge	LC	FAC	Tex	Tot
Bailey, Tony	1												
Boulton, Colin	42		2		5		2						
Bourne, Jeff												1	1
Butlin, Barry													
Daniel, Peter									3				3
Davies, Roger									5				5
Durban, Alan	31		1		5				4		6	1	11
Gemmill, Archie	40		2		5		2		3		3		3
Hector, Kevin	42		2		5		2		6	4	12	3	17
Hennessey, Terry	17						1				1		1
Hinton, Alan	38		2				2		8		15	2	20
Lewis, Alan		1											
McFarland, Roy	38		2		5		2		2		4		4
McGovern, John	39	1		1	5		1		6		3		4
O'Hare, John	40		2		5		2		5		13	4	17
Parry, Tony		2					1						
Powell, Steve	2	1					2						
Robson, John	41		2		5		2		6		4	1	4
Todd, Colin	40		2		5		2		6		2	1	3
Walker, Jim	3	3							2		1	2	3
Webster, Ron	38		2				2	2	5				1
Wignall, Frank	10	1	2						3		5	1	6
(own-goals)									2		2		2
22 players (16 in Lge)	462	7	22	2	55		22		88	3	69	10 18	97

LEAGUE DIVISION 1 — Manager: Dave Mackay — SEASON 1974-75

314

No	Date	Att	Pos	Pt	F-A	H-T	1	2	3	4	5	6	7	8	9	10	11	12 sub used	Scorers, Times, and Referees
1	A EVERTON 17/8	42,293	12	D	0-0	0-0	Boulton Lawson	Webster Bernard	Nish Seargeant	Rioch Clements	Daniel Kenyon	Todd Hurst	Powell Buckley	Gemmill Harvey	Davies Royle	Hector* Latchford	Lee Connolly	Bourne	Ref: T Reynolds. Francis Lee's debut, three days after signing for £100,000. Boulton saves well twice to foil Joe Royle. Bob Latchford nets, but is called offside. Hector is tripped after the interval and exits with an injury. McGovern and O'Hare are missing as they are about to join Brian Clough at Leeds.
2	H COVENTRY 21/8	25,717	14	D	1-1	0-1	Boulton Ramsbottom	Webster Hindley	Nish Cattlin	Rioch Mortimer	Daniel Lloyd	Todd Dugdale	Powell Craven*	Gemmill Alderson	Davies Stein	Hector* Cross	Lee Hutchison	Bourne Coop	Lee 68 Mortimer 20 Ref: R Capey. Powell tries to clear a John Craven centre but directs it to Denis Mortimer, who sends a dipping volley past Boulton. From Nish's corner-kick, Powell's first-time drive is flicked in at close range by home debutant Lee. Neil Ramsbottom makes good saves to frustrate Rioch and Powell.
3	H SHEFFIELD UTD 24/8	23,088	7	W	2-0	1-0	Boulton Brown	Webster Badger	Nish Hemsley	Rioch* Eddy	Newton Colquhoun	Todd Franks	Powell Woodward	Gemmill Speight	Davies Cammack	Hector Currie	Lee Field	Bourne	Hector 4, Davies 78 Ref: G Kew. Good approach work by Nish and Gemmill sets up Hector, who slips the Rams into an early lead. A powerful shot from Len Badger is headed off the line by Webster and a long-range shot from Micky Speight hits the top of the bar. Lee finds Davies who nets a spectacular second goal.
4	A COVENTRY 27/8	18,586	7	D	1-1	1-0	Boulton Ramsbottom	Webster Hindley	Nish Cattlin	Rioch Mortimer	Thomas Lloyd	Todd Dugdale	Powell Carr	Gemmill Alderson	Davies Stein	Hector McGuire	Lee Hutchison		Davies 22 Carr 70 Ref: J Williams. Thomas finds Todd who splits the Sky Blues defence for Davies to shoot firmly into the corner of City's net. A misunderstanding between Thomas and Powell allows Willie Carr to nip in to level. Gordon Milne's men look stronger after the break and Derby are happy with a point.
5	A TOTTENHAM 31/8	20,770	10	L	0-2	0-0	Boulton Jennings	Webster Evans	Nish Naylor	Rioch Pratt	Daniel England	Todd Beal	Newton Neighbour	Gemmill Perryman	Davies Chivers	Hector Peters	Lee* Coates	Bourne	Neighbour 46, 58 Ref: R Crabb. Ralph Coates' cross gives Jimmy Neighbour the chance to blast in from an acute angle. John Pratt's headed pass sets up a second, also forced in from a tight angle. Home fans give a standing ovation to Bill Nicholson, who has just announced his retirement after 16 years as manager.
6	H NEWCASTLE 7/9	21,197	10	D	2-2	1-1	Boulton McFaul	Webster Nattrass	Nish Clark	Rioch Gibb	Daniel Keeley	Todd Howard	Newton Burns	Gemmill Cassidy	Davies Macdonald	Hector Tudor	Lee Hibbitt		Davies 41, Lee 53 Macdonald 29, Burns 70 Ref: A Hart. Malcolm Macdonald heads home Micky Burns' cross. Nish hits a post before Davies blasts home a Lee pass to equalise. Lee gives Derby the lead, his free-kick deflecting off the wall. Burns levels with a marvellous solo goal and nearly adds a winner, but Todd's tackle saves the day.
7	A BIRMINGHAM 14/9	27,795	14	L	2-3	0-1	Boulton Latchford	Webster Martin	Nish Styles	Rioch Kendall	Daniel Gallagher	Todd Page*	Powell* Campbell	Gemmill Francis	Davies Burns	Hector Hatton	Lee Taylor	Newton Hynd	Rioch 83, Davies 87 Hatton 29, Francis 64p, 79p Ref: D Nippard. Trevor Francis skilfully creates the opener for Bob Hatton. Fred Goodwin's men win two disputed penalties much to Derby disgust. Davies is penalised for hands and Daniel for a foul on Francis. With Howard Kendall injured and the sub already on, Derby hit back late against ten men.
8	H BURNLEY 21/9	21,377	10	W	3-2	0-1	Boulton Stevenson	Webster Newton K	Nish Brennan	Rioch Ingham	Daniel Waldron	Todd Rodaway	Newton Noble	Gemmill Hankin	Davies Fletcher	Hector Collins	Lee James*	Flynn	Hector 46, Rioch 55p, Lee 64 Todd 19 (og), Daniel 89 (og) Ref: J Brent. Todd gives Jimmy Adamson's side the lead when meaning to head for a corner. A fine attacking display turns the tables. Newton hits the goal angle before Hector volleys in. Billy Rodaway handles for the second. Lee's acrobatic third precedes another own goal, via Daniel's deflection.
9	H CHELSEA 25/9	22,036	7	W	4-1	3-1	Boulton Phillips	Webster Locke	Nish Houseman	Rioch* Hollins	Daniel Droy	Todd Harris	Newton Hay	Gemmill Garland	Davies Cooke	Hector Hutchinson	Lee Sissons		Rioch 10, Webster 23, Daniel 34, Hutchinson 14 [Hector 84] Ref: K Burns. Rioch nets from Todd's precise pass. Defenders stop, thinking the ball has gone out, allowing Peter Houseman to set up a leveller. Webster's diving header is followed by a rare Daniel goal after a corner. A well-timed run sees Hector grab a fourth. Todd and Rioch are in superb form.
10	A STOKE 28/9	23,589	8	D	1-1	0-1	Boulton Farmer	Webster Marsh	Nish Pejic	Rioch* Mahoney	Daniel Smith	Todd Dodd	Newton Haslegrave	Gemmill Greenhoff	Davies Hurst	Hector Hudson	Lee Salmons	Powell	Lee 75 Hurst 27 Ref: A Jones. Rioch's foul on Geoff Salmons leads to a Mike Pejic free-kick being converted by Geoff Hurst. Davies misses a fine chance to equalise. Derby finally create a deserved equaliser when Hector's centre is met by Nish, whose header is fumbled by John Farmer. Lee is the quickest to react.

11	A	WEST HAM	9	D	2:2	1-1	Lee 30, Hector 72	Boulton	Webster	Nish	Todd	Daniel	Rioch	Newton	Gemmill	Davies	Hector	Lee
5/10		32,938	12	12		Robson K 9, Bonds 59	Day	McDowell*	Lampard	Lock	Taylor	Bonds	Jennings	Paddon	Gould	Brooking	Robson K Holland

Keith Robson appears to handle before scoring a fine opening goal. Derby bounce back in style, Lee equalising from a corner that resulted from Mervyn Day's fine save from Nish. Billy Bonds converts Frank Lampard's centre, but Hector's curling cross-shot wins a deserved point.

Ref: P Walters

| 12 | H | LEICESTER | 5 | W | 1-0 | 1-0 | Rioch 32 | Boulton | Webster | Nish | Todd | Daniel | Rioch | Newton | Gemmill | Davies | Hector | Lee |
| 12/10 | | 24,753 | 19 | 14 | | | Shilton | Whitworth | Yates | Sammels | Munro | Cross | Weller | Earle | Worthington | Birchenall | Glover |

Keith Weller breaks clear of the otherwise resolute Derby defence only to shoot wide. Steve Yates, in his first full league match, is put under heavy pressure by Davies and the ball falls for Rioch to crack home a blockbuster. Peter Shilton makes a great save to deny Derby a second.

Ref: D Nippard

| 13 | A | SHEFFIELD UTD | 3 | W | 2:1 | 1-0 | Lee 10, 83 | Boulton | Webster | Nish | Todd | Daniel | Rioch | Newton | Gemmill | Davies | Hector | Lee |
| 15/10 | | 21,882 | 9 | 16 | | Field 58 | Brown | Faulkner | Hemsley | Eddy | Colquhoun | Franks* | Woodward | Speight | Dearden | Currie | Field | Bradford |

Gemmill's cross is headed home by the diving Lee. Boulton makes a great save from Micky Speight's deflected volley. Webster heads off the line before Tony Field's cross-shot finds it way in. Near the end Webster's cross is headed down by Hector and Lee swoops to nick the winner.

Ref: R Perkin

| 14 | A | CARLISLE | 7 | L | 0:3 | 0-1 | | Boulton | Webster | Nish | Todd | Daniel | Rioch | Newton | Gemmill | Davies | Hector | Lee |
| 19/10 | | 13,353 | 14 | 16 | | Train 43, Martin 65, Clarke F 70 | Clarke T | Carr | Gorman | Balderstone | Green | Parker | Martin | Train | Clarke F | Owen | Barry |

Hector misses a chance when Tom Clarke fumbles a cross. Boulton saves from Frank Clarke, but Ray Train is on hand. Clarke hits a post and Dennis Martin pokes the second. A miserable day is complete when Boulton collides with Daniel, drops John Gorman's cross and Clarke nets.

Ref: R Mathewson

| 15 | H | MIDDLESBROUGH | 7 | L | 2:3 | 1-2 | Hector 37, Hinton 89 | Boulton | Webster | Nish | Todd | Daniel | Rioch* | Newton | Gemmill | Davies | Hector | Lee |
| 26/10 | | 24,036 | 4 | 16 | | Hickton 11, Foggon 36, Mills 48 | Platt | Craggs | Spraggon | Souness | Boam | Madren | Murdoch | Mills | Hickton | Foggon | Armstrong |

Derby boss Mackay is absent due to car crash injuries. Jack Charlton's newly-promoted side forge ahead when off-form Boulton lets a John Craggs' cross slip and John Hickton scores. Foggon grabs another from David Armstrong's cross. David Mills cleverly chips the decisive third.

Ref: E Wallace

| 16 | A | LEEDS | 7 | W | 1:0 | 0-0 | Lee 78 | Boulton | Webster | Nish | Todd | Daniel | Rioch | Newton | Gemmill | Davies | Hector | Lee |
| 2/11 | | 33,551 | 19 | 18 | | | Harvey | Reaney | Cooper | Yorath | McQueen | Hunter | Lorimer* | Clarke | O'Hare | Giles | Madeley | McKenzie |

Leeds are struggling in the wake of the amazing short reign of Brian Clough. They apply massive pressure but find Boulton back at his best. Lorimer clips the bar and ex-Ram O'Hare is denied by Boulton. Derby are ecstatic when Lee picks up Nish's pass and buries a dipping shot.

Ref: H New

| 17 | H | QP RANGERS | 5 | W | 5:2 | 2-1 | Hector 33, 55, 68, Rioch 35, Lee 78 | Boulton | Webster | Nish | Todd | Daniel | Rioch | Newton | Gemmill* | Davies | Hector | Lee |
| 9/11 | | 23,339 | 18 | 20 | | Leach 43, Bowles 88 | Parkes | Clement | Gillard | Hazell | McLintock | Webb | Thomas | Francis | Leach | Bowles | Givens |

Inspired by the midweek shoot-out win in Europe, Derby show Rangers no mercy. The only hiccup is Rioch missing a twice-taken spot-kick. Stan Bowles nets a wonderful solo goal late on. Hector poaches a hat-trick. A disappointingly low crowd gives the side a deserved ovation.

Ref: I Smith

| 18 | A | ARSENAL | 10 | L | 1:3 | 0-0 | Rioch 75p | Boulton | Webster | Nish | Todd | Daniel | Rioch | Newton | Gemmill | Davies | Hector | Lee |
| 16/11 | | 32,286 | 18 | 20 | | Ball 52, 79p, Kidd 72 | Rimmer | Rice | McNab | Kelly | Mancini | Simpson | Storey | Ball | Radford | Kidd | Brady |

Alan Ball breaks the deadlock from John Radford's pass. Derby scream for offside, but Brian Kidd's goal stands. Two dubious penalties (Lee seemed to take a dive) complete the scoring. The table is highly congested and Derby are only two points off the top despite dropping to tenth.

Ref: J Rice

| 19 | H | IPSWICH | 5 | W | 2:0 | 2-0 | Hector 8, Rioch 28 | Boulton | Webster | Nish | Todd | Daniel | Rioch | Newton | Gemmill | Davies | Hector | Lee |
| 23/11 | | 24,341 | 3 | 22 | | | Sivell | Burley | Harper | Talbot | Peddelty | Mills | Hamilton | Viljoen* | Johnson | Whymark | Woods Osborne |

Bobby Robson's league leaders are shocked by early goals in muddy conditions. Hector's header is followed by Rioch's left-foot shot flying in off a post. Newton made both and is man-of-the-match. Laurie Sivell saves from Hector and Lee. Colin Harper misses Ipswich's best chance.

Ref: B Homewood

| 20 | A | LIVERPOOL | 8 | D | 2:2 | 1-2 | Bourne 13, Davies 83 | Boulton | Webster | Thomas | Rioch | Daniel | Rioch | Newton | Gemmill | Bourne | Hector* | Lee |
| 7/12 | | 41,058 | 4 | 23 | | Kennedy 18, Heighway 22 | Clemence | Smith | Lindsay | Thompson | Cormack | Hughes | Keegan | McDermott | Heighway | Kennedy | Callaghan Davies |

Bourne is preferred to Davies at Anfield and he puts the Rams ahead from Rioch's cross. Ian Callaghan hits the crossbar and Ray Kennedy nets the rebound to equalise. Tommy Smith's firm cross is flicked past Boulton by the head of Steve Heighway. Sub Davies nods in Todd's centre.

Ref: P Willis

| 21 | H | EVERTON | 9 | L | 0:1 | 0-0 | Latchford 65 | Boulton | Webster | Thomas | Rioch | Daniel | Rioch | Newton | Gemmill | Bourne* | Hinton |
| 14/12 | | 24,891 | 1 | 23 | | | Davies | Bernard | Seargeant | Clements | Kenyon | Hurst | Jones | Telfer* | Lyons | Latchford | Connolly Pearson |

Not long returned from the tie in Mostar, Derby are out of luck as Lee twice hits the framework. Rioch and Davies also go agonisingly close. Garry Jones, who also hit the bar, runs from deep to supply lethal Bob Latchford. Everton go top — the tenth change of leadership this season.

Ref: T Spencer

LEAGUE DIVISION 1 — Manager: Dave Mackay — SEASON 1974-75

No	Date		Att	Pos	Pt	F-A	H-T	1	2	3	4	5	6	7	8	9	10	11	12 sub used	Scorers, Times, and Referees
22	A	LUTON	12,862	10	22	L 0-1	0-0	Boulton	Webster	Thomas	Rioch	Daniel	Todd	Newton	Gemmill	Davies*	Bourne	Lee	Hinton	Ryan Jim 81p
	21/12				23			Horn	Ryan John	Buckley	Anderson	Faulkner	Futcher P	Ryan Jim	Husband	Spiring*	West	Aston	Fuccillo	Ref: A Lees
								Derby lack punch without Hector and turn in an uninspired display. Harry Haslam's outfit battle hard after six straight losses to grab only their second league win of the season. Peter Spiring, a recent signing from Liverpool, is hauled down by Todd and Jim Ryan slots in the late winner.												
23	H	BIRMINGHAM	26,121	10	15	W 2-1	1-0	Boulton	Webster	Nish	Rioch	Daniel	Todd	Newton	Gemmill	Davies	Bourne	Lee	Lee	Bourne 37, Rioch 65
	26/12				25			Latchford	Page	Kendall	Styles	Gallagher	Pendrey	Campbell	Taylor	Burns	Hatton	Calderwood	Calderwood	Hatton 88
																				Ref: R Lee
								Dave Latchford saves twice from Davies, before the big striker fires in a low centre which Bourne hits into the net. Rioch exchanges passes with Lee and hits a fine second goal from a tight angle. Jimmy Calderwood's cross eludes Bourne and Bob Hatton swoops in for a consolation.												
24	A	MANCHESTER C	40,188	9	8	W 2-1	1-0	Boulton	Webster	Nish	Rioch	Daniel	Todd	Newton	Gemmill	Davies	Bourne	Lee		Newton 21, Lee 65
	28/12				27			Corrigan	Hammond	Donachie	Bell	Doyle	Oakes	Horswill	Royle	Marsh	Hartford	Tueart		Bell 63
																				Ref: W Gow
								Newton breaks from defence and fires his first of the season into the top corner of Joe Corrigan's net. Boulton saves well from Mike Doyle, but Colin Bell nets a fine first-time shot after a neat move. Ex-City man Lee, given a great welcome earlier, cuts in to shoot a thunderous winner.												
25	H	LIVERPOOL	33,463	7	6	W 2-0	1-0	Boulton	Thomas	Nish	Rioch	Daniel	Todd	Newton	Gemmill	Davies	Hector	Lee	Hector	Newton 39, Lee 80
	11/1				29			Clemence	Neal	Lindsay	Thompson	Cormack	Hughes	Keegan	Hall	Heighway	Toshack	Callaghan		Ref: M Sinclair
								Thomas is recalled due to Webster's injury and he helps create the vital opening goal - another cracking shot from Newton. The points are safe after Daniel releases Lee and he beats Ray Clemence. Boulton's saves are a key factor in this fine win, which keeps Derby in the title race.												
26	A	WOLVERHAMPTON	24,515	5	14	W 1-0	1-0	Boulton	Thomas	Nish	Rioch	Daniel	Todd	Newton	Gemmill	Davies	Bourne	Lee		Newton 32
	18/1				31			Parkes	Palmer*	Parkin	Bailey	Munro	McAlle	Hibbitt	Daley	Richards	Kindon	Wagstaffe	Powell B	Ref: A Hart
								Boulton saves well from John Richards and Thomas heads off the line early on from Steve Kindon. After Hector hits the bar with a volley, Derby move ahead when Newton surges forward onto Lee's pass to force home a fierce drive. Just two points now separate the top eight clubs.												
27	A	QP RANGERS	20,686	8	11	L 1-4	1-1	Boulton	Thomas	Nish	Rioch	Daniel	Todd	Newton	Gemmill	Davies	Hector	Lee*	Bourne	Rioch 3
	1/2				31			Parkes	Clement	Gillard	Masson	McLintock	Webb	Thomas D	Francis	Beck	Bowles	Givens		Givens 9, 80, 89, Thomas 87
																				Ref: I Jones
								Rioch's early strike is quickly cancelled out when Don Givens forces the ball in, despite Nish's desperate attempt to clear. Derby play well for 80 minutes, but an amazing late burst by Dave Sexton's side wins the points. Givens completes his hat-trick and Dave Thomas slips in another.												
28	H	LEEDS	33,641	9	10	D 0-0	0-0	Boulton	Thomas	Nish	Rioch	Daniel	Todd	Newton	Gemmill	Davies*	Bourne	Lee*	Bourne	
	8/2				32			Harvey	Reaney	Gray F	Bremner	McQueen*	Madeley	McKenzie	Clarke	Lorimer	Yorath	Gray E	Cherry	
																				Ref: D Richardson
								David Harvey makes a fine save from a thunderous Lee drive and also keeps out goalbound efforts by Newton and Rioch. Leeds have two reasonable penalty claims turned down and Derby one, when the ball hits Trevor Cherry on the hand. Boulton is the less busy of the keepers.												
29	H	ARSENAL	24,002	7	18	W 2-1	2-1	Boulton	Thomas	Nish	Rioch	Daniel	Todd	Newton	Gemmill	Davies	Bourne	Lee		Powell 2, 28
	22/2				34			Rimmer	Rice	McNab!	Storey	Mancini	Simpson	Armstrong	Ball	Radford	Kidd	Brady		Radford 23
																				Ref: J Yates
								Gemmill's suspension lets Powell back in to become hero of the hour. He loops a header home early on, before John Radford catches Derby napping to level. Powell swoops again as Jimmy Rimmer fumbles. In a stormy game Alan Ball and Bob McNab are both dismissed for dissent.												
30	A	IPSWICH	23,132	7	4	L 0-3	0-2	Boulton	Thomas	Nish	Rioch	Daniel	Todd	Newton	Gemmill	Bourne	Lee*	Powell	
	25/2				34			Sivell	Burley	Mills	Talbot	Hunter	Beattie	Hamilton	Viljoen	Johnson*	Whymark	Lambert	Woods	Johnson 12, Hamilton 43, Beattie 67
																				Ref: R Perkin
								On a bitterly cold night, David Johnson rises to head in Mick Lambert's corner. Bryan Hamilton is unmarked as he increases the lead when Lambert touches on Johnson's cross. Allan Hunter heads a corner against the bar and Kevin Beattie bundles in the third. Lee goes off injured.												
31	H	TOTTENHAM	22,995	7	19	W 3-1	2-1	Boulton	Jennings	Nish	Rioch	Daniel	Todd*	Newton	Gemmill	Davies	Hector	Hinton	Powell	Rioch 30, Daniel 37, Davies 63
	3/3				36				Kinnear	Knowles	McAllister	Pratt	Naylor	Conn	Perryman	Jones	Coates	Duncan		Jones 10
																				Ref: R Matthewson
								Hinton and Davies are recalled and ultimately help pep Derby's attack. Ralph Coates' long pass sets up Chris Jones to open the scoring. Rioch levels with a volley through a crowded area. Nish's corner is met by Davies and Daniel nips in to net. Hinton's cross finds Davies for a third.												

316

#	Date	Opponent	Result	W/D/L	Pos	Pts	Attendance	Scorers / Subs	Referee
32	8/3	A CHELSEA	2-1	W	3	38	22,644	Daniel 57, Hinton 62, Hollins 63	Ref: D Biddle	0-0
33	15/3	H STOKE	1-2	L	6	38	29,985	Hector 49, Greenhoff 75, 88	Ref: R Toseland	0-0
34	22/3	A NEWCASTLE	2-0	W	7	40	31,201	Nish 34, Rioch 87	Ref: R Capey	1-0
35	29/3	H LUTON	5-0	W	6	42	24,619	Davies 9, 13, 33, 78, 86	Ref: R Tinkler	3-0
36	31/3	A BURNLEY	5-2	W	5	44	24,276	Rioch 1, Nish 20, Dav'29, Hec' 78, 88; Hankin 18, James 75p	Ref: J Taylor	3-1
37	1/4	H MANCHESTER C	2-1	W	3	46	32,966	Rioch 44, 53; Bell 83	Ref: G Kew	1-0
38	5/4	A MIDDLESBROUGH	1-1	D	4	47	30,066	Hector 89; Mills 35	Ref: A Grey	0-1
39	9/4	H WOLVERHAMPTON	1-0	W	3	49	30,109	Lee 69	Ref: J Bent	0-0
40	12/4	H WEST HAM	1-0	W	1	51	31,336	Rioch 66	Ref: M Lowe	0-0
41	19/4	A LEICESTER	0-0	D	1	52	38,943		Ref: T Reynolds	0-0
42	26/4	H CARLISLE	0-0	D	1	53	36,882		Ref: A Morrissey	0-0

Average Home 26,718 Away 27,446

---

32 — A CHELSEA (8/3)
Boulton Phillips Thomas Nish Rioch Hollins Daniel Newton Todd Hector Hinton
                                Locke Sparrow   Harris Britton Hay Garland Cooke

Derby dominate early on but do not break through until Phillips pushes Davies' second-half header against the bar and Daniel forces home the rebound. David Hay brings down Hector and Hinton's free-kick is deflected in by Steve Finnieston. John Hollins' rising drive makes it close.

33 — H STOKE (15/3)
Boulton Thomas Nish Rioch Daniel Todd Newton Hector Hinton
Shilton Marsh Lewis* Mahoney Smith Dodd Skeets Greenhoff Hudson
                                                                Salmons Hurst

Gemmill's short corner finds Thomas, whose shot is deflected into Hector's path for the opening goal. Geoff Salmons' centre finds Jimmy Greenhoff in space and he equalises with a volley. In the dying moments Greenhoff dives through the mud to head a shock winner for City.

34 — A NEWCASTLE (22/3)
Boulton Thomas Nish Rioch Daniel Todd Newton* Gemmill Davies Hector Hinton
McFaul Kelly Hibbitt Smith Keeley Howard Barrowc'gh Nulty Macdonald Tudor Craig T
                                                                                Bourne

A Hinton free-kick rebounds to Nish, who sends in a curling shot that is pushed against the bar by Iam McFaul and then gathered as he falls. To the Geordies' horror, the ref says it crossed the line. Late in the day Rioch powers forward from deep to thrash in a classic clinching goal.

35 — H LUTON (29/3)
Boulton Thomas Nish Rioch Daniel Todd Powell Gemmill Davies Hector Hinton
Barber Ryan John Buckley Anderson Faulkner Futcher P Husband* Futcher R West Aston
                                                                                      Seasman

A day Davies will never forget: He nets five, has two disallowed and other efforts well saved. He heads in Hinton's corner, converts Thomas's cross and then buries a cross-shot for the hat-trick. He pounces on a back header by John Ryan and finishes off by converting Hinton's pass.

36 — A BURNLEY (31/3)
Boulton Thomas Nish Rioch Daniel Todd Powell Gemmill Davies Hector Hinton
Stevenson Newton K Brennan Noble Waldron Thomson Flynn Ingham Hankin Parker James

Rioch sets the tone, pouncing on Billy Ingham's square pass to net after just 28 seconds. Ray Hankin heads an equaliser, but Nish soon curls in a lovely free-kick. Davies hooks in a low centre before Leighton James pulls one back. Hinton's spadework creates a late double for Hector.

37 — H MANCHESTER C (1/4)
Boulton Thomas Nish Rioch Daniel Todd Powell Gemmill Davies Hector Hinton
Corrigan Hammond Donachie Doyle Booth Oakes Hartford Bell Marsh Royle Tueart

Rioch dives to head home Hector's centre. He extends the lead with a typically powerful left-foot drive. Tiredness then sets in, for this is the third game in four days. Good work by Daniel twice foils City, before Bell nets a fine goal from a Marsh pass near the end. Derby rise to third.

38 — A MIDDLESBROUGH (5/4)
Boulton Thomas Nish* Rioch Daniel Todd Newton Gemmill Davies Hector Hinton
Platt Craggs Cooper Souness Boam Madren Murdoch Mills Hickton* Foggon Armstrong
                                                                                Brine

An astute pass by David Armstrong sets up David Mills to put Boro ahead. Amid rain, hail and snow, subdued Derby nearly go further behind but Boulton saves well from Alan Foggon. Out of the blue Hector nets a Davies pass in the final minute. Mackay calls it 'the great escape'.

39 — H WOLVERHAMPTON (9/4)
Boulton Thomas Nish Rioch Daniel Todd Newton Gemmill Davies Hector Lee
Pierce Palmer Parkin Bailey Jefferson McAlle Hibbitt Carr Withe Farley* Daley
                                                                                Gardner

As the title race hots up, Derby welcome back the injured Lee. He breaks the deadlock in a tense game by pouncing when Mike Bailey can only help the ball goalwards from Gemmill's inswinging corner. Luton beat Everton, which means Derby hit the top for the first time this term.

40 — H WEST HAM (12/4)
Boulton Thomas Nish Rioch Daniel Todd Newton Gemmill Davies Hector Lee
Day McDowell Lampard Bonds Taylor T Lock Jennings Paddon Taylor A* Brooking Gould
                                                                                    Holland

It is tense at the top and only when Hinton replaces Davies do Derby look likely to score. Soon after he comes on, the winger floats over a corner which ends up being fired home by Rioch. Derby remain two points clear.

41 — A LEICESTER (19/4)
Boulton Thomas Nish Rioch Daniel Todd Newton Gemmill Davies Hector Lee
Wallington Whitworth Rofe Lee R Blockley Cross Weller Sammels Worthington Birchenall Garland*
                                                                                              Stringfellow

Rival boss Billy Bingham of Everton plays mind games, tipping Leicester to win this. Derby cling on dangerously for a point and their fans celebrate as news comes through that all three main rivals (Everton, Ipswich and Liverpool) have lost. The title looks to be there for the taking.

42 — H CARLISLE (26/4)
Boulton Thomas Nish Rioch Daniel Todd Newton Gemmill Davies Hector Lee*
Ross Carr Spearritt O'Neill Green Parker Martin Train Clarke F Laidlaw Balderstone
                                                                                Hinton

Ipswich can only draw in midweek, meaning the title is Derby's. In a carnival atmosphere on a sunny day, there is a parade of former players and a lap of honour by the new champions. Perhaps inevitably, the game is an anti-climax and relegated Carlisle pick up an unlikely point.

SEASON 1974-75

Manager: Dave Mackay

LEAGUE DIVISION 1 (CUP-TIES)

League Cup

		Att	F-A	H-T	Scorers, Times, and Referees	1	2	3	4	5	6	7	8	9	10	11	subs used
2 A PORTSMOUTH 11/9	10 W	13,582 2:20	5-1	2-0	Hector 10, 50, Lee 30, Rioch 47, Marinello 70, [Roberts 81 (og)] Ref: R Toseland	Boulton	Webster*	Nish	Rioch	Daniel	Todd	Powell	Gemmill	Davies	Hector	Lee	Newton
						Best	Roberts	Wilson	Piper	Went	Stephenson	Marinello	Kellard	Davies	Ron* Reynolds	Hand	Ellis

Derby County are completely dominant throughout against the Fratton Park side, and manager Dave Mackay reckons had they scored fifteen it would not have flattered them. The only downside is Ron Webster being carried off unconscious after receiving an accidental blow in the face.

| 3 A SOUTHAMPTON 8/10 | 9 L | 14,911 2:18 | 0-5 | 0-2 | [Osgood 71] Stokes 9, Channon 26, 67, 82, Ref: T Reynolds | Boulton | Webster | Nish | Rioch | Daniel | Todd | Newton* | Gemmill | Davies | Hector | Lee | Bourne |
| | | | | | | Turner | McCarthy | Peach | Fisher | Bennett | Mills | Stokes | Channon | Osgood | Holmes* | Steele | Chatterley |

Derby are thrashed by an energetic Second Division side, whose fans recently called for the head of manager Lawrie McMenemy. Error-prone Derby are passed by Hector. It is the club's worst defeat in two years and another early exit from the League Cup. Even an easy consolation chance is passed up by Hector. It is the club's worst defeat in two years and another early exit from the League Cup.

UEFA Cup

| 1:1 H SERVETTE 18/9 (Switz'land) | 14 W | 17,716 | 4-1 | 3-0 | Hector 12, 64, Daniel 25, Lee 43 Petrovic 76 Ref: A Segura (Spain) | Boulton | Webster | Nish | Rioch | Daniel | Todd | Newton* | Gemmill | Bourne | Hector | Lee | Hinton |
| | | | | | | de Blaireville | Schnyder | Morganegg | Martin | Guyot | Marchi | Pfister | Castella* | Riner | Wegmann | Petrovic | Sund^/Andrey |

Derby look comfortable after going two up through Daniel's first goal for the club in nine years and 142 senior games. They surge four ahead through a fine Hector effort. He evades two tackles before steering a shot home. After 12 lackadaisical minutes, sub Sundermann is hauled off.

| 1:2 A SERVETTE 2/10 | 8 W | 9,600 | 2-1 | 1-1 | Lee 44, Hector 72 Martin 19 Ref: H Woehrer (Austria) (Derby won 6-2 on aggregate) | Boulton | Webster | Nish | Rioch | Daniel | Todd | Newton | Gemmill | Bourne | Hector | Lee | |
| | | | | | | de Blaireville | Schnyder | Morganegg | Martin | Guyot | Sunderm'n^ | Pfister | Andrey* | Riner | Wegmann | Petrovic | March/Bar'qu'nd |

Servette give themselves a chance with an early lead, but Lee hit back before the break, Lee knocking in a simple goal after the goalkeeper fumbled Rioch's cross. Guyot hits a post, but Hector is on hand to win the tie when Rioch's free-kick and Bourne's follow-up are both parried.

| 2:1 H ATLETICO MADRID 23/10 (Spain) | 7 D | 29,347 | 2-2 | 1-1 | Nish 15, Rioch 88p Ayala 13, Aragon 78p Ref: R Helles (France) | Boulton | Webster | Nish | Rioch | Daniel | Todd | Newton | Gemmill | Bourne* | Hector | Lee | Hinton |
| | | | | | | Reina | Capon | Diaz | Marcelino* | Benegas | Eusebio | Leal^ | Adelardo | Garate | Irureta | Ayala | Bermejo/Aragon |

Two extraordinary penalty awards dominate this tie. Aragon nets after Boulton is penalised for gathering the ball cleanly at Garate's feet. The referee evens things up, rewarding Derby when Lee falls dramatically as Eusebio closes in. Hinton nearly wins the game when he hits a post.

| 2:2 A ATLETICO MADRID 6/11 | 7 D | 35,000 aet | 2-2 | 0-1 | Rioch 54, Hector 64 Luis 4, 76 Ref: F Biwersi (West Germany) (Agg: 4-4; Derby 7-6 on pens) | Boulton | Webster | Nish | Rioch | Daniel | Powell | Newton | Gemmill | Davies | Hector | Lee | Marc'lin/Salc'do |
| | | | | | | Reina | Capon | Diaz | Adelardo* | Benegas | Eusebio | Alberto^ | Luis | Garate | Irureta | Ayala | |

A fascinating tie is deadlocked after starring displays by Gemmill and young stand-in Powell. Rioch, Hector, Nish, Lee, Gemmill, Newton and Powell are all successful in the shoot-out, but Davies misses. Boulton dives to push Eusebio's kick against a post and Derby squeeze through.

| 3:1 H VELEZ MOSTAR 27/11 (Yugoslavia) | 5 W | 26,131 | 3-1 | 0-1 | Bourne 74, 87, Hinton 80 Vladic 3 Ref: P Mannig (East Germany) | Boulton | Webster | Nish | Rioch | Daniel | Todd | Newton | Gemmill | Davies* | Hector | Lee^ | Bourne/Hinton |
| | | | | | | Mrgan | Colic | Hadziabdic | Primorac | Glavonic | Pecelj | Topic | Vadic^ | Vukoje | Ledic | Hodzic | Okuka |

On a mud-clogged pitch, Derby fall behind after just 142 seconds to the Yugoslavs. It is a long wait but Derby fans are rewarded as Mackay's two substitutes score three in the closing stages to get the Baseball Ground rocking. Hector then has a late goal disallowed by Herr Mannig.

| 3:2 A VELEZ MOSTAR 11/12 | 8 L | 15,000 | 1-4 | 0-2 | [Bajevic 86p] Primorac 11p, Pecelj 30, Vladic 51, Bajevic 86p Ref: C Corver (Holland) (Derby lose 4-5 on aggregate) | Boulton | Webster | Thomas | Rioch | Daniel | Todd | Newton | Gemmill | Bourne* | Hector | Lee^ | Davies/Hinton |
| | | | | | | Mrgan | Meter | Hadziabdic | Colic | Primorac | Pecelj | Topic | Halhodszic | Bajevic | Vladic | Vukoje | |

On another sticky surface, the tie looks headed for extra-time after Vladic's shot is tipped onto the bar by Boulton but rebounds against his back and trickles in for 3-1. Referee Corver awards a disputed penalty when the ball hits Todd's body near the end. Derby go close late on.

FA Cup

3	A	ORIENT	9 D 2:15	1-2	Todd, 34, 83		
	4/1		12,490		Possee 13, Queen 16		
					Ref: R Crabb		
3R	H	ORIENT	9 W 2:15	2-1	Lee 6, Rioch 88		
	8/1		26,501		Fairbrother 5		
					Ref: R Crabb		
4	H	BRISTOL ROV	5 W 2:16	2-0	Hector 16, Rioch 82p		
	27/1		27,980				
					Ref: A Jones		
5	H	LEEDS	9 L 2:16	0-0			
	18/2		35,298		Nish 83 (og)		
					Ref: K Burns		

ORIENT (A): Boulton, Jackson, Webster, Fisher, Nish, Downing, Rioch, Allen, Daniel, Hoadley, Walley, Todd, Newton, Fairbrother, Gemmill, Bennett, Davies, Queen, Bourne*, Grealish, Lee, Possee, Hinton

Derek Possee and Gerry Queen set up a possible giant-killing but, in his 200th appearance for The Rams, Todd manages his first goals for over two years. Queen hits the bar for the lively Londoners, Possee has a good claim for a penalty waved aside and Barrie Fairbrother hits a post.

ORIENT (H): Boulton, Jackson, Webster*, Fisher, Nish, Downing, Rioch, Allen, Daniel, Hoadley, Walley, Todd, Newton, Fairbrother, Gemmill, Bennett*, Davies, Queen, Bourne, Grealish, Lee, Possee, Hinton Cunningham

Barrie Fairbrother puts George Petchey's side ahead but they are pegged back almost immediately by the wily Lee. The mid-table Second Division outfit play some excellent football, but find Boulton in good form in goal. Webster and Hinton both bravely play on despite injuries.

BRISTOL ROV: Boulton, Eadie, Thomas, Bater, Nish, Parsons*, Rioch, Aitken, Daniel, Taylor, Prince, Todd, Newton, Stephens, Gemmill, Coombes, Davies, Warboys, Bourne*, Fearnley, Lee*, Bannister, Staniforth

Heavy rain puts the game in jeopardy but hours of work on the notorious pitch saves it. A goal in each half wins the tie. Boulton has just two hairy moments: when Don Megson's side claim a penalty for holding and later when his clearance nearly rebounds off Gordon Staniforth.

LEEDS: Boulton, Stewart, Thomas, Reaney, Nish, Gray F, Rioch, Bremner, Daniel, Madeley, McKenzie, Todd, Newton, McCueen, Powell, Clarke, Davies, Jordan, Bourne*, Yorath, Lee, Gray E, Davies

New Leeds boss Jimmy Armfield praises goalkeeper David Stewart, deputising for car crash victim David Harvey, who keeps Derby at bay. Eddie Gray's cross bobbles in off Nish's leg for a late own-goal. A chance to equalise is spurned when Davies nods Rioch's pull-back wide.

League Table

	P	W	D	L	F	A	W	D	L	F	A	Pts
1 DERBY	42	14	4	3	41	18	7	7	7	26	31	53
2 Liverpool	42	14	5	2	44	17	4	9	8	16	22	51
3 Ipswich	42	17	2	2	47	14	6	3	12	19	30	51
4 Everton	42	10	9	2	33	19	6	9	6	23	23	50
5 Stoke	42	12	7	2	40	18	5	8	8	24	30	49
6 Sheffield U	42	12	7	2	35	20	6	6	9	23	31	49
7 Middlesbro'	42	11	7	3	33	14	7	5	9	21	26	48
8 Manchester C	42	16	3	2	40	15	2	7	12	14	39	46
9 Leeds	42	8	7	6	34	20	6	5	10	23	29	45
10 Burnley	42	11	8	4	40	29	5	6	10	28	38	45
11 QP Rangers	42	10	4	7	25	17	6	6	9	29	37	42
12 Wolves	42	12	5	4	43	21	2	6	13	14	33	39
13 West Ham	42	10	6	5	38	22	3	7	11	20	37	39
14 Coventry	42	8	9	4	31	27	4	6	11	12	29	39
15 Newcastle	42	12	4	5	39	23	2	5	14	10	35	39
16 Arsenal	42	10	6	5	31	18	3	5	13	18	33	37
17 Birmingham	42	10	4	7	34	28	4	5	12	19	33	37
18 Leicester	42	8	7	6	25	17	5	4	12	21	43	36
19 Tottenham	42	8	4	9	29	27	6	4	11	23	36	34
20 Luton	42	8	6	7	27	26	3	5	13	20	39	33
21 Chelsea	42	4	9	8	22	31	5	6	10	20	41	33
22 Carlisle	42	8	2	11	22	21	4	3	14	21	38	29
	924	235	124	103	753	460	103	124	235	460	753	924

Odds & ends

Double wins: (5) Burnley, Chelsea, Manchester C, Sheffield U, Wolves.
Double losses: (0).
Won from behind: (5) Burnley (h), Tottenham (h), Servette (a) (UEFA), Velez Mostar (h) (UEFA), Orient (h) (FAC).
Lost from in front: (2) QPR (a), Stoke (h).
High spots: Winning a 'wide open' League title for a second time.
Twelve goals and maximum points from the three Easter fixtures.
Spectacular goals from the boots of Bruce Rioch and Henry Newton.
Roger Davies' five-goal extravaganza against Luton.
The sight of that dreadful pitch being replaced in late April.
The dramatic penalty shoot-out victory in Madrid.
Low spots: Departing from the FA Cup thanks to an unlucky own-goal.
Bowing out of the UEFA exit due to a last-gasp controversial penalty.
Being hammered in the League Cup by Second Division Southampton.

Player of the Year: Peter Daniel.
Ever-presents: (2) Colin Boulton, Bruce Rioch.
Hat-tricks: (2) Kevin Hector (v QPR, h), Roger Davies (v Luton, h).
Opposing hat-tricks: (2) Don Givens (v QPR, a), Mick Channon (v So'ton, a, LC).
Leading scorer: (21) Kevin Hector.

Appearances / Goals

	Lge	Sub	LC	Sub	FAC	Sub	UC	Sub	Lge	Sub	LC	FAC	UC	Tot
Boulton, Colin	42		2		4		6							
Bourne, Jeff	7	10	1		3	1	4	1	2			2		4
Daniel, Peter	37		2		4		6		3					4
Davies, Roger	39		2		3		5		12	1	2	1	1	12
Gemmill, Archie	41		2		3		6							
Hector, Kevin	38		2		2		6		13	2	1	5		21
Hinton, Alan	8	5							2			1		3
Lee, Francis	34			2			6		12		1	1	2	16
McFarland, Roy	4													
Newton, Henry	35	1	1		4		6		3					3
Nish, David	38		2		1	1	5		2		1			3
Powell, Steve	12	3	1		1		1							2
Rioch, Bruce	42		2		4		6		15			2	2	20
Thomas, Rod	22				3		4							
Todd, Colin	39		2		4		5				2			2
Webster, Ron	24		2		2		6		1					1
(own-goals)											1			1
16 players used	462	19	22	2	44	4	66		5	6	14	92		